Editors
Seamus Deane
Breandán Mac Suibhne

Editorial Assistants
Heather Edwards
Cormac Ó Duibhne

Publishing Consultant
Sara Wilbourne

Copy
Hilary Bell

Design
Red Dog Design Consultants
www.reddog.ie

Copyright © 2005 by the contributors and Field Day Publications

Field Day Review is published annually by
Field Day Publications in association with
the Keough Institute for Irish Studies
at the University of Notre Dame.

ISSN 1649-6507
ISBN 0-946755-26-4

Field Day Review
Keough Institute for Irish Studies
86 St. Stephen's Green
Dublin 2
Ireland

fieldday@nd.edu

www.fieldday.org

FIELD DAY REVIEW
2005

The Thin Man

An Interview with Brendan Behan

Sylvère Lotringer

I did this interview in Dublin in January 1961; it has never been published before.[1] At the time I was twenty-three and my spoken English was still rudimentary.

1 The interview was transcribed by the writer Mark von Schlegell; footnotes by the editors.
2 The well-known poet Derek Mahon.
3 *Les Lettres françaises*, no. 1022, 26 mars au 1er avril, 1964.
4 The Théâtre National Populaire at the Palais de Chaillot facing the Eiffel Tower was a major avant-garde institution at the time and a huge theatre.

I was writing regularly for *Les Lettres françaises*, a weekly literary magazine close to the French Communist Party, but somewhat more liberal; my boss was Louis Aragon. I was also very involved with the students' movement against the French war in Algeria. I had come to Ireland to gather material for a long essay on James Joyce for the twentieth anniversary of his death. In Dublin I met with friends of Joyce, like Padraic Colum, who graciously took me for a tour of Eccles Street, the National Library, the bars mentioned in *Ulysses*, and the famous tower. That was, of course, long before the regular Joyce 'tour' had been initiated.

Behan was a well-known figure in Paris then. *The Quare Fellow* and *The Hostage* had been a resounding success on the stage. His *Borstal Boy* had just been published in French and I was about to review it. I decided to get some background information directly from Behan. He was kind enough to meet me at his home on a Sunday morning. He seemed a little dazed at first, although already smoking a fat cigar. We sat in his living room, which looked a bit disorderly. On the floor there was a half-eaten carcass of an animal, a chicken probably, lying on a plate.

Behan's eyes were red and puffed up, his face a bit crumpled. He must have stayed up pretty late the night before.

Our conversation wasn't exactly meant to be an interview, although it turned out to be one. It was a strange interview really. Although Behan was full of goodwill, he was obviously trying *not* to talk about *Borstal Boy*, which he didn't seem to remember very well. As a consequence, he kept introducing anecdotes about the history of Ireland, the IRA, the Communist Party, his years in prison, and the time he spent in France as a young writer. I didn't mind a bit. These digressions became the main story, regularly framed by the mostly unanswered questions, circling back time and again to where we began. So the exchange ends up having some kind of a shape, a digressive structure *à la* Sterne or Diderot. While in Dublin I stayed with a fellow student, Derek, at Trinity College. Derek accompanied me to Behan's house and shows up occasionally during the interview.[2]

When Behan died in 1964, I put together an *hommage* to him for *Les Lettres françaises*.[3] It had a short piece on Behan by Sean O'Casey on the front page, and inside, a short note by Joan Littlewood, the director and producer, who in effect had made Behan famous by her productions of *The Quare Fellow* (1956; with Gerry Raffles) and *The Hostage* (1958), and a longer piece by Georges Wilson, then director of the Théâtre National Populaire (TNP).[4] It also included the translation of a scene from *The Great House*, Behan's last play (written for BBC radio). I wrote two different pieces for the issue, one a general presentation of Behan's work and life, '*Laissons hurler les Loups …* ' [Let the Wolves Howl …'], and the other '*L'Homme maigre*' [The Thin Man]. This latter piece, from which our present title is taken, included some quotations, in French, from the 1961 interview.

*From '*L'Homme maigre*' (1964):*

Il est assis dans son fauteuil, col ouvert. Il n'arrête pas de parler, passant outre sa toux et un léger bégaiement. Ma présence lui fait plaisir. Elle lui rappelle la France. Sorti de prison, il n'a eu qu'un désir, gagner Paris. Il y arrive en 1948, sans travail, sans argent. Il me cite Emerson: «La plupart des hommes vivent dans un état de désespoir tranquille». En privé, continue-t-il, je suis une personne plutôt morose. «Je n'ai rien d'un exhibitionniste. Je préférerais de loin être tranquille. Je me trouve placé dans une situation qui ne me plaît qu'à moitié. Vous savez, dans chaque homme gros, il y a un homme maigre qui cherche à s'échapper.»

He is seated in his armchair, his collar wide open. He speaks in a husky, halting voice which occasionally catches and starts again. He's clearly pleased to have me here; I remind him of France. When he got out of prison, he had wanted one thing only — to get to Paris. He arrived there, without a job or money, in 1948. At one point he quotes Emerson: 'Most men live a life of quiet desperation.' In private, he assures me, he's a rather gloomy person. 'I am not at all an exhibitionist. I wish I were. I find myself in a situation I don't exactly like. You know, inside each fat man there's a thin man who's trying to escape.'

In Paris with a poster for the 1959 French adaptation of his play *The Quare Fellow*.
Photograph: Hulton Archive/Getty Images.

5 *I Knock at the Door* (1939) was the first volume of O'Casey's *Autobiographies* 6 vols. (1939–54).

Sylvère Lotringer: *How did you come to write* Borstal Boy?

Brendan Behan: Actually, I forget the fucking thing.

Did you enjoy writing it?

If you write a book and it goes off while you're working on it, it's the happiest time of your life. A writer will never spend better time than when he's working. Provided he's got money, he's going to get food and he's going to get a certain amount of sex. He doesn't even need a lot of that. Proust said one time that the two greatest allies that a writer has are chastity and water.

You had water?

Gotta have a woman knockin' round the place. Well, it's preferable. Say if you were two blokes about nineteen or twenty you'd probably get on OK together. But usually a woman is better. I got no prejudices one way or the other. But you got to have heat. You've got to have a reasonable amount of drink, if you're able to drink. Yeah, when I started to write I was OK. I could drink a good jar. Good to live in France — in Paris — because you meet other writers.

It's only in Paris that one meets writers?

A young writer needs a small time in France because, first of all, he doesn't know whether he's a writer at all or not. I mean, coming home and announcing to your friends that you're a writer is rather like changing your name. All of a sudden you come in and say, 'Listen you guys, from now on my name is Chuck' or 'I want to be called Lefty.' Well, it's a bit embarrassing at the start, isn't it? The same way when you're a writer, you've got to get everybody used to your being a writer. Someone says to you, 'What are you?' You say, 'Well, I'm a writer.' I never said it. I just had people say it for me. Actually, I didn't think I'd ever be anything else. I decided long since that I would not be anything else.

You wrote Borstal Boy *in France then?*

Sure, some of it in France. I wrote some of it at the Hotel Louisiane, at the corner of the rue de Bucy. And this proprietor — the patron of the hotel — was a great soccer man. He was very much interested in association football — what you call football or soccer. He was very sympathetic to my work, which he couldn't read of course. But I wrote it then, all over the place.

How did you come to write it?

The principal difficulty in writing a book was getting some place to write it if you didn't have any money. I didn't have any dough and no place to go. I lost the bloody manuscript of it lots of times. So weary just looking for a place to sleep, I forgot the goddamn thing. But how did I come to write it? Don't know how I came to write it ... I just wrote it, that's all.

Was it difficult to start?

Well, I'll tell you, I made a number of false starts. I started it off by writing some old bullshit, by writing an orderly progression of events in time. I think my writing was fundamentally influenced by Joyce. But the writing of *Borstal Boy*, in form, I think, was finally decided by my reading Sean O'Casey's *Autobiographies* ... One of them, *I Knock at the Door*, where he brings in characters and sometimes they've got phoney names and sometimes they've got real names.[5] He doesn't worry very much about time; he just tells you the story. And tells you what happened as he imagines it had happened. O'Casey's a great man. O'Casey could have done anything in the world of letters. I can't think of anyone anyplace to compare O'Casey to, except possibly Victor Hugo, whom I don't read very much. Hugo was born in rue de Florentine. Which is up by the Luxembourg — let me see, my memory! — in rue Pascal, I think. It's in the middle of the rue Saint-Jacques, you know it?

The fascist militia from the Law School is further up in rue Saint-Jacques and we keep fighting them. The police are in on their side. They want to keep Algeria French.

Well, Hugo was born there in what had been a convent which was sacked. They did away with the convent during the Revolution. I'm all for convents, but if you can't have a revolution without sacking convents, well then, sack the convents. That's hard, but it's fair.

You left Ireland just after they let you loose?

Sure. I was out for a bit. I was released in 1946 in Ireland. Then I was arrested in England in 1947 and I got four months, because somebody had escaped from jail. A man called Richard Cohen, alias Timmons. Or Timmons alias Cohen.[6] I came to France at the end of '48 or '49, I forget which. But I had been to France on little trips before. I'd been to Rouen on horse boats. I used to go with sailors. They knew me — used to give me a lift over. But I finally arrived in the Latin Quarter and I didn't know any French. I said to a fellow, 'Where's the Latin Quarter?' He said, '*Comment?*' I said, 'Where's the Latin Quarter?' I had never learned any French at school so I didn't know any. Finally, I looked along the métro to see if it said *Quartier Latin*. I'd have probably called it at the time 'Quarter Latin.' I didn't see anything, but I did see Saint-Michel. Everyone knows Saint-Michel. So I got a métro. I think it was ten francs at the time. How much is it now?

Forty-five francs.

Well, it was ten francs then. I got my ten francs worth of métro and I came off at Saint-Michel. And finally I dug up an Englishman and an American. I might knock the English occasionally but I like having them around. I might knock also the Americans. As I'm on the subject of America, I might say that a great number in France think that being anti-American is a leftist thing, that they're of the *Gauche* if they're anti-American. But as a matter of fact most French anti-Americanism is like English anti-Americanism. It's founded on the fact that the Americans have got more money and have got better manners in a hotel than Europeans. And also they're more sophisticated. A Frenchman will go across to England and he says there's nothing to eat there. There are *plenty* of things to eat in England. And in Ireland. They've got salmon; they've got chicken; they've got beef; they've got mutton — if you're willing to pay for it. Of course, anyone who says they can't eat better in France than they can anywhere else has a hole in their head. But if you fuck around in London, you can get it. London's a big city. Soho's a good spot. You can get food and you can get wine. You can get any goddamn wine if you know anything about wine. Which a great number of French people, of course, don't.

While in France, what did you do for a living?

I worked with French housepainters. The best — the working people of Paris and the housepainters especially. I was a member of the *section bâtiment*, Confédération Générale du Travail. It was in the Place de la République. I remember I was amused by the fact that they were all communists. They had *L'Humanité* and sold it all over the place. And if I went into a French trade union office and they were not selling *L'Humanité*, I'd think it was the wrong fucking office; I'd think it wasn't the proper union. I'm not saying I agree with everything there is in *L'Humanité*. I think a lot of it is silly. A lot of the stuff they write about the United States is obvious bullshit. And they're only playing the game of the French bourgeoisie and the French petit-bourgeois, who hate Americans because Americans are people with dough. I mean

6 Richard Timmons, Dublin-born participant in IRA bombing campaign of 1939; sentenced to fourteen years in November 1939 for possession of explosives; escaped from Wakefield Prison in 1947; dismissed from IRA in 1950; further estranged from republicans by writing a series of articles for a British newspaper that claimed to be an authentic account of the bombing campaign.

7 Members of Behan's social circle in Paris and Dublin. Michael Heron, associate editor of *Envoy: An Irish Review of Literature and Art* (1949–51); also translator and author of travelogues and books of curiosities. Gainor Stephen Crist, hard-living American; studied in Trinity College Dublin under the GI Bill in the late 1940s; remained in Dublin into the 1950s, where he became ubiquitous in the city's literary circles; the model for Sebastian Dangerfield, the main character in J. P. Donleavy's *The Ginger Man* (1955).

«here with a loaf of bread
a flask of wine-a book of

they're successful capitalists — a few are unsuccessful ones — and they come to France if they go anywhere else. They're courteous and civil to staff in hotels. At least, any of them I've ever seen ... They're a little bit loquacious some of them. Mostly a kindly and a well-disposed people. Anyway, they've got *L'Humanité* everywhere in sight at the CGT. So I went out and I started to work and by this time I had a room with a man called Michael Heron, an Englishman, and a man called Gainor Crist, an American.[7] And while I'm exceedingly fond of the French, I orbited principally amongst English-speaking French people and native speakers of English in the *Quartier Latin*. Because I'm not Samuel Beckett, I don't love to be funny in two languages. Though I *am* funny in two — I'm funny in Irish and I'm funny in English. But anyway, I worked for a little while as a housepainter. Drank anything I got. Wasn't much.

You liked living in France?

The French system is OK for the French. If you'vc got a homc, if you've got a wife and kids, you don't do too bad. The standard of living is good, as good as anywhere I know. You've got cheap charges and allowances. You've got cheap travel on the métro. Once you're established. Once you're a citizen and you've got a house and so forth and so on. But anyway — about *Borstal Boy*. You want to know about writing it?

No ...

So I'll tell you how to write it. First, to write you've got to have some place to fucking write. You've gotta have paper, you've gotta have ink.

How did you happen to belong to a terrorist organization to start with ...

I was not a member of a terrorist organisation. I was a member of the

In a Dublin bar, early 1950s.
Photograph: Picture Post/Hulton Archive/Getty Images.

Irish Republican Army. It's not a terrorist organization.

I mean ...

The Deuxième Bureau is a terrorist organization.[8] The Gestapo was a terrorist organization.

It may be true, but that's state terrorism.

So how did I become a member of the Irish revolutionary movement?

Yes. That's what I meant to say.

Well, my grandfather was a member of an organization called the Invincibles, who were peculiar. They used to run off to France whenever they were on the lam — when they were on the run. They did what was called the 'Park Murders'. They stabbed Lord Frederick Cavendish who was a Chief Secretary of Ireland and the other Chief Secretary, a fellow called Burke. They bumped them off in the Phoenix Park in eighteen hundred and eighty-three.[9] The day before there had been fifteen people, including a child of twelve, murdered in the West of Ireland by England's Royal Irish Constabulary.[10] There wasn't fucking anything said about that, of course, but there were great tears of lamentation for Lord Cavendish — Lord Frederick — and for Mr. Burke. My great grandfather was in the revolutionary movement, the Irish republican movement, which was founded by a Protestant — by a Presbyterian — by people who were fundamentally deists — some of them were under the influence of the French Revolution — by Wolfe Tone, who was a Protestant — by Robert Emmet, whose brother's grave I saw in New York City when I was there.[11] And it was a republican movement. My people were republicans; they were socialists. They still are. Brother of mine was a member of the National Executive of the British Communist Party. He went to Hungary —

I don't know the rights and wrongs of the Hungarian situation — but he gave an interview to *The Daily Express*, and then left it. I don't know that he really cares about Hungary, about Russia, about the ordinary people anywhere. I don't think he knows ... I don't think he's sufficiently intelligent to have any heart. I don't think my brother should have done that.[12]

You'd like Ireland to be a socialist country?

To me the ideal is a socialist thirty-two county republic. It's a very old one; it's not new. Our flag, the flag of the Irish Republic — it's the national flag now — the orange, white and green came from revolutionary France in 1848. It came from the Communards and was brought here by a man named Thomas Francis Meagher who, incidentally, became a big general on the Union side in the American Civil War later on. He led something called the Pennsylvania Line.[13] But my uncle who wrote the Irish national anthem also wrote a song for the October Revolution in 1917. Radio Éireann was doing a radio programme about him here. Now he's an accepted part of what they call in England 'the Establishment', but they didn't give him very much when he was alive.[14] They gave him a military funeral when he was dead — they gave him a state funeral — and they repaid him for his long devotion to Ireland by having all the traffic lights green for the funeral. Em, I should go and eat something ... (*Goes out the back. A woman's voice can be heard in the kitchen. Behan returns wiping his mouth and sits back in his chair. He's still puffing his cigar.*) Now about this book ...

Un Peuple Partisan. *That's the French title for* Borstal Boy.

By the way, what does *peuple partisan* mean? I know what *peuple* means — means 'the people'. And a *partisan* means 'a partisan'...

8   Deuxième Bureau, the French secret service.

9   Lord Frederick Cavendish, newly-appointed Chief Secretary of Ireland, and Thomas H. Burke, Under Secretary, were stabbed to death on 6 May 1882 close to the Viceregal Lodge in the Phoenix Park, Dublin. The assassins were members of the Invincibles, a small republican grouping. James Carey, a member of the group, turned informer. His information led to the execution of five men in summer 1883; eight others were sentenced to long terms of imprisonment. Carey sailed for Australia but was assassinated off the coast of South Africa. His assassin was hanged in London that December. These events loom large in oral histories of Dublin and feature in Joyce's *Ulysses*.

10 On 5 May 1882, the day before the assassination of Cavendish and Burke, the RIC fired into a group of boys in Ballina, county Mayo, fatally wounding twelve-year-old Patrick Melody, a member of a children's band.

11 Thomas Addis Emmet (1764–1827), physician and barrister; United Irishman; brother of Robert Emmet (1778–1803); arrested before 1798 Rising and exiled after it; distinguished lawyer in New York; buried in St. Mark's-in-the-Bowery; there is an obelisk commemorating him in the graveyard of St. Paul's Chapel, Broadway.

12 Brian Behan (1928–2002), activist and author; convicted of juvenile delinquency and sent to the Christian Brothers' Industrial School in Artane, Dublin; emigrated to Britain to work as labourer; joined the British Communist Party; travelled extensively in communist states but split from the party over the Soviet invasion of Hungary; lectured in media studies at the London School of Printing; published works include *With Breast Expanded* (1964), *Mother of All the Behans* (1984) and *Kathleen* (1988).

13 Behan here confuses the revolutionaries of 1848 and the Communards of 1871. Thomas Francis Meagher (1823–67), leading figure in the Young Ireland movement; brought the tricolour from Paris in 1848 and adapted it as the flag of Irish nationality; transported to Tasmania after the 1848 Rising; escaped to the US; led the Irish Brigade for the Union in the Civil War; appointed governor of Montana; drowned in obscure circumstances in Missouri River.

14 Peadar Kearney (1883–1942), housepainter and songwriter; worked behind the scenes in the Abbey Theatre; fought in the 1916 Rising and was afterwards interned; he wrote many well-known songs, including 'The Tri-coloured Ribbon' and 'The Soldier's Song' (1911), adopted as the national anthem of Ireland in 1922.

15 Fianna Éireann or Na Fianna, the youth organization of the IRA.

16 Tommy Woods (1919–36), Irish republican and member of the International Brigade; killed in action near Córdoba.

17 The Blueshirts, popular name for the Army Comrades Association (est. 1932), later the National Guard (1933–36), a half-cocked fascist organization associated with the new Fine Gael party; led by Eoin O'Duffy (1892–1944), retired Free State general and ex-Garda commissioner; O'Duffy's theatrics became an embarrassment to the party leadership, which ousted him in 1935; the following year some seven hundred supporters followed him to Spain to fight on behalf of Franco.

18 Behan may here be referring, inter alia, to Diana Mitford (1910–2003), wife of Bryan Walter Guinness (1905–92); married in 1929, Mitford deserted Guinness for British fascist leader Sir Oswald Mosley (1896–1980); married Mosley in 1936 in the home of Joseph Goebbels with Adolf Hitler among the guests; interned in Britain during World War II; lived in Ireland before settling in Paris; editor of right-wing journal *The European* and author of several books.

I wish English always were that easy.

(Behan starts singing a full-throated version of the 'Song of the Partisans': La-la-la-la-la-la ... La-la-la-la-la-la-la ...) We were starting about the book ...

... and the IRA ... In France they say that the title of Borstal Boy *is a bit disingenuous because you were in fact an IRA prisoner.*

Oh yeah, well, I joined an organization called the Fianna, which was a boys' organization, in 1932, when I was nine.[15]

You joined the IRA at nine? That's kind of early.

It's a youth organization! The only youth organization anywhere you could join except you joined the boy scouts, which were a British and an imperialist organization where you salute the flag and all. I don't see what else you could join if you were a kid. I was in the Fianna until I was fourteen. In 1937 a lot of friends of mine went and fought in the International Brigade in Spain. One of them, a boy called Tommy Woods, was two years older than myself when he went away. He was sixteen. He was killed when he was seventeen in Spain.[16]

My own uncle was killed in Spain too in 1936.

The people who were opposed to us, called the Blueshirts, they sent away people to fight for Franco.[17] They didn't do any fighting. They're the only military expedition in history that came back with more fucking men than they went away with. They went away with six hundred and they came back with six hundred and six because they picked up some Irish fellows who just wanted to come home. The Spanish used to call them *los turistas irlandéses*, the Irish tourists. They used to call General O'Duffy, who was their leader, 'the flying postman'. It must be remembered that fascism in Ireland had a very interesting

origin. It was largely supported by the British elements, supported very heavily by the Protestants, I'm sorry to say. Naturally, they got support from the Catholic priests — from some of them; some of them were against. But I'd say the hierarchy, I'd say the bishops were for it. Which is an unholy alliance of people — some of whom are friends of mine. The Guinness organization backed it with money. The big industrialists — it happens that in Ireland they are mainly Protestants — they didn't mind Catholic fascism, providing it was the same as the French bourgeoisie under Hitler.[18]

Now tell me, when did you first think of becoming a writer?

Well, if you look up the genealogies ... It's a contradictory feature of my character that I'm a great snob. My snobbery takes peculiar forms. For instance, one of the greatest men I ever saw in my life was André Marty. He was the secretary of the French Communist Party. I heard him speak in that Colombes Stadium. I didn't know what he was saying, but he was a good speaker and seemed to me to be a good man. Is he alive or dead? I don't know. I heard Jacques Duclos speak. He struck me as a good fellow — a fellow with a lot of humour — a very funny fellow. I heard de Gaulle speak at a place called Avenue d'Orléans, now the Avenue du Général Leclerc. At least I was at the opposition meeting. De Gaulle's not a bad guy; he's a good fellow.[19] He's trying to do the best he can. In some ways, I think the Communists ought to give him a rest — they ought to leave him alone. But eh, the Communists ought to give themselves a rest sometimes too.

Have you ever thought of living in France permanently?

I don't know what country I could live in except here; I only live here because they can't ... Well, they treat me OK here. The prime minister insults me, of course.

Because of what you wrote?

Well, to get back to that book ...

You wanted to say something about genealogies ...

My name in Irish means 'people who tend bees'. The Behans are an ancient literary family from south Leinster, a few miles south of Dublin. But they were never able to produce anything. The best-known member of this clan is, eh, Brendan Behan. It's the first piece of evidence you fuckin' got that we were a literary family. (*Sylvère laughs.*) Well, on my mother's side, my grandmother wrote and recited Gaelic and English verse. She was, of course, a native speaker of Irish. She came from county Meath.[20] And my father ... It's a very strange thing, the heaviest concentration of Roman Catholics in the entire world — that is to say Catholics that work at it, as the Yank says; people who go to mass every Sunday — is to be found in North Dublin. I never met a priest from North Dublin ... Well, I met a priest geographically from North Dublin, but not by what is famous in literature, in *Ulysses* and in the plays of Sean O'Casey. I never met one person from it who was a priest. I never met a person from it who was a policeman. I never met anyone from it was a schoolteacher. As they say, there's snobbery in hell, and there's snobbery in Ireland.

I assume you were born among the upper-classes ...

We were from tenement houses. My father is a very witty, smart man. He is a housepainter. And he used to read a lot. My uncle Peadar Kearney, my mother's brother, wrote a lot. He wrote songs. Some of them have become the songs you hear Irish people singing all over the world, no matter where you go. At least everywhere in the world I've ever been where there were Irish people. Ordinary Irish people. I don't mean

diplomats. I don't mean the type of people who go to the Sorbonne. They probably wouldn't know very much about him.

I didn't know much about him, I'm sorry to say. But then I go to the Sorbonne. Actually you can't be too snobbish about it. Anyone graduating from high school can be admitted there.

The ordinary Joes, anywhere they go, even the Protestants from the north-east, from the Shankill Road, the ordinary Belfast worker, if he gets drunk enough, and gets amongst a lot of his countrymen from other parts of Ireland, he sings 'Glory-o, Glory-o, to the Bold Fenian Men', which is a song written by my uncle and was in a film called *Down with the Rio Grande*.[21] I don't know whether he got any money out of it. I didn't know as much about Hollywood then as I do now. I would have seen he got more.

So you were born in culture after all. There always were books around. That's how you got the idea of writing Borstal Boy?

Anyway, I was always surrounded by books, although we lived in the slum. My father used to steal books, mostly from convent libraries, or from the libraries of such Protestants as can read. I don't like employers. And since a lot of my employers happened to be Protestant, I didn't like a lot of Protestants. The Protestants produced great writers — Yeats, Sam Beckett and others too numerous to mention, as the saying has it. But most of the Protestant people around Dublin that had any money were business people who didn't read anything except the Bible and the bank-book. Mostly reactionary in politics and snobbish. Kindly for the most part, except if you were working for them.

You kind of stole your way into literature?

I read Rabelais when I was very small, about Pantagruel coming out of his mother's

19 André Marty (1886–1956), naval engineer and communist activist; led a mutiny against French intervention in the Bolshevik Revolution; involved in the establishment of the International Brigade to fight in the Spanish Civil War. Jacques Duclos (1896–1975), quondam editor of Communist Party's underground journal *L'Humanité*; organizer of communist resistance group in World War II. Charles de Gaulle (1890–1970), leader of Free French in London during war years; later conservative statesman and president of the fifth republic, 1958–69. De Gaulle ended the French war in Algeria by signing the peace treaty at Evian with the Front de Libération Nationale in 1962.

20 Kathleen Kearney (1889–1984), known in her later years as a singer and broadcaster; she had seven children; twice married, both her husbands — Jack Furlong (d.1918) and Stephen Behan (c.1888–1967) — fought in the 1916 Rising; she was a messenger for the insurgents. Stephen Behan, housepainter, republican; imprisoned, 1922–24.

21 *Rio Grande* (1950), directed by John Ford, starring John Wayne and Maureen O'Hara, writing credits James Warner Bellah and James Kevin Mc Guinness.

22 Thomas Davis (1814–45), native of Mallow, county Cork; nationalist poet, songwriter and journalist; co-founder of *The Nation* and key member of the Young Ireland group that developed around it; critic of Daniel O'Connell's Catholic nationalism, attitude to higher education and venality.

23 Patrick J. Bourke (1883–1932), actor-manager and playwright; produced one of the first full-length films made in Ireland, *Ireland a Nation* (1913).

24 Dionysius Lardner Boucicault (1820–90), Irish-American actor, actor-manager and famous dramatist; his best-known melodramas include *The Colleen Bawn* (1860) and *The Shaughraun* (1875).

25 Behan went to England in 1939 to participate in an IRA bombing campaign; arrested within hours of disembarking at Liverpool, he was sentenced to three years in borstal in February 1940. Deported to Ireland in November 1941, he was arrested again in April 1942 for firing at a Special-Branch detective after an Easter Rising commemoration in Glasnevin Cemetery; sentenced to fourteen years penal servitude, he spent four years in the Curragh before his release in 1946 as part of a general amnesty for IRA prisoners. He served a short sentence in Strangeways prison for his participation in an IRA jail-break in 1947 and was jailed for a month in Ireland in 1948 for a breach of the peace.

26 Elizabeth Cleghorn Gaskell (1810–65), novelist; works include *Mary Barton* (1847), *Cranford* (1853) and *North and South* (1855).

27 Possibly James Hadley Chase's *No Orchids for Miss Blandish* (1939), a crime novel popular in Britain during World War II, despite its alleged fascist sympathies.

28 Frank Harris (1856–1931), Irish journalist and biographer who had a brilliant career in London; his *Oscar Wilde* appeared in 1916. Lady Jane Francesca Wilde (1826–96), poet; published under the name Speranza.

fuckin' ear or whatever he did. I remember my father stole a copy of Rabelais in two volumes. It was a beautiful edition. And he stole it from a Dominican monastery at Castleknock. And he brought it out under his coat. I said, 'How did you get away with it?' 'How?' he says, 'Those fuckin' druids' — which was his familiar way of referring to the clergy of his Church — 'they'd never suspect that a housepainter would take Rabelais. If I pinched a bottle of whiskey, they'd go for it quick enough.' But they didn't think a housepainter, an ordinary Joe, was going to knock off Rabelais. So that was only one book. He had the *Decameron* of Giovanni Boccaccio. My mother used to read his Thomas Davis, who was a great Protestant patriot who came originally from Cork.[22] The only thing I can say about him as a poet is that he never used the word *thee* or *thou* or *thine* or *thy*. I mean he had a sufficiently good knowledge of the English language as she is spoke not to give us any thees or thys or thous. But there were always books around where I was. And even the business of royalties was familiar to me because then my mother's sister was married to a man called P. J. Bourke, who ran the Queen's Theatre in Dublin.[23] He used to put on this great playwright ... was perhaps the most famous playwright in the English speaking world — which is to say in the theatre generally — about the year 1900. He was a man called Boucicault. It was a French name because he was a Dublin man, but, like many another good Dublin man, he was of Huguenot descent. We called him 'Busycot'.[24] But my uncle used to put on his plays and he used to put on revues, sometimes French revues which were very popular. I'm fucked if I know why because the French don't know how to dance. They don't get a good line number. You don't get good chorus girls from France. You get them from the north of England ... from Birmingham and places like that. You won't get any French girls to lift up their legs in unison. And the real test of a line number is that when one cunt opens, they should all open. When one cunt

shuts, they should all shut. Up down, *dum da dum dar um da.* (*He sings.*)

Derek: *When you were in prison, what did you read?*

Anything I could get. When I was in prison ... Prison and borstal, Derek, are two separate transactions.[25] When you were in prison, you got whatever books the librarian cared to leave in to you. When you were in borstal, I read Sean O'Casey; I read Bernard Shaw — I stick pretty close to my own land's men, you know — I read Dickens; a woman called Mrs. Gaskell.[26] I read a book from Miss Blandish, which was discovered to be a fraud, snare, a delusion, a very silly book.[27] We'd a good library there. I read Frank Harris's *Life of Wilde* — the first time I discovered what Oscar Wilde had done. I'd always thought he was an Irish rebel because his mother — Speranza was the name she wrote under — she was an old rebel.[28] Wilde was an Irish gentleman, as he said himself. I can see no reason for an Irish gentleman being put into prison by a lot of fucking base-born troglodytes from the London suburbs except it was for being an Irish rebel. And I suppose he was a rebel, of sorts. But then I don't like Wilde's writing very much, I'm afraid.

Derek: *Reading in prison did sort of stimulate your desire to write?*

No, I always wanted to be a writer. When I was a kid and saw a piece of paper on the street I'd kick it in front of me so it stopped there and read it before I'd walk on. The idea that I became a writer in jail is a fallacious one. Nobody becomes a writer in prison. The only kind of writer you become in prison is a bad writer. There was one book written in jail, *Pilgrim's Progress*. It was not a part of my education as a child. I was raised a Catholic and a Red. There was no place for pilgrims and progress in my childhood, I'm happy to say. I read the fucking thing afterwards. They should have stuck him back in Bedford prison for writing it.

In much of your work, The Hostage, *for instance, prisons always seem to be very present.*

Well, the world is a prison for anyone who hasn't got any money. You know what Albert Camus said? He said, 'The duty of the writer is not to those who are in power, but to those that are subject to them.'[29] In the same way, an awful lot of people go to prison and it doesn't seem to fundamentally matter much what you go to prison for. It's not an important point. People get into jail for all sorts of situations. I mean, I don't try to shed tears for everybody in prison. The troubles of Mr. Eichmann, for instance, weigh very lightly on my shoulders. I go to sleep quite well and sleep without worrying very much about what is happening to him.[30] But a great number of people get into jail as kind of an inconvenience. A great number of people live in the shadow of imprisonment for one reason or another.

And you seem to have had plenty of reasons yourself. Good ones too.

Oh jails, workhouses and whorehouses.

Same sort of things?

Oh no, I should hope not the same sort of things. But actually, *Borstal Boy* was a very innocent kind of a book. It's as innocent as it seems to be. A lot of kids in together; they were all healthy kids because they had to be healthy to go to that particular place. They had the normal sort of fear and wonder of kids. They had also the bravado by which we all live. Man lives in a strange environment. He hasn't been here very long. He does the best he can. Does better all the time. Old people are not so decrepit as they used to be when I was a kid and I don't see any children with bare feet. I know tourists tell me, or people who've been to Ireland on a visit tell me, that they met lots of barefoot children. I didn't meet any barefoot children — not in a long time. I never went barefoot myself, incidentally, but plenty of kids

round our way did. I'm also told you meet a lot of beggars in Dublin. But I've seen lots of beggars in Paris; I've seen lots of them in New York. I've seen people sleeping on the métro in Paris. And the only reason you don't see them in London is they're not allowed to sleep on the métro. But there are beggars in London and plenty of them. And there are plenty of them that sleep out in Hyde Park. But ... em ... you were asking me something about ...

About Borstal Boy ...

Eh, the sympathies of any writer are actually with the world at large. The world at large is not such a happy place as it might be. But these kids were healthy. Sexually, of course, they masturbated, which, of course, everybody does at that age. I think the only people who don't masturbate are people who've been married for a good number of years. They sort of don't bother with it. Not because it's distasteful, but just because it doesn't fucking mean anything. But at that age, of course, they do. Mr. Justice Frankfurt and Mr. Justice Brandeis went to a lecture by Kinsey — this is the story I was going to tell you — and Mr. Justice Brandeis, who seems to be a bit of an old ballocks, comes out and he said, 'Frankfurt, this man says that all Americans boys between the ages of thirteen and twenty-three they masturbate. I never masturbated.' 'Well,' says Frankfurt, 'You missed a damned good thing.'[31] But there was nothing very physical about sex in borstal. Sometimes fellows got into bed with other fellows. But once they got into bed they didn't exactly fucking know what to do. They didn't know what way to go about whatever they were after. And once or twice a fellow fell asleep and another bloke joined his bed and was caught. Of course, he was caught. Ah, they didn't make a big song and dance over it. How do you expel him? (*Laughs.*) Told him never to do it again, or some fucking thing. I think fellows used to pull each other off and things of that sort. But mostly they were fond of each other,

29 Albert Camus (1913–60), novelist, essayist and playwright; awarded the Nobel Prize for Literature in 1957; delivered a much-admired acceptance speech on literature, truth and liberty. Behan here paraphrases: 'By definition [the artist] cannot put himself today in the service of those who make history; he is at the service of those who suffer it.'

30 Adolf Eichmann (1906–62), Gestapo official; played a key role in the extermination of Jews and Gypsies; escaped from an American internment camp in 1946 and fled to Argentina; identified and abducted by Israeli secret service agents in May 1960; his trial in Jerusalem in summer 1961 attracted international attention; executed in May 1962.

31 Alfred C. Kinsey (1894–1956), biologist; led pioneering research project at Indiana University on human sexuality, the findings appearing in *Sexual Behavior in the Human Male* (1948) and *Sexual Behavior in the Human Female* (1953). Louis Brandeis (1856–1941), Associate Justice of US Supreme Court; Felix Frankfurter (1882–1965), appointed to the US Supreme Court in 1938.

32 Behan is playing here on *foi*, faith and *foie*, liver.

rather like young animals. They fought — not so much as they do in ordinary schools, because they were a tough lot of boys. The first thing you learned was to keep your hands down, because if you didn't keep your hands down some fellow would bang you one in the fucking head. The real way of fighting, of course, was you struck a man with your head and then you kneed him in the ballocks at the same time. This was known as the Knee-and-Nut. But they were a good crowd of kids. A lot of them were Cockneys, and Cockneys are from a big city. It's not much of a city, but it's a city. It's a big expanse of built-up area. They were very kind people, very witty and very funny, very entertaining. They wouldn't be entertaining to me now, but they were entertaining to me then. They were all kids. They were healthy. I won't say they were happy. I don't know who's fucking happy. I'm happy. Sometimes. The French say *question de foi*. Well, we all are good livers; don't know we have much faith.[32]

With theatre director Joan Littlewood (1914–2002) on the set of *The Hostage*, Theatre Royal, London, 1958; Littlewood's 1956 production (with Gerry Raffles) of *The Quare Fellow* brought Behan critical acclaim and celebrity.
Photograph: Joe Waldorf/ The Observer/Getty Images.

So there was nothing much wrong with borstal itself?

Well, broadly speaking, I was as happy in borstal as — I don't say in prison, prison was where I was when I was brought in first — but broadly speaking I was as happy in borstal as I was anywhere else. And, you know, a lot of them — it was very sad — a lot of them were killed during the war. Quite a number of them. I think a bigger proportion than any similar group of people.

What's the experience you remember most vividly from all your years in prison or in borstal?

All my years? I don't remember. People forget; they don't remember. Except I remember professionally. If you were to stick a thousand dollars under my nose, or two hundred and fifty pounds, I'd remember quick enough. That'd jog my fucking memory. But it's an effort. I remember I had great health. I used to box at nine stone and two. I wasn't a very good boxer. Gene Tunney, who was perhaps the greatest boxer that ever lived, was the only man who ever looked at me and accepted the fact.[33] He said, 'Yeah.' He says, 'Yeah.' Other people say, 'Oh I'm sure you were better than you think you were. You're just saying that. You're just being modest.' Well, I was a very bad boxer for two reasons. I couldn't fight except I was in a temper and I don't get in a temper unless I get scared. And when I was in the ring I wasn't scared. I guess I wasn't ferocious enough. Basically, I had a short reach — too short a reach for my weight, do you understand? And I remember everybody; they were a decent crowd. The people in charge of the place were English intellectuals. Any kind of intellectual is better than no intellectual. You can't get along without the fucking intellectuals. Nobody can.

How old were you when you left school?

Twelve. I was at school with the French

Sisters of Charity. Les Soeurs de St. Vincent de Paul. They were mostly Dublin girls and some French girls. Dublin girls in a convent are very unusual because you don't get many Dublin priests and you don't get many Dublin nuns. Well, these were mostly Dublin girls, from north-east Dublin near the docks. I went from there to the Christian Brothers when I was eleven. They were the biggest crowd of fucking bastards that I have ever met in my life. If I had a child I would not send him to anywhere except to where there were married men. I don't give a ballocks as to whether the men were young or they were old, but they gotta be married. No unmarried man is entitled to have children under his control. A woman perhaps, when the woman is getting screwed good enough, she's OK. Nuns seem to me to be an exception. They were very nice people. They were very good-humoured people. Whether they're especially blessed by God or not, I don't know, but apparently the blessing seems to extend only to the female section of the religious communities. The men were just nuts. They used to beat kids up. It was obvious that they weren't getting laid often enough. And I don't like religious people to have charge of children either. Well, I like children to have a bit of religion, maybe, but not too much. If I was given the choice between having a very religious person and an atheist that was well-read and had advanced and progressive ideas, if I was given the alternative of having, say, a very religious person who only read *La Croix* — is that what you call it? — and having an atheist that read *L'Express* or *France-Observateur*, well I'll take the reader of *France-Observateur* or *L'Express*.[34] I'd get religion somewhere else if I wanted to. But anyway, I always wrote, and I always wanted to write. Then when I was twelve I got published for the first time. I wrote an article for a republican magazine called *Fianna*. It was the paper of the scout organization I was a member of. I wrote an article then for a left-wing paper called *The Irish Democrat*, when I was about twelve. The editor of it was a man that was killed

33 James Joseph Tunney (1897–1978), American heavyweight boxer; defeated Jack Dempsey to become world heavyweight champion in 1926; retained his title in 1927 in a famous and controversial return bout; retired as champion in 1928 with 65-1-1 record and 47 KOs; successful businessman.

34 *La Croix* is a liberal Catholic journal; the other two weekly magazines were on the far Left at the time.

35 Éamonn McGrotty (1912–37), b. Mount Street, Rosemount, Derry; joined Christian Brothers teaching order; left and took up journalism in Dublin; advertising manager for *An tÉireannach*, Irish-language republican newspaper; member of the IRA; involved in Na Fianna; prominent in Conradh na Gaeilge; joined International Brigade; killed in action at Jarama.

36 Sean O Faolain (1900–91), short-storywriter, novelist, man of letters; took republican side in the Irish Civil War; became disenchanted with republicanism; founded and edited (1940–46) the literary journal *The Bell*.

37 O Faolain visited Behan in Mountjoy Jail after his arrest for firing at a Special Branch detective in April 1942; Behan's 'I Became a Borstal Boy' appeared in *The Bell* in June 1942.

38 *Cúirt an Mheán-Oíche* [The Midnight Court] (1780) is a bawdy tour de force about sexual relations; the poet, Brian Merriman (c.1749–1805), imagines a court of women sitting in judgement on men for failing to satisfy their sexual needs.

39 The poem consists of 1,026 lines; Behan here recites an extract from the introductory section. The translations listed are Ussher (1926), O'Connor (1945) and Marcus (1953); O'Connor's translation had first appeared in *The Bell* (1941). Behan claimed to have translated the poem in its entirety but lost his only copy of it; a section of his translation is in *Borstal Boy*.

40 Republican Congress (1934–35), radical umbrella group; established in March 1934 after the IRA army convention voted against adopting a more radical position on social issues; key figures included George Gilmore (1898–1985), Peadar O'Donnell (1893–1986) and Frank Ryan (1902–44); split into republican and socialist factions at its first convention in September; dissolved 1935.

41 Liam Tumilson, Irish republican and member of International Brigade, formerly member of the Orange Order; radicalized by outdoor relief riots; joined IRA and adopted Irish-language form of his Christian name (William); left IRA to join Republican Congress, 1934; killed in action at Jarama, 14 March 1937.

afterwards in Spain, a man called Eugene McGrattan.[35] He was from Derry, incidentally. I always wrote these things. Then when I'd come out of jail in 1942 — when I'd come out of borstal — I wrote an article for a magazine called *The Bell*. It was published by Sean O Faolain.[36] I think he's a well-known writer, at least he's well-known in England and America. I don't know about France. And O Faolain taught me a lot about writing. He told me, first of all, to cut out this shit where I was trying to get a bit of sympathy for myself. I was trying to get a bit of glory for myself as a republican martyr. So he cured me of that very effectively. And I suppose I just started writing.[37] I started to write exactly what happened. The defeats, the cowardice ... and you know, they're important too.

Derek: *I believe you write very good poetry in Irish. Have you ever written any in English?*

No. Except the translation of a poem called 'The Midnight Court'. Have you ever heard of it?[38]

Derek: *No.*

Never heard of 'The Midnight Court'? You should be ashamed of yourself as an Irishman. W. B. Yeats said, 'It's a violent, extravagant and an altogether remarkable and glorious poem.' Would you like to hear a bit of the translation? Well, I'll say the Irish too:

Siolla de mo shúil dar shamhlaíos uaim,
Chonacas chugam le ciumhais an chuain
An mhásach, bholgach, tholgach, thaibhseach,
Chámhnach, cholgach, ghairgeach, ghaibhdeach;
A hairde ceart, má mheas mé díreach,
Sé nó seacht de shlata is fuílleach,
Péirse beacht dá brat ag sraoilleadh
Léi sa tslab le drab is draoibeal...

I saw as I suddenly looked around approach from the bay with titanic strong sound a big-bellied bitch — well-arsed, gigantic, fierce, fearless, furious, formidable, frantic;
If my terror-struck gaze could estimate right, six or seven full yards or more was her height.
A mile of her mantle behind her trailed ...

That's a bailiff summoning the poet to the court, presided over by the Queen of the Fairies, where the women of Ireland protest against the men of Ireland. The men of Ireland aren't screwing them often enough. It's a good poem. You ought to read it. There are three translations. One is by a bad Catholic like myself, Frank O'Connor. The other is by Percy Arland Ussher who is a Protestant. The third is by David Marcus who is a Jew. They're all very good. They're all available. And they're all worth reading.[39]

You mentioned before that you belonged to a youth nationalist organization ...

I was in a republican organization. Besides being a nationalist organization it was a republican organization and it was a socialist organization. The IRA since that time has not been socialist. It's not been anti-socialist; it's just not been anything politically.

You were nine then. What happened to you when you were sixteen and got arrested?

Oh, I was thrown out of the IRA because I was accused of left-wing activity. By that time there had been a split in the IRA and the left wing had started an organization called the Republican Congress, most of whose members fought afterwards in the International Brigade in Spain.[40] It was a Dublin crowd. A lot from the country too. One fellow was from Belfast that was killed. A fellow called ... Jesus ... Tommelson, I think.[41] What else do you want to know?

What happened after you left the prison?

So I went to France. In France I was writing — in English, of course. I wrote a bit. Finally, I got a job working for Mr. de Valera's newspaper, *The Irish Press*. A friend of mine who'd been in prison over the IRA became editor of it, McGuinness.[42] He gave me a column to do every week, which I did. And I lived on the column while I finished *Borstal Boy*. So Mr. de Valera did this much good for literature, that he enabled me to finish *Borstal Boy*. I didn't have it finished, but I had most of it. And a man called Iain Hamilton from Hutchinsons who was a friend of mine ... I don't like publishers as a rule.[43] I would certainly never get into a motor car with anyone belonging to Gallimard; it doesn't seem to be very fortunate for writers in motor cars. But Hamilton was in the Shelbourne Hotel and he saw some of it and he said, 'Can I have

it?' I said, 'You can if you give me a hundred and fifty pounds for it in advance.' He said, 'Sure.' He gave me two hundred fifty pounds to finish it.
And that was that. (*Brendan seems relieved.*) Ça va?

Well, I'm glad we got this far. But you didn't quite finish telling me ...

What? (*Getting angry.*) I can only finish by writing the damn thing ... again. Is that what you mean?

... what you did before you wrote Borstal Boy ...

(*Exploding.*) I can't talk well about writing!

I meant what you did before you went *to jail.*

42 Jim McGuinness, London editor of Irish News Agency and editor of *The Irish Press* in the 1950s; subsequently senior editor at Radió Teilefís Éireann.
43 Iain Hamilton (b.1920), publisher and author; books include *The Irish Tangle* (1970).

In the National Library of Ireland, 1952.
Photograph: Daniel Farson/Hulton Archive/ Getty Images.

44 Camus died in a car accident on 4 January 1960; the car was driven by Michel Gallimard, a relative of his publisher.

45 Françoise Sagan, pseudonym of Françoise Quoirez (1935–2004), vivid supporter of left-wing causes; opposed French war in Algeria; works include *Bonjour tristesse* (1955) and *Aimez-vous Brahms?* (1959). Sartre's play *Les Sequestrés d'Altona* (1959) used Nazi atrocities to attack French torture in Algeria; Camus, who came from Algeria, retreated into an uncharacteristic silence on the topic of the Algerian War.

46 The quotation is usually attributed to Thomas Jefferson (1743–1826), president of US (1801–09).

(*Calming down somewhat.*) Before that, I was in the IRA. And then I went back into it. They had to take me because I'd been a messenger boy for years. I knew more about that than just about anybody else.

Was that a full-time job with the IRA?

Well no, but it became a full-time job. And I knew more about the IRA than possibly any man living. I don't know about what happened lately. I don't bother myself finding out.

Now, did you know that Borstal Boy *has been translated in French?*

No, I didn't know. Who are the publishers, Gallimard?

Yes.

Gallimard are good publishers. It's a pity that Albert Camus was travelling with someone of that family when he was killed.[44] Big loss. I didn't agree with everything Camus said. Several of his attitudes I didn't like, but he made a great statement when he got the Nobel Prize. And he said, 'The duty of a writer is not to those who are in power, but to those who are subject to them.' France has very good reasons to be proud of her writers. I don't speak as a literary critic; I don't speak even from the point of view of my own taste in literature, but as writers — I mean *hommes et femmes de lettres*, which is a phrase not properly translated by the English word 'man of letters' — your *hommes de lettres* in France, from Jean-Paul Sartre to Françoise Sagan, they have remembered that the only certificate a writer can possibly receive for his own integrity — the only genuine certificate he can receive — is being accused of being a traitor to his country.[45] The first duty of a writer is to let his country down. If he can't let his own country down, I don't see how he can let any other country down. His own is the one

he can let down most effectively. By that I do not mean that he lets down the people of his country. But in their attitude to Algeria, Jean-Paul Sartre and Françoise Sagan and the other writers there, they are the conscience of France; they are the *true* France. Even from a purely economic view, nobody goes to France to spend money to look at a lot of bastards with uniforms strutting up and down around the place like a comic opera of fucking heroes, wearing *képis* and blowing Gauloise smoke into the faces of the public. We can see those kind of tramps *anywhere*. You can get them anyplace. You can get old cabalistic, old chauvinistic — it's not even chauvinistic, it doesn't relate to the country as a whole — you can even get that sort of rubbish about the honour of the army and the traditions of the army from countries which have only had an army for five minutes. I have no doubt that the Kentucky Colonels take themselves just as seriously as this marshal that was in Algeria and is now retired, Marshal eh …

Maréchal Juin.

Juin. Yeah. You can get this sort of comic opera Charlie Chaplin *anywhere*. They're all over history. Sometimes they become dangerous. When they become Hitler, or when a Hitler comes along to employ them. But no person loves France for these comic opera thugs. You can get them anywhere. Even if you do happen to like them, you probably prefer your home variety to the foreign sort. There's no need to go across the water, or even across the front yard to look at 'em. You have 'em in *every* country. They're as easy got as a wet foot! But the real France, the France of whom it was said that 'Everyman has two fatherlands, his own and France', that is the France that has been very well represented by my *confrères* in writing.[46] And I'm extremely proud of them.

Your French confrères *certainly are in need of support because the war is really dragging the country down. There's widespread torture in Algeria and political censorship at home. But Ireland has had its share of violence as well, and readers in France are aware of that.* Borstal Boy *wouldn't have been written ...*

Well, I'm very glad first of all that it's been printed in French. I thought it was about time. My other work is in French — two of my plays are. I've not yet seen the French edition. In any event, I cannot read French. Such small French as I have I got it by standing around Les Halles market. I got my first lesson in French when I asked a fellow ... I said to him, 'Où est le bistro, le café de Le Nouvel Siècle dans Les Zalles?' '"Les Zalles", non!' he said to me, '"Les zommes", oui! "Les Zalles", non! "Les Halles".'[47] That's where I got my French grammar from — from a fish porter, a fellow carrying fish around the place. I don't know what you call him in French. I don't know what you call him in English either because I've always avoided hard work as much as I possibly could. But what were we talking about?

About Borstal Boy.

I wrote *Borstal Boy* many years ago.[48]

That was long before The Hostage?

Oh sure. It's a work of affection. There's a man, Mike Todd Jr., who was talking about making a film of it in New York. We're going to get Sal Mineo. Don't know if he's known in France. He's in a movie called *Exodus* now.[49] It's not a good film, but it's a film with good intentions and it's going to make a lot of money so I suppose it's got something to be said for it.

Can we speak a bit more in details about the matter of the book?

The matter of the book ... Sylvère, that's a thing I find very difficult to do. For a

garrulous man, I very seldom talk about my own work. Not that I'm reticent, but because I get bored by talking about it when I'm not actually doing it. However, you've been so good as to go to all this trouble, I've no doubt I can say something. You ask me questions and I'll answer them.

Borstal Boy *is an account of three years of your own life?*

Um, two.

And you spent eight years in prison?

Well, a lot of years. Yeah, eight.

So why did you choose to write only about those two?

Oh, well, they were the first two. It's chronological. And I may never write about the other time because ... First of all, my imagination was not exactly ... Politics, for instance, bore me. I have certain likes and I have certain dislikes in politics. Active members of the Communist Party in Ireland ... For the most part, I didn't find them very satisfactory people. For instance, they would not send me to the USSR because I came out of a slum. They're usually lower-middle-class people, at least the leadership ... At the same time I think the communists are very necessary, they're very necessary to the working class. Whether the people I know, or the people anybody knows as the leaders of the Communist Party would be good people to live under, I don't know. I shouldn't think so, myself. But I think the Communists are a necessity to the working-class, as I think the Irish Republican Army is a necessity to Ireland. But the second period of my imprisonment, which was spent in Ireland, was a period when I was involved in, well, sort of active political agitation inside. The IRA was split. It was split three ways. You see, the IRA had a very long and respectable anti-fascist tradition — a thing that is deliberately

47 Behan had mistakenly assumed *Les Halles* was pronounced like *les hommes*, with a liaison between the 's' and the following vowel; the fish porter was correcting him.

48 *Borstal Boy* was first published in 1958 but Behan had worked on it since the early 1940s, see note 37.

49 Mike Todd Jr. (1929–2002), film producer; b. Los Angeles, son of innovative film producer; stepson of actress Elizabeth Taylor; assistant to his father on *Around the World in 80 Days* (1956); produced *Scent of Mystery* (1960), a film employing Smell-o-Vision technology which piped smells featured in the film's scenes, such as pipe smoke, from tiny tubes beneath the theatre's seats; d. Borris, county Carlow, Ireland. Sal Mineo (1939–76), American actor and theatre director; nominated for Academy Awards for his performance opposite James Dean in *Rebel without a Cause* (1955) and opposite Paul Newman in *Exodus* (1960), Otto Preminger's adaptation of Leon Uris's novel; his career suffered due to rumours about his sexual orientation; developed a new career in theatre; stabbed to death outside his home in Los Angeles.

50 Frank Aiken (1898–1983), an IRA commander during War of Independence and Civil War, later senior Fianna Fáil politician; Minister for Defence (1932–43); Minister for Coordination of Defensive Measures (1943–45); Minister for Finance (1945–48); Minister for External Affairs (1951–54; 1957–69). Frederick Henry Boland (1904–85), diplomat; first Irish ambassador to the United Kingdom (1950–56) and Permanent Representative of Ireland at the UN (1956–63); President of the UN General Assembly (1960–61).

51 Henri Alleg was the editor of the underground left-wing periodical *Alger Républicain*. Arrested in June 1957, he wrote *La Question* (1958) while in prison, exposing the widespread use of torture by the French military; Sartre contributed an introduction to the first edition, which was banned in France.

misrepresented. But they had a very anti-fascist tradition and numbers of them, as a matter of fact one hundred of them, were killed in the defence of Madrid in 1936–37. The founders of the International Brigade and the International Column were members of the Irish Republican Army. They were the first over there. I knew some of them personally, though I was only a child. But during the time I was in jail we were so actively *engagé*, it was sort of ... Perhaps I'll write later about it, but I don't think my time has yet come to write about the second part of my imprisonment. Somehow it doesn't *send* me. Do you understand that expression? It's an American expression. It's a good expression too. Perhaps my period in borstal was a little unreal to the extent that it was in a way, I suppose, a little rest — a rest from Ireland. I find Ireland a very upsetting place because I happen to care a lot about it and am one of the very few people here who knows every part of Ireland. And my position has always been a very ambivalent one, if that's the word I want.

In what way?

For instance, when I had the first night of *The Hostage* in New York, the Irish Minister for External Affairs, Mr. Frank Aiken, and the President of the United Nations who had just been elected that day, Mr. Freddy Boland, and the entire Irish delegation came to my first night.[50] This greatly upset the New York Irish middle classes. The recent Irish arrivals there of the past forty years — those who had made money but were still born in Ireland — were kind of upset. Well, they didn't know what to do. They thought that, of course, if I was good enough for a cabinet minister, then I must be OK. It might seem as if I was accepted. But in actual fact they said that my play was irreligious and blasphemous, that I attacked the Catholic Church. Despite the fact that the Minister of External Affairs and the President of the United Nations

attended my first night. But the week before I left Ireland to go to America, the prime minister — the premier, or *taoiseach* as we say here — Mr. Sean Lemass — good old French name, from an old Huguenot family incidentally, and he was a good soldier himself, a good Irish republican in his time — he attacked me publicly in Tipperary. And he said there were Irish playwrights that were holding their country up to ridicule in rather the same way that some extreme right-wing people would say that Jean-Paul Sartre or Henri Alleg were letting the side down sort of thing.[51] But in actual fact I happen to know more about the people of Ireland than Mr. Lemass. An old woman had a letter to the newspaper last night about her troubles (she was an old-age pensioner) and she said she was going to write to Brendan Behan about it. She didn't say she was going to write to Sean Lemass about it or to de Valera, although I've no desire to go into competition with either of those gentlemen as a politician. The fact remains that she wrote that. On the other hand, in the six counties — in what I consider the occupied part of Ireland — I've gone across the border from Donegal ... When I was making a tour last year, I was received at the border by the Royal Ulster Constabulary. The inspector came down and shook hands with me, said — actually, my car broke down and they actually pushed my car — and some English customs man (the customs is a reserved occupation, I mean the customs in Northern Ireland is manned by London) ... the man came down says, 'Hey, what about his stuff? We gotta examine his stuff.' The Ulster Constabulary man said, 'This is Brendan Behan.' They said, 'Well, we don't care who he is.' 'Nonsense,' he says, 'Sure, he's a great man.' And I went into Derry city and I had a meal. Before I'd been in the hotel, I was at lunch. I sat down to my lunch. And by the time I went out on the street for a walk round the city *The Belfast Telegraph* was out. And it had on the front page that I was in Derry city. And going on the street, people kidded me a bit. They said, 'Do you see the walls?' They're in the centre of Derry where the richer people live, or the business part, where the Protestant population are the majority, though the majority of the people of Derry are Catholic. And a man, obviously a respectable upper-class or middle-class Protestant *bourgeois gentilhomme*, said to me, 'Do you see our walls?' — they had a siege there in 1690, a Williamite war — 'They withstood the greatest siege in history.' Says I, 'What about Stalingrad?' So he didn't quite know what to make of that. That was not the answer he was expecting. And therein lies the key. In that little incident in Derry lies the key to my whole attitude to my country and my country's whole attitude to me. I was greeted on the streets with affection, with respect, and at the same time this man mentioned the siege of Derry — which was where the Williamite or Dutch forces held the city against the Jacobite or French-backed forces, which was, I suppose, our forces. A reverse position had happened during the same war at Limerick, where the Irish and the French under Sarsfield and Saint-Ruth held the city against the Dutch and the English, in other words, against the Protestants — though it was a bit more complicated than that, if you read history; it was largely over an amount of money, like most wars. But this man thought that when he mentioned the siege of Derry, I would immediately say, 'Well, what about the siege of Limerick?' Instead of which, I said 'What about the siege of Stalingrad?' (*Laughs*.) Naturally, but for writing I couldn't possibly live. I like to live well, you see. Those cigars are Hauptmann's. They come from Dunhill's in Fifth Avenue. And even before I ever saw Dunhill's I was still fond of a good cigar and you don't exactly find them growing on trees up in the Phoenix Park. But I couldn't possibly live on what I would make by selling books to the people of Ireland. They banned *Borstal Boy*, as you know; it's banned here.

I wanted to ask you about that. In France they considered it a book about Ireland, that's why they called it Un Peuple Partisan. *I assume it also has to do with the PP alliteration, like BB for Borstal Boy. Why would a book about Ireland be banned there?*

Why is it banned? Because we have censorship here, which is a product of English Victorianism. Usually the people who become priests in Ireland are pretty bad people, even amongst the Catholics — amongst the patriotic Catholic population. And my uncle, remember, wrote the national anthem of this country; he wrote 'A Soldier's Song'. All my people fought in the 1916 Rising — such of them as were available to do so and some of them were. Among the nationalist population, priests are not very much loved. They may be necessary when you're a'dying or getting married or getting born, but you're usually able to get born or buried without anybody's assistance. They believe in the Catholic faith and all, but they don't like priests for the following reasons. Usually the priest is a son of a family who collaborated. They're *collabos* from way way back. They were permitted to be as Catholic as they liked so long as they weren't anti-imperialist. And there was an Irish leader, the leader of the 1916 Rising, Padraic Pearse, who said about the Irish censors — well, there wasn't a censor at the time, but about the kind of people who ban books here — Pearse described that type of person as the 'rotted man'. And this man had such a filthy mind that when he saw a girl putting a bandage on her father's ankle, he'd said, 'Oh no, you must not do that, that's immoral.' And Pearse said when that man died he was so filthy that they wouldn't let him into hell.[52]

You seem ambivalent about the Church as well.

The Church has a somewhat two-faced

52 Patrick H. Pearse or Pádraig/Pádraic Mac Piarais (1879–1916), educationalist, political activist and writer; editor (1903–09) of Irish language journal *An Claidheamh Soluis*; founded two schools; leader of 1916 Rising; executed; his many publications include short stories, plays and essays in Irish and English.

53 Ian Maclennan (1909–86), British ambassador to Ireland (1959–63).

54 Daniel Cohalan (1858–1952), bishop of Cork (1916–1952).

55 Aedan W. McGrath (1906–2000), Columban priest and Legion of Mary organizer in China; imprisoned for subversion in 1951, he was expelled from the country on his release in 1954. See Leo Roberts and Aedan McGrath, comps., *Mary in Their Midst: The Legion of Mary in Action in China, 1948–1951* (Dublin, 1958).

FORTY FOOT
GENTLEMEN
ONLY.

attitude in the matter. If I met a priest in the street he'd say, 'Oh how are you Brendan? Any chance of reading *Borstal Boy*?' Incidentally, a friend of mine, a Protestant clergyman from Donegal, told me he spent a night in the Protestant bishop's house in Derry, the town I was in, and he said he wanted to read something. The Protestant bishop showed him a line of devotional magazines and of devotional books and my friend said, 'I don't want to read them.' And he asked, 'Have you got anything ...' 'Nonsense,' the bishop said. 'There's a shelf below that where I keep the real things I read.' And the first book he saw there was *Borstal Boy*. Incidentally, Sir Ian Maclennan, the British ambassador to Ireland, told me — this is to make matters very clear to anybody who wants to know what my political affiliations are — that there's one place in Dublin that you're always sure to get a copy of *Borstal Boy*, and that's the British Embassy.[53] They have my works in practically all the British embassies all over the world.

You were brought up a Catholic?

Yeah, a very easy one ...

And you also are a nationalist. For what reason exactly do you think your book has been banned then? Is it because you show the Church in agreement with the English?

Ah yes, I show the Church as being *collabo*. And it's a very sore point with 'em because they have always been collaborationists. I mean, the bishop of Cork, Doctor Cohalan, in 1920–21, openly backed the Black and Tans who were the English Gestapo here.[54] And he was under sentence of death by Tom Barry, the leader of the Irish Republican Army in that area. And Cohalan lived on to be about ninety-eight and he was a great embarrassment to the government of Ireland and to the Church, of course. The Church, you see, they tell lies. There was a missionary that was

At Forty Foot male-only bathing pool,
south county Dublin, 1954.
Photograph: Daniel Farson/Hulton Archive/Getty Images

expelled from China. I'll give you his name. His name was Fr. Aedan McGrath and he was expelled by the Chinese government; he was expelled with some other priests.[55] When he came home the newspaper started off by saying that his father was killed in 1920. And then it went on a little further and it said his father was murdered by the British forces in 1920. And it went on, at last, and said his father was an IRA leader who was killed in action. But, in actual fact, his father was shot in Dublin because he was a collaborationist. And he was shot by the Irish Republican Army. Of course, in Ireland as in everywhere else, there are divisions. There's a lower-middle-class, a suburban kind of snobbery about Belfast in Ireland. But Belfast is a much more Irish city. If I went into, say, the Grand Central Hotel in Belfast, I would be accepted as I was years ago very simply as another fellow, as a bit of landscape. They'd say, 'Well 'ow are ye Brendan?' Just because I'm another man that they know and happen to come from Dublin. And they would kid me a bit about the Free State and about the Pope. In any Dublin hotel, by Jesus, they'd send for me. They'd pay me money to go into the Russell or the Shelbourne or the Hibernian, because they've seen my name in *France-Observateur*, in *Le Monde* — not *Le Figaro Littéraire*, that would tax their brains a bit too much. But they've seen my name in *The New York Herald Tribune*, in *The New York Times* and *The Daily Express* and *The Daily Mail* and so forth and so on. But as myself, as a native son of the city, I don't believe I'd be welcomed in those places. The difference is the centre of this city, *le centre-ville*, is a kind of tourist resort. Of course, we have the same kind of tourism as England. We get the leavings of English tourism. Well, Lenin made a statement once when he said the Russian army was for peace. Someone said, when did they vote for peace? How did they vote for peace? He said they voted with their feet. Well, in the same way, the Dublin Catholic, Protestant, Jewish, but mainly Catholic population vote for me at the box office. Now, two theatres

this year — one was the Abbey for *The Quare Fellow* and the other was the Olympia for *The Hostage* ... But my attitude to the powers that be in this country is the attitude of a writer anywhere to the ruling class. If I get a piece of praise abroad they're eager to use it, but I don't get anything from them.

When did you start writing Borstal Boy?

Borstal Boy I started about 1948, but, you see, I started it in Paris. Would you like to know the address of the place I started it in?

Sure, I'd love to know everything that has to do with Borstal Boy ...

I started it in the Hotel Louisiane — which is the corner of the rue de Bucy — in an apartment occupied by a man called Desmond Francis Ryan who for some reason was called by the patron of the hotel '*Monsieur Rien*'.[56] But Desmond Francis Ryan lives in Paris. He lives in the rue Molière. And he's a great — well, he's still a very literary, entertaining man — he is the Paris correspondent of *The Irish Times*. I then left Paris and had no home, no place to go. I was skint in Paris — had no money — and I heard everybody saying you should have been here in Hemingway's time, 1920 and so forth and so on. But the ex-GIs were there and those American guys; they were OK. They were very good to me. One of them who I knew very slightly was Norman Mailer, the man who wrote *The Naked and the Dead*. He bought me ham and eggs in the Pergola. Do you know the Pergola? It's in the boulevard Saint-Germain. Well, he bought me ham and eggs at a time when I had not eaten some ham and eggs for a long long time. I scrounged from Americans who were on the GI Bill of Rights, from a great number of French people. One of them was a lady called — she didn't set up to be a literary sort of a patron or anything of that sort — her name was Dame Housty. She lived in the rue de Grenelle. How I came to meet her was I had been out all night in

56 Desmond Francis Ryan (1893–1964), republican activist, journalist and author; educated by Christian Brothers and at Pearse's Scoil Éanna; later secretary to Pearse and, after his death, his biographer; fought in 1916 Rising; Paris correspondent for *The Irish Times* in the 1950s; author of many books, including a history of the 1916 Rising and biographical studies of John Devoy, James Connolly, Michael Collins, and de Valera.

57 Sean T. O'Kelly (1882–1966), republican activist, later popular politician and statesman; member of Irish Republican Brotherhood and Conradh na Gaeilge; founding member of Sinn Féin (1905); participant in the 1916 Rising; interned; elected MP in 1918; chairman of first Dáil; unsuccessfully sought admittance to Versailles peace conference as official representative of the Irish Republic; took republican side in the Civil War; jailed by Free State; followed de Valera when he left Sinn Féin to found Fianna Fáil; Minister for Local Government and Public Health (1932–39) and Minister for Finance (1939–45); elected President of Ireland 1945; re-elected 1952; retired 1959.

Paris. Paris is a city where you can be out all night. At least you could at that time. I never had trouble with the police in France until I became rich and famous ... Well, not rich but famous. I had been walking around all the night because I had nowhere to go and I called into a couple of cafés to see would I meet anyone who would give me a drink and I couldn't find anybody. So anyway, it was a summer's morning and I went down and ... You go along windowsills in Paris, you're always sure to find something. People are in the habit of leaving odd pieces of food up in the place, so I found some old stuff. I went across the Place de la Concorde where they were making a film at the Cleopatra's needle, the Obélisque. I went and stood with a crowd there. Finally, I wound up walking across the Champs de Mars at about six in the morning. No, I went to Les Halles and I scrounged a swig from a bottle from a *clochard*, from a couple of *clochards*, and I got a couple of pennies and a couple of francs there. I didn't quite get a bowl of onion soup though. Onion soup was always comparatively dear. A lot of foreigners think onion soup is nothing. But then a good onion soup and you're fed for the day. A person living on a diet of one onion soup and a litre of *rouge*, say *treize degrés*, well he's set for the day. He's fit for action. Into bed and out of barracks!

To go back to Borstal Boy ...

Allow me to finish this ... I was going across the Champs de Mars and I met a boy of about eighteen and his name was Jean Chevalier. And he brought me to the house of his aunt and his cousin Nicole and we had breakfast. His aunt's name was Madame Housty. She lived at the rue de Grenelle. And I was in Paris last year or the year before. I had a great success; I was a big shot. I don't remember very much because I was drunk most of the time, I'm sorry to say ... I must have missed a lot of things ... Still, I had some good fun too. We were on the top of the Martini terrace on the Champs-Elysées.

We were supposed to drink martinis but the Martini people are not Jansenists. I mean there was a fair amount of merry gin went into the transaction. But I went searching for Jean Chevalier and Madame Housty and just couldn't find them. And I want to make sure you get this name right. H-O-U-S-T-Y. And if your newspaper could find them for me I'd be very pleased if they would contact me through the newspaper. I'd like to see them again.

I'll do my very best.

I discovered all sorts of contacts like that in Paris. There's a great respect for writers there. I was in a bar called the Breton Bar in the rue Dauphiné. I think the Bretons were the only peasants I ever liked anywhere. I got on very well with them. A woman came in said, 'Who's he? What does he do?' And I said, '*Je suis un peintre en bâtiment.*' And the old concierge, whom I thought hated my guts — he'd never spoken to me before — said, '*C'est un écrivain anglais aussi.*' There was a respect for letters. You don't get that here. In Dublin they'd shout after you in the street. This is a semi-colonial country. North and South there's very little difference, I'm sorry to say. The fact that four hundred linen weavers have to leave Belfast and go work in Europe doesn't please me. I don't get any kick out of that. Ireland's great export, amongst a lot of other people, is a lot of university graduates. Every university graduate that sees me come home and is running around unemployed or is stuck in some civil service job says, 'I hate that bastard. He only gets there because he's a loud-mouth, an obscene Dublin guttersnipe from the slums.' What they forget, of course, is that I'm a man of the cities. My grandmother had smaller hands than I have. She was a seamstress.

There's an old nationalist tradition in your family.

Nationalist tradition? Sure. My family? Good Jesus, my father was a prisoner

Addressing a theatre audience, probably in Berlin or Paris, 1959.
Photograph: Robert Lackenbach/Time Life Pictures/Getty Images.

58 Bertolt Brecht (1898–1956), German poet, playwright and director; developed theatre as a forum for political debate; founded (with Helene Weigel) the Berliner Ensemble in 1949; they staged many of Brecht's most famous plays; hounded by the House Un-American Activities Committee; recipient of the Stalin Peace Prize, 1954. Jarolsav Hasek (1883–1923), Czech novelist whose satiric masterpiece was *The Good Soldier Schweik* (1935).

59 Eugene Ionesco (1912–94), Romanian-born avant-garde dramatist and critic of communism; settled in Paris in 1938; key figure in the Theatre of the Absurd; major works include *La Cantatrice chauve* (1950), *La Leçon* (1951), *Les Chaises* (1952), *Le Nouveau Locataire* (1955) and *Rhinocéros* (1960).

60 The CNR was a committee, composed mostly of communists, that co-ordinated the resistance to German occupation during World War II.

when I was born. The first place my father ever saw me as a baby I was outside of Kilmainham prison. He was inside the prison with Sean T. O'Kelly, the ex-president ... [57]

And yet from Borstal Boy *to* The Hostage, *you seem to have changed your mind somewhat about the national movement.*

My ideas on Ireland have never altered. My idea about Ireland is that it's a separate country from England. And it's only in the interests of a section of the English capitalist class and a section of the Northern Irish capitalist class — in the interest of a section of the people I'd describe as extreme Tories, extreme conservatives — to keep Ireland divided. My political *opinions* about Ireland may have changed, but my hopes and ideas of what is best for Ireland haven't altered.

Has your attitude towards the IRA changed much?

I regard the IRA as a regrettable necessity, but it is a necessity. I must explain that I consider some members of the IRA to be figures of fun, but if someone asked me to condemn the IRA for an attack on a British barracks anywhere in the thirty-two counties of Ireland, I'm not going to do it.

Some people in France found your depiction of the member of the IRA in The Hostage *to be a bit artificial. He behaved more like a West End type, a fashionable fellow, a character in a comedy.*

Well, it's artificial only to people who do not understand the theatre. Only to people who do not know music-hall, vaudeville. Only to people who are such peasants, such Parisian peasants in this context, that they have never seen the Berliner Ensemble by Bertolt Brecht. I don't imitate Brecht but ... Have you ever read *The Good Soldier Schweik* by Jaroslav Hasek?[58] Did you ever read Dickens, for Jesus's sake? What do you want me to do? Have them all sitting around a table? Have a

rhinoceros running round the place like your adopted chum, Eugene Ionesco, who is a client of the United States?[59] I am a friend of the United States and I love the United States. *Je ne suis pas un client, je suis un ami.* The only thing that your question convinces me of, Sylvère, is that you've got bogmen everywhere. Do you know what a bogman is? A *paysan.* You've got them in *France-Observateur.* You've got them in *The Irish Press.* But the people who say that sort of thing about me they ought to go to the theatre more often. And I'll tell you what they ought to do. They ought to go to Paris more often. Not have their minds stuck on their own stupid garbage-faced old mother up in the Vosges, stuffing truffles up a duck's ass. That might make for a very good peasant's wife, not for a good drama critic. Though I shouldn't say anything about the Vosges. A very good friend of mine comes from there. A man called Marcel. He was a member of the CNR — the Comité National de la Résistance.[60] We used to go the Club des Assassins. Do you know it? It used to be at the back of the boulevard Saint-Michel and it was full of the sort of company that I love. Rich Reds. People suspect writers but I got ammunition.

This wasn't a criticism, but you certainly deal with the IRA much more lightly.

What do you want me to do? Write a play about the Western World again?

But you believe the theatre can exert a political influence.

Well, sure I do. A writer influences. But you don't influence like the communists do. In the communist theatre in London, and indeed when they had one in Dublin, there was a drama about cement workers. They'd have a big stack of sacks of cement bags on one side of the stage and they'd all carry them to the other side and that was Act I. And they'd carry them back again and that was Act II. And they'd put them in the middle and someone would drop dead and rupture himself and that was Act III, and the finish.

And it was called Reinforced Concrete?

Well, maybe that's what they called it ... Jesus, but I call it having the balls bored off me.

Many people in France know about Ireland mostly from Sean O'Casey's plays and yours.

I'm in honoured company. O'Casey's a great man.

But you aren't following exactly in the same way.

Oh well, I'd like to follow in the same way and to be a great playwright but I don't follow in the same path, naturally. He's got his way of doing things and I've got mine. But I think every Irish writer is very much influenced by him. If I said I wasn't influenced by him I'd be very ungrateful as well as very untruthful. But they are different streams ...

You said that you're not really writing for the Irish ...

Sure, I'm writing for the Irish. Of course, I'm writing for the Irish. When did I say that? Once somebody said to me, 'How would this suit a Dublin audience?' And I said, 'The Irish are not my audience, they are my material.' When I say a thing, I don't talk in parables. I'm not a fucking clergyman, not a juggler, not a magician. I simply say what I mean ... I meant it economically. *The Quare Fellow* ran for ten weeks at the Abbey, which is a very long time for Ireland. *The Hostage* packed out for two weeks at the Olympia and as many Dublin people as could go went. But it wouldn't be enough, Sylvère, to keep me alive. Well, it would be enough to keep me alive if I was writing the *Journal d'un curé de campagne* but as I'm not writing that

sort of thing I've got to be out and about; I gotta meet my friends and walk in the sun and that's what I'm about to do.[61]

A last question about your language. You've written sometimes in Gaelic?

Sure.

And some shrewd French critics, just by reading your book translation, figured that you're writing in a special Anglo-Irish language.

First of all, I know more than your goddamn French critics, and I know more than any living person about the language — not just of Ireland — but about the spoken language. I'm not going into any philological arguments about nationalist languages — whether Breton or Provençal or the *langue d'oc* or Welsh. I know more about the language of the people that inhabit England, Ireland, Scotland or Wales than any other man living. I'm the only person living here that can say hello in every language spoken, apart from dividing it into dialects. (*He says: 'Hello how are you?' in many languages.*) All those languages are spoken in these islands, but that's simply a kind of tour de force, a bit of a show off. I'm simply calling to your attention the fact that besides English, they also speak Irish Gaelic, they speak Scotch Gaelic, they speak Welsh, fewer people speak Manx and they speak French. French is spoken in the Channel Islands. Maybe you think they belong to France, I don't know. But in any event, the English language is, of course, the language of these islands and a very great and wonderful language it is. Now the first person to put a Cockney — to write Cockney dialogue for the West End stage within living memory — was me. I have been attacked on all sorts of grounds. Nobody has ever said that my Cockney is not authentic, that it is not just as Cockneys speak it, and that goes for Cockneys themselves. I can write the way that the north of England people speak. The Irish for

61 *The Diary of a Country Priest*, a famous Catholic novel by Georges Bernanos (1888–1948), first published in 1936.

62 Evelyn Waugh (1903–66), satirical novelist; author of *Brideshead Revisited* (1945). Behan had a particular dislike of Waugh.

63 John Osborne (1929–94), actor-manager and playwright; enjoyed considerable celebrity in late 1950s and early 1960s on account of his phenomenally successful *Look Back in Anger* (1956); other works include *The Entertainers* (1957) and *Inadmissible Evidence* (1965).

the most part speak English the same all over Ireland. There's not very much difference.

Gaelic also is a literary language.

Let's stick to one thing at one time. Your critics allege that I had kind of fashioned a language of my own in English?

Yes.

What I write is English. I write English as she is spoke. Perhaps one person speaks English one way and another person speaks it another. But Evelyn Waugh, when he went to write Cockney, was an abysmal failure.[62] Cockney is a speech like any other. For instance, the use of the word 'fuck' is very important. Because it's an important part of the speech of the majority of people in these islands. Now if you were to ask Mr. Samuel Beckett about that, who is a friend of mine incidentally, he would say that what I was saying is not true. That's because he hasn't been in the habit of hearing it. Even when he lived here he didn't — he would meet students. Poverty is not the test. He could say he met fellows that were ever as poor as Brendan Behan was. The fact is that the urban population of these islands, culturally, are very closely knit together. Most of the impulse comes from, I'd say, Ireland and Scotland. Wales not so much. Manners come from the East End of London. With the result that I could be speaking English, if I had anyone here understood it, and I would speak English. I would be using English words and you wouldn't know what I was talking about. Neither would Derek, perhaps. Say I was saying something like (*Says it very softly.*): 'I'll give that Richard the Third a daisy up in her shop if she don't mack her rabbit.' See? Well, perhaps John Osborne might.[63] A peasant can attack me on many grounds, but not on that. ∎

At Democratic Party headquarters in New York on election night, November 1960.
Photograph: Al Fenn/Time Life Pictures/Getty Images.

The last dying Words of
PATRICK RACK FORRISTAL,

OF RHADUFF, IN THE COUNTY OF WEXFORD,

Who is innocently to suffer for the Murder of JOHN JAMES.

FRIENDS AND FELLOW-CITIZENS,

I WAS born in *Rhaduff*, in the Parish of *Killan*, County of *Wexford*, and must this Day suffer for a Murder of which I am Innocent.—It is true I am an United Irishman, and held a Commission in the United Irish Army, from its Commencement, which I had to its Dissolution continued in : since I was put into Confinement I have been made several Offers, which would have saved my Life; but such dishonourable and improper Proposals should never basely influence me, for had I a thousand Lives with that I am to lose, they should all be forfeited in the same Cause, as the spirit of a Republican should never leave my Breast (were I to live a Century), and hope it will not die with me.

I declare it to be true that I was with my Party at the time JOHN JAMES was murdered ; but I solemnly declare, that I never murdered him, nor did any of the Party that were with me, to my Knowledge ; and that I was the only Person who prevented them taking his Life, prior to the Time I understand he had been murdered.——And I declare I am an entire Stranger, except by hearsay, of what is laid to my Charge, and for which I now must suffer ; and I hope every other Man who may hear of me, and who has any spirit towards the Cause, may think nothing of what is past, but may, if it comes to their turn, as cheerfully suffer as I do. I therefore, good People, forgive my Prosecutor, and I die a Martyr in the Cause, in the Twentieth Year of my Age ; and request all Christians will pray that the LORD will have Mercy on my Soul.

PATRICK RACK FORRISTAL.

August 19*th*, 1799.

The Last Dying Words of Patrick Rack Forristal (1799), declaring his commitment to republicanism. National Archives of Ireland, State of the Country Papers Series II 3341/1

The Tree of Liberty

Republicanism: American, French, and Irish

Philip Pettit

In the mid-1790s, when the United Irishmen, the leaders of Irish republicanism, sought to make their ideas known among the populace at large, they had recourse to primers and catechisms.

1 Kevin Whelan, *The Tree of Liberty: Radicalism, Catholicism and the Construction of Irish Identity 1760–1830* (Cork, 1996), 57

2 For my earlier work on related issues, see Philip Pettit, *Republicanism: A Theory of Freedom and Government* (Oxford, 1997). For historically more authoritative research, see Quentin Skinner, *Liberty Before Liberalism* (Cambridge, 1998) and Maurizio Viroli, *Republicanism* (New York, 2002). See too Iseult Honohan, *Civic Republicanism* (London, 2002) and John W. Maynor, *Republicanism in the Modern World* (Cambridge, 2003).

3 Philip Pettit, 'Liberty and Leviathan', in *Politics, Philosophy and Economics* (forthcoming 2005)

4 Thomas Hobbes, *Leviathan*, ed. E. M. Curley (Indianapolis, 1994), 143

5 Thomas Hobbes, *On the Citizen* [*De Cive*, 1642], ed. Richard Tuck and Michael Silverthorne (Cambridge, 1998), 111

The drill of a catechism was a familiar and effective way of instilling belief in the people they wanted to lead. Thus we find the following published in Cork in 1797:

> What is that in your hand? It is a branch.
> Of what? Of the tree of liberty.
> Where did it first grow? In America.
> Where does it bloom? In France.
> Where did the seeds fall? In Ireland.[1]

I want to comment on each of these answers in turn and then ask after what, if anything, was distinctive about the doctrine of liberty — republicanism as it is commonly called — that arose in Ireland.[2]

Of what? Of the tree of liberty

The image of the tree of liberty having a branch in Ireland serves to convey both an historical and a geographical fact. Historically, republicanism was a plant with ancient roots. And geographically, it was not just an Irish phenomenon; it had roots and branches in many different places. In order to understand what people in the 1790s would have understood by liberty, it may be useful to focus initially on an alternative view of freedom developed by one of the harshest critics of republicanism, the seventeenth-century pro-absolutist thinker, Thomas Hobbes, the author of *Leviathan* (1651).

Hobbes tried to introduce a way of thinking about liberty under which it was opposed to physical obstruction and legal coercion: in short, to interference of any kind.[3] Liberty, he maintained, prevailed in the 'silence of the laws' — that is, coercive laws — and in the absence of physical restraint.[4] He was breaking new ground in introducing this way of thinking, as indeed he himself claimed; and he was doing so in a way that served his pro-absolutist purposes.[5] The representation of freedom as non-interference enabled him to argue that people could be just as free under an absolutist régime as under one in which citizens play an active part in formulating the law. If liberty is non-interference, then coercive law always initially takes away liberty. There is no *necessary* difference, then, between absolutist and non-absolutist régimes. Whether the law-giver be a dictatorial prince or a popular assembly, the laws given will always initially reduce people's liberty; and they may do this while serving equally well or badly the overall promotion of that liberty.

The key to understanding the republican way of thinking about liberty is to recognize that, in the eyes of republicans, Hobbes was defending an absurd position. James Harrington, an enthusiast of the English republic of the 1640s and 1650s, was prompted to write: 'The mountain hath brought forth and we have a little equivocation!'.[6] He suggested that Hobbes was confusing liberty under the law — true civil liberty — with the sort of natural liberty that we might imagine people enjoying in a solitary existence: liberty *from* the law rather than liberty *under* the law.

But if, contrary to Hobbes, true civil liberty does not consist in the absence of interference, what *does* it involve? Republicans believed that liberty does not rule out subjection to law as such, only subjection to the arbitrary or uncontestable law of an absolute ruler. More generally, they thought that the antonym of freedom was not interference but rather domination — exposure to the arbitrary, uncheckable power of a *dominus* or master in one's life. Being free, they insisted, meant being no one else's subject or servant or slave; it meant enjoying the status that allowed one to be one's own man or woman, acting without fear or deference according to one's own will.

If freedom requires the absence of an arbitrary master in one's life then two things follow immediately, both of which would have been rejected by Hobbes. First, as mentioned, it follows that being subject to the law — being subject to taxation and coercion and the prospect of penalty — will not take away one's freedom if the law is not uncheckable and arbitrary; if, as republicans hoped it might be, it represents an impartial, impersonal, essentially contestable régime that the citizens of a republic can embrace. And second, it follows that being subject to the arbitrary power of others, even if they are kindly masters — even if they never look likely to interfere — will still make one unfree. Such kindly masters may give one 'free rein' (in the received expression) but, like the rider who gives a horse free rein, they will remain firmly in the saddle, enjoying the position of a *dominus*.

The Roman republicans gave early, fairly explicit expression to this view of freedom, saying that liberty, *libertas*, was the antonym of *dominatio*, or mastery. The free person, or the *liber*, was someone who did not live *in potestate domini*, in the power of a master. That Roman theme was embraced at the time of the Renaissance by the burghers of Florence and Venice and other northern Italian cities. It carried over into the language of the English revolutionaries of the 1640s and their successors in the 'Glorious Revolution' of 1688. And it became a mainstay of the rhetoric of gruff independence that was celebrated in eighteenth-century England and America, and rendered in a somewhat more egalitarian key in revolutionary France. This initially Roman theme persisted in the Irish tradition. As the Bantry Bay Proclamation of 1796 put it: 'True republicans fight only to vindicate the rights of equality and detest ever the name of a Master.'[7]

It is not difficult to see how freedom could have been cast as the antonym of domination or mastery. In the long republican tradition, living under the thumb of others, being exposed to their arbitrary power of interference in one's life, was the very epitome of unfreedom. It was to live at the mercy of those others, dependent on their grace and favour, and thus inclined, in servile fashion, to keep them sweet, whether by the caution of self-censorship or by the fawning and toadying associated with self-ingratiation. Freedom, in contrast to such subjection and servility, was presented as a condition in which one could walk tall and look others in the eye, knowing that one could not be pushed around with impunity, and knowing that this knowledge was shared among the members of one's community.

The tree of liberty to which the United Irish catechism directs us is the tradition in which such independence — 'independency upon the will of another' — was celebrated, and all forms of involuntary subordination deplored.[8] The tradition focused, as did all traditions down to the end of the eighteenth century, on propertied, mainstream males, but it identified a rich and commanding ideal of human life and relationships. The

6 James Harrington, *The Commonwealth of Oceana* and *A System of Politics*, ed. J. G. A. Pocock (Cambridge, 1992), 20

7 Quoted in Seán Cronin and Richard Roche, *Freedom the Wolfe Tone Way* (Tralee, 1973), 78

8 Algernon Sidney, *Discourses Concerning Government* [1698], ed. T. G. West (Indianapolis, 1990), 17

9 Richard Price, *Political Writings*, ed. D. O. Thomas (Cambridge, 1991), 78
10 Joseph Priestley, *Political Writings*, ed. Peter N. Miller (Cambridge, 1993), 140
11 See Pettit, *Republicanism*, ch. 1.

tradition also extended the ideal from individuals to whole communities. In the late eighteenth century, Richard Price argued that the free community, like the free individual, is the community of individuals whose shared fortunes are not subject to arbitrary determination by a foreign power.[9]

The extension of the ideal of freedom to the communal level gave it relevance and impact, not just in the critique of absolutist rule, but also in the critique of any form of colonial rule. It made it applicable, not just in condemnation of the more or less absolute rule of the French king, but also in castigating the rule of the British government — a moderate, practically republican government, as it was generally seen — in the affairs of the American colonists. Even if the British government dealt relatively generously with the colonists — even if it taxed them for just one penny, as Joseph Priestley said in explicating their grievances — it had the arbitrary power to deal with them as it wished: 'For by the same power, by which the people of England can compel them to pay *one penny*, they may compel them to pay the *last penny* they have. There will be nothing but arbitrary imposition on the one side, and humble petition on the other'.[10]

I have concentrated on the republican conception of freedom as non-domination because, while the ideal involved is easy to grasp, the Hobbesian view of freedom as non-interference systematically displaced it in liberal traditions of thought. While Hobbes had little influence in his own time, his idea of freedom as non-interference became the mainstay of utilitarian and liberal thought in the eighteenth and nineteenth centuries. Thus Jeremy Bentham could write in 1776:

> As against the coercion applicable by individual to individual, no liberty can be given to one man but in proportion as it is taken away from another. All coercive laws, therefore, and in particular all laws

creative of liberty, are as far as they go abrogative of liberty.

This thought would have been anathema to republicans; they would have seen an enormous gulf between the rule of a non-arbitrary law and the régime of law imposed by an absolute or colonial ruler.

How did the liberal tradition of the nineteenth century ever come to embrace a conception of liberty associated with absolutist thought? Two considerations are pertinent.[11] First, it served well in defence of the colonial rule that the American revolutionaries wished to combat. Thus John Lind (1776) could invoke the notion of freedom as non-interference, which he admitted to borrowing from Bentham, as a ground for resisting American claims. He argued that if freedom is non-interference, then all law takes away freedom, whether it be imposed by a domestic or colonial government; thus he held that the Americans cannot claim that just because law is imposed on them by a foreign government, they are thereby made unfree.

A second consideration that may have helped to usher in the new way of thinking about freedom relates to the fact that by the end of the eighteenth century it was generally conceded that the citizenry of the state could not be confined to mainstream, propertied males, but would also have to include women and servants. This expansion of the constituency of state concern would have led to an almost impossible radicalism, had the older ideal of freedom as non-domination continued to prevail; it would have required an overturning of contemporary domestic and master–servant law. But if freedom meant just non-interference, then the inclusion of women and servants would not have called for removing the power of masters in their lives; women and servants would be perfectly free, under the new way of thinking, provided they happened not to suffer actual interference. It may be this observation that led one of the most influential of the utilitarians, William Paley, to argue in 1785 that the traditional, pre-Benthamite way of thinking about freedom was, ironically, too radical. He saw it as one of those definitions of liberty 'which, by making that essential to civil freedom which is unattainable in experience, inflame expectations that can never be gratified, and disturb the public content with complaints, which no wisdom or benevolence of government can remove'.[12]

Where did it grow? In America

To answer the second question, we have to return to the republican conception of liberty. In the third line, the catechism says that the tree of liberty — the republican way of thinking about freedom — grew in America. Is this fair? I am inclined to answer: yes and no. No, because in celebrating freedom, and in giving it institutional form, the American rebels drew on what was already a very well-established tradition. Yes, because the Americans did indeed develop the first, fully worked-out version of what is required for a country and a constitution to be free.

The reason for saying 'no' is that the comment overlooks the fact that the republican tradition was a creation of ancient Rome, built out of Greek ideas; that it had been used in the Renaissance period to describe and shape the politics of northern Italian city-states like Florence and Venice; and that it had been exported from Italy to conceptualize the aspirations of the Polish republic in the sixteenth and seventeenth centuries, the Dutch republic of the seventeenth century, and the English republic of the 1640s and 1650s, as well as the English settlement after the Glorious Revolution. While Britain remained a monarchy in the wake of that settlement, it did very well by republican ideals — 'commonwealthman' ideals, as they were

often called — ensuring, better than any contemporary régime, that law could not be imposed arbitrarily on people.[13] Thus the Baron de Montesquieu could say in his great work, L'Esprit des Lois (1748), that England alone had a constitution — an unwritten, conventional way of doing things — that made freedom its primary end. Indeed he could go so far as to describe England, in an unmistakable reference, as 'a nation where the republic hides under the form of monarchy'.[14]

This favourable picture of Britain as a country where at least the mainstream, propertied males enjoyed a high degree of freedom — freedom as non-domination — was widely shared in the eighteenth century and was adopted enthusiastically in Britain itself. It was even shared by the leader of the United Irishmen, Theobald Wolfe Tone. He wrote of England as a country 'where, if anywhere, constitutional liberty is studied and known, where the influence of the Crown is, comparatively, much weaker than with us, and where there is, out of doors, a jealous vigilance, a fund of knowledge, and a spirit of resistance not yet to be found in Ireland'.[15]

It is worth emphasizing the standing of eighteenth-century Britain as a republic hidden in the form of a monarchy, with a constitution devoted to the value of liberty, since it certainly did not have that aspect in Ireland at that time. Just as republican Rome had been a very repressive taskmaster in the rest of Italy and in its Mediterranean colonies, so this freedom-loving Britain presided over Ireland, or at least over Catholic and Dissenting Ireland, with a will that was no less arbitrary and dominating than that of the most absolutist régime. If the Westminster government was a kindly master in the American colonies — albeit, still a master, and still an objectionable ruler — it was a very unkindly master indeed in its Irish manifestation. The penal laws were surely among the most arbitrary laws ever

12 William Paley, *The Principles of Moral and Political Philosophy, Collected Works*, vol. 4 (London, 1825), 359

13 Caroline Robbins, *The Eighteenth-Century Commonwealthman* (Cambridge, Mass., 1959)

14 Charles de Montesquieu, *The Spirit of the Laws*, ed. and trans. Anne M. Cohler, Basia Carolyn Miller, and Harold Samuel Stone (Cambridge, 1989), 70

15 Cronin and Roche, *Freedom the Wolfe Tone Way*, 87

16 Polybius, *The Histories*, trans. W. R. Paton (Cambridge, Mass., 1922–27)

17 Fergus Millar, *The Crowd in Rome in the Late Roman Republic* (Ann Arbor, 2002)

imposed, especially by a parliament that claimed to advance the cause of freedom.

So, strictly speaking, America was not the country where the tree of liberty first grew, nor even the country where it had first grown in the period leading up to 1798. But my answer to the question about America was both yes and no. And the reason for saying 'yes' is that, notwithstanding the extent to which Britain — or Poland or the Dutch provinces — could lay claim to republican credentials, the rebellion of the American colonies in 1775, and the ratification of the United States Constitution in 1787, marked a whole new beginning in the development of republican thought and practice.

From its origins in classical Rome, republicans had argued that, foreign or colonial rule apart, the two great dangers to freedom — freedom as non-domination — came from private power or *dominium* and public power or *imperium*. They did not doubt the capacity of a well-run régime of law — a state, as it would later be conceived — to curb the danger from private power, incorporating citizens into a legal and cultural framework of equality. But they saw very keenly that, while a state might serve to reduce private domination in people's lives, it could itself represent an even more threatening source of public domination. Their central problem then was how to devise a state that would reduce private domination without becoming a source of public domination. They expressed that problem in the well-known question. *Quis custodiet ipsos custodes?* Who will guard against the guardians? Who will police the police? Who will govern the governors?

The Roman solution to this problem involved four elements:

- a dispersion of public power among different bodies and authorities, leading to a system of checks and balances;

- a rule of law — 'an empire of laws, not of men', as James Harrington (1656) described it in the seventeenth century — that would treat no one as special;
- an electoral régime in which appointments were made by more or less popular will for limited periods, and often on a rotational basis;
- a contestatory dispensation in which a virtuous citizenry would invigilate government relentlessly, on the assumption that power may corrupt the most high-minded of rulers: the routine expression of this idea is 'the price of liberty is eternal vigilance'.

The dispersion of power in classical Rome was described as a mixed constitution by the Greek slave-historian, Polybius, who first told the Romans that they were really special.[16] It was perhaps the most striking aspect of the Roman republic. For under the constitution that had emerged slowly over centuries, there were at least three public forums, each with its distinctive powers (the centuriate assembly, the tribal assembly, and the senate); there were many different officials, each with his own domain of action, and, at the top of that hierarchy, two consuls, not just one; and there were, finally, a group of plebeian tribunes who had a power of veto over many public proposals.[17] The system represented a mixed constitution, insofar as it contained elements of monarchy, aristocracy and democracy.

The ideas of the mixed constitution, the rule of law, election to office and civic, contestatory virtue became the markers of republican modes of thinking. The mixed constitution and the rule of law represented ways of containing the governors. The electoral and contestatory elements exemplified ways of empowering the governed: electoral processes empowered the governed, considered collectively, and contestatory dispensations empowered the governed, considered individual by individual, or grouping by grouping. It was in America that republican constitutionalism was first developed and articulated in the systematic way required for establishing a new régime. The unwritten ways of doing things among the Romans, in the Renaissance Italian cities, and in eighteenth-century Britain had been praised by republican writers for allowing citizens to have a reasonable hope of enjoying freedom as non-domination, both in relation to private and in relation to public power. But in none of those countries had republican ideas served comparably to ordain the explicit design of social institutions; at most they had had a degree of influence in reshaping them in face of changing circumstances. In the classic instance of republican utopian writing — Harrington's *Oceana* (1656) — there had been a series of recommendations for the design of Oceana's (Britain's) institutions and practices. But this was a utopian work. It was in America that recommendations on this scale were actually realized in practice.

So, America was different. It was a creation of individuals who rejected foreign rule and designed for themselves a set of institutions that were meant to create, as if out of nothing, a truly republican society. The founders were focused explicitly on the ideal of freedom as non-domination and they devoted themselves to working out the implications for their new country of ideas like those of the mixed constitution, the rule of law, electoral control and contestatory virtue. The exercise gave rise eventually to the constitution of 1787, in which these different institutional ideals all have a presence. The bicameralism of Congress, the separation of legislative, executive and judicial bodies, and the embrace of federalism sat well with the idea of the mixed constitution. The emphasis on due process, on the protection of rights, and on the judicial policing of the legislature expressed a commitment to the rule of law. And of course the commitment to a

democracy of equals answered well to electoral and contestatory ideals. The courage and the impudence of the American colonists in rejecting their traditional rulers and in seeking to build this new political world stunned their contemporaries in Europe. They were not people of the traditional ruling class nor, in the main, members of the Established Church. They ranged from lawyers to men of trade, from clerks to carpenters, and they brought to their revolution a wide variety of religious and philosophical ideas. They exemplified a faith in the capacity of human beings, just in virtue of their human nature, to build from scratch a new world in which everyone could enjoy a full measure of freedom. Or if not everyone, at least those in the mainstream and male. Women remained outside the republican pale, even in this new dawn, and of course so did the African-American slaves who would have to wait nearly a century longer for their emancipation.

Prior to the emergence of America as an independent republic, people might have thought that the extent to which a country and its institutions enabled members to enjoy freedom (as non-domination) was a matter of fortune — something in the lap of the gods. All of that changed after 1775. Now it appeared that human beings could make their own political destiny, sitting down together to pool their intelligence and using their common reason in the invention of new institutions. The marker of this fresh beginning was the idea of devising a document of understanding, be it a declaration of independence, a written constitution, or a bill of rights, behind which people could rally in opposing their foes and around which they could hope to build a new life among themselves. This was heady stuff and it aroused passions and enthusiasms across the world, not least of course in Ireland.

18 Quentin Skinner, *Visions of Politics. Vol. 2 Renaissance Virtues* (Cambridge, 2002), 394–99

19 J. P. Canning, 'The Corporation in the Political Thought of the Italians Jurists of the Thirteenth and Fourteenth Century', *History of Political Thought*, 1 (1980), 9–32; 'Ideas of the State in Thirteenth and Fourteenth Century Commentators on the Roman Law', *Transactions of the Royal Historical Society*, 33 (1983), 1–27

Where does it bloom? In France

The French Revolution gave a prominent place, like the American, to the notion of the rule of law — due process, natural justice, respect for rights — and like the American it emphasized the need for an electoral, contestatory democracy: a democracy in which any citizen could vote and stand for office (again, the citizenry remained a male preserve) and where the people were expected to monitor those in power and be ready to protest every abuse or semblance of abuse. But France differed from America, especially after the execution of the king and the rejection of monarchy, in its emphasis on the central and unique authority of *le peuple souverain* — the sovereign, self-ruling people. Through this difference, the central feature of the mixed constitution, its dispersion of authority, was severely reduced in importance. There might be a dispersion of authority and power at lower levels but at the top of the governmental hierarchy, according to the French vision, there stood a single supreme sovereign — the people.

It was no accident that French republicanism should have introduced this novel theme. In order to explain why, however, it is necessary to go back to the sixteenth century and to see how the notion of sovereignty arose and gained a hold on French political thought. The St. Bartholomew's Day Massacre of 1572 in Paris, in which thousands of Huguenots were killed, led to the development of what came to be known as the monarchomachian movement in France.[18] This movement drew on medieval legal theory to argue that, provided it was represented by authorized spokespersons, a people, like a guild or a university or any corporate body, could be a legal agent with a will of its own: a *persona ficta* or artificial person.[19] The Huguenot monarchomachs drew on that theory to argue that the people they constituted, with their own local representatives, were a single, consolidated entity that must be presumed to

have made a contract with the French king to be governed on certain terms. But they maintained that the king's campaign of religious persecution had surely violated the terms of any presumptive contract. And thus they had the right, as a corporate people, to rise up and reject that king. It was because of this claim that they came to be known as 'monarchomachs' or 'king-killers'.

The monarchomachian claims caused consternation in a France that was already riven by civil and religious dissension and, famously, they prompted Jean Bodin in *Six livres de la république* (1576) to argue that in every régime there had to be a single, sovereign power, with supreme authority over every aspect of life. It might have appeared to many contemporaries that Bodin, in taking this line, was rejecting the traditional republican view that there need not be any one sovereign — that sovereignty, if we are to speak of sovereignty, can be divided out among different individuals and bodies, as under the mixed constitution. But Bodin, making use of the notion of a corporate agent, maintained that even in the Roman republic there was an ultimate sovereign — the *populus Romanus* itself. Thus from outside the republican tradition he offered a radical rereading of republican claims, casting the doctrine as one in which the corporate, collective people are the last court of political authority and power.

Thomas Hobbes was equally concerned to undermine the radical monarchomachian movement and he found a particularly clever and effective way of doing so. He took over the medieval and monarchomachian view that the people could exist as a group agent in its own right only so far as it was represented. But he then argued that representation required a single voice and that the only effective representative or 'personator' of the people — the only one who made them into a 'civil person', as he said — was the sovereign.

The upshot was that the people as a whole could not be thought of as having made a contract with the sovereign such that the sovereign might be in breach of its terms; the people would dissolve themselves into a multitude, as he put it, should they kill or reject the sovereign: corporately speaking, regicide would be suicide. Hobbes, like Bodin, had a strong preference for a monarchical sovereign but he admitted that in principle the people in assembly — a committee of the whole, as we might say — could serve as well as an individual king to represent or personate the multitude, effectively transforming them into a people or *populus*. The main thrust of his argument was that whether the sovereign was a king or a people, sovereignty had to involve a more or less absolute kind of authority and power. Whether government was monarchical or popular, he said, it had to be absolute in character if it was to do its job of keeping the peace; and like Bodin, he associated popular or democratic government with the republican tradition. He took the republican dalliance with the notion of dispersing power to be a nonsense that failed to recognize the requirements of politics.

Both Bodin and Hobbes were influential in France and their influence probably explains why the most influential of French republican thinkers, Jean Jacques Rousseau, developed a version of republican doctrine — a renegade or heretical version — in *The Social Contract* (1762) in which the idea of popular sovereignty was given pride of place. Like all republicans, Rousseau took domination or dependency to be the great ill that the state should rectify and he believed that the law — the impartial rule of law — was the most important instrumentality in achieving this end. But unlike others, he argued that the law could not be expected to achieve the required impartiality, or to be established in common awareness as having that impartiality, unless it emanated from the citizenry as a whole.[20] Viewing the citizenry or people as a corporate entity in the monarchomachian manner, he claimed

that that body could have a will of its own and that this will, if allowed to form and issue in legislation, would inevitably support the impartial rule of law required for individuals to be protected and empowered against domination. He thought, moreover, that this will would not be a dominating presence in people's lives, since it would belong in a sense to each; it would represent the *general will* of the corporate people, as distinct from the particular wills of individual members of that body.

Rousseau had an enormous influence on the ways in which French revolutionaries thought and he gave French republicanism a very different cast from the traditional or the American version of the doctrine. In this variety, republicanism came to represent not just a belief in the democratic rule of law, but a belief in the democratic rule of the collective people. Democracy had always been an important aspect of republicanism, of course, both in its electoral and contestatory senses; both in the sense in which it validated the collective election of those in government and in the sense in which it permitted and encouraged the invigilation of government by ordinary citizens. But prior to Rousseau, republicanism had never given central place to the idea of popular, unchecked rule; on the contrary, it had set up an opposition between republicanism and any such image of popular democracy. Polybius, for example, had contrasted the Roman republic, in which he found power dispersed among many bodies and authorities, with the sort of unregulated democracy that he associated, rightly or wrongly, with Athens; this city he described, in a received phrase, as a ship without a captain, buffeted by the winds of public opinion. The contrast between republic and democracy remained in place right down to the French Revolution, with the collective *demos* being cast as having the capacity to be just as despotic as the absolute prince. It was in this context, for example, that republicans in America worried — as republicans had

20 Jean-Fabien Spitz, *La Liberté Politique: Essai de Généalogie Conceptuelle* (Paris, 1995)

21 Thomas Bartlett, ed., *Life of Theobald Wolfe Tone* (Dublin, 1998), 714
22 The reference is to Henry Flood. See A. T. Q. Stewart, *A Deeper Silence: The Hidden Roots of the United Irish Movement* (London, 1993), 41–43.

always worried — about the possibility of a tyranny of the majority.

The United Irish catechism says that the tree of liberty blooms in France, though grown in America. Wolfe Tone might not have agreed with these words. Conscious of the excesses of the reign of terror, he described America in 1796 as 'the best governed spot on the face of the earth'.[21] But 'blooming' suggests life and wildness — something resistant to control, with a momentum of its own — and the French celebration of the sovereign, triumphant people certainly released that kind of energy. The republican flame may have burned strongly in the austere determination of the American settlers but in France it achieved levels of popular combustion unequalled before then in human history.

The combustible potential of French republicanism increased even further as the doctrine of the sovereign people became a doctrine of the self-determining nation. The growing romanticism about nationality — a romanticism to which Rousseau's own doctrines had contributed — now transformed republicanism from a sound, if sometimes staid, ideal into a vision that attracted public passion and devotion. The austere figure of the virtuous republican citizen, ever ready to do his duty in the practice and invigilation of government, gave way to the rather more gripping image of the hero ready to die for love of his people. This was the stuff of which public enthusiasm and fervour were made, heightened further by the sight of the French *patrie* threatened by the surrounding, unreformed régimes of Europe. This was the political image that played a crucial role in the embrace of republicanism by those national groupings all over Europe that found themselves, like the Irish, under the heel of a colonial or imperial power. No wonder, then, that the tree of liberty should be said to bloom in France, even if it grew in America.

Where did the seeds fall? In Ireland

We have identified three different strands in the brand of republicanism emerging in America and France in the late eighteenth century — a classical rhetoric of independency or freedom, individual and communal, that was common to both countries; a constitutional ideal of establishing 'an empire of laws, not of men' that was particularly associated with the American rebellion; and an ideal of popular or national sovereignty that emerged with particular force in the context of the French Revolution. All of these themes had a presence in Ireland of the 1790s and played a role in shaping the republicanism of the United Irishmen.

The rhetoric of independency and freedom — freedom as non-domination — was part of the *lingua franca* of two important groups in Ireland of the 1780s: the Whig Clubs that attracted those who identified with the British commonwealthman tradition, including Wolfe Tone who penned pamphlets as 'A Radical Whig' and 'A Northern Whig'; and the Volunteers who were formed in 1778 to defend the country in the event of a French or Spanish invasion. These groups, composed in great part of Dissenters, became forces of reform that argued domestically for the repeal of legislation under which the resolutions of the Dublin parliament could be overridden in London. They were successful in achieving the repeal of this legislation in 1782, thereby ushering in a new constitution for Ireland, as it was seen at the time.

The Volunteers' insistence on the importance of freedom in the sense of independency can be seen particularly well in their reaction to the observation of a rather cold-eyed lawyer on what had actually been achieved in the repeal of this legislation.[22] He pointed out that while the British parliament was no longer overruling its Dublin counterpart, it had not given up the right to assume an overruling role, should it choose. It had decided to behave in a kindly or beneficent manner towards the Irish parliament, to put the point in republican terms, but it remained still the master of that body. It had given the Irish parliament free rein but it still sat in the saddle. The reaction of the Volunteers to this observation was exactly what one would expect of people steeped in republican thought. Led by Henry Flood, they demanded, not just *repeal* of the offending legislation — this had already been achieved — but *renunciation* of the very right to overrule Dublin's laws. And this they achieved in 1783 in a British parliament that must have feared the possibility of its Irish subjects — not just the native Catholics but the Dissenting and even the Anglican settlers — rising in the manner of the American colonists.

The 1782 constitution, and 'Grattan's Parliament' of the 1780s and 1790s, proved to be a great disappointment for the Volunteers and more radical Whigs. Its business was effectively manipulated by Dublin Castle, with the lord lieutenant having a far more effective degree of control over who would rule there than the king had in relation to Westminster. It was despair over the prospects of ever realizing republican ideals through this parliament

that led Wolfe Tone and others to establish the United Irishmen in 1791, and ultimately to seek full independence for Ireland. As Tone said in commentary on that parliament: 'We are free in theory, we are slaves in fact.'[23]

The United Irishmen embraced the rhetoric of independency and freedom with a fervour equal to that of the Americans or the French, as indeed this language of slavery suggests. Tone, as we saw, gave expression to the core idea when he said that true republicans 'detest ever the name of master'. He personally exemplified the attitude when he wrote from Princeton in a letter of 1795 that he could never live in a country where he had to depend on the leave or permission of others for doing so. 'I would exist in no country *permissu superiorum*.'[24]

The second theme — republican constitutionalism, as it crystallized in America — also had a powerful influence on the Volunteers, the more radical Whigs, and the United Irishmen. In the 1791 Declaration of the Society of United Irishmen the target explicitly opposed is 'that mortal disease which corrodes the vitals of our constitution'; and the

23 T. W. Moody, R. B. McDowell and C. J. Woods, eds., *The Writings of Theobald Wolfe Tone, 1763–98*, vol. 1 (Oxford, 1998), 115; cited hereafter as Tone, *Writings*

24 Tone, *Writings*, vol. 2 (2001), 30

Francis Wheatley
The Dublin Volunteers on College Green, 4th November 1779
1780
oil on canvas
175 x 323 cm
National Gallery of Ireland, Dublin

25 Tone, *Writings*, vol. 1,
    107
26 Tone, *Writings*, vol. 2,
    33
27 Tone, *Writings*, vol. 1,
    111

symptoms of that illness are said to be 'the rejection of a place bill, of a pension bill, of a responsibility bill, the sale of peerages in one house, the corruption publicly avowed in the other' and 'the notorious infamy of borough traffic between them both'.[25]

These are exactly the sorts of constitutional complaints that one would expect of a movement that tracked the American colonists in opposing departures from the idealized 'empire of laws, not of men', and that looked with horror on factional manipulation and financial corruption and abuse. We find the same constitutionalist, even legalistic, temper in 'a plaguey long letter' that Tone writes from America in 1795:

> Governor Mifflin (the General) told me that in a very short time the State (of Pennsylvania) would be able to pay all their expenses by the interest of the money which they were daily lodging in the bank without drawing a dollar from the people. What do you say to a State not mortgaging its revenues to an irretrievable amount, but growing rich and living like a wealthy individual on their money in the funds? Then go and

Mick O'Dea
The Split
1997
computer print
29.5 x 52.5 cm
private collection;
courtesy of the artist

look at Ireland borrowing two million in one year — and for what? I have not the temper to go on. *These are the things that make men Republicans.*[26]

But if republican constitutionalism was an important source of inspiration for the United Irishmen, as it was in America, the republican patriotism and nationalism that emerged so powerfully in France had an equal and perhaps even more salient presence in their minds. The linkage came about in the more or less Rousseauvian thought, certainly present in the work of Wolfe Tone, that there cannot be an 'empire of laws' — there cannot be a satisfactory constitutional settlement — except so far as it is realized through the rule of the people, a form of government in which the popular will is sovereign. Even in Britain the secret of constitutional success, according to Tone, was that 'the people are very powerful, though they have not their due power'. He argued by contrast that in Ireland 'the people are utterly disregarded and defied' — this is why he thought independence from England essential — and that it is for this reason 'that we see Peculation protected, Venality avowed, the Peerage prostituted, the Commons

corrupted'.[27] The background thought, phrased in appealing understatement, is that 'it is not a bad pledge for the good conduct of rulers, that they should have a wholesome fear of the spirit of a people united in interest and sentiment'.[28]

Driven by republican outrage at constitutional violations in Ireland, then, Tone calls for power to be given to the people. He looks more concretely, in the capitalized words of the United Irishmen Declaration, for 'AN EQUAL REPRESENTATION OF ALL THE PEOPLE IN PARLIAMENT'. Here, and in Tone's private writings, 'the people' is understood in a completely inclusive sense: 'Our whole people consists of Catholics, Protestants, and Presbyterians, and is, therefore, greater than any one of these sects, and equal to them altogether.'[29]

Tone argues in this spirit for the need to unite the Irish people, to overcome sectarian division, and to make possible an effective resistance to rule from London. His sense of the need to unite the people moves him in two directions. On the one hand, it leads him to make a plea, on behalf of Catholics, to other Irish people:

> We prate and babble and write books and publish them, filled with sentiments of freedom, and abhorrence of tyranny, and lofty praises of the *Rights of Man*! Yet we are content to hold three millions of our fellow creatures and fellow subjects, in degradation and infamy and contempt, or, to sum up all in one word, in *slavery*.[30]

On the other hand, it prompts him to make a call to national feeling, almost in the fashion of a nineteenth-century romantic nationalist:

> Irishmen are brave, generous, and determined. Courage and prudence will establish independence, liberty, and equality in their native soil, under the shade of their own mountains.[31]

How distinctive was Irish republicanism?

I have tried to locate Irish republicanism, particularly as it emerged in the late eighteenth century, in a broader tradition that encompasses America and France, and the longer Roman, Renaissance and English tradition. I want to suggest that there is one radically new theme in the Irish version of republicanism, particularly in the version associated with Wolfe Tone. It consists in a different, more ecumenical attitude to religion than was to be found in America, France, or Britain.

The American Revolution had been marked by a Dissenter spirit, as we might expect from the land of the Pilgrim Fathers. It could even be seen as the expression of an ideology of Dissenter independence that came to be embraced by American Protestants generally; and the colonists, of course, were mainly of Protestant stock. Tone himself associated republican thought and attitudes with the Dissenting tradition, finding it plausible as well as politically useful to hail the role of northern Presbyterians:

> The Dissenters of the north, and more especially of the town of Belfast, are, from the genius of their religion, and from the superior diffusions of political information among them, sincere and enlightened Republicans.[32]

The American response to religious difference, in particular to the many differences among the Protestant churches, was to declare, ultimately in a spirit of friendship towards religion, that no one church should have the sort of connection with the state that the Anglican Church enjoyed in England. Given that the founders and their followers belonged to different sects themselves, it is not surprising that they preferred a separation of church and state; they proposed that the state should be forced to be neutral between rival denominations. But while this neutrality

28 Tone, *Writings*, vol. 1, 101

29 Tone, *Writings*, vol. 1, 100

30 Tone, *Writings*, vol. 1, 125

31 Bartlett, *Life of Theobald Wolfe Tone*, 692

32 Tone, *Writings*, vol. 2, 298–99

33 Jean Jacques Rousseau,
*The Social Contract and
Discourses* (London,
1973), ch. 4
34 Tone, *Writings*, vol. 1,
125; vol. 2, 12
35 Tone, *Writings*, vol. 2,
386

would prove in eventual practice to be hospitable to Catholics, and indeed to the members of other religions, it was a Protestant sort of neutrality that saw merit only in distinctively non-Catholic attitudes of religious independence. It remained hostile to Catholicism and, in particular, to the suspect idea of giving allegiance to a foreign Pontiff and of acknowledging the authority of his priests.

Because of the contrasting religious profile of France, the response of French republicans to religion was very different from that of their American counterparts. Here, Roman Catholicism had been entirely dominant — after the Revocation of the Edict of Nantes (1685), tolerance towards Protestants had been guaranteed only in legislation of 1787 — and the Church had been closely and supportively connected to the *ancien régime*. In rejecting that régime, therefore, it is not in the least surprising that republicans should have seen themselves as enemies of the Church, nor indeed that the Church authorities should have seen them as such. Like American republicanism, then, the French variant was anti-Catholic too. But its anti-Catholicism was not grounded in a generally friendly disposition towards protestant churches, or towards religion of any kind. French republicans embraced, not the sort of separatism about church and state that appealed to Americans, but a downright secular or laicist attitude. The keyword was not neutrality but rather hostility.

The hostility to religion, which still shows up in the character of official France's attitude to religious symbolism, may have had theoretical as well as sociological roots. For Rousseau had argued forcibly and influentially that religion and the Christian religion in particular, was inherently hostile to republican independence and freedom:

Christianity preaches only servitude and dependence. Its spirit is so favourable to tyranny that it always profits by such a *régime*. True Christians are made to be

slaves, and they know it and do not much mind: this short life counts for too little in their eyes.[33]

All of this said, it is relatively easy to see in what regard the republicanism of the United Irishmen was genuinely novel. Unlike the anti-Catholic separatism that prevailed in America, and unlike the anti-religious secularism of France, Irish republican separatism of this period was not particularly hostile to Catholics, and its secularism was accepting of religion in general.

Tone laid the ground for reconciling Catholicism and republicanism in arguing that 'Protestantism is no guard against corruption', believing as he did — and as republicans in general would have believed — that 'power long exercised would corrupt an angel'.[34] He devoted much of his work to countering sectarian division, praising every sign of Dissenter support for the cause of Catholics; where the political situation of Dissenters had been greatly improved, the standing of Catholics remained decidedly second class. And he continually held out the prospect of a society in which religious toleration would prevail while the linkage between confessional allegiance and political power would be broken. This vision of reconciliation and respect is expressed by Tone with romantic, practically eschatological, enthusiasm:

The memory of religious dissensions will be lost, when no sect shall have an exclusive right to govern their fellow citizens. Each sect will maintain its own clergy, and no citizen will be disfranchised for worshipping God according to his conscience. To say all in one word, *Ireland shall be independent*. We shall be a nation, not a province, citizens, not slaves.[35]

Hasten the day. ∎

This is a version of a lecture given at the Notre Dame Irish Studies Summer Seminar in 2004.

THE MAN WHO TRIED TO GET THE HANG OF A JACK YEATS PICTURE.

Republics of Difference
Yeats, MacGreevy, Beckett

David Lloyd

Two puzzled observations: first, virtually every study of note devoted to Jack B. Yeats invokes the testimony of Samuel Beckett to the artist's singular greatness.

1 See Hilary Pyle, *Yeats: Portrait of an Artistic Family* (London, 1997). The epithets are selected more or less at random from her descriptions of the paintings.
2 Bruce Arnold, *Jack Yeats* (New Haven and London, 1998), ch. 6–8
3 *Dublin Opinion*, 8 (May 1929), 73

There is nothing peculiar in that: Beckett's are eloquent and authoritative statements, for reasons that have perhaps to do more with his stature than with the attention paid to his insights. Yet sketchy as Beckett's statements are, the accounts that invoke his authority make little effort to elaborate or to engage with the writer's quite idiosyncratic and solitary apprehension of Yeats's achievement and value. The invocation of the authority seems in no way to influence the approach to the paintings. Second, and no less puzzling, given the present general acceptance of the singularity and originality of Yeats's painterly technique in his later work, is how rarely critics undertake the formal analysis of it. Hilary Pyle, in her numerous and indispensable catalogues, gives us detailed accounts of each of the works reproduced, but even these remain essentially descriptive rather than analytical and are marked by the impressionistic, tonal vocabulary that has been the hallmark of Yeats criticism to date: 'exuberant', 'ruminative', 'elated', 'sombre', even 'Wordsworthian.'[1] Such impressionistic accounts of the paintings seek to render their undoubted force, but they do so at great cost. On the one hand, they do not pause to attend to the remarkable artifice, the compositional exactitude, of Yeats's most powerful work, giving instead an impression of Yeats's virtually naïve, notoriously untaught, spontaneity in his medium. In related ways, Bruce Arnold's peculiarly extended emphasis on the youthful artist's childlike fascination with miniature theatres and paper boats eclipses attention to the mature artist's reflections, political or aesthetic, in a way that ultimately sells short the seriousness of his engagements.[2] On the other hand, those impressionistic readings and the fascination with the apparent spontaneity of the artist's procedures, foreclose all too rapidly on the almost belligerent orneriness of the paintings and the unabashed difficulty with which they refuse to resolve to the viewer's gaze. Not for nothing did Yeats decline to permit reproductions of his works: prints, transparencies and digital images alike soften and flatten the sculpted dimensions of his brushwork, the stark transitions between virtually, sometimes even actually, bare canvas and astonishingly thick impasto, the unstable oscillation between the emergence of the figure and the foregrounding of the medium that dissolves even as it reveals. This difficulty that confronts the viewer has on occasion provoked hostility and mystification in face of the work and, precisely for that reason, should not be ignored or diminished. Indeed, if one wishes for an account of the difficulty of seeing a Yeats painting, an antagonistic and satirical cartoon in *Dublin Opinion* (Fig. 1) may serve better than much of what passes for art criticism.[3]

Where the latter seeks to make the work explicable and palatable, the cartoon has at least the virtue of capturing the labour of

Fig. 1: *Dublin Opinion*, 8 (May 1929), 73. Courtesy of the National Library of Ireland.

attention that the paintings exact and concludes, however sardonically, with an acknowledgement of their possibly unsettling effects.

But if we wish, as I believe we should, to take Yeats's not-so-modest claim to be 'the first living painter in the world' with some seriousness, we have surely to pay the paintings the more exacting attention they demand and begin at least to decipher the grounds of their originality and their continuing difficulty for the eye.[4] Beckett's valuation of him as being 'with the great of our time', which places him in the company of Kandinsky, Klee and Braque, amongst others, is scarcely to be dismissed: he was not given to flattery and his associations are hardly conventional.[5] The harder task is to decipher what Beckett's acute eye saw in Yeats's work (or, for that matter, to understand what Joyce meant in claiming that Yeats and he shared a 'method' or why an artist of the international stature of Oscar Kokoschka might have estimated Yeats so highly).[6] Beckett's remarks in his two published notices are not only too brief but also characteristically too enigmatic and reserved for us to do more than speculate on the grounds for Yeats's apparently powerful impact on him. This essay is, nonetheless, an attempt to understand Beckett's homage to Yeats through an approach to what he may have seen as formally significant in the paintings. Beckett's capacity for *attention* to visual work is notorious, and it is clear that his regard for the paintings that he valued was based on the significance of their forms rather than on any symbolic or allegorical meaning they might hold. Indeed, as we shall see further, the whole tendency of Beckett's writings on art (and not solely on Yeats) was antagonistic to either symbolism or allegory and even to representation itself. That antagonism places him, rightly or wrongly, in direct opposition to the predominant reception of Yeats, whether he be seen as the painter who gives expression

to the spirit of the nation or as one whose works are achieved, if enigmatic, symbols of emotional states or of individual memories. The question here is not so much whether Beckett was correct in his readings as it is to see what in Yeats's paintings might lend itself to such a radically antithetical vision.

The dominant view of Yeats in Beckett's own moment, which gave occasion for his first extended remarks on the painting, was that of their mutual friend Thomas MacGreevy. According to Beckett, the leading conviction in MacGreevy's short essay is that Jack B. Yeats is, in every sense, the most representative painter of the Irish nation. Beckett quotes MacGreevy as follows:

> What was unique in Ireland was that the life of the people considered itself, and was in fact, spiritually and culturally as well as politically, the whole life of the nation. Those who acted for the nation officially were outside the nation. They had a stronger sense of identity with the English governing class than with the people of Ireland, and their art was no more than a province of English art. The first genuine artist, therefore, who so identified himself with the people of Ireland as to be able to give true and good and beautiful expression to the life they lived, and to that sense of themselves as the Irish nation, inevitably became not merely a *genre* painter like the painters of the *petit peuple* in other countries, and not merely a nation's painter in the sense that Pol de Limburg, Louis le Nain, Bassano, Ostade or Jan Steen were national painters, but *the* national painter in the sense that Rembrandt and Velasquez and Watteau were national painters, the painter who in his work was the consummate expression of the spirit of his own nation at one of the supreme points in its evolution.[7]

4 Arnold, *Jack Yeats*, 234

5 Anthony Cronin's dismissive comments on the relationship between the two are especially egregious in this respect. Finding Yeats's work Romantic, he is surprised at Beckett's admiration and attributes it to personal needs: 'conceived as it was at a time in Beckett's life when he sadly needed someone to admire or look up to, it is a triumph of personal affection over critical or aesthetic considerations'. See Cronin, *Samuel Beckett: The Last Modernist* (New York, 1997), 140.

6 For Yeats's relation to Joyce and to Kokoschka, see Arnold, *Jack Yeats*, 235–36 and 220–21 respectively.

7 Samuel Beckett, *Disjecta: Miscellaneous Writings and a Dramatic Fragment*, ed. Ruby Cohn (New York, 1984), 96; apart from adding a couple of commas, Beckett's citation substitutes 'a nation's painter' for MacGreevy's 'a national painter'. See Thomas MacGreevy, *Jack B. Yeats* (Dublin, 1945), 10. Beckett, *Disjecta*, hereafter cited in text as D, and McGreevy, *Jack B. Yeats* as *JBY*.

8 MacGreevy, *Jack B. Yeats*, 32. On representation, see David Lloyd, *Nationalism and Minor Literature: James Clarence Mangan and the Emergence of Irish Cultural Nationalism* (Berkeley, 1987), 95–98.

9 MacGreevy, *Jack B. Yeats*, 28

10 MacGreevy, *Jack B. Yeats*, 27

11 Though one might be tempted in each case to echo Gabriel Conroy's perplexed query, 'Of what was it a symbol?'. See James Joyce, 'The Dead', in *Dubliners* (Harmondsworth, 1975), 207.

MacGreevy's reading of Yeats's painting as 'the consummate expression of the spirit of his own nation' may itself be the consummate expression of a cultural nationalist aesthetic. Intrinsic to this aesthetic, which in Ireland dates back at least to the Young Ireland movement of the 1840s, is the conception of both the artwork and the artist as representative. As MacGreevy puts it:

> Actually the peoples [sic] are represented only by disinterested men, and more particularly by artists. In resurgent Ireland the pioneer and first representative man in the art of painting was Jack B. Yeats.[8]

The play on the relation between the political and the mimetic usage of the term 'representation' is deliberate and explicit. The artist himself becomes representative of the national spirit by representing the life of the nation in painting. Not, as MacGreevy makes clear, that representing the national spirit requires 'strict adherence to the observed fact'; on the contrary, for a nationalist aesthetic, the transformative capacity of imagination redeems a damaged nation. One might say, drawing again on familiar Romantic precepts, that the act of representation is redemptively transformative in itself, in so far as it raises the scattered particulars to the permanent and universal, or to what MacGreevy terms 'the unchanging elements of reality'.[9] In such terms, re-presentation is not mere depiction of the particular but an always transformative elevation of the particular to the universal that is a return of the nation to its essential self. The poetry of this painting is 'the splendour of essential truth'.[10] Even without MacGreevy's emphatic evocation of the symbolic dimensions of paintings like *In Memory of Boucicault and Bianconi*, the insistent deployment of a vocabulary of translucence — 'glowing', 'mystic brilliance', 'light and fire', 'inward intensity', 'radiance' — would be sufficient to betray MacGreevy's investment in a symbolist reading of Yeats, a reading which has certainly been influential in subsequent readings of Yeats's work.[11]

In the terms of this nationalist/symbolist aesthetic, the representation of the particular is the outward manifestation of an inward spirit — the '*expression* of the spirit of [the] nation', as MacGreevy puts it. An expressive aesthetic of this order thus assumes as given a discrete spirit or essence. This spirit is translucent in the outward form. The fragmented particular becomes consubstantial with the whole of which it is part. Representation here has the double sense of standing in for and of manifesting something. Thus the very process of representation restores the fragmented elements of the nation to wholeness by making each an aspect of the expression of the national spirit. In MacGreevy's account, Yeats's work answers to the need of the Irish in the early twentieth century 'to feel their own life was being expressed in art.' [JBY, 19] The very term 'life' here marks the threshold at which the expressive act is situated — on the boundary that marks the difference between and the fragile continuity of the inner life of a people (its spirit or vital force) and the outward manifestations of a more or less unreflective 'daily life' — the labours, pleasures, and habits of a people. Painting, as it were, opens a door between the damaged life of a heretofore hidden Ireland and the secret realm of its spirit.

The nationalist view of art, in which a political and an aesthetic *parti pris* are combined, that governs MacGreevy's essay on Yeats, could only be anathema to Beckett. His review of the work articulates what appears to have been a longstanding and a well-understood difference in the two writers' approaches to Yeats and to art in general. Pointedly distinguishing in the subtitles of his review between the aspect of Yeats that MacGreevy emphasizes as *The National Painter* and that which he himself promotes as *The Artist*, Beckett insists that the 'national aspects of Mr. Yeats's genius have … been overstated' and proceeds to imply, briefly, curtly even, both the interested or aesthetically 'impure' grounds for that overstatement and reasons to suspect the validity of ascribing to Yeats an 'imaginative sympathy' with the Irish people ('How sympathetic?', the review almost maliciously enquires). In fact, the term Yeats himself invoked was 'affection'. As he puts it in 'The Future of Painting in Ireland', a brief lecture included in the appendix to this essay, 'And every day there are more Irish artists painting their own country and their own people, with the greatest equipment of the artist, affection. That affection for their fellows and for every rock, every little flash of water, every handful of soil, and every living thing in Ireland.' There is little doubt that in his sceptical approach to the question of 'imaginative sympathy', Beckett reads Yeats against his grain, if only to shed light on other qualities in his work. [D, 96] In what must be one of Beckett's most resonant locutions, he dismisses any notion that Yeats's paintings might represent a doorway between inner truth and outer reality, preferring instead a powerful image of closure: Yeats 'is with the great of our time … because he brings light, as only the great dare to bring light, to the issueless predicament of existence, reduces the dark where there might have been, mathematically at least, a door.' [D, 97] Beckett's image here is at once deft, succinct, and devastating. The very valence of light, as that which shines through the particular to imbue it with possibly universal meaning, is reversed here, as the light becomes a dismally demystifying force, reducing darkness only to expose the absence of communication, of doors in or out. Not only does the image uncannily predict Beckett's later short texts and plays, like *Lessness* (1970) and *The Lost Ones* (1970), *Not I* (1972) or *Eh Joe* (1966), it also catches the ambiguous quality of many of Yeats's paintings, where the angled beam of light seems to be no conventional

indicator of optimism or hope, but a baleful and melancholy illumination, that serves only to enhance the gloom.

Clearly, for Beckett, what is illuminated in the imaginative glow of Yeats's painting is not the particular restored to wholeness, but a series of disjunctive images deprived either of connection or determinate significance and expressive only of the missed encounter:

> The being in the street, when it happens in the room, the being in the room when it happens in the street, the turning to gaze from land to sea, from sea to land, the backs to one another and the eyes abandoning, the man alone trudging in the sand, the man alone thinking (thinking!) in his box — these are characteristic notations … [D, 97]

Beckett's terse and uncompromising statement of his utterly different apprehension of the painter can scarcely have surprised MacGreevy. Beckett had already made his understanding of Yeats clear in letters (to some of which MacGreevy alludes) that emphasize, in similar tones, his perception of the paintings as images of alienation, suspension, disjunction — anything but representations of the continuity of artist and people, inner and outer, spirit and body. Beckett's view of Yeats resonates rather with the post-Cartesian predicament of scission and disaggregation, between mind and matter, subject and object, that notoriously informs all of the writer's work. As he wrote to MacGreevy, even as the latter was composing the first draft of the essay on Yeats:

> I find something terrifying for example in the way Yeats puts down a man's head and a woman's head side by side, or face to face, the awful acceptance of 2 entities that will never mingle. And do you remember the picture of a man sitting under a fuchsia hedge, reading with his back turned to the sea and the thunder

12 Beckett to MacGreevy,
   14 Aug. 1937, cited
   in James Knowlson,
   *Damned to Fame: The
   Life of Samuel Beckett*
   (New York, 1996),
   267–68
13 Beckett to MacGreevy, in
   Knowlson, *Damned to
   Fame*, 267
14 Knowlson, *Damned to
   Fame*, 755n.

Fig. 2:
Jack B. Yeats
A Storm
1936
oil on canvas
46 x 61 cm
private collection

clouds? One does not realize how still his pictures are till one looks at others, almost petrified, a sudden suspension of the performance, of convention of sympathy and antipathy, meeting and parting, joy and sorrow.[12]

It is probably impossible to tell to which of Yeats's paintings Beckett is referring to in recalling 'puts down a man's head and a woman's head side by side, or face to face', though the second painting is identifiable as *A Storm* (1936; Fig. 2). But it is clear that what holds his attention is precisely not what MacGreevy celebrates in the painter — 'movement and colour', fluidity and, of course, translucence of expression. [*JBY*, 27] It is, rather, this quality of petrification and suspension that seems to him quite antithetical to the 'sympathy' that

MacGreevy names as a dominant quality in Yeats. In the same letter, Beckett insists on the separateness, not only of human beings from one another, but also of the human and the natural in Yeats's work: 'What I feel he gets so well, dispassionately, not tragically like Watteau, is the heterogeneity of nature and the human denizens, the unalterable alienness of the 2 phenomena.'[13] Unlike the painting of Constable or Turner, whose 'nature is really infested with "spirit"', Yeats's 'final quale' is 'the ultimate *inorganism* of everything'. This inorganism is for Beckett not merely a quality of the represented of the paintings, but a matter of what the *forms* of the paintings articulate: 'A painting of pure inorganic juxtapositions, where nothing can be taken or given and there is no possibility of change or exchange.'[14] Nothing could be further it seems, from MacGreevy's assertion that Yeats's 'concern with the natural scene itself was a human concern. He occasionally depicted it unpeopled, a solitude, but such a solitude as could clearly provide an enlargement of one's human experience.' [JBY, 12]

Such intense differences in perception and in the evaluation of the paintings signal, perhaps, the capaciousness of the paintings themselves, their openness to divergent readings that Yeats himself is known to have desired. At the same time, they derive from a marked difference in the aesthetic *and* the political assumptions of each writer. For MacGreevy, as we have seen, Yeats is the first and quintessential national painter; for Beckett, Yeats explores rather what he had described in a 1934 review, 'Recent Irish Poetry', as 'the new thing that has happened, or the old thing that has happened again, namely the breakdown of the object' or 'the breakdown of the subject' — in either case, the rupture of communication. [D, 70] Awareness of this situation makes it the artist's task to achieve a statement 'of the space that intervenes between him and the world of objects.' And, already in 1934, it is 'a picture by Mr. Jack Yeats' that he invokes, alongside T. S. Eliot's *The Wasteland*, as exemplary of this awareness. MacGreevy appears to assimilate Yeats to a nationalist agenda, emphasizing the representative status of both the artist and his figurations, foregrounding those elements of his work that can be read as expressive of the national spirit, appropriating Yeats to an aesthetic that affirms the continuity of the spirit in the face of the disintegrative force of an *unrepresentative* colonial power. Beckett emphasizes rupture and discontinuity and the radically unreconciled relation of subject and object, and appropriates the painter no less forcefully to his apprehension of the 'issueless predicament of existence'. Yeats's paintings become the contested zone of two radically opposed conjunctures of aesthetic and political principles.

But doubtless, in following the terms that Beckett establishes in his review of MacGreevy on Yeats, one is drawn to exaggerate the differences, stark as sometimes they are. MacGreevy's essay is in some ways a much less coherent production than at first appears, and is marked by contradictions and countercurrents that trouble its ostensibly nationalist agenda. While Beckett's contempt for the Saorstát (the post-treaty Irish Free State) has often been emphasized, less has been made of the longstanding republicanism that MacGreevy and Yeats shared and which forms a barely occluded subtext of the essay. In the wake of the Civil War, which pitted republican radicals against the forces of the new Free State — to which MacGreevy refers disparagingly as 'the little almost republic of Ireland' — the identification of nationalism and republicanism is no simple matter.

Indeed, MacGreevy's essay on Yeats not only makes no secret of his own political affiliations, but insists on articulating both a republican interpretation of recent Irish history and his sense of the relation of Yeats's work to republicanism. This subtext ranges from references to 'the tanks and lorries of imperial terrorists' to an openly republican interpretation of partition:

> The end of the prolonged struggle was that Ireland had not the one parliament that it wanted but the two it didn't want imposed on it. *Divide and rule*. The country was partitioned. The imperial connection remained. And with the adroitness of experienced politicians the imperialists laid the final odium of moral defeat on the Irish themselves. Ireland was launched on a civil war. [JBY, 25]

In this context, the discussion, or even the invocation of several paintings of Yeats's, gains implicit political significance: *Bachelor's Walk, In Memory* (1915), with its reference to the murder of Irish nationalists by the British army; *Singing the Dark Rosaleen, Croke Park* (1921), which

15 On this episode, see Mike Cronin, *Sport and Nationalism in Ireland: Gaelic Games, Soccer and Irish Identity since 1884* (Dublin, 1999), 87–88.

16 See Philip Pettit, *Republicanism: A Theory of Freedom and Government* (Oxford, 1997). Sean Kennedy, in his essay '"The Artist who Stakes His Being is from Nowhere": Beckett and Thomas MacGreevy on the Art of Jack B. Yeats', in *Samuel Beckett Today / Aujourd'hui*, 14 (Fall 2004), 61–74, collapses this crucial distinction between the official nationalism expressed in the Free State and the more recalcitrant republicanism espoused by MacGreevy and, it appears, Yeats. He also collapses both Yeats and MacGreevy with the views of Daniel Corkery which a reading of MacGreevy's text or Yeats's paintings does not really sustain. For Beckett's critical relation to Corkery, see my 'Writing in the Shit: Beckett, Nationalism and the Colonial Subject', in *Anomalous States: Irish Writing and the Post-Colonial Moment* (Dublin, 1993), 41–58.

depicts the singing of that patriotic ballad at the Gaelic sports arena that had become infamous for the Black and Tan massacre of Bloody Sunday the year before the painting's completion;[15] *Communicating with Prisoners* (c.1924), which represents a group of women shouting up to republican women prisoners in Kilmainham Gaol during the Civil War; *The Funeral of Harry Boland* (1922), commemorating the death of the prominent republican leader; and, in the postscript of 1945, the peculiarly sombre painting *Going to Wolfe Tone's Grave* (1929), of which MacGreevy parenthetically and somewhat redundantly remarks 'the national note is struck as clearly as ever in the past'. [*JBY*, 37] As if it were necessary, that last remark serves to underline the significance of this canon of Yeats's paintings and the kind of historical and political claim that is entailed in the assertion that Yeats is the preeminent Irish painter. In the first place, by establishing that the painter's work affiliated him with republicanism and that his claims as an historical painter rest on paintings that commemorate the high points and the defeats of republican struggle, MacGreevy links Yeats's own trajectory as an artist to disaffiliation from the present order and to a more or less proleptic relation to the nation he represents. Betrayed by the collusion with its imperial saboteurs of the nation that claims to be 'once again', the republican artist represents the nation that is 'yet to be', the still damaged but recalcitrant people. If, in the immediate aftermath of the Civil War, 'fact and poetry had parted company', it becomes inevitable that 'Jack Yeats's work became a passionate recall to poetry'. [*JBY*, 27] It is to this moment also that MacGreevy dates the major 'modification of technique' that begins to constitute Yeats's later, more aesthetically uncompromising style. Both stylistically and politically, MacGreevy suggests, Yeats's work is a refusal of the *status quo*, of the state that is in being. This trajectory of Yeats's work, which

MacGreevy understands as belonging with the 'subjective tendency' of post-war Ireland, correlates to an 'objective tendency' both in the painter's work and in Ireland itself. In these tendencies, we might say, republicanism withdraws into a kind of permanent if 'obscure' and dispersed opposition. The objective tendency, which is 'to insist on the need for a definitive solution of Ireland's political and, more particularly, social problems', maintains the legacy not only of Pearse, but also of Connolly. Its oppositionality, in the moment, is 'that it fulfills the perennial need to check up on authority's liability to abuse its privileges.' [*JBY*, 26] What may appear here as a strangely muted version of republican ideals in fact embodies an understated but no less significant principle of non-domination that, as Philip Pettit has argued, is critical to the specific understanding of freedom that is articulated throughout republican political thought.[16]

If the 'subjective tendency' of the movement manifests itself in the formal changes in Yeats's work, the objective tendency appears in the content of his work. However, the changes are less marked than the continuity. Yeats's longstanding devotion to depicting the common people of Ireland links him to the radical tradition of republicanism. MacGreevy's implication, scarcely muted here, is that Yeats's work has always allied him to the left-wing republicanism of 'the sociologist [*sic*], James Connolly':

> It is not likely that Jack Yeats has remained untouched by this objective tendency. But as he has always painted the people, 'the workers,' in town and country, it would be difficult to trace any such influence as a new thing in his art. It is not yesterday or today that Jack Yeats discovered labouring humanity. At the Celtic Race Congress in Paris in 1923, he read a paper in which he gave it as his opinion that the most stirring sights in the world are a man ploughing

and a ship on the sea. He still paints the people, and with an even more passionate directness in recent years than in his earlier days. Sometimes there is more outward calm but more inward intensity, fire and imagination than there used to be. I think here particularly of the timeless figure of *The Breaker-Out*. Impassive now, but still desperate, he might be the child of *The Big Turf Fire* painted twenty-five years later.
[*JBY*, 26–27]

MacGreevy's final allusion connects the 1925 oil of a departing sailor, *The Breaker-Out*, with an early sketch of unmistakable political import that he analyzes earlier in the essay:

Jack Yeats found no occasion to go outside of the everyday scene for his material and there is no excess of emphasis in his statement. We may read satire and revolution into that early sketch in which a ragged boy tries to gain a few coppers standing on the roadside on a stormy night singing, of all songs, *The Big Turf Fire*. His arms are raised above his head in a wild gesture of desperation as he marks the rhythm with a pair of bones in his hand. But the artist was more than a satirist or revolutionist in the everyday sense. The incident was one of a variety of incidents he noted, and he perceived the import of it and found the appropriate statement of it as he perceived the import and found the appropriate statement of others that were utterly dissimilar. Of course every genuine artist is a revolutionist by the mere fact of being a genuine artist. Genuineness, truth, however peaceable, is always revolutionary — it is usually the counter-revolutionaries who make revolution bloody. [*JBY*, 23]

The 'truth' that is so revolutionary, and that the Irish counter-revolution of the Civil War period had bloodily suppressed, entails a different Ireland than that established and made respectable by the official and conservative Catholic nationalism of the Free State. The Ireland mobilized by the left wing republicanism of Mellows, O'Malley, O'Donnell, Markievicz and Gonne was not that of the big farmers and graziers, the 'nation building' class of the new order, nor that of the small and larger business interests that, as Connolly had always predicted, would ultimately continue to serve the interests of British capital — what MacGreevy termed 'imperial masters' — even in a formally independent nation. It was, rather, the Ireland of the dispossessed, of the landless labourers and the workers who had fought for unionization and, in some cases, for soviet-style co-operatives, of the marginal people, the 'tinkers' and tramps, the rogues and derelicts, the ballad singers and roving musicians that populate Yeats's pre-war images of Ireland and who, in actual practice, so often proved recalcitrant to assimilation into the official nationalist movement with its need to refine and purify the spirit of the nation.[17] In this respect, Yeats's art could be seen to continue the traditions of recalcitrance to the law that MacGreevy sees as characteristic of an Irish anti-colonial mentality, so that his later painting projects decolonization as a process beyond the moment of formal independence. MacGreevy was right; Yeats saw his own work as an act of decolonization of the Irish visual imagination. As he puts it in 'The Future of Painting in Ireland', 'If he is a free man in a free country his eye is open and free. If he become a slave in a slave country he need never open a full eye. His masters will see all for him, and he becomes unable to express himself, except as the earth and stones express themselves.'

It is, indeed, no accident that when MacGreevy seeks to characterize the mentality of the dispossessed Irish on the eve of the War of Independence, it is not to a conventional historian that he turns but to the recently published memoir of Ernie O'Malley, the republican guerrilla,

17 See David Lloyd, 'Adulteration and the Nation', in *Anomalous States*, 88–124.

18 *JBY*, 17, cites O'Malley's *On Another Man's Wound*, published in 1936.

19 Terence de Vere White remarks: 'Most people by then [1920s] knew a drawing of a donkey by Jack Yeats. It was printed by the Cuala Press, which his sisters managed. The people who were disapproving of Bohemians would have wished that one Yeats should continue to reproduce that pretty little donkey, and the other the lake-isle of Innisfree, over and over again.' See 'The Personality of Jack B. Yeats', in Roger McHugh, ed., *Jack B. Yeats: A Centenary Gathering*, (Dublin, 1971), 23.

20 For example, Luke Gibbons, 'Synge, Country and Western: The Myth of the West in Irish and American Culture', in *Transformations in Irish Culture* (Cork, 1996), 23: 'The equation of rural life with all that is truly Irish has dominated the work of many modern Irish painters, but is particularly evident in the work of Jack Yeats, Paul Henry and Seán Keating.' Gibbons associates this with 'the idealization of the west', though his essay does much to complicate that equation in the case of Synge. Yeats's difference from either Henry or Keating will be suggested later in the present essay.

imprisoned by the Free State during the Civil War, who became a close friend of the painter and one of the earliest commentators on his work.[18] The pointers throughout the essay ask us to re-examine the pre-1922 body of Yeats's work in Ireland, on which — rather than on the later and most formally innovative paintings — his reputation as Ireland's foremost national painter is still based. Indeed, in so far as its broad public acceptance is concerned, that reputation probably rests on a mere handful of works, and principally those most frequently reproduced under his sisters' Cuala Press imprint and in subsequent mass-produced reproductions. Little wonder that in the 1930s he refused to permit reprints of those editions and, indeed, virtually repudiated them. Even his determined, if fruitless, attempt to ban reproductions of his work beyond his own death signals his vivid appreciation of the function of selection in defining — and domesticating — the reception of his *œuvre* as much as it does his desire to preserve the artistic integrity of his paintings *as* paintings.

The most cursory survey of Yeats's earlier drawings, paintings and illustrations of Irish material indicates how the selection and dissemination of his work has operated to contain and limit its range. The tendency of the reproductions is to emphasize the element of gentle whimsy in his depictions of Irish rural life, or the elements of fanciful, even boyish romanticism in the Cuala Press prints and broadsides.[19] A full sense of his engagement with a certain demotic, or even daemonic energy in the margins of Irish life (the sort of energy MacGreevy indicates in his description of *The Big Turf Fire*, an energy of contradiction and deprivation) seems to slip away through the refining filters of selection. This loss is not merely a matter of the *content* of the representations, though it is true that a principle of selection that emphasized his rogues and derelicts would give a quite different impression of his

understanding of the 'national spirit'. It is also a matter of what gets lost if one overlooks the compositional qualities that underwrite the scenes that energize him, qualities that emphasize an unruliness and insubordination that MacGreevy may be right to find more deeply internalized in the post-1922 paintings. As with his friend and travelling companion J. M. Synge, whose works on Aran and west Kerry and whose articles on the Congested Districts of Connemara he illustrated, it would prove too easy for even the most acute of critics to dismiss Yeats's work in this area as mere ethnographic romanticization.[20] The ethical comfort with which by now we dismiss the supposedly ethnographic gaze of early twentieth-century nationalists, as if they were simply primitivizing in the manner of Robert O'Flaherty, or as if the undoubted element of projection in their critiques of modernity fell on nothing more than a blank screen, risks missing their perception of more complex and subversive dynamics in the West's negotiations with modernity. But even as gently comic a drawing as *The Poteen Makers* (1912; Fig. 3), with its deft caricatures of the magistrates and of the onlookers — at once sympathetic and malicious — secretes an observation on Irish social life that easily passes unnoticed. For its focus on the magistrates' bench distracts from the peculiar fact that the accused themselves, whom the picture claims by its title to depict, are strangely absent from the scene. Their backs are turned to us; it is as if they abscond from our gaze as, perhaps, they seek to elude the force of the law that condemns them. Or in *The Wake House* (c.1908; Fig. 4), the scene of the crowded room frames the intent figure of a speaker occupying the vital site of the hearth, the mourning of the dead deflected, or, it may be, more fully realized in what seem to be the passions of political speech.[21] The faces of the crowd are again turned from artist and viewer, disregarding the act of representation as if the focus of the action is tangential or oblique to the gaze that seeks to render and make sense of the occasion.22 Or, to end with but one more of dozens of such images, in *The Felons of our Land* (1910; Fig. 5), as in the later *Singing the Dark Rosaleen*, the action of the ballad-singing is depicted at the margins of the sporting event, the ragged and derelict-looking assembly taking place at the edges of the main social gathering in which a nationalist like Daniel Corkery, or even MacGreevy himself on occasion, would have traced the image of the nation performing itself.23 The title of the drawing in turn nicely poses the ambiguity as to whether 'felons' refers to the ballad itself or to those who sing and listen to it.

My point is, of course, that there is something in such works, modest in their 'appropriate statement' as they are, that already exceeds the merely ethnographic, as it does the simply nationalist, precisely by foregrounding what MacGreevy seems also to have observed, that 'in Ireland, the whole people were below the law'. [*JBY*, 15] There is something in these events that defies the force of the law, the social order of the state and the gazes of its representatives, whether the police, the magistrate, or the ethnographic stranger — including ourselves as viewers. As these are representations of those who 'cannot represent themselves' and therefore 'must be represented', they are also no less representations of that which

eludes representation, which disappears from representation even in the glare of what it renders visible.24 It is no paradox, then, as MacGreevy seems to suggest, that the condition under which Jack Yeats becomes the representative national painter is precisely one of a failure of representation in which the *petit peuple* is set over against 'an unrepresentative possessing class' and in which 'those who acted for the nation officially were outside the nation.' [*JBY*, 9, 17] The counter-revolutionary Free State does not, from a republican perspective, overcome that rift in representation, but in a sense exacerbates it, dividing the people from itself rather than unifying it, as a decolonizing nationalism seemed to, against the imperial power. The rift cannot be healed by the official nationalist means of offering a symbolic common ground, an idealized West, for example, in which difference might appear to be sublated. For this reason, MacGreevy could never consider Paul Henry as a potentially representative Irish artist in the same way as he did Yeats. For in Henry, more often than not, the effect of Irishness (the spirit of Ireland, in nationalist terms) is rendered through the evacuation of the landscape of the population that works it, fights over it, fights for it, that makes it a site of struggle rather than of reconciliation or repose. Or, where the peasants are represented, they are represented as an element, if a naturally

21 Travellers in Ireland, like Thomas Croker and Mrs. S. C. Hall, who witnessed keening and wakes in the nineteenth century, generally regarded them as probable sites of sedition, political talk, and general impropriety. See David Lloyd, 'The Memory of Hunger', in David L. Eng and David Kazanjian, eds., *Loss: The Politics of Mourning* (Berkeley and Los Angeles, 2003), 208–12.

22 See John Barrell, *The Dark Side of the Landscape: The Rural Poor in English Painting 1730–1840* (Cambridge, 1980).

23 For Daniel Corkery's use of such a scene as an instance of the 'life of this people', see his classic *Synge and Anglo-Irish Literature* (Cork, 1966), 22. I have commented on Corkery's cultural nationalism and on Beckett's distance from it in 'Writing in the Shit: Beckett, Nationalism and the Colonial Subject', in *Anomalous States*, 43–44.

24 Gibbons, 'Synge, Country and Western', 27, in the context of the American homesteader cites this famous formula of Marx's *18th Brumaire*. All this suggests that, for Yeats, to be outside representation, in the position of the 'subaltern', is in no unambiguous way to occupy a position of disempowerment.

Fig. 3:
Jack B Yeats
The Poteen Makers
1912
pen, ink and
watercolour on card
30.5 x 19.5 cm
National Gallery of
Ireland, Dublin

Fig. 4:
Jack B. Yeats
The Wake House
c.1908
pen and ink on paper
22.5 x 29.4 cm
National Gallery of
Ireland, Dublin

embattled element, of the landscape itself, as in *The Potato Diggers* (1912; Fig. 6).

Refusal of the subordination of the human figure to the landscape or, by the same token, of the heroic domination of the landscape by the human, is intrinsic to Yeats's work, according to both MacGreevy and Beckett. Indeed it is precisely here that both critics converge, in their recognition of Yeats's recalcitrance to any mode of premature reconciliation. Where Beckett apprehends this in terms of the 'petrification' of figure and landscape, MacGreevy approaches it through what he understands as Yeats's singular innovation in the history of painting, the striking of 'a new balance between the landscape and the figure':

> With Jack Yeats, the landscape is as real as the figures. It has its own character as they have theirs. It is impersonal. They are the reverse. But the sense of the impersonal is an enrichment of the humanity of the figures. And conversely, the opposition heightens the sense of the impersonal character of the landscape ... I do not think I am claiming too much for Jack Yeats when I say that nobody before him had juxtaposed landscape and figure without subduing the character of either to that of the other ... Association and apartness at one and the same time have never been more clearly stated in terms of art. [*JBY*, 13–14]

This is an extraordinary insight by MacGreevy into what provides the underlying dynamic of so many of Yeats's later works. It is an observation that I would want to extend from the relation of landscape to figure (its justness here being exemplified by any number of paintings, from *O'Connell Bridge* [1925], where the landscape is urban, to *Men of Destiny* [1946] or *Many Ferries* [1948]) to other relations, formal and figurative, in the paintings — from the relationships among figures themselves to the relation of figuration to the material aspects of the medium itself. What MacGreevy variously comprehends as balance, or as 'association and apartness', seems to me to lie at the heart of the dynamic tensions that trouble the viewer's gaze before the most achieved of these canvases. It is as if the recalcitrance to representation that was depicted over and again as a quality of the figures *in* the early works is drawn into the very process of figuration, as if, to bend MacGreevy's terms only slightly, an objective tendency in relation *to* representation becomes a subjective tendency *of* representation.

It is well known that the most immediately striking aspect of the transformation of Yeats's style through the 1920s and 1930s is his gradual abandonment of line. The early oils are marked by the predominance of sharp outlines bounding the figures and the visual foci of the image, what Bruce Arnold aptly refers to as '*drawing* in oil paint'.[25] This is true not only for the illustrations to *Irishmen All*, whose technical qualities Arnold nicely analyses, associating them with the line drawing of *A Broadside* or with Yeats's experience of poster-work. It is no less true of free-standing oil paintings like *Bachelor's Walk* or *The Double Jockey Act* (1916; Fig. 7). In the former, the figures of the flower girl and the boy at her side stand out starkly from the street, the pavement and the walls behind them, as if backlit, or even as if collaged onto the already-painted scene (Yeats's miniature theatres come to mind at once). Facial features and the divisions of skin from fabric, as well as from the background, are clearly delineated. Here figure stands out from its ground emphatically. In *The Double Jockey Act*, painted only a year later, already *within* the figures a freer brushwork seems to be emerging — the different tones of the skewbald horse and the features and clothing of the jockeys and the clown have lost sharpness of definition and boundary in a way that

And though they sleep in dungeons deep,
    Or flee, outlawed and banned,
We love them yet, we can't forget
    The felons of our land

Fig. 5:
Jack B. Yeats
*The Felons of
Our Land*
1910
ink and watercolour
on card
30.5 x 19.5 cm
National Gallery of
Ireland, Dublin

Fig. 6:
Paul Henry
The Potato Diggers
1912
oil on canvas
51 x 46 cm
National Gallery of
Ireland, Dublin

25 Arnold, *Jack Yeats*, 180.
See also 198 and 229–30
for further remarks on
the transition in Yeats's
work away from line
and on the later oil
technique that emerges
with that break.
26 Pyle, *Yeats*, 204,
comments on a number
of these features in the
painting.
27 Arnold, *Jack Yeats*, 191

contributes to the demotic sense of energy that radiates from the painting. The effect of the very visible brushstrokes here, and of the pointillistic texture of the arena floor, begins to oppose the tendency to bounding line.[26] Nonetheless, the overall composition is strongly delineated, the red-striped canvas of the tent and the upright poles clearly distinguishing and outlining the various fields and depths of vision. There is a distinct tension in the work between the impulse of the draughtsman and that of the painter.

Just as the sharp illustrator's outlines make the often-reproduced drawings of *Life in the West* and other Irish scenes susceptible, if wrongly, of an ethnographic or a sentimentalizing appropriation, so the clear outlines and the relief into which they throw the figures against the background predispose a painting like *Bachelor's Walk* to being 'used as a nationalist ikon, and a symbol'.[27] The very 'standing forth' of the human figures projects them into a representational status that is both their 'standing for' the nation as its types *and* a mode of pictorial clarity or accessibility. Nothing obscures the significance of the act and its pathos. Indeed, by a kind of visual pun one might say that the clarity of outline correlates with the clarity of expressive visual communication, the translucence of the meaning in the image, of the general in this particular, that composes the symbol. In such a painting, in fact, Yeats comes closest to the formal qualities of an epic historical and unambiguously national painter like Seán Keating, whose canvases are marked by strong typological figuration, deliberate symbolic, even allegorical significance, and, above all, a stark outlining of figure against background.

This is not intended as a reductive comparison, but rather to mark the technical and formal transfiguration of Yeats's work in both its radical nature and its political significance. Neither of them lies simply in a shift in content or subject matter, from 'a perception of countrymen in relaxation' to 'the loneliness of the individual soul', as Ernie O'Malley put it, or from specificity to images 'less firmly fixed in time and space', as John Rothenstein claimed.[28] There is, obviously, nothing intrinsically less poetic or less lonely and individual, or even more specific, in *The Circus Dwarf* (1912) or *Derelict* (1910) than in *No Flowers* (1945) or *A Morning in the City* (1937). We are obliged, rather, to turn to the significance of the actual mode of representation rather than to the objects represented to grasp the import of the paintings, the way in which they seize and work on the viewer's gaze.

Any number of Yeats's later paintings would serve to exemplify the activity of the gaze that his canvases demand and provoke. We will focus on two here that manifest somewhat different aspects of the painter's technique and its effects. *Two Travellers* (1942; Fig. 8) is one of Yeats's better-known paintings, partly because the Tate Gallery purchased it, partly because it has been associated with the set of Beckett's *Waiting for Godot*.[29] Thematically, the painting resumes many of Yeats's visual preoccupations. Two men, in well-worn clothing, encounter one another on a rough track in a coastal landscape. Heavy clouds suggest an imminent rainstorm, though the skyscape is lighter over a choppy sea in what is presumably the West, where a faint

rose light illuminates the clouds and falls on one traveller's face. The encounter remains an enigma: are they strangers or acquaintances? Of what do they speak? How far are they travelling? What brings them to this otherwise desolate and apparently uninhabited terrain? Where is each headed? In this respect, the painting is of course susceptible either of Beckett's understanding of Yeats's images as disjunctive and suspended, or of MacGreevy's reading of this painting as 'an apparently casual encounter in a world of mystery', revealing a new 'exalted tragic consciousness'. [*JBY*, 37] It is also potentially open to Brian O'Doherty's dismissive criticism of Yeats's romanticization of the figure of the traveller, in the course of which he effectively reduces the later work to identity with the early illustrations and broadsides, all equivalent in their representation and mythologization of the national character as that of the outsider.[30] And yet to turn from the thematic paraphrase of the painting (the aspect of the painting that reproduction tends to foreground by flattening out the texture of the medium) to its formal and technical qualities is to engage with a much less stable phenomenon that obliges what Beckett calls the 'labour' that is engaged 'between such a knower and such an unknown'. [*D*, 95] The obligation to labour constitutes the difficulty that obtrudes in almost every instance of the later painting between a thematic statement that can be reduced for conventional consumption or, as O'Doherty complains, national self-flattery, and the work itself, in every sense of that word. That labour evoked by the work departs markedly from the lucidity of representation that makes earlier paintings like *Bachelor's Walk* so much more readily available for iconic use.

Confronting *Two Travellers*, one is almost certainly struck at once by the paint surface itself and by the difficulty of resolving the image out of the paintwork. The same effect

28 Ernie O'Malley, 'The Painting of Jack B. Yeats', in McHugh, *Centenary Gathering*, 68; John Rothenstein, director of the Tate Gallery, quoted in Arnold, *Jack Yeats*, 231

29 See, for example, Knowlson, *Damned to Fame*, 378–79. Peggy Phelan, in her article 'Lessons in Blindness from Samuel Beckett', *Proceedings of the Modern Language Association*, 119, 5 (Oct. 2004), 1279–92, which appeared as this essay was in press, sees Yeats's *The Graveyard Wall* (1945) as a possible source for the play. I cannot corroborate her sense, but am pleased to see how closely her description of Beckett's 'rhythm of looking' correlates to my own sense both of Beckett's gaze and of Yeats's mature style and the demands it makes of the viewer. She writes: 'It oscillates between seeing and blindness, between figuration and abstraction, between the void at the center of sight and the contour of the slender ridge that brooks it.'

30 Brian O'Doherty, 'Jack B. Yeats: Promise and Regret', in McHugh, *Centenary Gathering*, 80–81 and *passim*

Fig. 7:
Jack B. Yeats
The Double Jockey Act
1916
oil on canvas
61 x 46 cm
National Gallery of Ireland, Dublin

can be observed in many of Yeats's late paintings, notably, for example, *Grief* (1951; Fig. 9) or *Above the Fair* (1946; Fig. 10): it is often extremely difficult to achieve a total image of the painting no matter where one stands before the canvas, and wherever one stands, one has the impression of seeing the work at a different depth of focus, so to speak. It is as if the represented of the painting continually dissolves back into the medium of the representation, resisting totalization and renewing the work of the gaze at every turn.[31] In *Two Travellers*, not atypically, the layering of the oils is at very different thicknesses, ranging from the thinnest of layers to a dense impasto. The grey cloudscape that stretches from the expanse of sky in the upper left corner across the line of the hill or mountain that becomes an abrupt cliff to the right is a thin film through which the bare canvas can at points be glimpsed. To the far mid-right, the dark blue of the sea is thickly layered, but scored at points by brush handle or palette knife to reveal bare canvas, producing the effect of lines of surf foam at the cliff's base. Just right of centre, along the side of the road or path that

bisects the painting, an extraordinary stretch of primary colours — predominantly yellow, red and green — is dashed unmixed and thickly on to the canvas and apparently, from the lack of brushmarks, applied directly from the tube or perhaps the finger to the canvas. Similar patches of bright primary colour appear to the left of the two figures, but in neither case do these vivid and heady patches of colour resolve into the conventional outlines of the vegetation they must be taken to represent. The thickest impasto composes the two figures. In evident contrast to the earlier oils, however, no firm bounding lines enclose them. On the contrary, they are composed largely out of the same oil tones as the landscape immediately surrounding them; at points, such as the right leg of the left-hand traveller, they are literally carved out of the depth of the paint by, presumably, the tip of the brush handle. The figures seem at one moment to be sculpted almost three-dimensionally out of the surface of the oil paint, at another to merge back into it, the figure becoming consubstantial with the medium. In such a technique, 'drawing in oils' takes on an entirely new meaning.

31 This is precisely the effort that the *Dublin Opinion* cartoon captures: see Fig. 1.

Fig. 8:
Jack B. Yeats
Two Travellers
1942
oil on wood
91.5 x 122 cm
Tate Gallery, London

Fig. 9:
Jack B. Yeats
Grief
1951
oil on canvas
102 x 153 cm
National Gallery
of Ireland, Dublin

The mobility of the gaze that is obliged by this highly plastic application of the oils is reinforced by the overall composition of the painting. With an effect that is again largely lost in the flattening of reproduction, the canvas appears to be constructed of overlapping and competing zones of focus. While at one moment the two figures in the foreground appear to dominate, the eye is almost immediately led either to the upper left quadrant of the lowering sky by the figure's vertical posture, or by the intense primary colours to the roadway and then, by a sharp rightward turn of the line described by those pigments at the base of the cliff and its continuation in a fine line of red, to the sea- and skyscape of the upper right quadrant. These various zones of focus are not discrete, however, but overlap and penetrate each other while being linked by the roadway whose line of sight projects diagonally from the lower left through the standing figures towards the upper right. The effect of these distinct but overlapping compositional zones is to prevent the eye from coming to repose. In this sense, the painting forcefully confirms MacGreevy's insight, based on earlier work of Yeats's, as to the 'balance' between figure and

landscape, but does so in a way remarkably more dynamic in every respect. It is not only that within the representation the eye moves without dominative hierarchy between what would otherwise be 'figure' and 'ground', but that the gaze moves, is obliged to move, simultaneously between the representation, the image in the painting, and the medium of the representation, the material of the painting. The dimension of artifice, the material that composes the image, is not subordinated to the image: rather, its surfaces, depths and plastic textures are foregrounded in a way that dissolves the figure even as they supply the medium through which it emerges. The oscillation of the eye between material and representation produces the paradoxical effect of suspension to which Beckett refers, like a sustained tremolo in musical composition.

In this relative autonomy of medium and representation, Yeats's rejection of reproductions is aimed at the preservation of the work *as work*, as the difficult locus of an unachievable labour of looking. The rejection does not have as its aim a reactionary preservation of aura, in which the symbolist translucence of the image through the transparent medium might be maintained. Instead it is based on the wish to retain the sometimes vertiginous oscillation between the image and its material medium. The relation here between the visual 'content' and the formal or technical means is much as Theodor Adorno describes the relation of content and technique with regard to the new music that was emerging more or less contemporaneously with Yeats's career as an artist:

> Content and technique are both identical and non-identical because a work of art acquires its life in the tension between inner and outer; because it is a work of art only if its manifest appearance points to something beyond itself … The unmediated identity of content and appearance would annul the idea of art. For all that, the two are also identical. For in composition, that which has been made real is all that counts. Only philistines can entertain the notion of a ready-made and self-contained artistic content that is then projected into the external world with the aid of a

technique conceived of in similarly thing-like terms. Inner experience and outer form are created by a reciprocal process of interaction.[32]

This dialectic of content and technique is less formally implied in Yeats's own remarks to interviewer Shotaro Oshima concerning the stylistic changes in his work: 'Things in the external world may seem always the same to some people, but an artist finds them different when a change is brought about in him. He must not try to go against this inner change.'[33]

What this conception of the mutual autonomy of content and technique suggests is no less that every occasion, every image to be produced, requires a different technical solution; that composition, in painting as in music, requires different modes of deployment of its medium, specific to that occasion. To turn from *Two Travellers* to *The Old Walls* (1945; Fig. 11) is to see Yeats deploy a similar repertoire of techniques modified for a quite different conjunction and to equally different effects. Here, a solitary figure stands enclosed by a

32 Theodor W. Adorno, 'Music and Technique', in *Sound Figures*, trans. Rodney Livingstone (Stanford, 1999), 197–98
33 Shotaro Oshima, 'An Interview with Jack Butler Yeats', in McHugh, *Centenary Gathering*, 52–53

Fig. 10:
Jack B. Yeats
Above the Fair
1946
oil on canvas
91 x 122 cm
National Gallery
of Ireland, Dublin

Fig. 11:
Jack B. Yeats
The Old Walls
1945
oil on canvas
46 x 61cm
National Gallery of
Ireland, Dublin

space of ruins, the whole being suffused by a yellow light that is totally appropriate to those melancholy light effects that I referred to earlier. If the dark patch to the left of the standing figure is, as it appears to be, his shadow rather than a bush or clump of weeds, then the light that enters the ruined structure is the low light of a rising or setting sun. This painting, which Beckett could have seen on his immediate post-war visit to Ireland, shares some of the colour tones of *A Storm*, on which he commented in his letter to MacGreevy and of *A Morning* (1935–36), that he had purchased from Yeats in the mid-1930s. Here, the variation in the application of the oils is no less marked than in *Two Travellers*, but to quite different tonal effect. The figure upper-centre and his shadow to the left are zones of thick, dark impasto while the walls that constitute the upper segment and the sides of the painting are composed of an astonishingly thin layer of paint, in many places consisting of virtually bare canvas. There is a certain bravura in this willingness to compose so much of the painting from the exposed canvas that underlies the image,

pushing what MacGreevy refers to as the 'swift and summary … brushwork' that shapes his figures to a further limit. [*JBY*, 15] Here, however, the treatment is not of the figure, but of the walls between which the figure stands, a structure that becomes attenuated to apparent translucence: it is virtually the formal antithesis of the two paintings that MacGreevy singles out on account of the disappearance of the figures into, respectively, background and motion, *Going to Wolfe Tone's Grave* and *The Salt Marshes* (n.d.). In *The Old Walls* it is the human figure that bears the substance of the painting, while the ruins around him seem to fade and dissolve from representation. It is an effect that recurs with remarkable frequency in the later paintings, where even what appear to be still-whole structures lose substance and solidity in relation to the light and to the human figures that move across them (see, for example, *The Breakfast Room* [1944], *A Silence* [1944], *The Music* [1946], *In the City's Heart* [1950], or *Grief* [1951]). The paradoxical effect of this is, on the one hand, to make the human figure seem more solid and substantial than its material environment: we might then see the contemplative figure of *The Old Walls* standing out against the structures he has outlasted; on the other, it is to make the human presence seem, by virtue of its very solidity, a ghostly remnant of things that have passed away, seeking to summon them once more to presence.[34] The very application of the paint thus enacts the oscillation of memory and loss, representation and the evanescent present, staging technically the insubstantiality of substance and the accumulated patina of perception and reflection that makes memory a filter or screen rather than a translucent medium. The formal as well as iconic tension that insists here between the figure and its ground transforms the 'balance' between landscape and figure that MacGreevy noted into a reflection on the medium of representation itself. The canvas as painted becomes in its technical bravura an index of the extent to which the opacity of the subject, with its dense layerings of memory, obtrudes between the representation and the object that eludes it, fading ultimately into ruination.

This rigorous foregrounding of the technical problems of representation constitutes the enduring difficulty of viewing Yeats's paintings as visual totalities: standing before his canvases, one is constantly forced to move back and forth between technique and image, figure and medium, undecided as to which dominates. This recalcitrance to visual consumption of the image belies equally those who seek to celebrate Yeats for his romantic nationalism and those who, like Brian O'Doherty, deprecate him for the same. Both appropriations of his work are as reductive of the aesthetic concept of romanticism as they are of the paintings themselves, levelling one to mere fanciful idealization and the other to mere iconic thematics. Yeats's painting defies every effort to reduce it to figurative translucence, whether in the form of the translucence of the symbol that informs a nationalist

aesthetic or in that of a classical painting in which, as Louis Marin has argued, 'the material "canvas" and "real" surface must be posited and neutralized in what is essentially a technical, theoretical and ideological assumption of transparency'.[35] On the contrary, Yeats's painting foregrounds its material conditions of representation with an effect that is the antithesis of mimetic reflection of the world. It is to this formal recalcitrance of Yeats's painting, rather than simply to any contingent affinity with his representations of tramps, clowns or derelicts, that we can most fruitfully trace Beckett's high estimation of the painter. The period during which Beckett befriended and engaged most closely with Yeats was also that in which he was beginning to articulate his own approach to art and was singularly exercised by the problem of representation and with the problematic relation, already cited, of subject to object. Where for Yeats the difficult relation of representation to represented was articulated in a painting that foregrounded the tension between figure and medium, for Beckett, most notably in his critical essays of this period and throughout the restless experimentation of his writing, an analogous tension first emerges in the relation between language and its objects. For Beckett, that relation later ceased to be phrased as a question of *two* distinct domains — whether of language and self-consciousness or of language and percepts — and became (as for Adorno and Yeats) more precisely a question of *one* domain in which medium and representation are undecidable aspects of the work. From at least *The Unnamable* on, there can be no distinction between medium and content: representation is what is represented; what can be represented is representation.

But through the 1930s and 1940s, Beckett continues to articulate the problem of the writer through what may have been for him at first a necessary distinction between the two. As he writes in 1937 to his German friend Axel Kaun:

34 This may be especially true of *A Silence*, which has been seen as an assembly of dead and living friends, including, in the foreground, J. M. Synge.

35 See Louis Marin, *To Destroy Painting*, trans. Mette Hjort (Chicago, 1995), 47.

And more and more my own language appears to me like a veil that must be torn apart to get at the things (or the Nothingness) behind it ... As we cannot eliminate language all at once, we should at least leave nothing undone that might contribute to its falling in disrepute. To bore one hole after another in it, until what lurks behind it — be it something or nothing — begins to seep through; I cannot imagine a higher goal for a writer today. Or is literature alone to remain behind in the old lazy ways that have been so long ago abandoned by music and painting? [D, 171–72]

Language for Beckett at this point remains conceived of metaphorically as a *veil* between the object external to it and the representation that it constitutes, although the counter-analogy with music and painting suggests that he may already be grasping for a notion of an art in which there is no distinction between form and matter.

As he proceeds, he articulates a project that, though the analogy here is to music, remarkably resembles Yeats's use of his artistic materials:

Is there any reason why that terrible materiality of the word surface should not be capable of being dissolved, like for example the sound surface, torn by enormous pauses, of Beethoven's seventh Symphony, so that through whole pages we can perceive nothing but a path of sounds suspended in giddy heights, linking unfathomable abysses of silence? [D, 172]

And it is, in fact, to painting that Beckett most consistently turns to find analogies for his own predicament as a writer. What is striking, however, is that despite the antagonism to representation and to expression that informs his criticism of MacGreevy and his art criticism in general,

Beckett does not turn for a solution to abstraction, as one might expect, but rather to artists who seem to be linked only in their exploration of the limits of figuration: Yeats, Bram Van Velde, and, later in his life, Avigdor Arikha. He remarks in his review of Denis Devlin's *Intercessions* that 'it is naturally in the image that this profound and abstruse self-consciousness first emerges with least loss of integrity ... First emerges.' [D, 94] That insistent repetition (separated from the first instance by several sentences, thus requiring a noticeable effort of recall) is also a qualification. Beckett's fascination with the qualities and paradoxes of the image remains a constant of his work, so much so that the images he isolates from Yeats's paintings remarkably anticipate those of the short texts and plays of the 1960s. But the condition of the image's emergence, as the representative of self-consciousness, is no less the condition of its fading, a point on which those texts, with their cyclical fadings in and out of visibility, insist. This is already for Beckett in his writings on painting, the crux of the gaze that painting obliges in its staging of the undecidable relation between image and medium:

Whence comes this impression of a thing in the void? Of artifice [*de la façon*]? It's as if one were to say that the impression of blue comes from the sky. [D, 125; *my translation*]

This perplexity as to the object of representation, in representation, and to its referents is bound up with the act of looking itself, in which the viewer's disequilibrium becomes a kind of self-referential slapstick. Beckett's 'amateurs' in the museum or gallery 'look first from far away, then close up, and ... in particularly thorny cases, assess with their thumbs the depth of the impasto.' [D, 120; *my translation*] Though this passage concerns painting in general and the Van Velde brothers in particular, perhaps no better or more succinct account of the process and difficulty of looking at a Yeats painting could be achieved.

But none of this resolves the question of the relation of the medium to the represented. Which is it that is recalcitrant, the figure that insists on its emergence or the medium into which again it dissolves before the oscillating gaze? For Beckett, this 'issueless predicament', the aporia into which so reflexive an artwork throws the viewer, is thoroughly melancholic. It is a condition that leads him to speak, writing still of the Van Veldes, Geer and Bram, of *le deuil de l'objet*, mourning for the object (or the mourning *of* the object — the ambiguity of the French genitive is carefully poised). This mourning is not one that can be alleviated, least of all by abandoning the attempt to represent:

> It seems absurd to speak, as Kandinsky did, of a painting liberated from the object. That from which painting is liberated is the illusion that there exists more than one object of representation, perhaps even of the illusion that this unique object would let itself be represented ... For what remains of representation if the essence of the object is to abscond from representation? [*D*, 136; *my translation*]

The persistence of an obligation to represent, because painting cannot be freed from the very object that eludes it, leads to a painting whose condition is a ceaseless unveiling that reveals only further veils, as if the medium cannot dispense with the medium that hinders its ends, any more than language, as the Unnamable will discover, can put an end to the obstruction of language: 'An endless unveiling, veil behind veil, plane on plane of imperfect transparencies, an unveiling towards the ununveilable, the nothing, the thing yet again.' [*D*, 137; *my translation*] This thing

that insists and is at once no-thing, this thing that eludes representation, remains the melancholic 'core of the eddy', encrypted beyond the reach of a subject that nonetheless cannot abandon the urge to capture it.[36] 'Siege laid again to the impregnable without,' as Beckett later writes of his friend Arikha. [*D*, 152] Though it may seem absurd to align Jack B. Yeats with the Van Veldes, whose work in quite different ways pushes the boundaries between figuration and abstraction to the very limit, yet it is the association that Beckett makes from the outset. All are painters whose work, like 'the best of modern painting', is a critique, a refusal 'of the old subject-object relation'. In each case, and not least in Yeats's, it is the dynamic oscillation between material and image that sets that critique in play.

The dynamic of Yeats's paintings, then, is the enactment of a failure of representation, a failure either to retrieve or to abandon the object. The formal means employed in this virtually obsessive work of representation are at once the analogue and the performance of that predicament. It is a predicament to which Beckett himself continually recurs in his writings and that links his own profoundly obsessive, or single-minded practice with Yeats's own. His critical works, from *Proust* (1931) to the *Three Dialogues with Georges Duthuit* (1949), repeatedly address it, and the early writings in English through *Watt* (1953), continually thematize it, but it is not until the trilogy (*Molloy*, *Malone Dies*, *The Unnamable*, 1951–53) that he will with assurance achieve the capacity to enact in writing the utter imbrication of medium and representation that Yeats's paintings assume in their own domain. It is well known that Yeats produced these paintings through acts of memory, the records of which are the voluminous sketchbooks that he mined for later treatment.[37] This is, of course, a remarkable transition for an artist whose

36 The phrase comes from Beckett's essay, 'Proust', in *Proust* and *Three Dialogues with Georges Duthuit* (London, 1976), 65–66.
37 Pyle, *Yeats*, 24, quotes a letter of Yeats to Joseph Hone: 'No one creates ... The artist assembles memories.' She also remarks on the collection of small notebooks in which he kept sketches from which later paintings could be 'assembled'; see *Yeats*, 26.

38 Pettit, *Republicanism*, 101

39 For an historical account of the emergence of this cultural and political formation, see Paul Thomas and David Lloyd, *Culture and the State* (London, 1997). For the Irish context, I have elaborated some of these terms in the introduction to *Nationalism and Minor Literature*.

early work was, often perforce, based on the rapid notation of daily events. Painting from memory, even without the intermediary of the retrieved sketch, is inevitably the representation of an object already internalized, the representation of a (mental) representation, rather than that of an object presented to view. It is painting as anamnesis rather than mimesis. Memory here is neither the retrieval of time past nor the repossession of a lost object, but the performance of that occultating light in which the figure merges and dissolves. Thus many of Yeats's later paintings foreground a figure watching, gazing, as if the painter's or the viewer's gaze passes perforce through another's. Beckett's term 'suspension' again seems utterly apt, rendering acutely not only the sense of the figure's apprehensive fixation before the scene, but also the suspension in turn of the viewer's gaze as the medium dissolves the specular image of the gazing figure, even as it emerges. In these paintings, memory is presented, not as the past regained, but as an enigma for the present. And that enigma is only reinforced by the teasing, highly literary titles affixed to the paintings, titles that seem to allude to an explanatory framework outside the canvases, to a tale in which they might become clear, but which yet eludes the viewer. They transform what might have been symbols into allegories, but into allegories that cannot be reduced to conceptual clarity, to interpretative mapping. This is a figuration without a possible turn to the literal.

We face, then, an *œuvre* that answers in advance to Beckett's desire for an art that abandons the 'possessional' drive that has continually renewed western representational art. [*D*, 135] The internal dynamics by which figure and ground, material and image, technique and content are held in suspended, oscillating equilibrium correlates to a refusal of domination that is the aesthetic counterpart

of a radical republicanism, a republicanism, that is, that remains profoundly at odds with the representational structures that undergird the cultural projects of nationalism and the modern state. I do not, evidently, mean to suggest that either Yeats or, least of all, Beckett, programmatically set out to subserve the political projects of Irish republicanism, though Yeats's commitment to depicting the marginal sectors of Irish social life, urban and rural, has often enough been understood in those terms. It is, rather, that the post-colonial disaffection of both artists from the nation-state that emerged stands not only as an acknowledgement of the failure of a certain political promise but also spells the disintegration of a coeval aesthetic project of representation. Pettit has suggested that the displacement of a long-standing tradition of republican thought by the emergence of political liberalism and representative forms of democracy in the early nineteenth century follows from the radicalization of republicanism in the late eighteenth century into a will to extend the principle of non-domination universally, rather than restricting it to white men of property.[38] This displacement in political thought coincides with the emergence, no less in reaction to radical republicanism, of an aesthetic and cultural philosophy that detours the antagonistic and potentially revolutionary claims of democratic social movements into and through representation. In this tradition, which runs most evidently from Kant and Schiller in Germany through Mill and Arnold in Britain, distinct domains of representation are conjoined and articulated together to produce a field of identities in which the disinterested ethical citizen willingly learns to be represented. Aesthetic representation prefigures political representation, regulating the identification of the subject with the common ground of the state.[39] One might say that the whole tendency of the aesthetic that is devoted to the moment of representation, in which the formal supervenes on the material, derives from and corresponds to the continuing anxiety provoked by the radical claims of a republicanism of differences. The need for an aesthetic education to produce in the spectator that disposition by which he (she) becomes representative of the species is no other than the moment in which Kant responds to the French Revolution by proclaiming a republic that would be restricted to the learned, to the philosophers. In each case, the subordination of the singular, potentially eruptive manifestation of difference to a narrative of representation establishes a trajectory whereby the spectre of intractable elements can be contained and assimilated to identity. Realism, in which the multiplicity of social forms is disciplined into narrative resolutions that integrate the individual into the 'second nature' of the social, and symbolism, in which the particular stands in, translucently, for the universal, are the twin stylistic modes of this trajectory.

Cultural nationalism by and large reproduces that model in forms complicated by the need that MacGreevy acknowledges to find in culture alternative institutions to those that the colonizer occupies politically. This at first insurgent cultural nationalism seeks to enter into representation a people that has never before been represented, and to regulate the forms of representation in such a way that the unity and identity of a heterogeneous population can be produced and affirmed. The failure of the national project thus throws into relief both the logical contradictions of the drive to representation, revealing the necessarily selective requirements of its inclusive claims, and the dominative ends that subtend it. The nationalism that proclaims the unity of the people in difference from the imperial state cannot accommodate the proliferation of difference that constitutes the inner space of the popular. And in so far as the

contradictions of nationalist culture repeat those of the metropolis, only in forms writ larger by the exacerbated conditions of the colony, the foundering of this model of representation in the periphery resonates at the centre also. It is no accident that the modernist critique of representation was so often generated from peripheral cultural locations, since it was at the margins and in sites of more or less violent struggle that the aesthetic politics of the nation-state began to unravel.

The critical aesthetic impulse that draws together Yeats the painter and Beckett the writer dwells, with a certain compulsion born of necessity, on the ruin of representation that follows in the wake of the national project. It is not that either artist promotes an immediately cognizable political aesthetic. On the contrary, it is rather the inevitable imbrication of the political with the aesthetic within nationalism that makes of their intense preoccupation with the conditions of representation a deeply implicit political affair. The disengagement of the aesthetic from apparent political ends serves in their case no longer as the means to furnish the separate space for aesthetic formation in a well-articulated state. We might view it rather, to borrow a term from Pettit, as the aesthetic correlative of a 'deontological republicanism', one that regards the foundations of 'freedom-as-non-domination' rather than the institutions that promote or safeguard its realization. In other words, where an aesthetic of representation that had become tied to a mode of political thinking becomes, along with the political state, a means to domination, only in the ruins of that aesthetic can an alternative be excavated. The excavation that follows is at once positive and negative: positive in its making space once more for the recalcitrant, for figures of those that had been denied representation: the tramps, rogues and derelicts that populate both artists' works;

negative, in the relentless interrogation of the means of representation that both engage formally and technically. However, it is precisely the tension between the act of figuration and its formal questioning that prevents the dimension of the political in either artist's work from ever congealing into a concrete utopian project. The space of their work is, rather, the place made over and again for the unfit in representation, for those that dwell only among the ruins. In the ruins of representation alone, where the nation meets its end, the anticipatory trace of a republic emerges as that thing that yet eludes representation. ■

This is a version of a paper given at the Notre Dame Irish Studies Summer Seminar in 2003.

1   Library of the National Gallery of Ireland, Jack B. Yeats Archive/Yeats Museum Y17-1: this four-page typescript, signed by Jack B. Yeats, is the text of a lecture given at the Celtic Race Congress, Paris, 1923; it was formerly in the papers of Robert Brennan, Irish ambassador to the US in World War II, whose granddaughter Yvonne Jerrold donated it to the library in 1993; transcribed by Heather Edwards.

APPENDIX

The Future of Painting in Ireland[1]

Jack B. Yeats

When a country lifts itself up under the sun, a country where the people live for Life in this world and beyond, where conventions for the sake of conventions are not appraised beyond their value, and where the old rules of the copyists and the new rules of the searchers for a *hokus pokus allacupain*, with which to open the treasure house door, are taken at the their face value only. In that country painting will rise also.

In the eastern loop of the Atlantic Ocean an island people are ready to rise up and take their own. This island and its people are better equipped to lead painting to the ground where it must stand if it is to be the mighty force it should be, for a mighty force it should and will be. Painting is the memory and communication of all which lives within the eyes' sweep. This nation, though some of its people are sometimes, for a little while, lead [*sic*] to accept what is forced upon them at the giver's valuation, always turns again with a bitter and assaying eye. In the end it looks every gift-horse in the mouth. And so this country has only staggered, not fallen, under the enervating waves of false ideas as to the meaning and end of painting.

Here is a curious little fact. The comic opera 'Patience' with its velvet-coated aesthetes has all over the world dealt a blow to the prestige of the painters from which they have not yet revovered [*sic*]. Before that they have been wild, impecunious, and tattered figures. But 'Patience' made them ridiculous. Now, that wave of ridicule did not reach Ireland with any force and the position of the painter in Ireland to-day is one of dignity.

For a time the Irish painters were anxious to do what was 'being done' in other countries, largely because most of the painters were of Dublin where the imitation mind of the children of the Pale still made the Pale pace. But though the said Irish painters of the past turned with humility to imitate the painters of other countries every now and then the native eye and the native memory would take charge. And every day there are more Irish artists painting their own country and their own people, with the greatest equipment of the artist — affection. That affection for their fellows and for every rock, every little flash of water, every handful of soil, and every living thing in Ireland. I believe this power of wide affection is racial with the Irish. All the finest Irish painters of the past — even when they painted other lands — had this affection.

The imitativeness of the artists of the Pale came partly from servile humility and partly from a feeling that it was more polite to have a something of the amateur about them than to be as the painter who painting from himself is ready to stand or fall by his work. Responsibility and irresponsibility meet in him. His eye sees and his spirit catches up the wonders which are about him. But he did not invent those wonders, how could he? He is himself a part of them. If he is a free man in a free country his eye is open and free. If he become a slave in a slave country he need never open a full eye. His masters will see all for him, and he becomes unable to express himself, except as the earth and stones express themselves. But if he has in him the spark of freedom he will lose nothing, but time, while silent in the soil. He will rise again strengthened and take up again the responsibility of the true painter, part of his own day and his own land, with whose flood he rises and with whose ebb he falls.

I read the other day in a review an extract from a book on the Evolution of Civilization:—

> Great Art — or periods of great Art — belong to the earlier phases of civilization. The possibility of them seems to grow fainter as the intellectual part of man grows stronger ... The Artistic future in general must consist of raising the sentiment for Art, the power of appreciating Art in the mass of the people. That would be an immeasurably greater service than a new galaxy of artistic Geniuses.

In fact UPLIFT, and I never fully realised before where the poison lay in Uplift. Under the Uplifter's banner mediocrity is to be encouraged and genius smothered, for the genius might take the bit in his teeth and clear for the mountain tops, beyond the reach of the Uplift instructor, and before his Department could get out a sedative pamphlet.

But the painters of Ireland will not be content to mildly and lazily browse in the valleys, occasionally enjoying a little feeling of superiority by drawing some dull one's attention to the distant and unattainable mountain top. We will not sit smirking over the old lovers' anthologies. We will make our own love-songs. But when this writer on Civilization wrote that Great Art belongs to the earlier phases of civilization I think, without knowing what his definition of civilization is, that perhaps he wrote the truth.

Now, Ireland's civilization as far as the pictorial arts are concerned is an arrested civilization. Before the Normans came an individual decorative Art had grown to power, but it sank away; and the native strength of the Irish painters has since lain under the weight of a super-imposed civilization. But the finest of the Irish painters had that selflessness which makes the painter look on himself not as the journey's end, but as the vehicle which conveys the wonders and the mysteries he meets upon his way. The danger lay where sometimes this very selflessness lead [sic] the painter to become the bravo of paint itself.

Literature is enfeebled. Words have been nearly squeezed dry in the linotype machines, and the hour has come for communication by the memory of the eye to take its rightful place. And painting is the poetry of the eye. It is not necessarily patriotism to paint your own country. It is but commonsense to paint the only country which you are part of. But it is patriotism to paint with all your power. True painting must be national and the true painter will be no compromiser. Now there is a something in the Irish nation which refuses to compromise, and its painters — springing from such a nation — will stand out boldly and paint what they see and what they feel. They will lead and not follow. They will cut out their own floatation [?]. ■

INJUSTICE TO IRELAND.

Is it there, yez are, ye two-faced Lyin' Blaguard wid yer mane Blarney
about the Sun; no Sun ivir riz anywhere, afore it did in Ould Ireland!
England afore Ireland! nivir!! Hurroo!!!

Fig. 1: 'Injustice to Ireland'. The politicization of time in Ireland is evident in this
comic postcard in which 'Pat' protests over the fact that under Greenwich Mean
Time, the sun rises in London before Dublin.

Spaces of time through times of space
Joyce, Ireland and Colonial Modernity
Luke Gibbons

'Joyce with his own material can do what no painter can within the limits of colour and flat surface. He can build up his picture of many superimposed planes of time'. — Frank Budgen[1]

1 Frank Budgen, *James Joyce and the Making of Ulysses* (New York, 1934), 42

2 Mahaffy's dismissal of Joyce has passed into literary folklore: 'James Joyce is a living argument in favour of my contention that it was a mistake to establish a separate university for the aborigines of this island — the corner boys who spit into the Liffey.' See Richard Ellmann, *James Joyce* (New York, 1965), 59.

3 Stephen J. Kern, *The Culture of Time and Space, 1880–1918* (Cambridge, Mass., 1983), especially 60–64

4 Michel Foucault, 'Of Other Spaces', *Diacritics*, 16 (1986), 22, cited in Edward Soja, *Postmodern Geographies: The Reassertion of Space in Contemporary Social Theory* (London, 1989), 10

5 Joseph Frank, 'Spatial Form in Modern Literature' [1945], in *The Idea of Spatial Form* (New Brunswick, NJ, 1991), 5–66

On one of his forays into the Irish countryside, J. P. Mahaffy, distinguished Provost of Trinity College, Dublin, and no friend of James Joyce, missed a train because the time on the clock outside the station differed from that on the clock inside. When he took one of the locals (or 'aborigines', as he might refer to them) to task for this affront to efficiency, he received the timely answer: 'If they told the same time, they'd be no need to have two clocks!'[2]

Even the clocks, as well as the trains, failed to run on time in this outpost of modernity. This resistance to synchronicity (if it can be so elevated) questions one of the key assumptions in theories of modernity, namely, that new technologies in transport and mass communications work their way inexorably through traditional communities, transforming their experience of time and space out of all recognition. According to the conventional understanding of modernity, the vagaries of local memory were abolished by the advent of railways, the postal system, the wireless telegraph, the telephone and, above all, by the greater accuracy and availability of clocks and watches. In his magisterial study of the culture of time and space at the beginning of the modern era, Stephen Kern argues that this realignment of sense of time affected all forms of public experience: what was left of diversity and contingency retreated into psychological space, exiled, as Hegel said of religion under modernity, to the private lair of the skull.[3] But what if it is not possible to make such a clear-cut division between inner and outer worlds in the first place? In Joyce's *Ulysses* there are indeed different senses of time, but it is not at all clear that they require, for the establishment of their difference, a separation of public and private experience. Instead, the difference occurs within these zones, as different temporalities and relationships to place cut across the routines of the everyday world of that day in Dublin, 16 June 1904.

In opening up the city to competing, unresolved temporalities, the experience of disjunctive or 'allochronic' time, *Ulysses* makes a significant departure from the new modalities of space and time that were coming to define modernity in the metropolitan centre. For the proponents of modernity, in Michel Foucault's account, the onset of the twentieth century saw the triumph of the 'determined inhabitants of space' over 'the pious descendants of time'.[4] Long before Foucault, Joseph Frank proposed his influential thesis on the 'spatialization' of form in the modern novel, according to which the unfolding of time through narrative is 'flattened out' by, and converted into, the co-ordinates of the spatial imagination.[5] The modern novel, on this reading, approximates to the flat two-dimensional plane of a modernist painting, or — more germane to *Ulysses* — to the layout and composition of the *newspaper*, in which events are related to each other, not through the linear progression of an overarching narrative, but solely on the grounds that they all took place on the same day.

The recourse to 'spatial form' in modern culture represents an attempt to register, in artistic terms, one of the most pervasive features of the machine age: the experience of *simultaneity*. The new transport and communications systems brought widely separated regions and different cultures into contact with a rapidity previously unimaginable. This process was greatly facilitated by the International Meridian Conference, convened in Washington in October 1884, which sought to universalize time by establishing Greenwich as the zero meridian in a longitudinal grid of twenty-four world-wide time zones. Through the narrative techniques of crosscutting and parallel action, transverse time was incorporated into the syntax of early cinema, providing the cue for the innumerable chases and last-minute rescues that enthralled popular audiences. According to Arnold Hauser, 'the new concept of time, whose basic element is simultaneity and whose nature consists in the spatialization of the temporal element, is expressed in no genre so impressively as in this youngest art'. Hauser goes on to argue that of the key modernist writers, none is more cinematic than Joyce:

> [Joyce] pushes the spatialization of time even further than Proust, and shows the inner happenings not only in longitudinal but also in cross-sections. The images, ideas, brainwaves and memories stand side by side with sudden and absolute abruptness; hardly any consideration is paid to their origins, all the emphasis is on their contiguity, their simultaneity. The spatialization of time goes so far in Joyce, that one can begin the reading of *Ulysses* where one likes, with only a rough knowledge of the context. ... The medium of the novel in which the reader find himself, is in fact wholly spatial, for the novel describes not only the picture of a great city, but also adopts its structure to some extent, the network of its streets and squares, in which people stroll about, walking in and out and stopping when and where they like.[6]

But a question arises here: is Dublin, or for that matter the Ireland out of which Joyce emerged as a writer, to be defined solely, or even primarily, in terms of space as conceived by high modernism? Certainly there have been enough studies of geographic and topographical relationships in Joyce, but for the most part they assume the sovereignty of space in Joyce's imagination, as if Dublin were simply another metropolis like Paris, Berlin or Boston. In *Ulysses*, Robert M. Adams writes, 'Joyce does not seem to have an antiquarian's eye for old Dublin', but is it indeed the case that Joyce's Dublin is confined to the extended present which modernists claimed to be the product of the spatializing drive of painting and of cinematic form?[7] Is the past simply erased and, thereby, are the disparities of time removed from the public sphere to the domain of what Edmund Husserl referred to as 'internal time-consciousness'?

The Past and Its Phantoms

> Francis was reminding Stephen of years before when they had been at school together in Conmee's time. He asked about Glaucon, Alcibiades, Pisistratus. Where were they now? Neither knew. You have spoken of the past and its phantoms, Stephen said. Why think of them? If I call them into life across the waters of Lethe will not the poor ghosts troop to my call?
> James Joyce, *Ulysses* (1922)[8]

6 Arnold Hauser, *The Social History of Art*, vol. 4 (London, 1972), 255. The comparison of the novel to a city that could be entered in any direction is derived from Edmund Wilson's pioneering discussion of Joyce's modernism in *Axel's Castle* (New York, 1950), 210.

7 Robert M. Adams, *Surface and Symbol: The Consistency of James Joyce's* Ulysses (New York, 1962), 199

8 James Joyce, *Ulysses*, ed. Hans Walter Gabler with Wolfhard Steppe and Claus Melchior (New York and London, 1984; London, 1986), 14.1110–14; hereafter cited in text.

9 Kern, *Culture of Time and Space*, 77

10 Stuart Gilbert, *James Joyce's* Ulysses (London, rev. edn. 1952), 200

11 Joyce's use of ellipsis and cinematic techniques to expose the gaps in both space and time in the 'Wandering Rocks' is signalled by Christopher Butler in 'Joyce, Modernism and Postmodernism', in Derek Attridge, ed., *The Cambridge Companion to James Joyce* (Cambridge, 1990), 270.

According to Kern, 'the highpoint of simultaneous literature' in the modern novel is *Ulysses*:

> In *Ulysses*, he [Joyce] improvised montage techniques to show the simultaneous activity of Dublin as a whole, not a history of the city but a slice of it out of time, spatially extended and embodying its entire past in an extended present.[9]

Echoing what is virtually a critical consensus, Kern points to the 'Wandering Rocks' episode as the most vivid example of 'spatial form'. Indeed, if we are to believe Stuart Gilbert, it is a microcosm of the novel as a whole.[10] In this episode, the action (such as it is) takes place in nineteen sections (or cross-sections), connecting by spatial contiguity and temporal coincidence a series of random and seemingly inconsequential activities happening all over Dublin. As Kern observes, several narrative devices are deployed to convey this effect: multiple accounts of an action in different sequences; recurrence of the same object in different places; cross-cutting and eventual convergence of movement to suggest the spatial interrelatedness of the city and to provide points of juncture for all that was happening.

In the light of these co-ordinates, the narrative shifts in the 'Wandering Rocks'

Fig. 2: Fr. John Conmee SJ, Rector of Clongowes College which Joyce attended as a young boy. Fr. Conmee later moved to Belvedere College and was instrumental in admitting Joyce to the school when the family had fallen on hard times.

episode may be examined, particularly as they affect that punctilious man of the clock, 'the very reverend John Conmee S. J.' (Fig. 2). The episode begins with Father Conmee resetting his 'smooth watch' (well-worn from regular use we conclude) as he leaves the presbytery near Belvedere College to walk to the orphanage at the O'Brien Institute in Artane, to secure admission for the late Paddy Dignam's son (motivated not just by compassion, we later learn, but also by a concern to prevent him falling into the hands of Protestant soupers). No sooner has he left the presbytery than he passes a one-legged sailor begging for alms, before crossing Mountjoy Square where he encounters the wife of a prominent Home Rule parliamentarian:

> He walked by the treeshade of sunnywinking leaves: and towards him came the wife of Mr David Sheehy M. P.
> — Very well, indeed, father. And you, father? [10.16–18]

This brief exchange introduces the kind of narrative ellipsis that acts as a stylistic marker of the chapter: the tendency for things to happen 'off the page', whether in the form of unspoken words, unseen presences, or actions which occur in 'off-screen' space.[11] As Conmee proceeds on his errand of mercy, he gives a letter to a young boy to post in the pillar-box at the corner of Fitzgibbon Street, an action followed by another that disrupts the apparently coherent visual field of the action:

> Master Brunny Lynam ran across the road and put Father Conmee's letter to father provincial into the mouth of the bright red letterbox. Father Conmee smiled and nodded and smiled and walked along Mountjoy square east. Mr Denis J. Maginni, professor of dancing, &c, in silk hat, slate frockcoat with silk facings, white kerchief tie, tight lavender trousers, canary gloves and pointed patent boots, walking with grave

deportment most respectfully took the curbstone as he passed lady Maxwell at the corner of Dignam's court.
Was that not Mrs M'Guinness?
Mrs M'Guinness, stately, silverhaired, bowed to Fr Conmee from the farther footpath along which she sailed. And Father Conmee smiled and saluted. How did she do? [10.52–65]

Everything in the episode up to this point has been within Father Conmee's field of vision, so we would expect the colourful Mr Maginni and lady Maxwell to be on his route alongside Mrs M'Guinness. In fact, the mention of Dignam's Court, close to O'Connell Street, indicates that they are a considerable distance away. The unity of space and time has already begun to disintegrate.[12]

Fr. Conmee's walk quickly takes him to North Strand Road, where he passes Corny Kelleher totting figures as he chews a blade of hay in O'Neill's funeral establishment, before making his way to Newcomen Bridge where he steps on board the Dollymount tram. The description of boarding the tram is repeated, as in a double-take, thus signalling another variant on spatial form identified by Kern, viewing the same scene from a different perspective:

> On Newcomen bridge the very reverend John Conmee, S.J. of saint Francis Xavier's church, upper Gardiner street, stepped on to an outwardbound tram.
> Off an inward bound tram stepped the reverend Nicholas Dudley C.C. of saint Agatha's church, north William street, on to Newcomen bridge.
> At Newcomen bridge Father Conmee stepped into an outward bound tram for he disliked to traverse on foot the dingy way past Mud Island. [10.107–14]

The boarding of the tram is replayed again in more abbreviated form in the next section of the chapter ('Father Conmee stepped into the Dollymount tram on Newcomen bridge' [10.213–14]), where it coincides with Corny Kelleher's relieving himself of the contents of his mouth, but also with another arc-like action:

> Corny Kelleher sped a silent jet of hayjuice arching from his mouth *while* a generous white arm from a window in Eccles Street flung forth a coin. [10.221–23; *my italics*]

This is the only explicit use of the preposition 'while' in a cross-cutting context, so central to the narrative techniques of early cinema ('Meanwhile, back at the ranch ...'), but its implicit presence underlies the unfolding of simultaneous action throughout the entire chapter. Apart from the visual resemblance, then, what has the gesture of throwing the coin to do with Corny Kelleher? We learn in the third section that a one-legged sailor has ambled up Eccles Street where a woman, whom we later take to be Molly Bloom, throws him a coin. Though we are not expressly told, we take it that the one-legged sailor who crops up in Eccles Street is, in fact, the same character Fr. Conmee has encountered a short while earlier. Other items that catch Conmee's attention, however, prove to be more enigmatic, and their interrelations take us far from the initially secure co-ordinates of his gentlemanly stroll through the northside of Dublin just before he steps on the tram:

> Moored under the trees of Charleville Mall Father Conmee saw a turfbarge, a towhorse with pendent head, a bargeman with a hat of dirty straw seated amidships, smoking and staring at a branch of poplar above him. It was idyllic: and Father Conmee reflected on the providence of the Creator who had made turf to be in bogs whence men might dig it out and bring it to town and hamlet to make fires in the houses of poor people. [10.101–06]

12 For a perceptive discussion of the incongruities of space in 'Wandering Rocks', see Ruth Frehner, 'Why a Thinsocked Clergyman Walks Through Other People's Kitchen: Simultaneity in "Wandering Rocks"', in Fritz Senn et al., eds., *James Joyce: 'Thought Through My Eyes'* (Basel, 2000), 176–89.

13 The leisurely pace of the *Bugabu* was the butt of the satirical ballad, 'On Board the *Bugaboo*', which imagines it as an ocean-going vessel, braving the high seas: 'We soon weigh'd anchor and set sail to plow the raging surf / We were bound for the Bog of Allen to get a full load of turf'; see Colm Ó Lochlainn, *More Irish Street Ballads* (Dublin, 1965), 225–26. In the *United Ireland* cartoon, it becomes a vehicle for the rudderless Home Rule party after the fall of Parnell, Mr. David Sheehy MP being one of those who defected to the anti-Parnellite side.

14 Shari Benstock and Bernard Benstock, *Who's He When He's at Home: A James Joyce Directory* (Urbana, 1980), 170

15 The 'brown straw hat' clearly echoes the 'hat of dirty straw' which Fr. Conmee sees, indicating they are one and the same turfbarge. This feature is taken from 'On Board the *Bugaboo*': 'The Skipper he wore a wide straw hat and a body coat of blue / He'd made a lovely figure head to adorn the *Bugaboo*'.

The language of Conmee's reflections is taken from his nostalgic pamphlet on his native county Westmeath, *Old Times in the Barony*, which he 'thought of' a little later. But what connects Westmeath with the turf barge? The cultural (and mental) geography of the episode becomes apparent if we revert to a moment earlier in the day, recounted in the 'Hades' chapter, in which Leopold Bloom sits in the hearse (supplied by O'Neill's funeral establishment, Corny Kelleher's workplace) as Paddy Dignam's funeral wends its way across the city to Glasnevin cemetery. Crossing the Royal Canal at Crossguns Bridge in Phibsborough, we get the following description:

> Water rushed roaring through the sluices. A man stood on his dropping barge, between clamps of turf. On the towpath by the lock a slacktethered horse. Aboard of the *Bugabu*. [6.439–41]

Is the legendary *Bugabu* (Fig. 3) recalled by Bloom the same barge perceived by Fr. Conmee later in the day?[13] Shari and Bernard Benstock think so, equating the two bargemen in their directory of Joyce characters, but while it is highly improbable that there were two one-legged sailors in the same vicinity that afternoon, it is very possible that there were two turfbarges on the Royal Canal.[14] There is no way of definitively settling whether the turfbarge(s) establish a *spatial* link between the two episodes, but as we shall see, they are linked through a *temporal* connection, albeit one that breaks up the intricate simultaneity of the action.

As the hearse passes the barge at Crossguns bridge, Bloom's thoughts turn to his fifteen-year-old daughter Milly, who has taken up a job as a photographer's assistant in Mullingar, county Westmeath:

> Their eyes watched him [the man on the barge]. On the slow weedy waterway he had floated on his raft coastward over

Ireland drawn by a haulage rope past beds of reeds, over slime, mudchoked bottles, carrion dogs. Athlone, Mullingar, Moyvalley, I could make a walking tour to see Milly by the canal. Or cycle down. Hire some old crock, safety. … Perhaps I will without writing. Come as a surprise, Leixlip, Clonsilla. Dropping down lock by lock to Dublin. With turf from the midland bogs. Salute. He lifted his brown straw hat, saluting Paddy Dignam.[15] [6.442–46; 449–52]

Bloom's desire to pay a surprise visit to his daughter Milly perhaps is motivated by his worries about her sexual precocity. These fears may not be entirely groundless, for we hear her suitor, Alec Bannon, boasting that he has procured what he euphemistically refers to as 'a cloak' to protect her from 'wetting' on their amorous trysts at Lough Owel, near Mullingar. [14.771–84] Bloom's anxieties about Milly are enmeshed with his deep distress over his wife's adultery with Blazes Boylan; Bannon, it transpires, also sings Boylan's risqué ditty about 'Those Lovely Seaside Girls', and when in 'Circe' Bloom is taunted about Molly's infidelity by Bello, the brothel owner, in the midst of the sexual delirium of the 'Nighttown' episode, he imagines he sees his wife on their first encounter years ago:

> I see her! It's she! The first night at Mat Dillon's! But that dress, the green! And her hair is dyed gold and he …
> BELLO
> *(Laughs mockingly)* That's your daughter, you owl, with a Mullingar student. [15.3162–66]

— 'owl', it would seem, being a particularly appropriate term of abuse, given the location (Lough Owel) of Bannon's seduction of Milly.

Can the barge linking these episodes, the *Bugabu*, heavily freighted with associations of an inner erotic economy, be the same as

that noticed by the highly un-erotic Conmee, with his sentimental thoughts of old times in the barony? Or, to revert to the original point, is the spatial logic of simultaneity sufficient to establish a link between them (Kern's 'multiple accounts of a character from different perspectives')?[16] As Fr. Conmee reads his breviary on the Malahide Road, he encounters a young man, later identified as Lynch, coming through a gap in a hedge with a young woman who 'with slow care detached from her light skirt a clinging twig'. ('Twig'?', we read later in 'Oxen of the Sun', 'Bold bad girl from the town of Mullingar. Tell her I was axing at her. Hauding Sara by the wame. On the road to Malahide ... '). [14.1493–96] Just before this incident, the priest's thoughts turn to the Malahide of long ago, and it is this which expressly calls to mind his pamphlet about life in the midlands. This is then followed by a strange, abrupt cut to a new paragraph rendered in the same tense as the 'objective' description of Conmee's perambulations:

Those were old worldish days,
loyal times in joyous townlands,
old times in the barony.
Father Conmee, walking, thought of his

little book *Old Times in the Barony* and of the book that might be written about jesuit houses and of Mary Rochfort, daughter of lord Molesworth, first countess of Belvedere.

A listless lady, no more young, walked alone the shore of lough Ennel, Mary, first countess of Belvedere, listlessly walking in the evening, not startled when an otter plunged. Who could know the truth? Not the jealous lord Belvedere and not her confessor if she had not committed adultery fully, *eiaculatio seminis inter vas naturale mulieris*, with her husband's brother?[17] [10.159–69]

The last paragraph appears to usher in a revenant from another time, the shadowy, tragic figure of the first countess of Belvedere, who underpins (or undermines) the narrative logic linking Belvedere College, Fr. Conmee, the turf barge, Bloom, Mullingar, Milly, Molly's adultery, and the 'nature lessons' of Lynch and the young woman on the road to Malahide.[18] In 1743, Mary Rochfort (Fig. 4) had been locked away by her husband, Lord Belvedere, on his estate near Lough Ennel at Mullingar, for an alleged adulterous liaison

16 Kern, *Culture of Time and Space*, 77

17 The Latin translates as 'ejaculation of semen within the natural female organ'.

18 Among the few studies to address Joyce's relation to the Irish midlands are Eoin O'Mahony, 'Father Conmee and his Associates', in John Ryan, ed., *A Bash in the Tunnel: James Joyce by the Irish* (Brighton, 1970), 147–55; Jane Ford, 'Why is Milly in Mullingar?', *James Joyce Quarterly*, 14, 4, (Summer 1977), 436–49; Tilly Eggers, 'Darling Milly Bloom', *James Joyce Quarterly*, 12, 4 (Summer 1975), 386–96; and Leo Daly's invaluable *James Joyce and The Mullingar Connection* (Dublin, 1975), a meticulous reading of Joyce through the lens of local history.

19 James Joyce to Stanislaus Joyce, 13 Nov. 1906, *Letters of James Joyce*, vol. 2, ed. Richard Ellmann (London, 1966), 193–94. John T. Gilbert's monumental *History of the City of Dublin*, 3 vols. (Dublin, 1854–59) was the bible of antiquarian lore about Dublin, and Joyce's interest in it is hardly consistent with Robert M. Adams's charge (note 7 above) that he lacked an antiquarian eye for old Dublin. William Dara owned a house near Belvedere College.

20 O'Mahony, 'Father Conmee and his Associates', 155

21 Benstock and Benstock, *Who's He When He's at Home?*, 182. Kathleen McCormick argues in favour of a 'similarity between the countess of Belvedere and the elderly female that goes beyond being involved in court cases ... three women become associated by the lines that are repeated about them and ... continue to act out the past events in the repetition and reenactment of phrases and stories as if they were present'. Kathleen McCormick, Ulysses, *Wandering Rocks and the Reader: Multiple Pleasures in Reading* (Lewiston, 1991), 120–21. McCormick's argument here draws on Leo Knuth, 'A Bathymetric Reading of Joyce's *Ulysses*, Chapter X', *James Joyce Quarterly*, 9, 4 (Summer 1972), 412.

with Arthur Rochfort, the lord's younger brother. Belvedere College, of which Fr. Conmee had once been rector, was built by the countess's son; it was said to be haunted by her. Joyce had attended Belvedere. This sad story of betrayal and revenge loomed large in his imagination, as is clear from as early as 1906 when he first conceived of writing a story about *Ulysses*. In a letter to Stanislaus, he states, 'I thought of beginning my story Ulysses, but have too many cares at present', and then he mentions another possible venture:

> You remember the book I spoke to you of one day in the Park into which I was going to put William Dara and Lady Belvedere? Even then I was on the track of writing a chapter of Irish history. I wish I had a map of Dublin and views and Gilbert's history.[19]

The story was of sufficient importance to the overall conception of *Ulysses* for Joyce to feel compelled, as late as 3 October 1921, when the novel was at the printers, to check again about its historical accuracy in a letter to Fr. Doyle, Conmee's successor as rector at the college. But as Eoin O'Mahony has pointed out, Doyle did not provide accurate information on the story. He confused Belvedere House on Lough Ennel with the family mansion at Gaulstown, miles away.[20]

Does the cutaway to Lady Rochfort's walking by Lough Ennel represent a sudden eerie intrusion of the historical past upon the present, thereby radically disturbing the simultaneity of events in the chapter — or can it be accounted for solely as a *memory* on Fr. Conmee's part, in keeping with Kern's demarcation between public and subjective time? Clearly it is precipitated by Fr. Conmee's meditations on history, but there are indications from subsequent apparitions (if such they are) in the chapter that Mary Rochfort's appearance may not be an entirely subjective phenomenon, and that

the reverberations of her transgression and punishment persist into the present. Just as there are two descriptions side-by-side of Fr. Conmee's boarding the tram at Newcomen Bridge, one objective, the other indicating his state of mind, so also there are *two* consecutive descriptions in one sentence of the countess walking by Lough Ennel — the first possibly objective, the second touching on her subjective responses to her environment:

> A listless lady, no more young, walked alone the shore of lough Ennel, Mary first countess of Belvedere, listlessly walking in the evening, not startled when an otter plunged. Who could know the truth? [10.164–66]

Moreover, this 'listless lady' is apparently linked to a mysterious woman who was involved in court proceedings in Dublin on 16 June 1904. Later in the episode, we read of a court case in Dublin on that day in which

> An elderly female, *no more young*, left the building of the courts of chancery, king's bench, exchequer, and common pleas ... [10.625–26; *my italics*]

In the Benstocks' directory, this woman is identified in turn with a woman in an earlier reference:[21]

> Lawyers of the past, haughty, pleading, beheld pass from the consolidated taxing office to Nisi Prius court ... and heard rustling from the admiralty division of king's bench to the court of appeal *an elderly female* with false teeth smiling incredulously and a black silk skirt of great amplitude.[22] [10.470–75; *my italics*]

These latter two women are considered identical, yet the 'semantic ghost' (to use Fritz Senn's insightful term) of the phrases 'no more young' and 'an elderly female'

Fig. 4: Mary Rochfort (1720–90), countess of Belvedere. Her portrait is painted in the style of Mary, Queen of Scots (mentioned earlier in the chapter [10.65]).

links them both to the anachronistic 'listless lady' at Lough Ennel — or at least establishes them as having as much in common as the two descriptions of Fr. Conmee boarding the tram, or his notice of the appearance of the *Bugabu* with the barge noticed by the priest.[23] The point is not that the truth can be finally ascertained but that, if we adhere to a register of simultaneity, it is essentially *undecidable*. Fr. Conmee, hitherto so sleekly chaste amid all the intimations of sexual misbehaviour and secrecy, is now shown to be a figure in whom the secret, internal world of the sexual can be locked up, via the confessional, and the outward show of respectability sustained. Even the act of reading his breviary, so outwardly respectable, connects him again to the nature of the inner world of sin and its relationship to holiness. Conmee is himself comically sexualized and transported back into 'old times' — 'Don Juan Conmee walked and moved in days of yore'. [10.173] Although a mock Don Juan figure, he is also seen as a confessor to the nobles, the priest who seals in public marriage the private sexual relationship, in a ceremony under a high ceiling in a splendid mansion. The inescapable references to the Rochfort story lead back, via sky and ground (inverted), to the Jesuit houses of Clongowes and Belvedere where Conmee had been rector. Even as he looks at the sky, and thinks of

22 The elderly female reappears at the end of the chapter in the crowd that watches the viceregal cavalcade. [10.625] My discussion of the enigma of the 'listless lady' is indebted to Jo-Anna Isaak, *The Ruin of Representation in Modernist Art and Texts* (Ann Arbor, 1986), 38–39 — a pioneering text which remains the best account of Joyce's highly distinctive modernist treatment of space and time.

23 Fritz Senn, 'Charting Elsewhereness: Erratic Interlocations', in Andrew Gibson and Steven Morrison, eds., *Joyce's 'Wandering Rocks'*, European Joyce Studies, 12 (Amsterdam, 2002), 176. As Senn points out, the 'lawyers of the past' passage was inserted in the margins of the early Rosenbach manuscript, and the 'elderly female, no more young' added in later revisions.

24 See Lady Maxwell's first appearance in this episode, cited above [10.56].

25 It may be that the dislocation is itself a brief interpolation, a cross-cut to the site of the Royal Canal that first introduced disturbances into the cross-cutting of the chapter. Fr. Conmee does indeed pass a poster of Eugene Stratton at Annesley Bridge [10.141], but this crosses the river Tolka, just above the Royal Canal.

26 Hugh Kenner, *Ulysses* (Baltimore, rev. edn. 1987), 73–75, 127, 151

the French verb 'Moutonner', 'to cover with white fleecy clouds', associates 'mouton' ('sheep') with 'sleep', as in 'counting sheep' and with 'covering' (secrecy), he associates sheep with grass (in French slang 'mouton' is also a 'grass', an informer) and the 'stubble' of the field, thereby coming back down to ground:

> Fr Conmee, reading his office, watched a flock of muttoning clouds over Rathcoffey. His thinsocked ankles were tickled by the stubble of Clongowes field. He walked there, reading in the evening, and heard the cries of boy's lines at their play, young cries in the quiet evening. He was their rector: his reign was mild. Fr Conmee drew off his gloves and took his rededged breviary out. An ivory bookmark told him the page. Nones. He should have read that before lunch. But lady Maxwell had come.24 [10.184–92]

At one moment Fr. Conmee is on the Malahide Road; the next moment he has travelled back in time to his period as rector at Clongowes: but whether the latter is a subjective memory on his part, or an objective flashback, remains unclear as intrusions from the past disrupt the apparently homogeneous spatial form of the present. That the logic of spatial form no longer applies amid the switching currents of time in the 'Wandering Rocks' episode is finally evident as the episode draws to a close with the slow procession of the viceregal cavalcade through the opposite side of Dublin. Mimicking Conmee's walk, the procession too crosses a canal, albeit under the gaze of the racialized face (white face, black mask) of the performer, Eugene Stratton, grinning from a poster:

> In Lower Mount street a pedestrian in a brown mackintosh, eating dry bread, passed swiftly and unscathed across the viceroy's path. At the Royal Canal bridge, from his hoarding, Mr. Eugene Stratton, his blub lips agrin, bade all comers

welcome to Pembroke township. [10.1271–74]

The difficulty here is that it is the *Grand* Canal Bridge that follows Lower Mount Street, not the *Royal* Canal. Just as everything is finally converging, as in a D. W. Griffith film, things fall apart. Both space and time are out of joint.25 Whatever the truth of the ghost in Belvedere College, Mary Rochfort herself haunts the pages of *Ulysses*, introducing tremors from the past into the apparently firm spatial logic of a city defined by the regulated circuits of the representatives of both Church and State.

The Parallax View

> Some differences of opinion exist as to whether the Free State is, indeed, free. There can hardly be freedom which ignores the laws of space and time and the profound implications of these, to which we have only recently awakened.
>
> J. F. Mac Cabe, 'Irish Time', *The Dublin Magazine* (1927)

The breakdown of simultaneity in Joyce's Dublin, the dislocation of synchronicity by aberrant senses of time, is nowhere more evident than in the phenomenon of *parallax*, which Hugh Kenner and others have rightly identified as one of the key organizing (or disorganizing) motifs in the novel.26 As Bloom approaches the Ballast Office (Fig. 5) from O'Connell Bridge in the early afternoon, he does his best to put the painful thought of Molly's impending rendezvous with Blazes Boylan out of his head:

> Mr Bloom moved forward, raising his troubled eyes. Think no more about that. After one. Timeball on the ballast office is down. Dunsink time. Fascinating little book that is of Sir Robert Ball's. Parallax. I never exactly understood, There's a priest. Could ask him. Par it's Greek: parallel, parallax ... [8.108-12]

A short time later, Bloom realizes he has made a mistake and that it is not in fact one o'clock:

> Now that I come to think of it that ball falls at Greenwich time. It's the clock is worked by an electric wire from Dunsink. Must go out there some first Saturday of the month. If I could get an introduction to professor Joly or learn up something about his family. That would do to: man always feel complimented. Flattery where least expected ... lay it on with a trowel. Cap in hand goes through the land. Not go in and blurt out what you know you're not to: what's parallax? Show this gentleman the door.
> [8.571–79]

As Bloom understands it, the timeball on top of the Ballast Office registered Greenwich Mean Time as an aid to shipping and for communications with England, but the clock on front of the building (Fig. 6) registered Irish (Dunsink) time, which was twenty-five minutes behind London, as established at the Washington Conference in 1884.[27] So while modernity sought to standardize time to facilitate synchronic timetabling at a global level, the imperial connection and the need to facilitate shipping from Britain imposed another time scale on Irish society, undermining that simultaneity. Perhaps this explained the double standards of the rural railway station where J. P. Mahaffy missed his train. Though Bloom's musings on parallax lead him into abstract speculations on astronomy (prompted by Sir Robert Ball's famous handbook on astronomy, *The Story of the Heavens* [1885], which he has on his shelf), discrepancies in time were in fact a bitterly contentious political issue in Ireland at the turn of the century, and particularly during the 1914–21 period that Joyce was writing *Ulysses*. In August 1916 — as if in retaliation for the Easter Rising four months before — the Time (Ireland) Act was passed by the British government, abolishing

Dublin (Dunsink) mean time, and replacing it by what Fr. R. S. Devane described as 'English or Greenwich Time'. 'So,' according to Devane, 'by a few lines of a British Act we lost our own Irish Time, conferred on us by an international congress, and, shall I say, an Irish sun was replaced by an English sun':

> It was not asked for by the Irish people, nor were they consulted as to whether they desired it or not. As a matter of fact the nation was too upset at that time to think of anything but arrests, raids, shootings and executions. This was the period immediately following the Rising of Easter Week, and fourteen of the leaders of the Rebellion had been executed the previous week. It is unnecessary to recall the mental state and strain of this country during these awful days to anyone who lived through. It was at this unforgettable time Daylight saving was imposed on Ireland.[28]

Nor was the alteration of Hibernian time restricted to twenty-five minutes. In 1907, following the innovation of Daylight Savings Time to facilitate early morning factory schedules in Britain, another hour was lopped off the Irish clock, thus leading to the incongruous situation in late 1916 where as many as four different time scales were operating in Ireland:

> Dunsink Time (11.35 am)
> Greenwich Mean Time (12.00 pm)
> Summer Time (Ireland) (12.35 pm)
> Summer Time (England) (1.00 pm)

This was one step too far for patriotic Irish sentiments and for those who sympathized with the plight of farmers of the Irish countryside who had to rise almost an hour and a half earlier to facilitate their British working-class counterparts. Stating that for rural dwellers, an early September morning was now little different than a cold

27 Deborah Warner, 'The Ballast Office Time Ball and the Subjectivity of Time and Space', *James Joyce Quarterly*, 35, 4 / 36, 1 (1998), 863 contends that there is no evidence for Bloom's and Hugh Kenner's (*Ulysses*, 74–75) assertion that 'the Ballast Office presents two different times simultaneously, "Greenwich Time" by the ball for mariners, "Dunsink Time" by the dial for pedestrians'. As we shall see below, the political issue was the perception that Irish national time was being subsumed into English imperial time.

28 Fr. R. S. Devane SJ, 'Summer Time: An Imposition and an Anomaly', *Irish Ecclesiastical Record*, 53 (Feb. 1939), 127–28

29 Rev. C. Mangan, 'Greenwich Time in Ireland', *The Catholic Bulletin*, 8 (Aug. 1918), 395

30 J. F. Mac Cabe, 'Irish Time', *Dublin Magazine*, 2, 1 (Jan.–Mar. 1927), 35

December one, another priest, the Rev. C. Mangan, remonstrated:

> Why should the body of the people be penalized by having to rise prematurely and to grope in the dark for a match which has a way of not being easily found on such occasions, and to face all the rawness of the elements on a winter's morning before the sun has come to shed his mellow influence on them, and to use artificial light for the preparation and taking of their morning meal to suit the fanciful convenience of a few ... The whole thing is utter retrogression ... it is due to no honest desire to benefit any Irish interest, but rather to the insufferable arrogance of the ruling caste in England and its complacent garrison in Ireland. There is a suspicion that it was motivated by a desire to check the national sentiment which the people might have in distinct Irish time.[29]

Ten years later the matter was still unresolved, provoking J. F. Mac Cabe in *The Dublin Magazine* to note that the conflict was indeed one of different tempos and rhythms in the life of the nation. His

comment raised wider questions about economic development and the insertion of Ireland into global capitalism. Drawing on the social distributivist critiques of industrial capitalism advanced by G. K. Chesterton and Hillaire Belloc, Mac Cabe pointed out that both agricultural labour and the Irish factory floor involved elements of craft and skill that did not answer to the automated routines of mass industrial production:

> Some differences of opinion exist as to whether the Free State is, indeed, free. There can hardly be freedom which ignores the laws of space and time and the profound implications of these, to which we have only recently awakened ... It cannot be disputed that the imposition of 'Summer Time' on Ireland was a definite invasion of our national habits of thought, work and outlook. It was, and is, the product of English town and industrial life.[30]

Ireland had broken free in name from British rule, yet not only Irish human beings but even Irish cattle were still held captive by the work disciplines of British industry:

Fig. 5: The Ballast Office and O'Connell Bridge. The timeball was positioned in the Ballast office so that ships at the Custom House Quay could see it — their view was blocked off by the building of the Loopline Railway Bridge in 1890.

The beginning of all these things is, necessarily, our own time standard. In itself it is an indication of our own separate, Irish entity ... It would also convenience our Irish cows and help our harvesters ... So let us blaspheme neither space nor times but combine them for Irish purposes.[31]

Notwithstanding the distributivist diction, Mac Cabe was drawing attention to a key issue relating to decolonization under capitalist modernity: whether the cultural logic of development in the West — in particular, the Protestant work ethic, time-discipline, Taylorism, and so forth — provides the only successful modes of entry into the modern world system. As Fredric Jameson argues, there is only one world system, and to that extent a 'singular modernity'; but Jameson himself is careful to point out that there are 'alternate historical paths' leading into, traversing, and indeed traducing, this global network of capital.[32] What may be anachronistic or dead weight in one society need not be so in another, and still less need it be a form of romantic regression. A famous advertisement by the Irish Development Authority (IDA), designed to attract the international investment that helped develop the Celtic Tiger economy, showed a sepia photograph of a grim, Victorian factory, with the caption: 'MISSING THE INDUSTRIAL REVOLUTION WAS THE BEST THING THAT EVER HAPPENED TO THE IRISH'.[33] Of course, Fordism, not to mention sweatshop labour, are still very much part of late capitalism, but it does not follow that this is due to the intrinsic laws of capital, rather than to the political/imperial aggrandizement policies of particular 'national capitals'.[34] As Dipesh Chakrabarty, in taking issue with E. P. Thompson's attribution of 'time-discipline' to the structural logic of market economies, argues:

> Even if ... a place like India suddenly and unexpectedly boasted human beings as averse to 'laziness' as the bearers of the Protestant ethic are supposed to be, we would still ... never know for sure whether this condition ... was a genuinely universal, functional characteristic of capital, or whether world capitalism represented a forced globalization of a particular fragment of European history in which the Protestant ethic became a value. A victory for the Protestant ethic, however, global, would surely not be a victory for any universal.[35]

31 Mac Cabe, 'Irish Time', 37. Mac Cabe goes on to stake a claim for an early Irish contribution to the theory of relativity, citing the Trinity College scientist G. F. Fitzgerald's discovery that 'a measuring scale in motion would be affected by its own motion' (38).

32 Fredric Jameson, *A Singular Modernity: Essays on the Ontology of the Present* (London, 2002), 218

33 I discuss this in greater detail in 'Coming out of Hibernation: The Myth of Modernity in Irish Culture', in *Transformations in Irish Culture* (Cork, 1996), 82–94.

34 For the argument that the post-September 11, and more generally post-Cold War, era has intensified new, nationally driven forms of globalization, dominated by American pursuit of global market hegemony, see Perry Anderson, 'Force and Consent', *New Left Review*, 17 (Sept.–Oct. 2002), 5–30.

35 Dipesh Chakrabarty, 'The Two Histories of Capital', in *Provincializing Europe: Postcolonial Thought and Historical Difference* (New Delhi, 2001), 69

Fig. 6: The Ballast Office, facing Westmoreland Street. The clock was only visible from the street, and is understood by Bloom as relaying Dunsink time, by contrast with the timeball above which followed Greenwich Mean Time. The clock in the present rebuilt office, however, faces the quays.

36 Pier Paolo Pasolini, 'Observations on the Long Take', *October*, 13 (1980), 5–6, cited in Mary Ann Doane, *The Emergence of Cinematic Time: Modernity, Contingency, The Archive* (Cambridge, Mass., 2002), 105

37 Max Horkheimer, *Critique of Instrumental Reason* (New York, 1994), 22, cited in Chakrabarty, 'The Two Histories of Capital', 66

38 Dipesh Chakrabarty, 'A Small History of Subaltern Studies', in *Habitations of Modernity: Essays in the Wake of Subaltern Studies* (Delhi, 2002), 12

39 See above, note 36.

40 Miriam Hansen, 'The Mass Production of the Senses: Classical Cinema as Vernacular Modernism', in Christine Gledhill and Linda Williams, eds., *Reinventing Film Studies* (Oxford, 2000); Mary Ann Doane, *The Emergence of Cinematic Time*, especially 103–07

41 Ruth Leys, *Trauma: A Genealogy* (Chicago, 2000), 241

Flashbacks and the Public Sphere

As soon as montage intervenes ...
the present becomes past: a past that,
for cinematographic and not aesthetic
reasons, is always in the present mode:
that is, it is a historic present.

Pier Paolo Pasolini[36]

At one point in his analysis of the psychic life of (western) capitalism, Chakrabarty has occasion to cite Max Horkheimer's famous dictum: 'Machinery requires the kind of mentality that concentrates on the present and can dispense with memory and the straying imagination.'[37] In the interests of calibration, uniformity and built-in obsolescence, part of this process was to remove the discontinuities and fragmentation of time under modernity from public space — political or economic — to an inner life, re-created in the image of the new culture industries. The paradox here, however, is that in the very sundering of the past from the present, new media technologies such as cinema also created — or articulated — ways of reliving memory with an unprecedented, almost visceral immediacy. The issue here is not one of residual traces of the past: remnants from other eras which have survived into the present, like the herding of those cattle through the streets of Dublin for the boat to Britain which the mourners at Paddy Dignam's funeral momentarily glimpse on their way to Glasnevin. [6.386–405] As Chakrabarty points out elsewhere, to speak of the 'survival' of such practices is not to challenge 'stagist' or stadial theories of progress, for it is clear that their days are numbered: they can 'be seen as leftovers from an earlier period, still active, no doubt, but under world-historical notice of extinction'.[38] By contrast, the instabilities of time that surface in Joyce's Dublin inhabit public space and co-exist with, or may even be actively produced by, the dislocations of colonial modernity. 'Time shocked

rebounds, shock by shock', according to Stephen, and it is this which recalls Pier Paolo Pasolini's argument that, with the introduction of cinematic montage, past and present are juxtaposed in hitherto unthinkable ways.[39] [2.316–17]

Moreover, it is not as if this is simply a cinematic or literary device, purely a new mode of *representation*, while 'life' carries on regardless, oblivious to such innovations in the art-world. As the recent work of film scholars such as Miriam Hansen and Mary Ann Doane suggests, one of the most radical changes brought about by new mass-media technologies of modernity is precisely the re-structuring of our senses, and our frames of knowledge.[40] The psychological diagnosis of trauma — or 'shell-shock', as it was initially called — in World War I, with its symptomatology of flashbacks, nightmares, broken narratives, and the like, coincides with the appearance of flashbacks and the aesthetics of shock in early cinema:

The term flashback implies the cinematic possibility of literally re-producing or cutting back to a scene from the past and hence expresses the idea that the trauma victim's experiences are exact 're-runs' or 'replays' of the traumatic incident.[41]

The reappearance of such shocking experiences are disturbing. They are like apparitions from another world. In the first Irish feature film, *The Lad from Old Ireland*, shot on location in Ireland for the American Kalem Company in 1910, the male hero, Terry (Sidney Olcott), emigrates to America to seek his fortune, and is shown on the deck of the ship overcome by nostalgia, pining for his sweetheart, Aileen (Gene Gauntier). She suddenly appears beside him, superimposed on the deck of the ship. Is this a flashback, an attempt to visualize his memory or inner life? Terry does not think so, for he reaches out to embrace her — at which point she vanishes

Ormond Quay, Dublin, 1904. Photograph: Clarke Collection 91, courtesy of the
National Library of Ireland

42 Maureen Turim, *Flashbacks in Film: Memory and History* (New York, 1989), 27

43 Turim points out that in Hugo Munsterberg's pioneering critical work, *The Psychology of the Photoplay* (1916), the use of dissolves or fades signals subjectively motivated flashbacks, as in memory: by contrast, 'flashbacks that are not subjective do not use dissolves or fades, but are simple cuts' (31) — which corresponds with Joyce's practice in 'The Wandering Rocks'.

44 Isaak, *Ruin of Representation*, 36

into thin air. As Maureen Turim argues of 'the early period of cinema, before 1910':

Flashbacks in this period are extremely difficult to distinguish from 'vision' scenes that are meant to be understood as imaginary, or actions that happen simultaneously, but are 'seen' by a character in no position to observe them ... A 1914 text called *Playwriting for the Cinema: Dealing with the Writing and Marketing of Scenarios*, gives us a section on 'visions' but none on flashbacks. It suggests abandoning the superimposition for the sequential presentation of dreams punctuated by fades-in and -out, a preference presented as more economical for producers.[42]

This latter 'scenario' corresponds to Joyce's interpolations of Mary Rochfort/lady Belvedere in the 'Wandering Rocks', except — crucially — there are no fades-in or -out to signal their imaginary status.[43] As Jo-Anna Isaak observes in her acute discussion of Joyce's dissident modernism, the various characters in *Ulysses* move around, not just in different spaces, but also through different time-frames or 'chronotopes' which overlap and interpenetrate each other: clock-time, psychological time, and the political time sedimented in the buildings and streetscapes encountered by the various characters:

Numerous planes of space and time have been superimposed. What distinguished this technique from the common novelistic technique of flashback is that Joyce, concerned with surface and texture, is not so much interested in entering the past as he is in having segments of the past (or the future) overlap upon the present.[44]

There is no regression in time here: but it is not abolished either. As Isaak notes, in the use of cinematic flashbacks there is a clear separation of *now* and *then*: what we find

in Joyce are *unannounced* flashbacks, or rather 'flash-cuts', in which the pressure of the past forces its way into the present. In the course of teaching his history lesson in 'Nestor', Stephen reflects that the past is over but it is not done with, and may contain narratives whose time has yet to come — 'Or was that only possible which came to pass?' [2.52] The realm of possibility is opened up rather than closed down by the contingency of fact, and draws on the unrealized past as much as the future. It is not that such possibilities only remain in 'thought' but that the boundaries between thought and reality, inside and outside, past and present, come apart in Joyce's Dublin. The alternative histories with which *Ulysses* abounds (many of which trace the genealogy of an independent Ireland) were still part of a contested *public* sphere in Ireland, and were not therefore in a position to accept their relegation by modernism to private, psychological space. Rejecting Kern's assertion of a clear boundary between inner and outer worlds, public and psychological space, the new mass media infiltrated not only the conscious but even the unconscious, leaving little space beyond the reach of art. It is not even a matter of finding in the public sphere the equivalent of trauma, or related notions of 'involuntary memory' that are normally allocated to personal experience; rather, the true measure of psychic dislocation under colonial modernity is that both public and private are permeable, and that the unrequited past comes across with the lived intensity of personal experience. Whatever about the ahistorical triumph of space over time in metropolitan modernism, in *Ulysses* space, both outer and inner, is historicized through and through. This is the true nightmare of history to which Stephen bears witness: 'Fabled by the daughters of memory. And yet it was in some way if not as memory fabled it ... I hear the ruin of all space, shattered glass and toppling masonry, and time one livid final flame. What's left us then?' [2.9–10] ∎

This is a version of a paper given at the Notre Dame Irish Studies Summer Seminar in 2004.

Chancery Lane, 1913. The street on which the Dublin Metropolitan Police found accommodation for Litvak immigrant Jacob Davis on his arrival in Dublin in the early 1870s. Courtesy of the Royal Society of Antiquaries of Ireland.

Settling In

Dublin's Jewish Immigrants of a Century Ago

Cormac Ó Gráda

At what period and by what devious ways the ... settlement came into being, it would be impossible to determine. — Hannah Berman, Litvak novelist[1]

1   Hannah Berman and Melisande Zlotover, *Zlotover Story* (Dublin, 1966), 25

2   Compare Simon Kuznets, 'Economic Structure and Life of the Jews', in *The Jews: Their History, Culture, and Religion* (Philadelphia, 1960); Maristella Botticini and Zvi Eckstein, 'From Farmers to Merchants: A Human Capital Interpretation of Jewish Economic History', Institut zur Zukunft der Arbeit (IZA): Discussion Paper No. 670, Dec. 2002.

3   For a brief but useful account of the Lurgan community, see Francis Xavier McCorry, *Lurgan: An Irish Provincial Town, 1610–1970* (Lurgan, 1993), 168. *Jewish Chronicle*, 18 Oct. 1895, reports services being held at Abbey Street Hall in Armagh, conducted by Bernard White, A. Glicksman, and S. J. Parkes, with the last-mentioned acting as president. For a popular account of the social life of Irish Jews, see Ray Rivlin, *Shalom Ireland: A Social History of the Jews in Modern Ireland* (Dublin, 2003).

For centuries, Jews have been more urbanized than any other ethnic or religious group. For observant Jews, living close together in clusters was a prerequisite for religious practice: the ten-man minimum needed for communal prayer (the *minyan*), the requirement that the faithful proceed to *shul* (synagogue) on foot, and the need to sustain even a part-time rabbi — who might also serve as butcher (*shochet*) and circumciser (*mohel*) — presupposed a community of ten or more households for viability. Their urbanization had religious origins, but it had socio-economic effects. The commercial world of the city created and demanded the specialized skills of traders and artisans. By the mid-nineteenth century the Jewish population of Eastern Europe was overwhelmingly *shtetl*-based, and most of those who emigrated west from the *shtetls* became town- or city-dwellers.[2]

Housing and Settlement

Virtually all of Ireland's post-1870 Jewish immigrants settled in urban areas. On the eve of World War I nearly nine in ten lived in the three main cities of Dublin, Belfast, or Cork. There were small settlements too in Limerick (119), Waterford (62), Derry (38), and — most surprisingly — in the Armagh linen town of Lurgan (about 75).[3] While Lurgan's Jewish presence lasted for several decades, neither Galway nor Kilkenny, both bigger towns, ever sustained

a viable community. Most of those who plied their trades outside these cities tended to return before sundown on Fridays for the Sabbath, or at least for the most important of the Jewish holy days.

The newcomers began arriving in the early 1870s. The big rise in the number of Russian-born residents in Ireland in the 1880s (from 198 in 1881 to 1,111 in 1891) was almost matched by the rise of 855 in the 1890s. Thereafter the Jewish population relied on natural increase rather than immigration for further growth, since the number of Russian-born was only marginally higher in 1911 than in 1901. Stricter controls on immigration into the United Kingdom in the 1900s, particularly in the wake of the United Kingdom's Aliens Act (1906), may be partly responsible for this. The arrival of the Litvaks increased the geographical dispersion of Irish Jewry for a time. Dublin's share of the all-Ireland total fell from 74.6 per cent in 1881 to 55.6 per cent in 1911, but has increased steadily since then. In 1926 it was 62.5 per cent, in 1936, 64.7 per cent.

The small pre-existing Jewish community did not make the newcomers welcome. The tension between 'English' and Litvak Jews, replicated wherever the Litvaks settled, was largely based on class. Ireland's small 'English' community was mainly middle class and English-speaking, its workplaces and residences well dispersed across the city. It was inconspicuous, and bent on integration. It regarded the Litvaks as rather ignorant and uncouth, and over-zealous in religious orthodoxy. According to novelist Hannah Berman, 'an old man in Dublin, Davis the glazier, often told father how, soon after he appeared in Dublin carrying his case of glass on his back, he was told by the self-appointed leaders of the community ... [that] he was a disgrace to Jewry, and they offered him the then colossal sum of £40 to betake himself elsewhere, America or wherever he liked, only to vanish from the Dublin horizon'.[4]

What would 'Davis the glazier' have looked like? Irish playwright Sean O'Casey (1880–1964) has left a pen-portrait of somebody like him, doing his rounds in Dublin in the late 1880s or early 1890s. His distinctive dress and lowly status would certainly have set him apart from his settled co-religionists:

The Jew was short and stocky; bushy-headed, and a tiny black beard, tinged with grey, blossomed meagrely on his chin. A pair of deep black eyes stared out of a white fat face. Long locks of jet-black hair straggled down his forehead. The trousers of a shabby black suit were well frayed at the bottoms; his boots were well worn down at the heels; his head was rasped with a high and hard and shining white collar, set off by a gallant red, green, and yellow patterned tie. The Jew's arms were held out in front of his body to strengthen the resistance to the heavy weight on his back. His body was so much bent that the back of his head was sunk into the back of his neck to enable him to look to his front and to see any possible need for his services. The sweat was trickling down his cheeks, and glistening patches showed where it had soaked through his clothes near his armpits and the inner parts of his thighs.[5]

The Dublin Metropolitan Police, it seems, found accommodation for some of the earliest arrivals next to the police station in Chancery Lane off Bride Street, about half way between Dublin Castle and St. Patrick's Cathedral. They lived 'in a little square wherein stood the police station, Chancery Lane, joining the other foreigners — Italian organ-grinders, bear-leaders, one-man-band operators, and makers of small, cheap plaster casts of the saints of the Catholic church'. Originally a small but elegant street of three- and four-storey buildings, by the 1870s Chancery Lane was in a state of dilapidation.[6] Two houses on the lane featured on a list of tenements condemned as unfit for human habitation, and therefore closed, between 1879 and 1882.[7]

Some of the first immigrants to arrive can be named. The register of births covering the pre-1880 period records children born to Jacob Davis of 28 Chancery Lane (29 September 1874), Marks Isaacs of 78 Bride Street (10 September 1875), and L. Rosenberg of Moore Street (18 November 1875). The last-mentioned is probably Levin Rosenberg from Tels, who arrived via Edinburgh in 1873.[8] Jacob Davis may well be the 'old man in Dublin, Davis the glazier' mentioned by Hannah Berman, or else the glazier's son. Jacob is listed as a painter in the marriage register of St. Mary's Abbey, where he married on 2 October 1873, and his father is listed as a glazier. Jacob's address then was given as 14 Chancery Lane. His next child was born while he was living at 12 Chancery Lane (26 August 1876), but by December 1878 he had moved to Peter Street, a few blocks away. These details corroborate Hannah Berman's remark that the pioneers moved first to 'streets and laneways not far from Jervis Street, Mercer Street, and Bride Street'. Molly Harmel Sayers, whose uncle would become for a time the richest man in the immigrant Jewish community, was born in a tenement house in Jervis Street; 'a delicate child, [she] survived only because of the tender care bestowed on her by a drunken applewoman'. She is presumably the Miriam Harmel recorded in the Jewish birth register

4 Hannah Berman, 'Berman Story' (unpublished typescript in the Jessie and Robert Bloom Collection, American Jewish Archives, Cincinnati), 8

5 Sean O'Casey, 'Vandering Vindy Vendhor', in *Autobiographies*, vol. 1 [1939] (London, 1981), 122–23. O'Casey's depiction bears comparison with William Bulfin's racist account in *Rambles in Eirinn* (Dublin, 1907), 307–09.

6 Berman, 'Berman Story', 8; Irish Folklore Commission/Urban Folklore Project, Ms. 0471. Even in mid-century the street consisted, apart from the police station at no. 31, entirely of either tenements or workshops; see Henry Shaw, *The Dublin Pictorial Guide and Directory* [1850] (Dublin, 1988). See too Peter Pearson, *In the Heart of the City* (Dublin, 2000), 135–37; Kevin C. Kearns, *Dublin Tenement Life: An Oral History* (Dublin, 1994), Plate 4.

7 Charles Cameron, *Report upon the State of Public Health and the Sanitary Work Performed in Dublin during the Year 1882* (Dublin, 1883); Jacinta Prunty, *Dublin Slums 1800–1925: A Study in Urban Geography* (Dublin, 1998), 136–37

8 Louis Hyman, *The Jews of Ireland* (Shannon, 1972), 146. Louis Wine, also from Lithuania, was another early arrival.

9   Berman, 'Berman Story',
     8; Berman and Zlotover,
     Zlotover Story, 25–26;
     Hyman, *Jews of Ireland*,
     136, 146, 155, 256–57

10   A Dublin Tourism
     plaque today marks the
     fictional birthplace of
     Leopold Bloom at 52
     Upper Clanbrassil
     Street.

11   Murray Fraser, *John
     Bull's Other Homes:
     State Housing and
     British Policy in Ireland,
     1883–1922* (Liverpool,
     1996), 72; F. H. A.
     Aalen, 'The Working-
     Class Housing
     Movement in Dublin
     1850–1920', in Michael
     Bannon, ed., *The
     Genesis of Irish Planning*
     (Dublin, 1985), 131–88

as having been born on 6 February 1878; if so, her family moved to 20 Upper Mercer Street around this time. Nos. 18 and 19 Upper Mercer Street were among the 'ruinous, deserted and uninhabitable' houses listed by the corporation in 1883. Jervis Street was not far from Moore Street where L. Rosenberg lived, or from St. Mary's Abbey where the city's only synagogue was located. Perhaps the presence, albeit temporary, of the Rosenbergs and Harmels in the Jervis Street area indicates the drawing power of a place of worship to these very observant Jews. The Church of Ireland national school on Bride Street, next to Chancery Lane, was the first to receive immigrant children. It is reckoned that the Lithuanian Jewish population numbered about twenty-five in the late 1870s.[9]

The newcomers did not remain long in the tenements. The earliest movers to the complex of small streets off Lower Clanbrassil Street and the South Circular Road on the southern edge of the city, where most of the community would soon settle, can be guessed at from *Thom's Directory*.[10] The 1881 *Directory*, referring to tenants resident in the city before the end of 1880, lists two Jewish householders living on Oakfield Place (the highly mobile Jacob Davis at no. 15 and Harris Lipman at no. 16), where there had been none in earlier directories. The 1884 *Directory* lists only two (at nos. 16 and 17), but there were four by 1886 and six by 1890. Nearby St. Kevin's Parade contained one Jewish householder (Meyer Schindler) by 1882, two by 1886, and four by 1890. These two streets would soon become heavily Jewish. Located in an area populated by semi-skilled and clerical workers, they were particularly favoured by recently arrived 'greeners', as newcomers were sometimes dubbed. The housing stock, mainly roadside one-storey terraced units, was new or almost new. Most units, however modest, contained outside flush toilets and running water. On streets off Lower Clanbrassil Street such as St. Kevin's Parade, Peyton's

Cottages, Arbutus Place, and Oakfield Place, dwellings containing three or four small rooms were typical. Lower Clanbrassil Street, which ran north–south, would become the heart of the community; the South Circular Road, which ran from east to west, crossed it at Leonard's Corner.

Much of the housing that would constitute Little Jerusalem was built in the 1870s and 1880s. In the late 1870s several small speculative builders were at work in the streets off Clanbrassil Street, building blocks of terraced houses, as few as two or three at a time. Their work is still evident in the streetscapes of St. Kevin's Parade, Oakfield Place, and Lombard Street West. The minor variations in house types along these streets, a by-product of their builders' lack of capital, are a pleasing architectural feature.

Just a few years later, the Dublin Artisans Dwelling Company embarked on a substantial building project on the other side of the South Circular Road, in Portobello. The DADC was run by a group of high-minded and energetic citizens interested in improving housing conditions in the city. They married profit and philanthropy, and the weekly cost of a DADC dwelling was high enough: 3s. 6d. to 5s. per week for a single-storey, and 6s. to 8s. for a two-storey unit. As its name implies, the DADC catered for 'respectable' households who could be relied upon to pay their rents regularly.[11] Their somewhat genteel reputation would quickly become part of their appeal. The brand-new houses in Portobello came on the market at exactly the right time for clusters of Jewish immigrants ready to pay the 6s. to 8s. weekly rent. Though more aesthetically monotonous than the housing on the other side of the South Circular Road, the DADC housing was of a very high standard. Just a few years later — in 1899–1901 — houses on Dufferin Avenue, north of the South Circular Road, came on the market. They would represent the upper end of the market as far as Little Jerusalem Litvaks were concerned.

The area that would soon come to be known as 'Little Jerusalem' included most of the streets between St. Kevin's Parade and the Grand Canal. At the turn of the century there were two small clusters with very heavy concentrations of Jews: one around St. Kevin's Parade/Oakfield Place/Lombard Street West, and the other across the South Circular Road, around Kingsland Parade/Walworth Road/Martin Street by the Grand Canal. In the following decade the concentration of Jewish families further west, between Raymond Street and Greenville Terrace, would become much denser. The spread of the community's small prayer houses or *hevroth* — Lombard Street West, Oakfield Place, Camden Street, Heytesbury Street, Camden Street, Walworth Road, St. Kevin's Parade, Greenville Hall on the South Circular Road — offers a good indication of its boundaries.[12] There was a hierarchy of streets within the ghetto: newcomers might opt for a street like Oakfield Place, while on Dufferin Avenue or Longwood Avenue 'the tone was one of middle-class assurance'. William (or Wolve) Nurock and his family thus started off in modest circumstances in Oakfield Place (1892–95), whence they moved to 8 Emorville Avenue (1895–1908), and then to the relative affluence of 79 South Circular Road. These houses were valued at £7 10s., £20, and £34, respectively. Nurock's different homes, within a short stroll of one another, all doubled up as moneylenders' premises.[13] Moneylender Oscar White moved from 1 Kingsland Parade (valuation £15) to 11a St. Kevin's Road in 1906 (£15), then to 17 Victoria Street (£24) in 1908, and finally across the canal to the upper-middle-class respectability of 57 Kenilworth Square (£46) in 1918.[14] Hyman Barron, who operated a thriving business on Camden Street selling house furnishings on credit, moved from a comfortable house at 7 Emorville Avenue to the more salubrious 38 South Circular Road in 1902–03. Jacob Davis whom we described earlier as starting off in Dublin as

an itinerant glazier/painter and living in a tenement house in Chancery Lane, is listed in the 1912 *Thom's Directory* as 'contractor, 8 Wynnefield Road, Rathmines' (valuation £30). Similarly, Nick Harris's parents moved from Greenville Terrace to Victoria Street in 1929, and Hannah Berman's household moved in rapid progression from sharing a small house with the Price family at the corner of Lombard Street West and Oakfield Place, to renting a room in one of the old houses on Upper Clanbrassil Street, to having houses to themselves, first at 25 Arnott Street and then, in 1894, at 37 Lombard Street West. Non-Jewish residents of Greenville Terrace got along well with their Jewish neighbours, but considered those living on nearby Dufferin Avenue 'a different breed' and 'arrogant' or 'higher up'.[15] The Jews sensed these class distinctions too. The 'rather snobbish Peisa Harmel, who was living in great style in Upper Clanbrassil Street', and who 'drove behind a prancing horse, a beautiful dapple-grey, in a grand car', 'had not much use for [his] naïve unkempt greenhorn of a brother-in-law'. Peisa and his family were 'snobbish, uppish, even towards their own relatives'. George Mitovsky refers to *The Eye-Opener*, 'as a scurrilous sheet in which the cream and leaders of the community — whom my mother always dismissed airily as "the rubbish" — were mentioned in blatantly libelous and deliciously scandalous terms'.[16]

The social gap between the 'old' and most of the 'new' Jews was also marked, although some of the more successful among the 'new' (such as the Wigoders and the Briscoes) were quick enough to bridge it. It is significant that when the Dublin Hebrew Congregation moved south of the Liffey in 1892, it located its new synagogue outside the Little Jerusalem area, almost a mile away from the poorer Litvaks of the Lower Clanbrassil Street area. Many of the latter continued to worship in their own small *hevroth* within Little Jerusalem. The

12 Excluding the small synagogue on Lower Ormond Quay, which was 'used mainly by people who had a business in the area'; see Nick Harris, *Dublin's Little Jerusalem* (Dublin, 2002), 119–20.

13 Mark J. Duffy, 'A Socio-Economic Analysis of Dublin's Jewish Community 1880–1911' (unpublished MA dissertation, National University of Ireland, 1985), 28, 32; Jessie Bloom, 'The Old Days in Dublin: Some Girlhood Recollections of the 1890s', *Commentary* (Jul. 1952), 21–32; Berman and Zlotover, *Zlotover Story*, 32, 39. Compare Laura Marks, *Model Mothers: Jewish Mothers and Maternity Provision in East London 1870–1939* (Oxford, 1994), 60–61, who suggests that Jewish households tended to be concentrated in the best streets in the East End of London.

14 One of the moneylenders in Joseph Edelstein's *The Moneylender* is Oscar Whitingstone: see Edelstein, *The Moneylender* (Dublin, 1908), 110.

15 Interview with Sheila and Carmel Cunningham, 21 Mar. 2003

16 Berman and Zlotover, *Zlotover Story*, 30; Berman, 'Berman Story', 8; Hannah Berman, 'Zlotover Story' (unpublished typescript in the Jessie and Robert Bloom Collection, American Jewish Archives, Cincinnati), 4–5; George Mitovsky, 'When Zionism was Slightly Traife', *Nachlath Dublin* (1959–60), 16–17

most upwardly mobile were more than willing to move out and switch to Adelaide Road, however.[17] Though the area north of the South Circular Road contained some middle-class streets, on the whole the Jews who lived there were less well off than those living south of the South Circular Road. Jewish-tenanted houses to the south were roomier, and more likely to contain a domestic servant. Jessie Bloom describes housing conditions in Dublin as follows:

> The … social strata of the children that played on the streets of Dublin might best be described by the type of home in which they lived. The children who lived in a house, and did not share that house with any other family, but had their own backyard and front garden, were on the highest level. Then there were those that lived in the 'shut-door' tenement, and the last were those that lived in tenements that always had the front door open.[18]

In *fin de siècle* Dublin it was unheard-of for a Jewish family to live in any kind of tenement accommodation, though the poorest lacked a back or front garden. It was also very unusual for a Jewish household to rent lodgings in a house owned by non-Jews. On the other hand, it was not uncommon for poorer Jewish households to keep a Jewish boarder, or for prosperous Jewish households to include a Catholic domestic servant.[19] Only four Jewish households (out of 329) in a database constructed as part of a larger study lived in one-room accommodation in 1911.[20] Three of these were elderly couples and the fourth a recently married brush-maker with one child.[21] The same database suggests that in 1911 Jewish households were

Chancery Lane, 1913.
Courtesy of the Royal Society
of Antiquaries of Ireland.

Dufferin Avenue. A prosperous middle-class street; the Mirrelsons lived at no. 25.

Greenville Terrace. Author Nick Harris grew up here in no. 14.

somewhat better-off than their non-Jewish neighbours, by two criteria. First, their houses were less congested; the number of occupants per room in Jewish households was 1.29, compared to 1.63 in Catholic households, and 1.16 in other non-Jewish households. Second, they were much more likely to contain a domestic servant (or a *shikse*, as she was often called in the Jewish community); the respective percentages were 27.7, 9.3, and 15.5.

An indicator of the material progress made by the immigrant community on the eve of World War I was its ability to collect, within a matter of months, over £2,000 in subscriptions towards the purchase of the site of the future Greenville Hall *shul* in 1913–14. Apart from £100 from Lord Rothschild and a few other much smaller foreign contributions, this sum was made up of the subscriptions of 264 members of the *hevroth* constituting the United Hebrew Congregation. Subscriptions ranged from a few shillings to three of £100 or over. The median contribution of five guineas, a sizeable sum at the time, is a measure of both the community's piety and its material progress.[22]

At the outset the Litvak community was too small to sustain a *kosher* butcher. For a time two Gentile butchers, Byrne's of Camden Street and McDonnell's of Wexford Street, paid *shochtim* 10s. to 12s. a week to slaughter livestock and poultry according to Jewish ritual. The *shochtim* were also supposed to attend while Jewish customers were being served. In 1895 the Jewish Meat and Provisions Company opened at 73 Lower Camden Street, but this attempt at founding a co-operative *kosher* butchery

failed.[23] Then one Naphthali Cristol opened a butcher-shop at 1 Walworth Road c.1900, and soon after Myer Rubinstein and L. Barron opened shops on Lower Clanbrassil Street. By that time Clanbrassil Street had already become Little Jerusalem's main shopping artery.[24]

The occupational and settlement profiles of Dublin's Jewish immigrants on the eve of World War I imply that they were in better circumstances than their co-religionists in London's East End. Many East Enders had also arrived penniless. Unlike their Dublin brethren, however, they had chosen one of the poorest parts of their adopted city to live in.[25] Their occupational profile was also different: many were employed as wage-workers in the sweated trades of tailoring and shoemaking. A factory inspector described conditions in the East End in 1903 thus:

> The alien is imprisoned day and night and kept in a semi-nude state for a semi-starvation allowance. Family and all sleep in the same room ... The effect of this is found in the anaemic and lifeless state of the workers.[26]

Though peddling remained an option, fewer than one in three of the immigrant labour force earned their living as small traders. There was also more social differentiation within East London Jewry than in Dublin's Little Jerusalem.[27] These factors may help explain why left-wing political activism was more characteristic of London's Jews.

Dublin's immigrants were also relatively well off when compared with the city's large underclass of casual unskilled labourers and

17 In Glasgow the tension between the 'old' community, focused on Garnethill *shul*, which was consecrated in 1879, and the 'new' based in the Gorbals, was analogous. There were no organized daily prayers at Garnethill, it being left up to groups who wanted to pray to provide their own *minyan*, whereas in the new *hevroth* daily services were standard. See Kenneth E. Collins, *Second City Jewry: The Jews of Glasgow in the Age of Expansion* (Glasgow, 1990), 48–56, 134.

18 Jessie Bloom, 'Dublin Notes', untitled typescript on childhood in Dublin, American Jewish Archives, Jacob Rader Marcus Center: Cincinnati (undated, but probably 1953–54)

19 Berman, 'Berman Story', 12–13; Bloom, 'Dublin Notes', 27; see too Duffy, 'A Socio-Economic Analysis of Dublin's Jewish Community', 47–48. Perhaps there was something cultural in this penchant for domestic servants: a local history of the US city of Wilmington, Delaware, describes most Russian Jewish households as having black maids: 'anyone could afford one — they only cost three or four dollars a week', and in a large sample of Jewish households constructed by the US Census Bureau in 1890 over three-fifths of

households had one or more servants. See David Goldberg, 'An Historical Community Study of Wilmington Jewry, 1738–1925' (in Lucy Davidowitz Papers, American Jewish Historical Society, Box 2/1); US Census Bulletin No. 19 (30 Dec. 1890), 'Vital statistics of the Jews in the US'.

20 Cormac Ó Gráda, *Jewish Ireland in the Age of Joyce: A Social Science History* (forthcoming). The database consists of households containing a married couple, and living on a street with a Jewish presence in the Clanbrassil Street–Portobello area in 1911.

21 The élite of the Jewish community lived south of the canal in Rathmines or Rathgar. In the 1900s few of the socially exclusive council of the Adelaide Road *shul* lived in Little Jerusalem proper.

22 Irish Jewish Museum, Minutes of the United Hebrew Congregation, 1914

23 *Jewish Chronicle*, 5 Apr. 1895

24 Bernard Shillman, 'The Dublin Board Shechita', *Jewish-Irish Yearbook* (1964–65)

25 Marks, *Model Mothers*, 16–18; D. Englander, 'Booth's Jews: The Presentation of Jews and Judaism in *Life and Labour of the People of London*', *Victorian Studies*, 32, 4 (1989), 551–73; William J. Fishman, *East End 1888: A Year in a London Borough among the Labouring Poor* (London, 1988)

26 Cited in Marks, *Model Mothers*, 22

their families. As Thomas Finlay SJ noted in 1893: 'nor are they given to the occupations of the "sweated" Jew of London. They are respectable in their way, well dressed and well fed, not at all likely to compete with our poor tradesmen for the "jobs" on which they depend for a livelihood'.[28] Even within Little Jerusalem, as we shall see, they had the edge economically on their Gentile neighbours. The same was true in Belfast and Cork.

Little Jerusalem was always a compact area. To the south it was bordered by the Grand Canal, which separated the city proper from the municipality of Rathmines and Rathgar. The rectangle defined by Camden Street to the east, Donore Avenue to the west, and Kevin Street to the north, contained virtually all the streets that were, to a greater or lesser extent, Jewish between the 1890s and 1930s. Most of the streets within this rectangle are included in our database. As noted earlier, some were almost completely Jewish at one point, while others never contained more than a minimal Jewish presence.

The immigrants' settlement patterns are of interest. Their determination to live close together is hardly surprising: ghettoes have always been a key feature of immigrant life. Though the long-run economic advantages of ethnic neighbourhoods or ghettoes are debatable, in the short run they confer several advantages on the recent immigrant. They reduce the costs of adjusting to life in a setting very different from home by providing less expensive lodging, friendship, and recreation. They offer better opportunities of finding work or starting a business quickly, and some security against prejudice and crime. In addition, living close to places of worship and scriptural learning would have weighed heavily with many in a very religious community like the Litvaks.[29] All these factors influenced the choices made by Dublin's Litvaks. Because the community was relatively small and lived in

an ethnically mixed neighbourhood, clustering did not retard host language acquisition.

Six Streets in Little Jerusalem

As noted earlier, the newcomers selected where to settle wisely. When they began to move into the little streets and lanes off the South Circular Road and Lower Clanbrassil Street in the early and mid-1880s, most of the housing stock in the area was newly or very recently built. Its quality was good; most units, however modest, had running water and an outside toilet. Moreover, the housing varied in size and cost, allowing the poor, the less poor, and the comfortably off to be part of the same community. Another crucial factor was the high turnover of tenancies in the early 1880s.

Here I focus first on the settlement of Jewish immigrants on six streets in the Little Jerusalem area: Oakfield Place, St. Kevin's Parade, Greenville Terrace, St. Kevin's Road, Longwood Avenue, and Dufferin Avenue. These streets housed a broad cross-section of the immigrants and their descendants. Four are located north of the South Circular Road, two to the south of it. All six streets still contained significant, if already declining, Jewish populations on the eve of World War II. To some extent our choice of streets was constrained by the information given in *Thom's Directory*: since *Thom's* usually did not report the names of individual householders on streets where the average house valuation was less than £7 or so, this ruled out heavily Jewish streets such as Peyton's Buildings and Arbutus Place.

[1] Oakfield Place. This compact cul-de-sac of twenty small single-storey units is where some of the earliest immigrants settled. Built in the mid-1870s, it was the most modest of the six streets selected. As far as can be ascertained, it was the first street in the

future Little Jerusalem to house immigrants. The first Litvaks, Jacob Davis and Harris Lipman, settled there in 1880, living next door to each other in nos. 15 and 16. Before long Oakfield Place would become one of the most Jewish streets in Dublin, favoured in particular by recent arrivals. The average valuation of houses — a useful guide to their relative size and comfort — was just over £9. Each unit, terraced and fronting on to the street, contained three or four rooms. In the early 1890s Wolve Nurock ran a moneylending business from no. 20; in the early 1900s 'Barron and Green' operated as *wholesaleniks* from no. 1A. In 1911 the Jewish male householders present on Oakfield Place included three tailors, a labourer, a cap presser, a traveller for a draper, a huxter, a dairyman, an illiterate antique dealer, two general dealers, a bootmaker, and a draper. In addition three husbands were away from home on census night, presumably 'travelling' either on their own account or for someone else. Several household heads would have been wage earners. Several households supplemented family income by taking in boarders. The Jewish presence on Oakfield Place remained considerable until the 1940s; today only one of its houses remains in Jewish hands. In mid-2004 the front window of no. 3, which had been occupied by Jews for nearly eight decades, contained a poster supporting a boycott on Israeli produce.

[2] *St. Kevin's Parade* is a labyrinth of twenty-five modest terraced houses, mostly single-storey, linking Lower Clanbrassil Street and Lombard Street West. A century ago all units on the parade were valued at between £13 and £15, except for nos. 10 and 11 (valued at £9 and £8, respectively) and no. 19 (£28). The typical house, again fronting on to the street, contained five rooms. The street's occupational profile in 1911 reflected its somewhat better housing relative to nearby Oakfield Place. On the eve of the Great War three-quarters of those living on the street were Jewish. Jewish male

household heads included two Hebrew teachers and a rabbi; two butchers; two retired peddlers; a 'general marine dealer'; a coal merchant; a bookseller; two tailors; and a traveller for a draper. The last three of these would have been wage earners. The street and several Jewish residents are mentioned in *Ulysses*. Moses Herzog, the one-eyed, bibulous peddler who features in the 'Cyclops' episode, lived at no. 13 between 1894 and 1906. In Episode 4 ('Calypso') Bloom muses about pleasant evenings in the company of 'poor Citron' in St. Kevin's Parade, with Molly Bloom seated in Citron's basket-chair. Louis Hyman identified 'Citron' as Israel Citron, a peddler who lived at no. 17 between 1904 and 1908. His next-door neighbour in no. 16 was Philip Masliansky, identified by Louis Hyman with 'Mastiansky [*sic*] with the old cither' in the same passage in 'Calypso'. 'Masliansky' was incorrectly rendered as 'Mastiansky' in *Thom's Directory*, and Joyce perpetuated the error.[30] The first southside *shul* was established there at no. 7 St. Kevin's Parade in 1883, at the instigation of Robert Bradlaw, Peisa Harmel, and some others. Harmel was its president 'for many years', and 'was presented with a silver snuffbox by the congregation when he was leaving for South Africa'.[31] This was where in 1890 some representatives of the long-established Mary's Abbey community 'found about two hundred persons assembled in a room in the upper part of a house, not more than 250 feet square, and of a height not exceeding eight or nine feet'.[32]

[3] *Longwood Avenue* is located south of the arterial South Circular Road. Its fifty houses, built between the late 1840s and the late 1850s, ranged in rateable value from £12 to £26, but most were valued at about £20. Longwood Avenue was a relatively affluent place. Its houses had gardens to the front and rear. More than half of its Jewish householders had domestic servants in 1911, whereas none on Oakfield Place had one. The first Jewish resident of Longwood

27 Todd M. Endelman, *The Jews of Britain, 1656 to 2000* (Berkeley, 2002), 130–32. The occupational profile of Dublin's Jews closely mirrored that of Liverpool. According to Bill Williams ('History of Liverpool's Jewish Community', (http://www.ljgs.org/Documents/Bill-Williams1.html:), downloaded 24 Jan. 2003, undated), 'A majority of [Liverpool's] newcomers took to some form of peddling, which underwent a marked revival in the city, to Scotch Drapery (that is, the sale of domestic textiles from house to house on a weekly-payment basis), or to itinerant glaziery, carrying panes of glass in frames strapped to their backs in search of broken windows.'

28 Cited in Dermot Keogh, *Jews in Twenthieth-Century Ireland: Refugees, Anti-Semitism and the Holocaust* (Cork,1998), 21; see too Kevin C. Kearns, *Dublin Voices: An Oral Folk History* (Dublin, 1998), 170.

29 David M. Cutler and Edward L. Glaeser, 'Are Ghettos Good or Bad?', *Quarterly Journal of Economics*, 112, 3 (1997), 827–72; David M. Cutler, Edward L. Glaeser, and Jacob L. Vigdor, 'The Rise and Decline of the American Ghetto', *Journal of Political Economy*, 107, 3 (1999), 455–506; Marianne Bertrand, Erzo F. P. Luttmer, and Sendhil Mullainathan, 'Network Effects and Welfare Cultures', *Quarterly Journal of Economics*, (2000), 1019–55; Barry Chiswick and Paul Miller, 'Do Enclaves Matter in Immigrant Adjustment?', mimeo, University of Illinois at Chicago, 2003

30 See Hyman, *Jews of Ireland*, 189, 329. For more on Joyce and Dublin Jewry, see Ó Gráda, 'Lost in Little Jerusalem: Leopold Bloom and Irish Jewry', *Journal of Modern Literature* (forthcoming).

31 Berman, 'Berman Story', 8

32 Cited in Bernard Shillman, *A Short History of the Jews of Ireland* (Dublin, 1945), 97

33 See Berman and Zlotover, *Zlotover Story*, *passim*.

34 Harris, *Dublin's Little Jerusalem*, 23

Avenue, Israel Leventon, was a representative of the 'old' community. Originally rabbi to the St. Mary's Abbey congregation, he moved south to minister to the newcomers, occupying no. 43 Longwood Avenue in 1889. The first Litvak tenant, Israel Ellis, settled on the street in 1895; he made his living as a draper. Louis Levitt followed in 1896, and Louis Mendelson, M. Copman, and T. Fridjohn in the following year. Joseph Zlotover, one of the leaders of the Litvak community, lived at no. 42.[33] By 1911 over one in four of Longwood Avenue's inhabitants was Jewish. The occupational profile of Longwood Avenue's Jews in 1911 reflected its better housing stock. They included five drapers and two travellers; a merchant, a financier (i.e. moneylender) (Michael Mofsovitz), and a furniture dealer, the rabbi in charge of Adelaide Road *shul* (Abraham Gudansky), a musician (Marks Rosenberg, one of several talented musical brothers), and a housepainter (37-year-old Isaac Rubin).

[4] *Greenville Terrace* is off the South Circular Road across from Portobello Barracks. It is another street of modest one-storey terraced houses, but with small railed-in front and more substantial rear gardens. It was built in the 1870s. This is where Nick Harris, author of *Dublin's Little Jerusalem*, grew up. The Solomons took over no. 14 from the Harrises in 1928. The Solomons were poor; neighbours remember representatives of the Jewish Board of Guardians (the Jewish 'Saint Vincent de Paul') calling to their house. Mrs. Solomons supplemented family income by putting cloth covering on buttons. Mr. and Mrs. Solomons later died tragically, from accidental gas poisoning.[34] Jewish occupants in Greenville Terrace in 1911 included a cabinetmaker, three tailors, two 'general dealers', four drapers, two commercial travellers, a painter, a Hebrew teacher, a dry cleaner, and a painter. They included Abraham Eppel, a draper, and Joseph Eppel, a 'general dealer'.

[5] *St. Kevin's Road* is located next to the Portobello complex of streets constructed by the DADC in the 1880s, close by the Grand Canal, and about half a mile from the original core settlement area around St. Kevin's Parade and Oakfield Terrace. The

Oakfield Place. Nos. 15 and 16, the first houses to be occupied by Litvaks.

housing on St. Kevin's Road consisted of thirty-five mostly identical on-street terraced two-storey units. Litvaks began settling on the road in the 1900s. Here too they were mainly self-employed in 1911: travelling salesmen (4), drapers (3), tailors (3), or dealers (4), but they also included another Hebrew teacher and a cap manufacturer. Henry Gilbert at no. 9 was listed as an auctioneer.

[6] *Dufferin Avenue*, at the western end of Little Jerusalem, was the most middle-class street north of the South Circular Road to be settled by Litvaks. The first Litvak family to settle there were the Weiners in 1901; Levi Berman followed in 1902. The street was almost brand-new then. The Jewish households living in its six-roomed homes on the night of the 1911 census were prospering: over half had a domestic servant (compared to two out of twenty-seven non-Jewish households). The seventeen Jewish male household heads included seven drapers, three general dealers, a master tailor, two tailors, a jeweller, a factory manager, a commercial traveller, and a capmaker. Talmudic scholar and able businessman Myer Joel Wigoder lived for a time at no. 53. The name 'Wigoder' would soon become synonymous in Dublin with wallpaper and interior decoration; in due course two other Jewish families also well known in the broader community — the Mirrelsons (at no. 25) for their cab service and gambling shops, the Mushatts (at no. 8) for their pharmaceutical remedies — settled in the avenue.

Within-Street Clustering

Only fleetingly, once or twice, did the Jewish community have a whole street to itself. What of within-street clustering? Here, using data taken from *Thom's Directory*, I describe settlement patterns on three streets in Little Jerusalem between the 1880s and the 1960s. These streets represent a socio-economic and geographic spread. On St. Kevin's Parade, among the first to house Litvaks, the housing stock was very modest. Longwood Avenue was affluent by comparison, while Lombard Street West occupied an intermediate position.

Panel I describes the density of Jewish settlement from the late nineteenth- to mid-twentieth century. The Jewish presence was strongest on St. Kevin's Parade, where it topped 80 per cent for a time. Panel II compares the actual proportions of Jewish households having a Jewish next-door neighbour in each year, with the expected proportions if Jewish households had been randomly distributed on the street. This is a crude measure: for example, comparing the actual and expected proportions living within two houses of another Jewish household would almost certainly accentuate the clustering. (There is also evidence of such clustering in Cork, at least in the early days. Half of the Jewish-occupied houses in Hibernian Buildings in 1893 were numbered between 79 and 93.[35] Jewish households also lived in nos. 30, 32, and 34.) For households used to living in an exclusively Jewish environment in the *shtetls*, this is only natural. But in assessing claims of mutual friendship and neighbourliness from both sides, this should be borne in mind.

Houses on these three streets changed tenants quite often, particularly in the early years. In the early 1880s, around the time when the first Jewish families moved in, about one house in four on St. Kevin's Parade changed tenants every year. Houses were rarely vacant for long. In this fluid market it was easy for the immigrants to make their mark in a relatively short time. Neither landlords nor existing tenants seem to have resisted the arrival of the Litvaks, and immigrant families already in residence kept an eye out for vacant properties on behalf of friends and relations.

35 Ó Gráda, 'Notes on the History of Cork Jewry', in Dermot Keogh, ed., *In Memoriam Gerald Goldberg* (forthcoming)
36 Harris, *Dublin's Little Jerusalem*, 23
37 Interview with Sheila and Carmel Cunningham, 21 Mar. 2003

Panel I Settlement Density

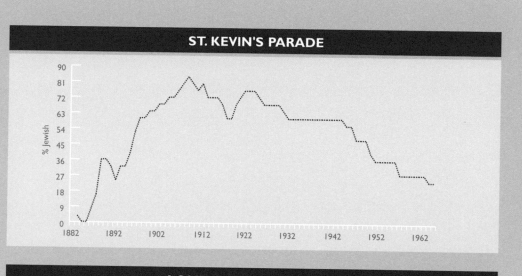

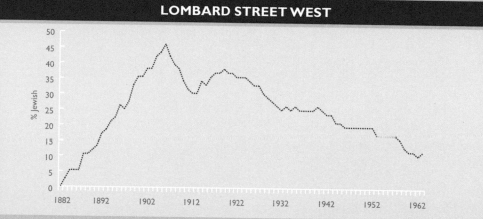

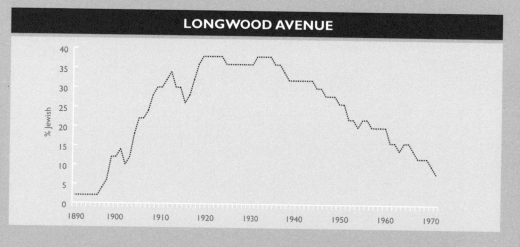

Panel II Expected and Actual Proportions with Jewish Next-Door Neighbours

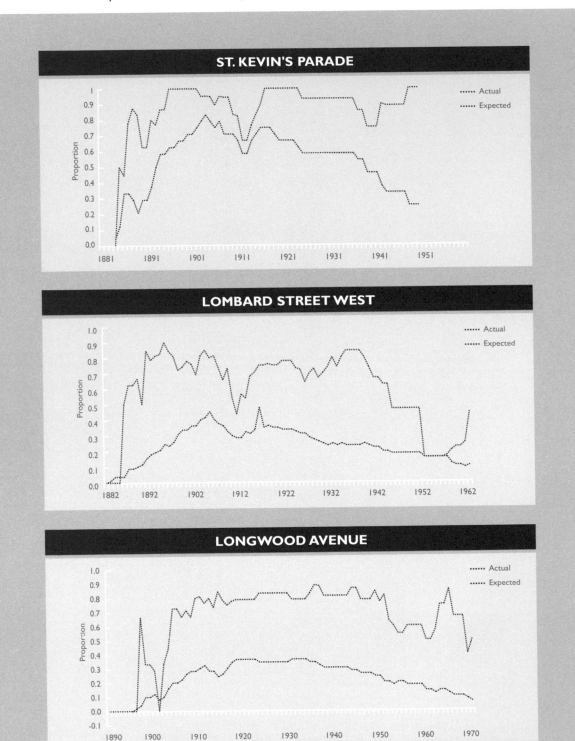

When a sitting tenant decided to move on, custom dictated that he had the right to select the incoming tenant.[36] This urban version of 'tenant right' inevitably led to offers and payments of key money. However, when Nick Harris's parents passed their house on Greenville Terrace to the Solomons, they took no key-money because the Solomons were poor. Shifts in tenancies in Little Jerusalem, as reflected in *Thom's Directory*, clearly indicate that Jewish tenants gave first call to co-religionists. When a Jewish-occupied house became vacant, the incoming tenant was very likely to be also Jewish. In many cases, the new arrivals were related to a family already on the street: for example, three of the Jewish families living in Greenville Terrace in the 1920s and 1930s (the Whites, the Orkins, and the Gudkins) were related by marriage, as were several of the families living on Martin Street.[37] The rapid turnover of tenancies on Oakfield Place and St. Kevin's Parade in the pre-1914 era is another indication of Jewish upward mobility. Over half of the Jewish households settling in either of these streets before 1914 stayed four years at most.

Little Jerusalem was in its heyday between the 1890s and the 1920s. By 1930 or so the upwardly mobile in the Jewish community were already moving south across the Grand Canal — 'across the bridge' — to Rathmines and Rathgar in numbers, leaving behind the elderly and the less well off. Both for their descendants and for most current residents of the old neighbourhood (now almost exclusively non-Jewish), the Litvak ethos of Little Jerusalem and the bustle of Lower Clanbrassil Street once the Sabbath was 'out' are but distant, mostly vicarious memories. ■

Longwood Avenue. Community leader Joseph Zlotover lived here at no. 42.

Form K.)

PARTICULARS relative to ~~Convict~~ *Thomas Barry* 25 & 33

Where Convicted,	County
At what Assizes or Sessions,	
Date of Conviction,	
Crime	
Sentence,	
Age on Conviction,	*20* years,
Read and Write,	*Read*
Religion,	*R C*
Married or Single,	*Single* Number of Children,
Trade or Calling,	*Cotton Spinner*
Prison Trade,	
Where Born,	*Liverpool*
Where Resident before ~~Conviction,~~	*About 5 weeks from England at Thomas Dublin*
Where his friends reside,	*Bolton England*

DESCRIPTION.

Hair,	*Brown*
Eyes,	*Brown*
Eyebrows,	*Brown*
Nose,	*Large*
Mouth,	*Regular*
Complexion,	*Sallow*

Fenians in the Frame

Photographing Irish Political Prisoners, 1865–68

Breandán Mac Suibhne and Amy Martin

The Dublin Metropolitan Police arrested Thomas Berry, a twenty-year-old cotton-spinner living on Thomas Street in the city's Liberties, on 17 February 1866.

1 On Berry, see National Archives of Ireland, Chief Secretary's Office Registered Papers 1866/16991; Fenian Photographs 16; Irish Crime Records 13. Although his surname appears as 'Barry' on the form opposite, most records give it as 'Berry'.

The arresting officers did not charge him with any offence; at most, they may have told him that they believed him to be a member of the Irish Republican Brotherhood or Fenians and that, under the terms of the *Habeas Corpus* Suspension (Ireland) Act (29 & 30 Vict., c. 119), he could be detained at the Lord Lieutenant's pleasure. Berry had probably never heard of the legislation; the bill that allowed his detention without charge had only been brought before parliament the previous evening, and it is possible that at the time of his arrest it had not yet received the royal assent, formally making it law. Initially confined in Mountjoy Jail in north inner-city Dublin, Berry was transferred four weeks later to Antrim County Jail on Belfast's Crumlin Road. Before his transfer, warders in Mountjoy recorded his basic biographical and descriptive information (Fig. 1). They asked him his age, occupation, residence, place of birth, religion and whether he could read and write; noted his facial features; measured his height and told him to strip for a physical examination. They also asked him to sit for a photograph. Berry answered the questions, allowed the examination and sat for his 'likeness.'

Berry's photograph is important. It may not have been the young cotton-spinner's first encounter with a camera; working-class men and women had increasing access to photography due to the proliferation of

cheap portrait studios in the late 1850s. But Berry's experience of being photographed as a *prisoner* was unusual. Prison authorities had been routinely photographing men and women entering convict prisons in Ireland since 1860, but photography would not become a routine part of the processing of convicts elsewhere in the United Kingdom until the 1870s. Moreover, Berry, unlike the prisoners photographed in Dublin over the previous six years, had not been convicted of any offence; he was an internee, a person arrested without charge and lodged in jail without the prospect of a trial on the basis of the authorities' suspicion about his political beliefs and activities. Berry was ultimately discharged from Crumlin Road after two hundred and six days in custody on condition that he leave for England and, it was understood, not return to Ireland. His photograph and descriptive details were retained, not only by the prison authorities but also by the Irish Constabulary, facilitating his identification and surveillance in the future.[1]

A few months before the Mountjoy authorities started to photograph internees (Fig. 2) like Berry, they had begun to photograph men on remand awaiting trial for Fenian-related activity; men sentenced to penal servitude for Fenian-related offences were already being photographed as convicted felons. Together, these 'Fenian Photographs' (internees, remand prisoners and convicts) form a remarkable archive of

Fig. 1: Detail of Form K and prison photograph filed for Thomas Berry, interned from February to September 1866. NAI, FP 16

images of mostly working-class men.2 Critically, they were not taken to satisfy a physiognomist's gaze, and hence they cannot be easily assimilated into histories of crime or photography in which criminal or racial anthropology provides the impetus for the photographing of prisoners. Rather, this systematic photographing of political prisoners was primarily for the purpose of intelligence, surveillance and the documentation of potential insurgents and, as such, it constituted a significant encroachment by the state on its subjects' rights and a radical shift in the use of photographic technology. Previously, photography had been associated with the staging of identity through portraiture and with the 'private' transactions of desire and affection that were signified by the exchange of such images. It now became another mode by which the state laid claim to the self and to the representation and disciplining of potentially unruly or 'terrorist' bodies.3 These photographs of Fenians, therefore, represent a critical moment in the history of photography and its deployment by the state. They also exist as an important genealogical fragment that illuminates the foundational connections between modern state-formation, anti-terrorism, the problem of rights, and the state's use of visual technology.

I

Photography was an invention of the late 1830s and early 1840s. By the mid-1840s, portrait studios were in operation in major cities across Europe and North America, and the exchange of 'photographic likenesses' was fast becoming a fashionable display of affection (Fig. 3).4 At the same time, practitioners of several branches of 'science' sought to codify various forms of deviance as they were written on the body, and photography became central to their efforts. Physiognomists, phrenologists, and racial anthropologists used the camera to document, classify and interpret the bodies,

particularly the faces, of subjects such as mental patients and indigents and to compare them to the bourgeois ideal of the 'average' or the 'normal'.5 In this context, police and prison officials were soon experimenting with the new technology and photographing people in their custody. The Brussels police took photographs of criminals in 1843–44; Mathew Brady photographed inmates of two New York prisons in 1846; and by the mid-1850s Louis Mathurin Moreau-Christophe, the inspector of prisons in Alsace, had proposed a *biométrophotographique* system for the documentation of convicts.

Such early efforts, however, were scattered and short-lived. Furthermore, they shared a physiognomic imperative, being largely concerned with the representation of a particular criminal *type* and with documenting the signs of criminality on the bodies of convicts. It was not until the 1870s that police and prison authorities began to institutionalize the use of photography for the purposes of identification, notably in France, England and New York City. The photographing of radical prisoners in France was a key event in this process. Communards in the prisons of Versailles were asked to sit for photographs after the suppression of the Paris Commune in 1871. These photographs generally showed the sitter from the waist up, as in a standard portrait, but they were intended for police files; portrait photography was being pressed into the service of intelligence. Although the Communards were initially allowed to buy their likenesses, the French Ministry of the Interior soon imposed restrictions on their sale; for photographs of prisoners to serve their new functions, their circulation as political portraits and as expressions of an insurgent ideology had to be controlled.6 Over the next decade, repressive agencies in several locations set increasingly rigid rules and guidelines for the photographing of prisoners. By the 1880s, the frontal-profile

2 There are photographs of republican prisoners in the 'Irish Crime Records' and 'Fenian Photographs' collections in the National Archives of Ireland. The latter collection contains 509 files but not all of them contain photographs and not all of the photographs are of Fenians; documents (many of them with photographs) concerning Fenians interned in 1866–68 account for 249 of the files; the remainder are mainly photographs of other Fenian prisoners (remands and convicts) in 1866–68; descriptions, rarely with photographs, of Fenians active in Britain in the late 1860s and early 1870s, and portraits of political figures in the 1880s. On the conservation of the collection, see Niamh McGuinne, 'The Fenian Photographs in the National Archives', *IPCRA Journal* (Spring 2004), 23–25. There are also photographs of republican suspects and prisoners among the papers of Dublin Castle officials and senior policemen: see National Library of Ireland, MS 5957 [Samuel Lee Anderson Album, 1865–71]; Larcom Papers MS 7698; Album no. 37.

3 John Tagg, *The Burden of Representation: Essays on Photography and History* (Amherst, 1988) documents this transition.

4 Jennifer Green-Lewis, *Framing the Victorians: Photography and the Culture of Realism* (Ithaca, 1996), 52–53; Audrey Linkman, *The Victorians: Photographic Portraits* (London, 1993), 30–31

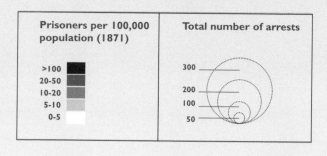

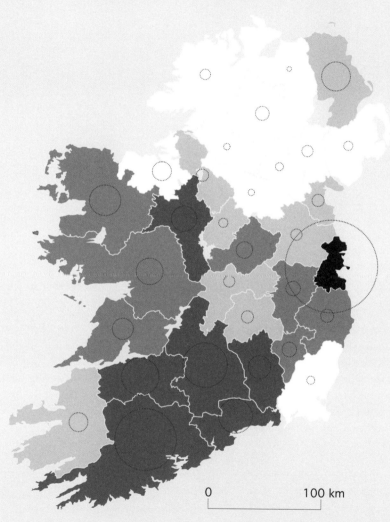

Prisoners per 100,000 population (1871)

>100
20-50
10-20
5-10
0-5

Total number of arrests

300
200
100
50

0   100 km

Fig. 2: HCSA Prisoners, 1866–68
Source: NAI, CSO ICR 13

The police made 1,153 arrests under the HCSA from February 1866 to mid-summer 1868; there were few internment orders from then until the restoration of *habeas corpus* in spring 1869. Over half of all arrests were made within a month of the enactment of the legislation; there were also large numbers of arrests in December 1866 (when the authorities believed a rising as imminent), in March 1867 (the aftermath of the Fenian Rising), and June 1867 (the aftermath of the *Erin's Hope* gun-running expedition). Men in their teens and twenties predominated among those interned but a surprising number of older men saw the inside of jails; the average age of internees was twenty-seven and 28 per cent of internees were over thirty. The youngest were two fifteen-year-olds and the eldest two seventy-year-olds. Periods of internment ranged from a few days to two years, the average internment lasting 157 days. Over half of the internees (607) were released on giving bail; 14 on condition that they 'leave Ireland' and a further 390 on agreeing to go to a named country, generally America (258), England (124), and Scotland (4). The most unusual destinations stipulated for released internees were Italy (Nicholas Walsh, a Dublin-based artist); Australia (Richard Rogers, a young Tipperary farmer); New Zealand (Darragh Daniel, a schoolmaster in Ballycastle, county Antrim); and Archangel, Russia (Thomas Whittle, a Waterford sailor). Four internees died in custody, three turned informer and one escaped. Revisionist historians have argued that internment 'wreaked havoc' on the IRB: see R. V. Comerford, *The Fenians in Context: Irish Politics and Society 1848–82* (Dublin, rev. edn. 1998), 133. Nevertheless, the detention of men without trial (and the death of men in custody) generated considerable public sympathy — 40,000 people attended the funeral of Belfast internee William Harbinson — and prison conditions became the subject of a public debate that energized the amnesty campaign of the late 1860s. Certainly, some Fenians saw advantages in the suspension of *habeas corpus*. Writing in summer 1867, 'A Looker-On' argued that it exposed the folly of constitutional activity: 'The suspension of *habeas corpus* act I regard with complaisance. It is an advantage to have unmasked a battery. The *habeas corpus* act can no longer be a trap; men know the worst, and stand prepared for it at all times. They know that personal freedom is not worth an hour's purchase in Ireland. In a word, they stand face to face with absolutism worse than Russian in Poland. Open and avowed speaking and agitation and so forth, thank heaven, is dead now; there is no real Irishman ignorant of what he owes to himself and to his country, or of the virtue of perseverance.' See *Irishman*, 10 Aug. 1867.

photograph of an individual against a blank background had been standardized, and all signs of any conflation of portraiture and prison photography had been purged. The state had developed the mugshot.[7]

The Irish experience is different, however. Britain's colonies often served as laboratories for new technologies of power before their deployment in the home-country and, much as colonial administrators in India pioneered finger-printing, those in Dublin Castle were precocious proponents of prison photography. With the Castle's support, the directors of the Irish convict prisons were experimenting with photography as early as 1857; from the end of 1860, all men and, apparently, all women condemned to penal servitude and processed through Mountjoy, the central convict depot, were required to sit for a photograph. Prison officials conceived these photographs as an 'appliance for the obstruction of crime'. By circulating prisoners' likenesses to the governors of county and borough jails, the Mountjoy authorities hoped to establish if they had any prior convictions; earlier misdemeanours would be added to their records, affecting both the conditions in which they were held and their hopes of early release. If a person were convicted a second time, the Mountjoy governor sent his photograph to the inspector general of the Irish Constabulary. By the mid-1860s, photographing was also part of the routine processing of convicts in many local prisons which held less serious offenders.[8]

Besides becoming part of the processing of *convicts* at a comparatively early date in Ireland, photography took a crucial turn when *untried prisoners* began to be photographed in Dublin jails in 1865–66. The photographing of Fenian remand prisoners from late 1865, and internees from the following spring, was part of a general tightening of prison security after the escape of James Stephens, head centre of

Fig. 3: An undated portrait (c. 1866) archived among the Fenian Photographs, presumably having been confiscated by the Irish Constabulary, inscribed 'Truly and fraternally yours Frank J. Brennan, 1st Lt. N.Y.V. Infantry' [New York Volunteer Infantry]. NAI, FP 29

the IRB, from Dublin's Richmond Jail in November 1865. But, more particularly, it was a product of the administration's need for enhanced surveillance to combat the unprecedented threat posed by the Fenians. The United Kingdom was now confronting an insurgent network that was organized internationally and intent on striking against the state's interests both within and beyond its borders. Moreover, the insurgents included citizens of a friendly state (mainly returned emigrants from the United States) whose lengthy detention without trial or severe punishment, including exile — particularly if not convicted of any offence — would be highly controversial (Fig. 4). Hence, the Castle approved new measures of intelligence and surveillance. Mountjoy warders received instructions to complete Form K — a form previously used to record biographical and descriptive details *after* a prisoner had been convicted — for 'untried prisoners' or more correctly for those untried prisoners suspected of involvement in the IRB;

5   For a discussion of early 'scientific' uses of photography, see Allen Sekula, 'The Body and the Archive', in Richard Bolton, ed., *The Contest of Meaning* (Cambridge, Mass., 1996), 342–89.

6   Donald E. English, *Political Uses of Photography in the Third French Republic, 1871– 1914* (Ann Arbor, 1984), 65

7   Here we draw on the discussion of the mugshot in Robert A. Sobieszek, *Ghost in the Shell: Photography and the Human Soul, 1850–2000: Essays on Camera Portraiture* (Cambridge, Mass., 1999), 113–19, and Michel Frizot, 'Body of Evidence: The Ethnography of Difference', in Frizot, ed., *The New History of Photography* (Köln, 1998), 259–71.

8   Our discussion here draws on Peadar Slattery, 'Uses of Photography in Ireland, 1839–1900', 3 vols. (unpublished PhD dissertation, Trinity College, Dublin, 1992).

9   For an overview, see Slattery, 'Uses of Photography in Ireland', vol. 1, 233–38. Slattery dates the photographing of internees to June 1866. However, prison photographs of internees released before that date survive; also Form Ks completed for some internees released before June note that they had refused to sit for a photograph. See for example, NAI, FP 347 (Michael McDooley, 15 Apr.); 122 (John O'Donoghue, 16 Apr.); 478 (John Sullivan, 16 Apr.); 257 (James Kinsella, 20 Apr.) and 322 (John Murtagh, 15 May); only Murtagh sat for a photograph. For the release dates, see NAI, ICR 13.

Fig. 4: Daniel J. Buckley, 23, single, jeweller and former Union soldier. American-born Buckley had sailed from New York on 13 April 1867 on the *Erin's Hope*, an 81ft brigantine carrying arms, ammunition and fifty American veterans. Weather had prevented the vessel from landing the weapons but many of the men on board came ashore, mainly at Helvic Head, county Waterford on 1 June 1867; most were soon picked up by the Constabulary and, despite being US citizens, detained under the HCSA. Buckley turned informer and acted as a crown witness in the trials of several participants in the expedition, including Augustine E. Costello (convicted of treason felony and sentenced to twelve years in 1867 but released in 1869 under a government amnesty) who later became the official historian of the New York police and fire departments. NAI, FP 37

Fig. 5: Joseph Byrne, 26, married with three children; brass-founder in Hibernian Gas Works, Great Brunswick Street, Dublin; resident at 2 Clarendon Street; arrested under HCSA on 19 December 1866 and released on bail on 4 February 1867; his Form K notes a 'mark or resemblance of a cut on top of forehead'. NAI, FP 47

10 Anon., *Things Not Generally Known Concerning England's Treatment of Political Prisoners* (Dublin, 2nd edn. 1869), 24; Seán McConville, *Irish Political Prisoners, 1848–1922* (London, 2002), 151n.46

11 NAI, FP 47 (Byrne)

the prison governor was to return a copy of the form to the inspector general of the Irish Constabulary with a photograph. For reasons that remain unclear, however, the administration initially balked at compelling the untried prisoners to sit for photographs like convicted men; warders could request but not require them to have their pictures taken.[9]

Completion of Form K — the written record of identity that accompanied most photographs — demanded the co-operation of the prisoner, who had to respond to a series of questions and then strip for an examination in which his physical features would be noted. There was occasional resistance to the questioning but nothing very serious. A number of prisoners, mainly Americans, persisted in the use of aliases even when the police and prison authorities were aware of their real names, while others refused to answer certain questions or gave false answers when asked for their address or the addresses of their friends. The question about religion — the only question about belief — caused particular friction. Remand prisoner John Murphy (an alias of the prominent Fenian John O'Leary), although not an atheist, refused to choose one of the designated religions (Church of Ireland, Presbyterian, or Roman Catholic) when being processed in Mountjoy; he was placed in a punishment cell on a bread and water diet.[10] Less defiantly, if more humorously, Joseph Byrne, a Dublin gas-worker and father of three children, interned in December 1867, responded 'Roman Catholic while in this place' when asked his religion in the same jail (Fig. 5).[11] Certainly, the issue animated discussion in the prisons. In autumn 1867, *The Irishman*,

a republican weekly, carried an account of life in Kilmainham by an internee who signed himself 'Mickey Halpin'; the author was most probably General William G. Halpin, an officer in the US army and one of the few internees convicted of any offence. Halpin singled out the question about religion as particularly vexatious:

> Strange enough, every newcomer has to register himself as professing some religion, and he is left the choice of embracing the established faith of England or Rome. Outside of these there seems to be no redemption; so we have to swallow either the Thirty-nine Articles and a she-Pope, or acknowledge the Babylonian lady as our guide.

Noting that many Fenian prisoners had little regard for chaplains, having encountered them in 'other branches of public service' (meaning the Union army), he gave the prison clergymen a back-handed compliment by saying that they were less than zealous in their efforts to flog their commodity (religion):

> One thing can be said in favour of the chaplains, that they do not persecute the prisoners with their orthodox teaching, seeming not to care too much whether the sheep of this fold stray to heaven by themselves, or take the broad road that is said to lead to the other place. With this tacit understanding, the prisoners are well-content, most of them having had ample experience of chaplains in other branches of public service, and believing that religion, like other marketable commodities, can be had at any time for its fair equivalent in hard cash.[12]

Fig. 6: John Cade, 22, single, bar boy and late of the US army. A native of Drogheda, county Louth, who had emigrated to New York, his Form K notes a gunshot wound on his left side. Cade had returned to Ireland on the *Erin's Hope* and was arrested on 5 June 1867 in Waterford; he was released on 3 March 1868 on condition that he would return to America. NAI, FP 51

Fig. 7: Anthony J. Gill, 22, single, grocer's assistant, formerly a sailor in the US navy. A native of Westport, county Mayo, Gill was arrested under the HCSA on 13 December 1866 and lodged in Castlebar Jail and later transferred to Mountjoy; he had a large hole in his right jaw and a heart, a cross and A. J. G. tattooed on his left arm. NAI, FP 185

Among the most obstructive prisoners were John Flood and John McCafferty, two American veterans centrally placed in the Fenian leadership, who were arrested under the HCSA in Dublin in February 1867. Flood, claiming his name was John Phillips, gave false answers to some of the questions on Form K. He said that he was a sailor, gave Dublin as his place of birth (but could not say what part of the city) and insisted that he was a resident of the Isle of Man and that his 'friends' all lived in Australia. McCafferty, processed after him, was even more uncooperative: he gave his name as William Jackson, answered the biographical questions — also claiming to be a seaman, 'lately travelling' — but refused to submit to the physical examination. After recording his hair colour and facial features (eyes, eyebrows, nose, mouth, complexion, visage) on a Form K, the turnkey noted that 'he now protests against his descriptions being taken' and left blank the spaces for his 'make' and height.[13]

Flood and McCafferty were exceptions; extant Form Ks indicate that most prisoners stripped for the physical examination. Concerned to identify individuals as unique, the turnkeys paid considerable attention to 'marks on the person', a category that included everything from pimples and dimples to blotches, scalds and scrofula marks, missing teeth, pierced ears, varicose veins and cupped breasts. For instance, the Form K completed for Patrick Andrews, an iron-founder's apprentice from Thomas Street, Dublin, records 'a small mole under left-ear on neck; teeth decayed in upper jaw in front of mouth; a small blue mark on left-hand; and small finger a little crooked'.

Likewise, the form filed on Thomas Barr of Killygordon, county Donegal, arrested in Dublin shortly after returning from America, notes a 'small mole over his right eyebrow' and a 'brown mole on the inside of right thigh'. Warders took great interest in wounds, common on the bodies of American veterans (Fig. 6). The warder who examined Michael McDooley, the son of a Waterford city shopkeeper and 'late of the American army', noticed a bayonet wound on his right jaw, a gunshot wound on his left shoulder and a fracture on the left side of his head; McDooley refused to sit for a photograph. Similarly, the warder who examined Anthony J. Gill, a native of Westport, county Mayo who had served in the American navy, observed a 'large hole' in his right jaw (Fig. 7). The turnkeys could be quite meticulous. It was a very alert warder, for instance, who noted a bullet wound on the left instep of John Dunne of Fethard, county Tipperary; Dunne had been a 1st Lieutenant in the 23rd Regiment, US Volunteers.[14]

Tattoos, considered by police and prison authorities to be among the most reliable distinguishing marks, also attracted the warders' attention (Fig. 8). The most common forms of bodily decoration were simple crosses, circles, stars and dots on the hands or arms and rings on the third or fourth finger of the left hand, a mark of attachment much like a wedding ring. A few men also had their initials tattooed on their arms. Gill, the man with the hole in his jaw, had the letters A. J. G. as well as a heart and a cross on his left arm. Seamen and men with associated occupations were the most heavily tattooed, anchors and ships

12 'A Voice from the Prison', a letter dated 1 Oct. 1867 in *Irishman*, 19 Oct. 1867. For another account of conditions in Kilmainham, see *Irishman*, 20 Jul. 1867. For an extended account of conditions in Mountjoy, see 'Mountjoy Prison Life', in *Irishman*, 11 Jan.; 18 Jan.; 25 Jan.; 1 Feb.; 8 Feb.; 15 Feb. 1868; the author had been arrested under the HCSA in Roscommon. Conditions were worse in prisons outside Dublin; on Ennis and Galway jails, see a letter from Corrofin in *Irishman*, 15 Feb. 1868.

13 NAI, FP 230 (McCafferty), 427 (Flood)

14 NAI, FP 7 (Andrews), 11 (Barr), 141 (Dunne), 185 (Gill), 347 (McDooley)

Fig. 8: Patrick Fitzsimons, 22, single, national schoolteacher, Dollymount, county Dublin; arrested under the HCSA on 22 December 1866, he was released on bail on 23 November 1867; he had a cross tattooed on the back of his left hand and a ring on the third finger of his left hand. NAI, FP 163

Fig. 9: William Grace, 25, single, labourer, remand prisoner in 1866. A native of Carlow, Grace was resident at 9 Upper Kevin Street, Dublin; he had an anchor tattooed on his left arm and a ring on his middle finger. NAI, FP 193

being common (Fig. 9); for example, Francis McClelland, a Belfast shipwright, had anchors on both hands, a ring on one of the fingers of his left hand and tattoos all over his arms. There were some quite elaborate designs, again mainly on seamen. James Lawless, a Dublin-born cooper, arrested near Dungarvan, county Waterford, had a woman, a bird and a ship on his right-arm while the tattoos on Edward Toomey, a native of Callan, county Kilkenny who had served as a storekeeper in the US Navy, hinted at political commitment: he had a woman, a harp and shamrock on his right arm (Fig. 10).[15]

Although the physical examination of prisoners was largely incident-free — perhaps as it had connotations of a medical examination — photographing proved controversial. From the outset, prisoners occasionally 'refused to sit' for their photograph when they were being processed in Mountjoy or Kilmainham. However, the authorities made it compulsory in summer 1867 when, in the aftermath of the Fenian Rising, numbers of untried prisoners objected to having their picture taken. The exact number who refused to sit is unknown: some men refused and then relented prior to their release; the files on many men do not survive. However, 13 of some 249 internees whose Form Ks are in the 'Fenian Photographs' collection in the National Archives of Ireland — just over 5 per cent of all such forms in the collection — are known to have refused to be photographed. Significantly, almost half of these men had served in either the Union or Confederate armies in the Civil War and, as such, may have had a more developed sense

than civilian prisoners of the rights of individuals in relation to the state-apparatus.[16] Moreover, several of them (like McCafferty and Flood) were processed through Mountjoy together, as indicated by their prison numbers, thus revealing their refusal to have been an organized action. In general, however, prisoners complied with the request (later the requirement) to sit for a photograph. Although some suspects glare at the camera, others seem to have enjoyed the experience. Morgan Burke, a butcher arrested under the HCSA in January 1867, laughed at the camera (Fig. 11); a native of Dunmanway, county Cork, Burke had recently returned from America. Patrick Waters, a poulterer from Great Britain Street, Dublin, also laughed (Fig. 12), while Patrick J. Haybyrne, a hairdresser on Dublin's Thomas Street, and Thomas Gallagher, a Roscommon student, struck fetching poses (Fig. 13).[17]

Notwithstanding their early adoption of the new technology, prison authorities (and the police authorities with whom they shared the images) were conscious that the camera did not always produce a perfect likeness. In other words, they understood that photographs, which seemed to have a strong claim to realism and empirical documentation, were just another, sometimes unreliable, form of representation. In March 1867, Patrick J. Murray, one of the directors of the Irish convict prisons, asked the Mountjoy authorities to supply him with a photograph of a prisoner who had been discharged the previous spring on condition that he return to America. The prison official who dealt with the request observed, 'the photograph

15 NAI, FP 185 (Gill), 264 (Lawless), 337 (McClelland), 487 (Toomey)

16 Here we are referring to Forms K in the 'Fenian Photographs' collection in the National Archives of Ireland.

17 NAI, FP 41 (Burke), 179 (Gallagher), 206 (Haybyrne), 504 (Waters)

is not a striking one; it is rather full in the face'. Similarly, an official noted on the file of William Hogan, an agent for St. Patrick's Sick Burial and Assurance Society, arrested in the late 1860s, that his voice was 'strong and coarse' and that he was 'not so gentlemanly looking as in photo'.[18] In the short term, however, the photographs improved prison authorities' capacity to do background checks on men in their custody. Photographs of sentenced Fenians, like those of other convicted men, were routinely circulated to jails near their former residences to establish whether they had any previous convictions. Likewise, photographs enhanced the surveillance of discharged internees, making it easier for the authorities to confirm that they were complying with the terms of their release. James Redmond, a ship's porter resident at 9 Bride Street, Dublin, was arrested on 20 February 1866 and photographed in Mountjoy before being transferred to Antrim County Jail. When he was released on 5 July 1866 on condition that he went to England, the governor forwarded his photograph and description to the Liverpool Constabulary which had been asked by the Home Office to visit 12 Dickinson Street, the address at which Redmond had claimed he would be living. Divisional Superintendent Benjamin Ride reported back that constables had visited that address and that Redmond was not known by the occupants, a family named McManus, who had been there for the past eighteen years.[19]

At the same time as warders in Mountjoy started to photograph internees in spring 1866, their Kilmainham counterparts began photographing Fenians in their custody. As well as requiring convicted men to sit for photographs on arrival in the jail — it remained optional for remands and internees — the Kilmainham warders appear to have initiated the practice of photographing prisoners immediately prior

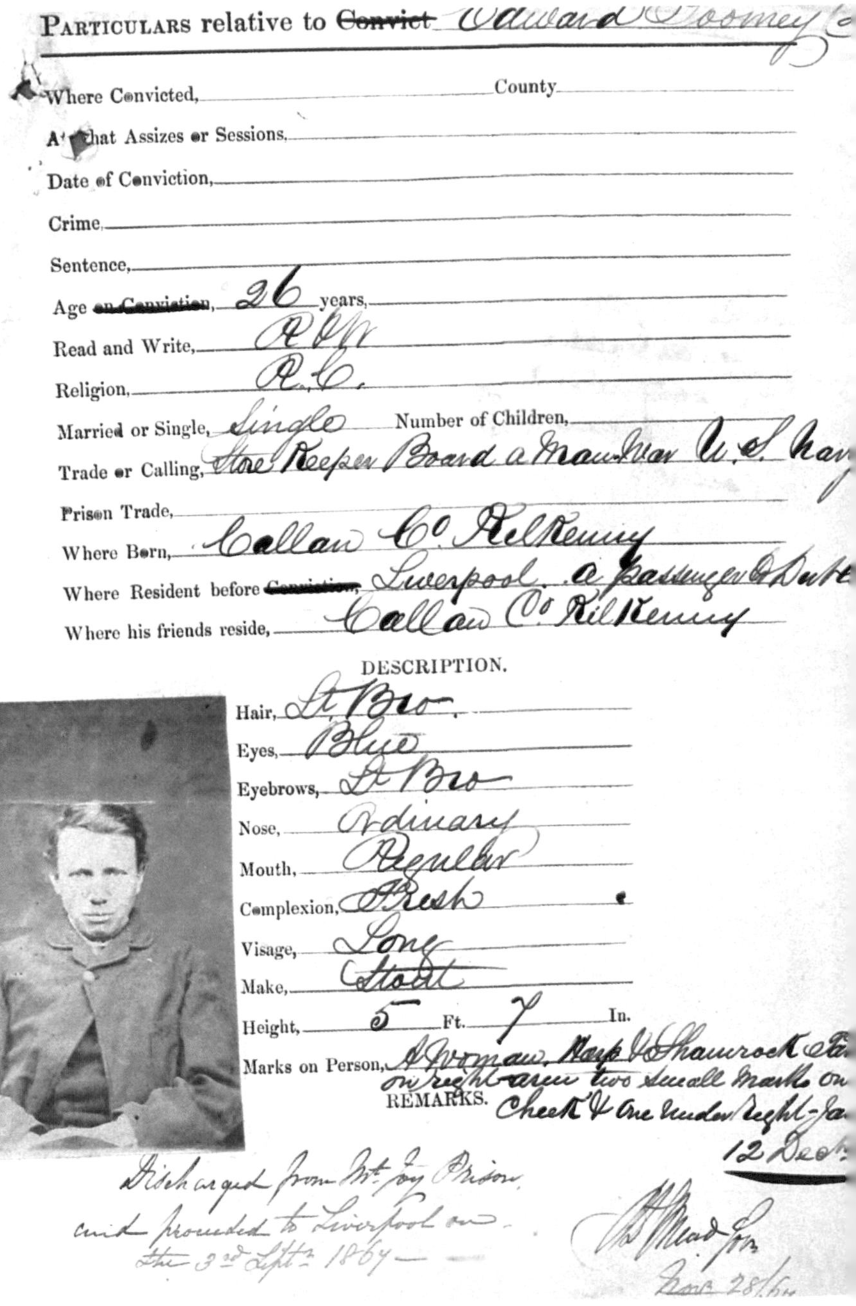

Fig. 10: Edward Toomey, 26, single, storekeeper on a man-of-war in the US navy. Born in Callan, county Kilkenny, he had a woman, harp and shamrock tattooed on his right arm, two small marks on his right cheek and one under his right jaw. He had recently arrived from Liverpool when arrested in Dublin on 12 December 1866. Discharged on 3 September 1867 on condition that he would return to America, he was allowed to return to Liverpool to work his passage to New York. NAI, FP 487

Fig. 11: Morgan Burke, 29, single, butcher. A native of Dunmanway, county Cork, Burke had arrived from the US about six months prior to his arrest under HCSA on 12 March 1867; he was released on 15 April 1868 on condition that he return to America. NAI, FP 41

Fig. 12: Patrick Waters, 20, single, poulterer, remand prisoner, 1866. Resident at Great Britain Street, he had a cut mark on his left eyebrow and left temple, pierced ears, and a burn mark on the back of his hand. NAI, FP 504

18 NAI, FP 141 (Dunne), 219 (Hogan)
19 NAI, CSORP 1866/14026
20 For an example, see the case of Henry Trodden, released from internment in Kilmainham in July 1866 on condition that he return to England: NAI, CSORP 1866/13990.
21 *Irishman*, 19 Oct. 1867. Price was an early proponent of prison photography. In 1864 he used photographs to identify nineteen prisoners in Kilmainham as recidivists; two of these men had thirteen previous convictions each. See Slattery, 'Uses of Photography in Ireland', vol. 1, 240. Smollen was a detective who had tailed James Stephens in 1865; acting detective Dawson participated in Stephens's arrest.
22 Breandán Mac Giolla Choille, 'Fenian Documents in the State Paper Office', *Irish Historical Studies*, 16, 63 (1969), 258–84, remains an important guide to official papers on the IRB. Also see Tom Quinlan, 'The Registered Papers of the Chief Secretary's Office', *Irish Archives*, (Autumn 1994), 5–21.

to their release. That 'likeness', attached to a new 'Photograph and Description' form, was, like the Mountjoy Form K, sent to Dublin Castle.[20] Initially at least, the Kilmainham prisoners saw nothing untoward in having their picture taken. In his smuggled letter, Halpin suggested that for some time they looked upon it as an eccentricity of Henry Price, the governor, a notoriously ugly man whom he sarcastically described as having 'cultivated a taste for the beautiful in early youth'. In time, however, the prisoners came to see photography as part of the 'happy system adopted by our keepers to keep us properly in the strings'. Halpin gave a sharp account of the change in attitude among the prisoners, arguing that the photographs were intended not for the present amusement of the governor but for future police purposes:

Until lately we were given to understand that his efforts in that line were merely for amusement, and under this plea many of the prisoners were seduced to sit for their likeness. Lately, however, some obstreperous fellows refused to be caught by chaff, whereupon the amiable Mr. Price, who is not supposed to be in the affair at all, waxed exceedingly wrath and flatly told the delinquents that they should never leave the prison until they submitted, thereby plainly intimating that the deputy's position was but a sham, and that the pictures are really to adorn the 'Rogues' Gallery' in the Lower Castle-yard. Threats have not yet been used towards the untried prisoners; but the tried fellows are claimed body and soul by our beneficent rulers. So those that have submitted to

the soft saulder of the deputy, have now the satisfaction to learn that Professors Smollen and Dawson are attentively studying their physiognomies with a view to future operations. This is a charming method for marking for future purposes all who come within the charmed influence of Kilmainham, and must be highly creditable to the government that adopts it.[21]

The prisoner had identified the value of his photograph to the state. The Form Ks and photographs from Mountjoy and 'Photograph and Description' forms from Kilmainham, archived in Constabulary headquarters, constituted the basis of the most extensive series of alphabetical files ever before compiled on Irish political activists. The Constabulary's system for accessing these files is somewhat unclear, due in part to the removal of 'Irish Crime Records' and 'Fenian Papers' from Dublin to London on the eve of partition, not all of which appear to have been returned. Still, surviving materials indicate that files on many men jailed in 1866–68 were copied into alphabetical ledgers in the late 1860s while others remained loosely bound.[22] Certainly, however, both the ledgers and loose files were updated during the next few years with information sent to Dublin by both Irish and British police forces. Arthur Forrester, an eighteen-year-old Lancashire-born printer, was arrested in Dublin under the HCSA in March 1867. The police found a revolver in his possession; Forrester was charged and convicted with having arms in a proclaimed district and served six months in Kilmainham. The Constabulary updated his file in Dublin in 1869, noting that he had assumed women's clothes as a disguise in Manchester (Fig. 14).[23] Similarly, they updated their description of medical student Edmund O'Donovan in January 1870, three years after his release from jail, when they received information from England that he had since grown light whiskers (Fig. 15). O'Donovan, son of the celebrated scholar John O'Donovan, had been interned twice under the HCSA, first from March to September 1866 and again from November 1867 to May 1868; on both occasions, he had been discharged on condition that he go to America.[24] The police had good reason to check up on these two men, both of whom remained active revolutionaries. Forrester, a quondam ballad-writer ('The Felons of Our Land' was his best-known production; see page 54), and O'Donovan both fought in the French Foreign Legion during the Franco-Prussian War before returning to Britain as the IRB organizers for, respectively, northern and southern England.[25]

Files on men no longer active in Fenian circles in Ireland or Britain were also reviewed in the early 1870s. The authorities reviewed the file on former internee John H. Gleeson of Borrisoleigh, county Tipperary, five years after his release from jail on condition that he return to the United States. The review of Gleeson's file in May 1871 may have been related to the recent publication of a book on the 1870 Fenian incursion into Canada; Gleeson, now styling himself 'general', had been one of the leaders of the 'invasion'.[26] In addition to updating existing records, the Constabulary continued to create new files on Fenian suspects, including men based overseas. There was a file in Dublin on Lancashire-based Michael Davitt, including his description and known haunts, as early as 1869; the Constabulary updated it several times prior to his arrest in 1870 with information received from their English counterparts via the Home Office in London. Davitt's file contained no photograph, but both captured photographs

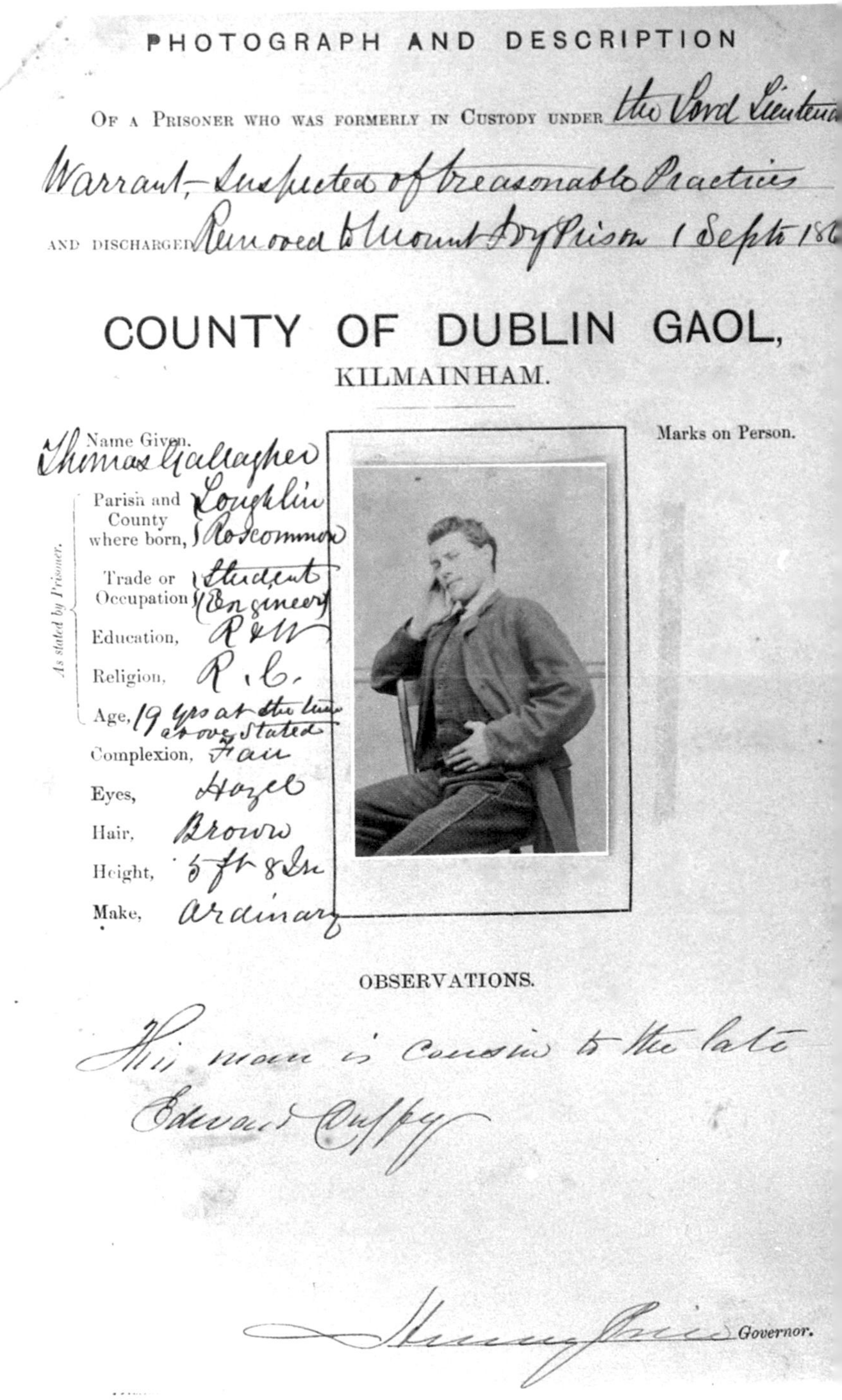

PHOTOGRAPH AND DESCRIPTION

OF A PRISONER WHO WAS FORMERLY IN CUSTODY UNDER the Lord Lieutena
Warrant – Suspected of treasonable Practices
AND DISCHARGED Removed to Mountjoy Prison 1 Septr 186

COUNTY OF DUBLIN GAOL,
KILMAINHAM.

Name Given. Thomas Gallagher

Marks on Person.

As stated by Prisoner.

Parish and County where born, Loughlin Roscommon
Trade or Occupation Student Engineer
Education, R & W
Religion, R. C.
Age, 19 yrs at the time above stated
Complexion, Fair
Eyes, Hazel
Hair, Brown
Height, 5 ft 8 In
Make, Ordinary

OBSERVATIONS.

This man is cousin to the late Edward Duffy

Governor.

Fig. 13: Thomas Gallagher, 19, single. A farmer's son from Aughrim, county Roscommon, Gallagher was a student of engineering when arrested under the HCSA on 27 February 1866; he was released on bail the following September. His Form K notes that he was a cousin of the Fenian organizer Edward Duffy. NAI, FP 179

23 NAI, FP 173; ICR 13; within a few days of his release, Forrester published a letter detailing the threats and blandishments used by the authorities in unsuccessful attempts to get him to turn informer, see *Irishman*, 12 Oct. 1867.

24 O'Donovan's brother, John, was also interned; he was a student in Trinity College. See NAI, FP 398 (Edmund); 400 (John).

25 On both Forrester and O'Donovan, see T. M. Healy, *Letters and Leaders of My Day*, vol. 1 (London, 1929), 116–18; O'Donovan is also mentioned in Katherine Tynan, *Twenty-Five Years* (London, 1913).

26 NAI, FP 189; Anon., *A Brief Account of the Fenian Raids on the Missisquoi Frontier in 1866 and 1870* (Montreal, 1871). On Gleeson's arrest, see *Irishman*, 24 Feb. 1866. For correspondence from the prisoner, his wife, doctor and the US consul in Dublin, see NAI, CSORP 1866/13784.

27 NAI, FP 63 (Carroll), 119 (Devitt [sic]). For a studio portrait of Davitt circulated in the 1880s, see NAI, FP 111.

28 For an excellent discussion, see Stephen A. Ball, 'Policing the Land War: Official Responses to Political Protest and Agrarian Crime in Ireland, 1879–91' (unpublished PhD dissertation, Goldsmith's College, University of London, 2000), 286–311.

(studio portraits provided by informers or acquired in some other way by the police) and photographs taken when the person was in custody were also archived. For instance, the Irish Constabulary added a photograph and descriptive details of William Carroll of Birkenhead to its Fenian files in 1870; local police had taken his photograph after his arrest in Liverpool for pawning a revolver.[27]

As the Irish republican threat to the British state receded in the mid-1870s, the Constabulary had fewer occasions to consult 'the "rogues' gallery" in the Lower Castle-yard,' as Halpin had dubbed the authorities' photographs and descriptions of political activists. In the early 1880s, however, mass-agitation on the land issue and, in particular, the Invincibles' assassination of the Chief Secretary and Under Secretary in May 1882 caused government to radically overhaul counter-insurgency activity in Ireland. The most far-reaching development was the creation of two distinct sections within the RIC's detective system, the Ordinary Branch and the Special Branch; the latter branch, initially conceived as an intelligence section concerned with the collection of information on secret societies and combinations that might countenance illegal activity, rapidly transformed itself into a semi-secret force-within-a-force that aggregated information on a much broader range of political activists. New faces appeared in the 'rogues' gallery' for the first time in several years.[28] The Special Branch acquired portrait photographs of prominent political figures, including MPs, who travelled the country on organizing or speech-making tours; these photographs were generally purchased from portrait studios where they were sold as political memorabilia.[29] These photographs were then circulated from Dublin to divisional headquarters to facilitate the identification, surveillance and arrest of these men if the need arose. Hence, portraits of Charles Stewart Parnell, Michael Davitt,

John Redmond, William Redmond and Fr. Eugene Sheehy ended up in the same files as the photographs and descriptions of the internees, remand prisoners and convicts photographed in the late 1860s and early 1870s; although very few of these new additions had any involvement in Fenianism, the extended collection would still be known as 'Fenian Photographs'. The Special Branch also sought out group-photographs of suspects, often taken at meetings of clubs believed to be republican fronts. There were some surprising sources for images. In 1882 a group of land activists had their photographs taken upon their release from internment in Dundalk Jail under the Protection of Person and Property (Ireland) Act; the photographer then mounted the portraits on a postcard adorned with shamrocks and the legend 'Dundalk Gaol, Christmas 1881'. Intended by the sitters as a memento of their time in jail or a propaganda piece, the image lingered in the mind of senior police officers. In November 1886 when the Constabulary was seeking one of the men in the photograph, the Special Branch obtained a copy of the card from Galbraith's photographic studio on Clanbrassil Street, Dundalk. An official in the Special Branch office noted that it included 'several important men, amongst others J. Butterfield, a Northern Fenian organizer'. 'I think it would be well to keep this with our photographs of suspects,' he wrote to one of his superiors, 'and to note on each file in which the suspect is referred to that such has been done.'[30]

Over the next few years, cheap portable cameras became part of regular police work, and photographs of crime scenes and covertly snapped images of suspects began to appear with increasing frequency in police files.[31] From 1890, the Special Branch had its own photographic department in the Constabulary Depot in the Phoenix Park, where a sergeant was employed full-time developing and copying

Fig. 14: Arthur M. Forrester, 18, single, bookkeeper and letter-press printer. Born in Lanchasire, England, Forrester was living at 43 Essex Street, Dublin, when arrested under the HCSA on 25 March 1867; a gun was found in his possession and he was sentenced to six months for having arms in a proclaimed district. He was discharged on 8 October 1867. For his literary productions, see Ellen Forrester (his mother) and Arthur M. Forrester, *Songs of the Rising Nation and other Poems* (Glasgow, 1869), reviewed in *Irishman*, 24 Apr. 1869. NAI, FP 173

photographs. The Dublin Metropolitan Police established a similar department in the same year. In late 1892, David Harrell, the commissioner of the latter force, reported to Dublin Castle that group photographs of suspects were hard to obtain; 'Dublin men have avoided being photographed for many years past,' he wrote of republican activists, 'and it is impossible to obtain copies from groups or otherwise.'[32] Twenty-six years after the state first systematically photographed suspects in Dublin jails, Fenians were again 'refusing to sit'.

II

The experience of being photographed in jail features in several Fenians' prison recollections, some of which were serialized in newspapers shortly after their release, while others appeared in book-form years later.[33] Republican icon Jeremiah O'Donovan Rossa provided two highly charged accounts of being asked to sit for photographs, first in Mountjoy Jail following his conviction for treason felony in December 1865 and then in Millbank Prison in England in 1867, while serving his sentence. In *My Years in English Jails*, Rossa describes how, upon conviction, he was returned to Mountjoy and photographed:

> After being shaven I was led to have my picture taken. The photographer had a large black-painted pasteboard prepared, with my name printed across it in white, and, pinning it across my breast, he sat me in position. I remained sitting and looking according to instructions till he had done, and he never had the manners to tell — what artists never failed to

tell me — that I made an exceedingly good picture.[34]

Rossa's humour here throws the transition to which he found himself subject into sharp relief. Specifically, photographing prisoners marked a key point in the transformation of photography from its early association with portraiture, 'a sign whose purpose is both the description of an individual and the inscription of social identity' and which is also 'a commodity, a luxury, an adornment, ownership of which itself confers status'.[35] Rossa's ironic comment about the photographer's refusal to acknowledge a 'good picture' points to the absence of aesthetic valuation and to the photographic subject's abstraction of self from the photographic transaction. In other words, it calls attention to the seizure of photography by the state, a harnessing of technology which was previously understood as a mode of representing one's own identity. Indeed, Rossa highlights how prison photographs — pictures which the subject does not ask to be taken and which he will likely never see — allow the state to assert power over the body through its documentation. Allen Sekula's depiction of photography as a 'double system' — 'a system of representation capable of functioning both *honorifically* and *repressively*' — is useful here. By insisting on an understanding of sitting for a picture as an 'honorific', aesthetic act, Rossa expresses his own recognition that, in the context of the prison, photography had become a disciplinary and repressive exercise of power.[36]

29 Dublin portrait studios had produced daguerreotypes and lithographs of Young Ireland leaders in the late 1840s but the sale of photographs of Irish political figures first became common in the 1860s; for a brief discussion, see Fintan Cullen, *The Irish Face: Redefining the Irish Portrait* (London, 2004), 203–04. Shortly after the release of the Fenian celebrity Stephen J. Meany, *The Irishman* advertised two large-sized portraits of Meany with a 'lithographed facsimile of his signature'; the advertisement noted approvingly that the signature, 'Yours most feloniously, Stephen J. Meany', was 'characteristic of the man'. Ironically, a photograph of James Stephens found in Meany's possession had been presented as evidence against him at his trial. See *Irishman*, 1 May; 8 May; 15 May 1869.

30 For the Dundalk photograph and associated correspondence, see NAI, FP 3.

31 The scene of the killing of District Inspector William Martin in February 1889 was one of the first crime scenes extensively documented by the RIC; photographers working for defence solicitors also photographed it. On the incident, see Breandán Mac Suibhne, 'Soggarth

Aroon and Gombeen Priest: Canon James MacFadden (1842–1917)', in Gerard Moran, ed., *Radical Irish Priests, 1660–1970* (Dublin, 1998), 167–69; for samples of the photographs, see Ulster Museum, James Glass Collection (1889). Slattery, 'Uses of Photography in Ireland', vol. 2, 15, relates the photographing of the scene to the establishment of the Constabulary's photographic department. For the contemporaneous and more ambitious uses of photography by the French police under Alphonse Bertillon, see Frizot, 'Body of Evidence', 264.

32 Quoted in Slattery, 'Uses of Photography in Ireland', vol. 2, 22. C. P. Crane, a key figure in the establishment of the department, had been involved in the Martin investigation.

33 For example, *The Irishman* serialized a biography of Stephen J. Meany (by John Augustus O'Shea) after his release in summer 1869; for Meany's recollection of being photographed, see *Irishman*, 15 May 1869.

34 Jeremiah O'Donovan Rossa, *Irish Rebels in English Prisons: A Record of Prison Life* (New York, 1882), 73

Rossa's recollection of his encounter with a prison photographer in Millbank documents this historical transition in greater detail. More particularly, it emphasizes that surveying, possessing and representing the potential insurgent's body had not yet been fully naturalized as the self-evident rights of the state over its subjects. The state's claim to these rights was sufficiently unstable that Rossa could use the photographic moment to reveal its contradictions and to interrogate its legitimacy; resistance was not only possible, but it had the potential for success. Significantly, Rossa connects being asked to sit for a photograph in Millbank with heightened surveillance in the aftermath of the Clerkenwell explosions of 1867. After the explosions, he writes, 'our rescue was apprehended, and our photographs were wanted for the detectives in case we were taken away'. Rossa 'refused to sit'; he recalls the resulting exchange with the photographer in the following passage:

'Come on, come on,' said Warder Power to me one day as he opened my door. On I went, and I was brought through the square to where the warders were on parade. I was soon landed in the room which turned out to be the photographic department of the establishment. The artist had his glasses ready, and sat me down on a chair opposite the picturing instrument. As soon as he had me fixed in position, and taken his hands off, he

Fig. 15: John O'Donovan, 23, single, student, Trinity College Dublin, and his brother Edmund O'Donovan (alias Edward Hunt), 21, single, medical student. John had been in custody since November 1865 when arrested under the HCSA in April 1866; he was released in August on condition that he go to America. Edmund was resident at Nelson Street, Dublin, when interned in March 1866; he was released in late September of that year on condition that he go to America but re-arrested under the HCSA in county Clare in November 1867; he was released in May 1868, again on condition that he go to America. O'Donovan was taken prisoner when fighting with the French Foreign Legion in the Franco-Prussian War (his third time in custody) and, after his release, fought in the Carlist War in Spain. He subsequently became IRB organizer for southern England and worked as a war correspondent. He travelled to Central Asia in 1879 where he was imprisoned by the Turks for several months and, on his release, he wrote a famous book, *The Merv Oasis* (London, 1882). He was killed in 1883 covering Hicks Pasha's expedition to the Sudan. NAI, FP 398, 400

made for the machine and I stood up.
'What do you stand up for?' he said.
'What would I sit down for?' said I.
'To take your picture.'
'My picture?'
'Yes, sit down there again,' and he made toward me to place me in my position.
'Now wait awhile. Who wants my picture?'
'We want it; sit down.'
'You want it? Do you know I have a wife?'
'What do you mean?'
'I mean I have a wife, and you have made her awfully jealous by circulating a report that I was holding an intrigue with another man's wife. I don't want to make matters worse than they are by sending my picture into the world; if my wife saw it with any other woman, it might cause a separation for life.'
'Why, what a foolish man you are! Don't you know that these photographs are for the prison authorities, and that they do not leave the prison?'
'Oh, I couldn't rely upon that, and my mind would be uneasy. The prison authorities have the original, and I will give them permission to come and look at me whenever they please.'
'Come now, come now, don't be so foolish; you will only bring additional trouble on yourself.' And he gently laid hands on me to coax me into the chair.
'Oh no, governor, no; there's no trouble to me as trouble of mind, and if I allowed you to take my picture I could not help thinking that it would get into the hands of other women, and that my wife would hear it.'
'Then you absolutely refuse to allow your picture to be taken?'
'Unless I see that it is absolutely wanted, and that I have a guarantee that it will not be improperly used.'
Here three or four of them pressed me to sit down. I sat down, and as soon as they had their hands off me, I stood up and replied to their persuasion thus:— 'See now, governors, there is no use pressing me further. There is only one condition on which I will allow my picture to be taken, and that is this — that the Queen write to me for it, and promise she will not let it out of her own possession.'
I was taken out of my cell, and the next day I was again taken to the photographer, with the same result as before … I would not give them the satisfaction of letting them make a picture of me.[37]

Here, Rossa again plays on the association of portrait photography with intimacy, romantic attachment, and the domestic sphere in order to signal the state's intrusion into these domains. He insists, much more explicitly than in his account of being photographed in Mountjoy, upon a prior understanding of photography in which women were the primary consumers of images of men and in which the exchange of photographs served as a romantic and sexual transaction. This feigned misunderstanding thus represents prison photography as an intrusion on the body and its intimacies and a materialization of the imperial state's claim to possess the body of the unruly or potentially unruly colonial subject. Moreover, with his introduction of Queen Victoria to the exchange, Rossa indicates that a formerly 'private' exchange has become an exercise of public power and exposes the flawed logic (from a Fenian perspective) inherent in his conviction for treason felony, namely, the assumption that an Irish republican owed allegiance to the British crown. By insisting on photography as private and personal rather than public, Rossa successfully resists both the authority of the British state which renders his politics illegal and treasonous and, more particularly, the further encroachment of state power.

35 Tagg, *Burden of Representation*, 37. Also see the account of the aesthetic and political effects of the replacement of portraiture by photography in Walter Benjamin's essay 'The Work of Art in the Age of Its Technological Reproducibility' [1939], in *Selected Writings*, vol. 4, 1938–40, ed. Michael W. Jennings (Cambridge, Mass., 2003), 251–83.
36 Sekula, 'The Body and the Archive', 345
37 Rossa, *Irish Rebels in English Prisons*, 262–63. The allegation that Rossa (while a prisoner) endeavoured to 'carry on an intrigue with the wife of another prisoner' had been circulated by the governor of Portland Prison; a letter he had addressed to 'Mrs. Mary Moore, Denzille Street, Dublin, For Mrs. O'Donovan' was the basis of the accusation. See *Irishman*, 16 Mar. 1867.

38 Tagg, *Burden of Representation*, 61

39 Tagg, *Burden of Representation*, ch. 2–3

40 For an extended version of this argument, see Amy E. Martin, 'Acts of Union: Representing Nation-States and National Identities in Victorian British and Irish Writing' (unpublished PhD dissertation, Columbia University, 2002).

41 The Oxford English Dictionary documents the emergence of these terms in histories of the French Revolution written as early as 1791.

42 See the Oxford English Dictionary entries for 'terrorism' and 'terrorist'.

Both of Rossa's accounts are a reminder that, if the photographing of Fenians marked a major transformation in the uses of photographic technology, it also constituted a key moment in British state-formation. Art historian John Tagg has produced a compelling history of photography's 'mobilization within the emerging apparatuses of a new and more penetrating form of the state' in nineteenth-century Britain.[38] Tagg argues that new uses of photography reveal much about the radical restructuring of the capitalist state in this period, in particular its use of surveillance and disciplinary technologies as new forms of power and knowledge over its subjects.[39] Tagg's history of these developments focuses on clinical photography of the criminally insane in asylums beginning in 1856, and then the production of mugshots and photos of criminal children in the 1870s. However, the photographing of Fenian prisoners suggests a missing link in this account of state photography. For notably, the deployment of this new technology against republican prisoners in Dublin prisons in 1865–66 occurred contemporaneously with the first appearance of the modern discourse of 'terrorism' to describe Fenianism and the earliest articulation of the British state's vision of itself as not just a counter-insurgent but as an anti-terrorist apparatus. Thus, before photography became a pervasive method of documenting and managing criminality in Britain in the 1870s, it was used systematically to collect evidence concerning those described as 'terrorists' in the modern sense of the word.

From 1865, newspaper articles, editorials and political cartoons, particularly in Britain but also in Ireland, began to represent Fenians using a new language of 'terror' which made claims about the causes and aims of insurgency.[40] The word 'terrorism' had first appeared in reactionary accounts and histories of the French Revolution of 1789-94: Jacobin power was

'the Reign of Terror', the Jacobins 'terrorists', and their system of government 'terrorism'.[41] Now, the historically specific word 'terrorism' was abstracted, becoming a comparative term to indicate an insurgency which had as its primary method the intimidation, terrorization and destruction of those against whom it was directed. In this shift of usage and definition, 'terrorism' shifts from a descriptive of an institutionalized mode of governance to a method of terrorization which is not necessarily centralized or institutionalized.[42] The logic of counter-revolutionary historiography, which argued that the Jacobin government degenerated into a reign of terror for terror's sake, reached a culmination. 'Terrorism' was characterized as having no political goal, as being dedicated to the sole object of creating 'terror'. Hence, the modern, less historically specific idea of 'terrorism' associated political violence with atavism and barbarism. The 'terrorist' became a figure of irrationality, alien to modern 'rational' forms of power rather than produced by them.

This new discourse of 'terrorism' crystallized immediately after the Clerkenwell explosion, the event that occasioned Rossa's second encounter with a prison photographer. For example, the London *Times* and many other mainstream newspapers repeatedly described the bombing as 'terror', 'terrorism', and 'terrorist'. They also represented it as something novel: it was 'a crime of unexampled atrocity' and 'the worst crime in English history'.[43] Although it was clear that the Fenians had planted the explosives to blow a hole in the prison wall, not to kill people, *The Times* wrote: 'Their object is now apparently to create a terror throughout the United Kingdom ... such is their unscrupulous ferocity'.[44] Even the liberal *Newcastle Daily Chronicle* declared, 'English liberalism cannot grasp a hand which smells rank with the blood of her children, slaughtered in mere wantonness of fanaticism'.[45] Such descriptions are consistent with the use of the term 'terrorism' in its modern sense — as an irrational, savage, racially and culturally atavistic programme of violence designed to kill innocent civilians, in particular women and children. As is apparent, this ideology quickly converged with the figure of the violent colonial 'fanatic' that had been elaborated and disseminated in imperial gothic fiction since the early nineteenth century.

In newspaper prose and visual images, Fenian 'terrorism' was most often represented as a masculine invisible threat, a monstrous presence lurking within the United Kingdom, an ever-present menace that warranted continual panic on the part of potential victims. In political cartoons, the inextricable relation between this new notion of terrorism and the transforming British state was most apparent. In *Punch* cartoons such as the exemplary 'Fenian Pest', which appeared in 1866, state violence and the suspension of rights and liberties in Ireland is rationalized in the interest of protecting subjects of the crown (Fig. 16).[46] Here, then, is an allegorical staging of one of the founding mythologies and paradoxes of the modern state. The condemnation of violence legitimates state violence and new modes of power, but presents this institutionalized violence as reactive and as designed to ensure the protection of citizens. The caricatured Fenian comes to legitimize and to naturalize the violence of the imperial state; such a gesture erases the historical context of anti-colonial violence, relocating its origins in the *ontos* of the Irish insurgent body and suggesting essential (racial and cultural) rather than contingent origins for Fenian politics.[47]

The racialism of newspaper narratives and cartoon art can also be read as a part of a drive to establish the *visibility* of the

Fenian, integral to any successful strategy of counter-insurgency. Without skin colour as the basis of racial identification, the possibility that Fenians could blend into an English crowd pointed up the failure of both racial classification and of policing structures. This failure was more profound because the IRB was a highly organized secret society with a cell structure that had penetrated even the ranks of the British Army. British authorities found it difficult to identify Fenians in any definitive way; those who were identified were often difficult to convict due to lack of admissible evidence, hence the 'necessity' of suspending *habeas corpus* in Ireland and interning suspects indefinitely. Texts which saturated the public sphere in the United Kingdom disseminated a racialized construction of Irish 'terrorism' which might work against such failures and against Fenian strategies of insurgency. In cartoons such as 'The Fenian Pest', the simianized and racialized body of the Fenian is reassuring to the extent that it makes him hyper-visible to British citizens and the state.

The tension in this developing modern discourse of 'terrorism' — its representation as a threat that is simultaneously frighteningly invisible and yet visible to the point of caricature — finds its counterpart in the material history of the photographing of

43 *Times*, 14 Dec.; 16 Dec. 1867. Similar descriptives can be found in contemporaneous issues of other British newspapers, such as *The Spectator*.

44 *Times*, 14 Dec. 1867

45 Cited in Charles Townshend, *Political Violence in Ireland: Government and Resistance since 1848* (Oxford, 1983), 65

46 For a study of the representation of the simianized Irishman in cartoon art, see L. P. Curtis, *Apes and Angels: The Irishman in Victorian Caricature* (Washington DC, rev. edn. 1997). A more recent reading of British cartoons of the Fenian can be found in Michael Willem De Nie, *The Eternal Paddy: Irish Identity and the British Press, 1798–1882* (Madison, 2004).

47 For a later period, see Joseph Conrad's *The Secret Agent* (1907), which presents the Russian/Irish basis for a 'terrorism' that aims to destroy Greenwich Mean Time itself; it also intimates the strange accord between policeman and terrorist. Michaelis, one of the figures in the novel, is based on the experiences of several Fenians, including Michael Davitt.

Fig. 16: 'The Fenian Pest', from *Punch*, London, 3 March 1866. Hibernia: 'O my dear Sister, what ARE we to do with these troublesome people?'; Britannia: 'Try isolation first, my dear, and then —'

48 David Lloyd, 'Regarding Ireland', in *Ireland after History* (Cork, 1999), 45–46

49 *Times*, 11 Dec. 1867, carried an article by 'Historicus', calling for an international code of citizenship in order to remedy the particular problems raised by Fenianism and more specifically to allow the British state jurisdiction over Irish-American Fenians. For a brief discussion of this article, see Catherine Hall, Keith McClelland, and Jane Rendall, 'Introduction', in *Defining the Victorian Nation*, 57.

50 David Lloyd and Paul Thomas, *Culture and the State* (New York, 1998), 136

51 Keith McClelland, 'England's Greatness, the Working Man', in Hall et al., *Defining the Victorian Nation*, 76–77

52 McClelland, 'England's Greatness', 98–99

Fenians. British popular culture disseminated an ideology of the menacing yet grotesque and easily-captured Fenian, enacting a paradoxical gesture of inciting viewers' fear yet reassuring the public of the state's efficacy in 'stamping out' the threat. In material practice, the British state transformed its modes of power in response to the Fenian movement. David Lloyd argues that 'what appears in statist narrative as pre-modern, atavistic and generally violent elements of colonial society are in fact reciprocally engaged in the emergence of the modern apparatus of the colonial state'.[48] Fenianism participated in such a transformation through its critical position in the development of the tactics, apparatuses and ideology of counter-insurgency that became defining features of the modern British state. The innovative use of photography to establish the visibility of both interned and released Fenians is a primary and telling example of this transformation. Such prison photography exemplifies the state's claims to assert power over bodies and the way that it extended such claims even beyond the nation-state's formal boundaries. For example, the exchange of photographs between Britain and Ireland, technically different police jurisdictions although both parts of the 'United Kingdom', suggests as much, as does the problems posed for authorities by Irish-American internees.[49] Thus, photographing Fenians was part of a mid-nineteenth-century consolidation and expansion of state power through the suspension of the rights of citizens, residents and foreign travellers at will as well as the use of new forms of surveillance as deemed necessary in the interest of 'public safety'. These images are products of a state that had begun to define itself in relation to politics and practices that it called 'terrorism' and, specifically, to a population of detainees suspected of producing or even simply supporting 'terror'.

Significantly, these developments coincided with the extension of the franchise to more working-class males in the Reform Acts of 1867 and 1868. That extension was itself associated with a change in the language and meaning of citizenship as 'docility or respectability' replaced ownership as the condition for voting; thus, assent to the state's authority and obedience before the law became the condition for full citizenship.[50] The enfranchised subject had to disavow all forms of anarchy, including the Reform agitation that produced this extension of suffrage, or his rights of citizenship would be revoked. Keith McClelland has argued that 'the axial figure within the controversies of 1866–67 about who was to be enfranchised was the "respectable working man"'.[51] This ideal of 'manhood' emphasized the moral role of the respectable working-class male subject as a law-abiding citizen who performed his 'proper' social function as father, economic head of the household, and protector of women and children.[52] The new ideology of citizenship reproduced the logic of the state — the duty to protect weaker subjects from threat — through a particular ideal of masculinity.

Located in this context, the representation of Fenians in cartoons stands as the antithesis of 'the respectable working-class man', the figure at the centre of debates about the extension of suffrage. In caricature, the Fenian is the inversion and negation of British national identity and its newest articulation, obedient male citizenship. This juxtaposition is expressed most often through gendered narratives in which the Fenian is a man who destroys women and children rather than protecting them. In other words, the Irish Fenian is the racial and cultural converse of the ethical citizen subject. He exists as a terrifying phantasmatic counterpoint to the newly defined ethically masculine working-class citizen.[53] Thus, at the very moment when the state seems to extend rights to more subjects, it consolidates and expands its power by justifying the suspension of those rights in the case of anyone who does not recognize the legitimacy of its authority. The caricatured Fenian serves as the limit of the state's frontier of citizenship and as the rationalization of its monopoly on violence. However, the photographed Fenians are a critical visual supplement to this discourse, that demonstrate exactly what was at stake in such rationalization — the expansion and retrenchment of the state's capacity to produce obedient subjects.[54]

III

I can discover no evidences of 'villainy' in the panorama of faces now before me. It appears that the originals are all conspirators — Fenians, or something of that kind. I look at portrait after portrait, and I say — '*There* is a man to whom I would trust myself, were I travelling on a dark night through an uninhabited country, with ten thousand pounds in gold under my charge.' Yet these men are inmates of English prisons, 'felons', 'criminals', 'traitors' and at home there are gentlewomen who have lain in their bosoms, and who (like me) refuse to believe this. But then the explanation lies behind: these men, kindly, amiable, good, who in good order of things, would make a high and honourable reputation, find themselves branded as traitors, and are herded with England's most foul and brutal scoundrels because they believed their country was cruelly wronged, and they thought to remove that wrong by physical force.

D[enis] H[olland], 'A Gallery of Irish Faces. A Study of the Portraits in *The Irishman*', in *The Irishman*, 7 April 1866

In spring 1866, journalist Denis Holland wrote a series of articles on engraved portraits of well-known Fenians, which had appeared in the republican press. The series challenged the discourse of 'terrorism' that rationalized both the physiognomical caricatures of Irish 'terrorists' then common in British newspapers and the photographing of Fenian suspects, which was, at that moment, being institutionalized in Dublin prisons. By emphasizing both the ordinariness and respectability of the men and women depicted in the engravings, Holland contested the idea that 'terrorists' are the antithesis of average citizens and, by including women, that they are all deviant males. The most remarkable feature of the 'panorama of faces' in the paper was that they *could not* be easily differentiated from the faces of other 'good' men, even from the writer himself; their humanity was proof of the rationality of their actions. In the passage quoted above, he invites his reader's identification with the men depicted in the portraits, inserting them into a recognizable narrative of masculinity, desire and family, while at the same time elevating them as national heroes; the noble-minded, politically motivated Fenians stand in contrast to 'England's most foul and brutal scoundrels'.[55]

A recognition that the state misrepresents average, respectable individuals as deviant in order to justify extraordinary repressive measures — internment and lengthy sentences for men convicted of treason — underpins Holland's series; likewise, there is an implicit warning that the state legitimates the expansion of its coercive capacity — including intrusions on the body — as an exception but that it rarely relinquishes powers claimed in exceptional circumstances. Certainly, the British state deployed visual technology against an ever-widening range of Irish people in the latter half of the nineteenth century. First, convicts, then men on remand for Fenian-related charges (Fig. 17), and then suspects (internees) were photographed in Dublin jails.[56] By the mid-1880s the state was archiving photographs not only of prisoners (convicts, remands, and internees) but also portraits and surreptitiously snapped photographs of political activists (often with

53 John Newsinger, *Fenianism in Mid-Victorian Britain* (London, 1994), 25

54 Sarah Jane Edge, 'Photographic History and the Visual Appearance of an Irish Nationalist Discourse 1840–1870', *Victorian Literature and Culture*, 32, 1 (2004), 35, argues that prison photographs of Fenians 'may have played a role in the formation of a shared identity of Irishness' and that 'they need to be seen as part of a more widespread institutional discourse on criminality, class, and racial/ethnic difference'. However, as Edge acknowledges, the photographs were not circulated to a wide audience, and they were taken because of the authorities' fear that the Irish 'difference' that produced Fenianism might not be recognizably expressed on the body. Lacking an audience, the photographs, therefore, are less an expression of racializing discourse concerning Irishness and more a counterpart to it.

55 Although Holland's reading of the portraits challenges British discourses concerning Irish masculinity, he relies on traditional gendered narratives that represent the Irish nationalist hero as male and as the protector of women. This problematic of the masculine runs throughout the writings of the Fenians, and points to the difficulties of countering the colonial state's narratives while retaining the visions of gender, race and nation that are central to them.

56 At the same time, the Irish experience became a model for the institutionalization of the mandatory mugshot in the British penal system in the 1870s, see Slattery, 'Uses of Photography in Ireland', vol. 2, 228–32, 242–43.

57 These issues are now modified by the conversion of Kilmainham into a museum in which the technology of surveillance is itself subjected to a later analysis in which the technology is further historicized. See Áine O'Brien, 'Marketing and Managing Colonial Spectacle: In the Belly of the Archive', in John Paul Waters, ed., *South Atlantic Quarterly*, 95, 1 (Winter 1996), 103–44.

58 Susan Sontag, 'The Photographs Are Us: Regarding the Torture of Others', in *The New York Times Magazine*, 23 May 2004, 27

friends with no political involvement) and even members of parliament. The suspension of rights and harnessing of technology in unusual circumstances had served as the foundation for the normalization of new apparatuses of power and knowledge to which all, rather than a few, were now potentially subject.[57]

The contemporary relevance of such an analysis is clear. The attacks of 9/11 and the wars and occupations that have followed in Afghanistan and in Iraq have brought seemingly disparate elements to the centre of a debate about the modern state's confrontation with insurgency and, more particularly, with 'terrorism'. This controversy raises questions about the suspension of civil liberties (particularly *habeas corpus*); the deployment of new technologies in the intensified documentation and surveillance of citizens and foreigners; the status and treatment of political prisoners and prisoners of war; and the physical limits of a state's power — specifically, whether its power ends at its border or may extend beyond it. One of the primary ways that these problems have literally and theoretically been brought into view is through the medium of photography, in large part due to the widespread dissemination of photographs of Iraqi detainees being tortured in Abu Ghraib. The late Susan Sontag, for example, argued that the central place of photography within the current crisis is a peculiarly contemporary phenomenon, one that is linked to the transformation of experience by the proliferation of visual culture in the late capitalist global economy of the twentieth and early twenty-first centuries.[58] But what seems to be peculiarly contemporary is not new. The 'rogues' gallery' compiled in Ireland in the mid-1860s is a reminder that photography was a foundational element in the 'war on terror' at its inception over a century ago. ∎

Fig. 17: Joseph Fortune, 18, single, labourer, Bride's Alley, Dublin, remand prisoner in 1866. NAI, FP 174

Photograph: Charles Hewitt/Picture Post/Getty Images.

Mapping the Narrow Ground
Geography, History and Partition

Mary Burgess

In 1952 J. C. Beckett wrote with a certain finality that 'the real partition of Ireland is not on the map but in the minds of men'.[1]

1 J. C. Beckett, *A Short History of Ireland* (London, 1952), 192

2 M. W. Heslinga, *The Irish Border as a Cultural Divide: A Contribution to the Study of Regionalism in the British Isles* (Assen, 1962). For the pervasive influence of Heslinga, see Arthur Green, 'Homage to Heslinga', in Joep Leerssen, ed., *Forging in the Smithy: Representation in Anglo-Irish Literary History* (Amsterdam, 1995), 145–59.

3 A. T. Q. Stewart, *The Narrow Ground: Aspects of Ulster 1609–1969* [1977] (London, rev. edn. 1989), 157. In the 1989 edition (159–60), Stewart went further: 'Nationalists may or may not be justified in their attempts to remove [the border] and annex the other six counties of Ireland to the Republic, but there is little point in doing so unless they can find a way to eliminate that other border of the mind.'

4 See, in a different context, Oliver MacDonagh, *States of Mind: A Study of the Anglo-Irish Conflict, 1780–1980* (London, 1983), 15: 'The Irish problem has persisted because of the power of geographical images over men's minds.'

Ten years later, M. W. Heslinga quoted Beckett as the epigraph to his *The Irish Border as a Cultural Divide: A Contribution to the Study of Regionalism in the British Isles* (1962), a book that did much to promote both the border and the companion theory of two nations as facts of nature and history.[2] And fifteen years after Heslinga, A. T. Q. Stewart, in an even more influential book, *The Narrow Ground: Aspects of Ulster 1609-1969* (1977), wrote: 'The truth is that partition is not a line drawn on the map; it exists in the hearts and minds of Irish people'.[3] Beckett, Heslinga and Stewart were arguing against the imagined geography of nationalism (an island 'limned by God in water') and for an alternative imagined geography of unionism in which the six counties would appear as a territorial unit separate from the island of which it formed a physical part, but closely bonded to an island from which it was separated by a stretch of sea.[4] In *Language and Symbolic Power*, Pierre Bourdieu contends that geographical '"reality" … is social through and through' and that 'the frontier, that product of a legal act of delineation, produces cultural difference as much as it is produced by it'. For Bourdieu, indeed, 'the most "natural" classifications are based on characteristics which are not in the slightest respect natural but which are to a great extent the product of an arbitrary imposition.'[5] This essay argues that, while partitionist scholars like Beckett and

Stewart have consistently used the past to explain and justify existing state divisions in Ireland, unionist conceptions of geography have been decidedly unstable, leading to a curious insecurity in the crucial marriage between unionist interpretations of history and the geography of the north of Ireland.

From the moment the Irish border was drawn, 'with a bland subordination of topography to self-interest', it hardened into permanence in northern unionist politics.[6] Certainly, the levels of violence and coercion which attended the birth of the state did not represent an auspicious beginning, or as natural a resolution to the 'Irish Question' as Stewart and Beckett, among others, would have us believe. The border would become one of the most contested and militarized state-boundaries in European history. It still retains the sense of unease, of impermanence and of contention that characterized its inception. This is so in spite of a long and complex effort by unionists to manufacture a sense in which the Northern Irish state has always 'really' existed.

The potential for violence in the very idea of the border has diminished. Especially since 1998, there has been such an enormous increase in cross-border initiatives — educational, commercial, economic, cultural and political — that it is widely claimed that it is losing both its relevance and its divisive potential.[7]

One of the great ironies of this situation for unionists is that, in the formative years of the state, regionalism added cultural density to the idea of partition. Now, in the 'Europe of the Regions' this is no longer the case; the border matters culturally only to an increasingly embattled and shrinking unionist community.

The earlier project of constructing Ulster accelerated after partition and was articulated in the works of geographers and historians in particular.[8] The relationship between regionalist geography and historiography in the construction of Northern Ireland has always been central.[9] Geography determined the history of the region, and the history finally realized the geographical imperative. In 1928, a young Welshman named E. Estyn Evans took up a lectureship in geography at Queen's University Belfast (QUB). At some point in that year, Evans met with Thomas Jones, sometime Professor of Economics in the university, and formerly David Lloyd George's private secretary. Jones had been the British Prime Minister's chief negotiator with Michael Collins and Arthur Griffith during the Treaty negotiations which ended in the partition of Ireland.[10] The content of their conversation is unrecorded. It had been Jones, however, who first mooted the idea of the Boundary Commission as a palliative to the Irish delegation; the possibility that the border was moveable, even 'temporary', was insinuated into the officially inflexible rhetoric of partition from the outset.[11] Given Jones's own interest in geography, it is possible that they discussed the border. Moreover, Evans's arrival in Belfast came at a time when unionists were intent on making the recently drawn border permanent; throughout his career, he remained close to the establishment and this central ambition.

Also in 1928, only three years after the Boundary Commission made the border permanent, D. A. Chart, the Deputy Keeper of Public Records in Northern Ireland, published *A History of Northern Ireland*. Unsurprisingly, since 'Northern Ireland' had then been in existence for less than a decade, Chart's book was relatively brief, yet it managed to confer on the recently formed 'Northern Ireland' a pedigree of antiquity stretching back to the fifteenth century and to make it identical with a new version of 'Ulster', now a six-county, not a nine-county, province. The new political formation became, at a stroke, 'an old country'. Events which could properly have fallen within the ambit of Chart's title — the violent political and sectarian events of 1920–22, for instance, or the passing of the Special Powers Act of 1922, or even the wrangles over the border — made no appearance in the book. The fact of partition was merely stated in the preface. Chart was resolutely unwilling to 'reopen recent controversies and recall ... many painful memories'.[12] The conclusion of the Boundary Commission's investigations had changed the atmosphere if not the rhetoric of Ulster; an editorial in the January 1926 issue of the new *Ulster Review* declared:

> The signing of the Border Agreement wipes the political slate for us in Ulster ... We are like a garrison so surprised to find a prolonged siege suddenly raised, and the enemy quietly withdrawn, that we cannot quite believe in our good luck.[13]

Chart's *History of Northern Ireland* suggested that the 'stagnant optimism', which G. K. Chesterton had observed in Belfast in 1918, was finally producing results.[14]

In this new mood of confidence and relief, born of the apparent gift of a clean 'political slate', the unionist establishment set about naturalizing its new state. A cancel line would be drawn through the troubled recent past, and an older history would instead gain prominence. Chart's history, a textbook produced under the auspices of the new

5 Pierre Bourdieu, *Language and Symbolic Power*, ed. John B. Thompson and trans. Gino Raymond and Matthew Adamson (Cambridge, Mass., 1991), 222

6 MacDonagh, *States of Mind*, 21

7 See, for instance, the large number of cross-border initiatives, projects and publications produced by the Centre for Cross Border Studies, based in Armagh, and also the work of the Institute for the Study of Social Change, based at University College Dublin.

8 Relatively recent books and essays by Ian Adamson, and by two-nations geographer Dennis Pringle, in which the partitionist position is reiterated, have their foundation in the work of earlier scholars. See Ian Adamson, *The Identity of Ulster: The Land, the Language and the People* (Belfast, 1982) and D. G. Pringle, *One Island, Two Nations: A Political Geographical Analysis of the National Conflict in Ireland* (Letchworth, 1985) and 'Diversity, Asymmetry and the Quest for Consensus', *Political Geography*, 17, 2 (1998), 231–37.

9 Under the umbrella of geography were also sheltered a regional study of 'folklife', archaeology and a nascent Ulster anthropology.

10 This meeting is referred to by Evans's widow, Gwyneth Evans, in 'Estyn: A Biographical Memoir', in E. Estyn Evans, *Ireland and the Atlantic Heritage: Selected Writings* (Dublin, 1996), 5, and by Matthew Stout in 'Emyr Estyn Evans and Northern Ireland: The Archaeology and Geography of a New State', in John A. Atkinson, Ian Banks and Jerry O'Sullivan, eds., *Nationalism and Archaeology* (Glasgow, 1996), 111–26.

11 Gwyneth Evans published a strong refutation of Stout's suggestion that Evans received 'tutelage' on the North of Ireland from Jones. See her 'Emyr Estyn Evans and Northern Ireland', *Ulster Journal of Archaeology*, 58 (1999), 134–42. Interestingly, however, she remembers Jones being a frequent visitor to her family home as she was growing up in Wales.

12 D. A. Chart, *A History of Northern Ireland* (Belfast, 1928), 1: 'In an old country such as Ulster there are few neighbourhoods that do not possess some actual relic of antiquity', and 'as Ulster is largely an industrial country, a section has been devoted to that aspect of its history'.

13 Editorial, *The Ulster Review*, 2, 8 (Jan. 1926), 337

14 G. K. Chesterton, *Irish Impressions* (London, 1919), 26

15 See Heslinga, *Irish Border as a Cultural Divide*, 36.

16 MacDonagh, *States of Mind*, 26

17 J. Logan, *Ulster in the X-Rays* (Belfast and London, 1924); Ernest W. Hamilton, *The Soul of Ulster*, (New York, 1917). Some other books of this type include: C. J. C. Street, *Ireland in 1921* (London, 1922); H. S. Morrison, *Modern Ulster, Its Character, Customs, Politics and Industries* (London, 1920); F. H. Crawford, *Why I Voted for the Six Counties* (Belfast, 1920); R. McNeill, *Ulster's Stand for Union* (London, 1922); Cyril Falls, *The History of the 36th (Ulster) Division* (London, 1922) and *The Birth of Ulster* (London, 1936); Henry Maxwell, *Ulster was Right* (London, 1924); D. J. Owen, *History of Belfast* (Belfast, 1921); H. C. Lawlor, *Ulster: Its Archaeology and Antiquities* (Belfast, 1928).

régime, exhibits several features shared by many publications similarly devoted to the naturalization of the partition of Ireland: the deployment of 'history' to legitimize the new state, a refusal to analyse too closely contemporary or recent political events and a whig-unionist narrative with its inescapable culmination in the present.

It is significant that even in the late 1920s, when a majority of the inhabitants of the new state believed the border would be permanent, they could not fix on a name for the area defined by it. That situation, of course, has not changed in the intervening years. The 'Six Counties' are not quite identical with 'Ulster'. Although many unionists were keen to jettison any 'Irish' connotations altogether, a movement to have the name 'Northern Ireland' officially changed to 'Ulster' was not successful.[15] Oliver MacDonagh has stated perceptively that 'the Treaty of 1922 had rendered the Northern unionist view of place more instead of less ambivalent'. Partition, rather than reflecting an already existing Irish *mentalité*, as later historians (Beckett, Stewart and F. S. L. Lyons) would have it, had created a confused, more divided new one:

> The very decision of 1921, confirmed in 1925, created in its turn a new mental geography. Once painted a different colour on the map Northern Ireland became a pictorial entity in men's minds, with fresh claims and counter-claims about territoriality. This reinforced the real internal separation of both the Irish Protestant and the Irish Catholic communities, when they were divided by the two states, and henceforth carried along, to a degree, in the streams of two separate 'national' histories ... What Northern Unionists usually mean by 'place' and 'people' is Protestant Ulster. Yet — apart from anodyne 'Northern Ireland', employable for official purposes — what alternative do they have to 'Ulster'? One cannot very well write 'Protestant Supremacy' on a map.[16]

Chart's *History of Northern Ireland* was neither the first nor the last of its kind. Books with titles such as *Ulster in the X-Rays* and *The Soul of Ulster* had proliferated in the years after 1912 (the year of Ulster's Solemn League and Covenant), and especially through the 1920s and 1930s.[17] These books form a miniature genre that achieved its highest definition in Stewart's *The Narrow Ground*.[18] Stewart's book did with more authority and style what the earlier texts had attempted to do — it 'explained' the contemporary Northern crisis by showing it to be integral to Ulster's long history, a history that was interwoven with elements of archaeology and geography. It was part of a sustained effort to create a unionist and partitionist hegemony.

Partition was, amongst other things, an attempt to reshape Irish space. And if, in Foucauldian terms, space is always a container of social power, then 'the reorganization of space is always a reorganization of the framework through which social power is expressed'.[19] The spatial structure of cultural partitionism was that of the region, a concept capacious enough to embrace both the recalcitrance and the political contingency of Ulster unionism. Irish geographical initiatives — the triangulation, the surveying and the mapping of the country — are central to the history of Irish colonization. Geographers T. J. Hughes and J. H. Andrews have told, in fastidiously impartial language, the story of the nineteenth-century Ordnance Survey of Ireland and Sir Richard Griffith's *General Valuation of Rateable Tenements* (1848–64); but what of the equally-militarized, more recent geography of partition?[20]

The *géographie humaine* of Evans, who imported an innovative emphasis on the *longue durée* from the French *annalistes*, provided a comfortably neutral landscape for liberal unionism. His work avoided overtly political issues. *Les événements*, including what Evans called 'the controversial realms of religion and politics', were replaced by a concentration on primarily rural material culture.[21] His style was charming, elegiac, generalized; his maps were crude. In Evans's work, history became 'heritage', and the folk-objects and practices he traced — 'plough and spade', 'hearth and home', 'turf and slane' — were constructed as museum objects or as dying arts in a curiously unpeopled landscape.[22] Irishness, in the work of Evans, became a set of innocuous rural practices whose time was past.

There were important differences between Evans's interest in 'Irish folkways' and the work being done on the other side of the border in the 1930s and 1940s to present the living voices of Irish speakers. No figure comparable to Peig Sayers appeared in Evans's landscapes. His generalized, more 'scientific' and abstract approach contrasted sharply with the extensive, detailed, voluminous, nationally conscious work carried out, after 1935, by the Irish Folklore Commission (IFC).[23] There were clear differences between the work of the IFC, chaired by Antrim-born James Hamilton Delargy, and Evans's concentration on 'folklife' studies. These differences tended to emphasize, once again, 'Ulster's' separateness from the rest of the island, but also to distance Ulster's 'folklife' (material culture and practice) from the Free State's 'folklore' (oral tradition). Delargy, a cultural nationalist, was firmly convinced of a line of continuity between Gaelic, pre-colonial folk culture and that of contemporary Ireland, something which Evans's folklife studies did not acknowledge.[24]

Stormont facilitated Evans's folklife studies just as various southern governments funded and promoted Delargy's work. When the southern Department of Education invited the Northern Ireland Education Ministry to participate in a schools' folklore collection project in 1937, it declined, only to support a similar project in the 1950s, covering the six counties alone.[25] Evans chaired the Committee on Ulster Folklife and Traditions (CUFT), set up in 1955, and one of his students, R. H. Buchanan, edited its journal, *Ulster Folklife*. Stormont financed the work of this committee and, steered by Evans, in consultation with Terence O'Neill, it culminated in the foundation of the Ulster Folk Museum at Cultra in 1958 under the directorship of G. B. Thompson, another of Evans's students.[26]

Ulster Folklife, the journal founded by the CUFT, was supposed to cover the whole of nine-county Ulster, and yet the very first number includes declarations of purpose such as 'The collection of the oral traditions of the people of the six counties of Northern Ireland is a work of great importance' and 'We are attempting to record and study the folklife of Northern Ireland as a whole.'[27] Furthermore, the journal did not make a clear distinction between material 'folklife' studies and oral 'folklore', suggesting the possibility that Evans, while interested in the southern effort, may have wanted to create an appearance of difference between the *practice* of northern and southern folklore studies when none in fact existed. It was in the area of *ideology* that the differences were clear. A comparison of *Ulster Folklife*, and its older southern counterpart *Béaloideas* (founded in 1927, with most of its early articles in Irish) reveals the very different approach to folklife/lore adopted by Evans's committee, which is notably regionalist, and lacks the strong sense of a Gaelic national identity that governs Delargy's work.

By 1948, Evans's geography department at QUB was the largest in Britain and Ireland. He left a lasting impression on the cultural map of Belfast and the North, having been involved in, among many other things, the founding of the Northern Ireland Tourist Board (1948), the Ulster Folk and Transport Museum at Cultra (1958), the Institute of Irish Studies at Queen's (1968), and the

18 Also important here is F. S. L. Lyons, 'Ulster: The Roots of Difference', in *Culture and Anarchy in Modern Ireland 1890–1939* (Oxford, 1979), 113–45.

19 David Harvey, *The Condition of Postmodernity: An Enquiry into the Origins of Cultural Change* (Oxford, 1989), 255

20 See J. H. Andrews, *A Paper Landscape: The Ordnance Survey in Nineteenth-Century Ireland* (Oxford, 1979). T. J. Hughes, whose scholarly reputation rested on a lifetime's work on Griffith's Valuation, never published a book, but produced many articles. A list of these can be found in W. J. Smyth and Kevin Whelan, eds., *Common Ground: Essays on the Historical Geography of Ireland*, (Cork, 1988), 320–23.

21 E. Estyn Evans, *Irish Heritage: The Landscape, the People and their Work* (Dundalk, 1942), 2

22 E. Estyn Evans, *Irish Folk Ways* (London, 1957)

23 In 1927, the Folklore of Ireland Society (An Cumann le Béaloideas Éireann) was founded in Dublin; in 1935, it was streamlined and professionalized into the Irish Folklore Commission (Coimisiún Béaloideasa Éireann) and continued the systematic collection, preservation, classification and study of Irish folklore until 1971.

24 Diarmuid Ó Giolláin, *Locating Irish Folklore: Tradition, Modernity, Identity* (Cork, 2000), 61–62, discusses the differences between folklife and folklore.

25 Ó Giolláin, *Locating Irish Folklore*, 134

26 Writing in 1970 of Evans's role in the creation of the Museum, Thompson tried — rather desperately — to place the museum in a wider cultural and political context: 'I have come to see the folk museum's likely role as generally relating to the absence of cultural identity in Ulster. Underlying the superficial complexities of the Ulster situation is the fact that by virtue of its chequered history Ulster has become a community in which political and religious identity supercedes cultural identity. The abnormal prominence of religion and politics, and the extent to which they are intertwined in Ulster, have stifled the natural emergence of any sense of regional cultural personality. Indeed, one might be tempted to conclude that no such personality exists now or ever existed in the past.' Perhaps sensing a mood of intemperateness here, Thompson goes on to say, 'I do not feel, however, that this is a theory to which Estyn Evans would subscribe.' See G. B. Thompson, 'Estyn Evans and the Development of the Ulster Folk Museum', *Ulster Folklife*, 15, 16 (1970), 236. The Ulster Folk Museum merged with the Ulster Transport Museum in 1967.

27 *Ulster Folklife*, 1, 1 (1955), 5, 7

28 Maurice Hayes, *Minority Verdict: Experiences of a Catholic Public Servant* (Belfast, 1995), 89

Ulster-American Folk Park at Omagh (1976), as well as in various government rural and urban planning committees. Though he played a vital role in the rural theme-parking of the province, Evans left a lighter impression on Belfast's urban landscape than he might have wished. Former civil servant Maurice Hayes, for instance, recalls Evans's involvement in the work of the Community Relations Commission in Belfast in the troubled late 1960s:

In this seminal stage, we were very much guided by Estyn Evans, the father figure of social geography and regional planning, who had written sensitively and perceptively about identity, tradition and folk culture. He rather shocked me by prescribing the use of bulldozers which would start at Castle Junction and flatten the segment of Belfast including the Shankill and Falls Roads; the area would subsequently be planted as an urban forest park which would effectively separate warring factions. We never got far enough into the discussion to find out what was to be done with the people so displaced.[28]

Evans's plan to transform the problematic sectarian landscape of west Belfast into a 'peace park' was characteristic of his career-long refusal to combine political and historical analysis with human geography. It was also characteristically deterministic: change the landscape and the ghetto-dwellers will change with it.

Evans's 'Ulster' was ultimately conceived as a sectarian landscape in which the land itself had somehow shaped the politics of division. In a lecture delivered in 1971, the year in which internment was introduced, Evans paraded sectarian division as indicative of 'diversity' and a kind of equilibrium:

Diversity is revealed of course in many other different ways; it is reflected often in different religious affiliations; the most fertile areas of fat drumlins have usually been occupied by newcomers. In Ulster where you find the drumlins you will hear the drums, for the Protestant planters usually *chose* the most fertile lowland areas, and I suspect that people living in such closed-in lowlands with restricted horizons tend to have a limited vision and

Photograph: Charles Hewitt/
Picture Post/Getty Images.

imagination. I always like to contrast that kind of hidden landscape — Protestant landscape, shall I say? — with the open, naked bogs and hills which are naturally areas of vision and imagination, which are poetic and visionary and which represent the other tradition in Ulster.[29]

This is an 'Ulster' regionalist redaction of Arnoldian stereotypes in which, it appears, the *longue durée* extends only as far back as the plantations. Evans's landscape replicates the religious and cultural divisions so necessary to the reproduction of partition.[30] As Matthew Stout points out, 'the unacceptable language of environmental determinism is heard in this grossly oversimplified explanation of divisions within Ireland'.[31] Stewart Parker parodied just such an approach (also a key element in Helsinga's work) in his play *Lost Belongings*, in which an Orangeman recites the geology of partition:

The bedrock of Ulster is just a continuation of the bedrock of Scotland. The rocks stretching across under the sea

... Now, along the southern edge of the Ulster bedrock there's what they call a fault. South of that fault there's an entirely disconnected type of a bedrock altogether. That's the foundations of the Free State. So the two parts of this island, you see, are different and separate right down in their very bones. You can't join together what God has set apart. We've got British rocks under the very soil of this province.[32]

This geologized environmental determinism, whereby the 'separateness' of Northern Ireland is both produced by and reflected in its physical features, is also present in the drafting of a regional Ulster archaeology. During the late 1930s and early 1940s, Evans conducted a series of digs along the northern side of the border with Oliver Davies, a friend and colleague at QUB. Davies and Evans had embarked on their excavations in 1932 in response to a characteristically partitionist suggestion by Sir Arthur Keith at the British Association meeting of 1928, that the ancient monuments of the North of Ireland differed

29 E. Estyn Evans, *Ulster: The Common Ground* (Mullingar, 1988), 7. Lecture first delivered in 1971, my italics. John Wilson Foster has more recently used this formula (i.e. that sectarianism is one kind of diversity) in his 'Radical Regionalism', *The Irish Review*, 7 (Autumn 1989), 1–15.

30 For an opposing view to that of Stout on the work of Evans, see Virginia Crossman and Dympna McLoughlin, 'A Peculiar Eclipse: E. Estyn Evans and Irish Studies', *The Irish Review*, 15 (Spring, 1994), 79–96. The most sustained and sophisticated account of Evans's career is Brian Graham, 'The Search for the Common Ground: Estyn Evans's Ireland', *Transactions of the Institute of British Geographers*, New Series, 19, 2 (1994), 183–201.

31 Stout, 'Emyr Estyn Evans and Northern Ireland', 120

32 Stewart Parker, *Lost Belongings* (London, 1987), 50

Photograph: Charles Hewitt/ Picture Post/Getty Images.

33 Evans and Davies assumed the editorship of *The Ulster Journal of Archaeology* in 1938. They immediately altered its cover logo from the seal of Hugh O'Neill to the state emblem of Northern Ireland, the red hand of Ulster surmounted by a crown. See Stout, 'Emyr Estyn Evans and Northern Ireland'.

34 See *A Preliminary Survey of the Ancient Monuments of Northern Ireland* (Belfast, 1940).

35 Oliver Davies left QUB for South Africa in 1945.

36 See E. Estyn Evans, 'Disputing with de Valera', in *Ireland and the Atlantic Heritage*, 210–15.

37 See Marcus Heslinga, *Geography and Nationality. The Estyn Evans Lecture no. 2* (Belfast, 1978), 22: 'It was professor Evans who in the late summer of 1959, guided my first steps through the North of Ireland'.

38 E. Estyn Evans, Foreword to Heslinga, *Irish Border as a Cultural Divide*, i, ii

substantially from those of the South. Predictably, the tendency of Davies's and Evans's 'scientific' conclusions tended to emphasize Ulster's archaeological difference from the rest of Ireland, and its links to other 'British' regions. The absurdity, from an archaeological perspective, of siting digs according to a line on a map drawn only a few years earlier to demarcate a local power-base is blatant. But the border marked the edge of the new political entity, and what was being exhumed was a 'state' archaeology.[33]

Evans and Davies also collaborated on the large survey of *The Ancient Monuments of Northern Ireland*, overseen by the government-financed Ancient Monuments Advisory Council for Northern Ireland.[34] This survey, directed by Chart, echoed in style and scale the rhetoric of nineteenth-century colonial-antiquarianism.[35] The non-political politics of the Evans–Davies collaboration re-emerged in the 1960s, when their thesis on 'horned-cairn tombs' in Ulster was questioned by de Valera's son, Ruaidhri — Evans misspelled it 'Rory' — a Professor of Archaeology at University College, Dublin. Evans and Davies, unsurprisingly, had argued that the tombs were an importation from Scotland (and were therefore implicitly 'British'). De Valera argued that the diffusion across Ireland of what he renamed 'court cairns' was from west to east. The politics of this debate are clear.[36]

Equally clear is the tactic Evans adopted in his foreword to Heslinga's *The Irish Border as a Cultural Divide*.[37] It is a simple and well-tested approach, that always begins with a disingenuous affectation of scholarly disengagement from partisan politics; '"the border",' he claims, denying and asserting its reality by the use of the scare quotation marks, 'is such a lively political issue that our motives would be suspect, on one side or the other, and probably both, if we were to concentrate our attention on it. Any

student who approaches the subject must pick his way delicately through the hard spikes of political prejudice.' By guiding Heslinga's 'first steps through the North of Ireland' in the late summer of 1959, Evans had helped him 'pick his way' and praises him for having 'pursued it with a high degree of objectivity'. The conclusion is that partition is, or appears to be, a natural not a political condition of the landscape: 'Dr Heslinga sees both sections of the Irish border, land and sea, as in the last resort, religious frontiers.'[38]

Heslinga combines a human-geographical definition of regionalism (the idea of regionally based imagined communities) and a physical-geographical emphasis on, for instance, similarities between the geological structures of north-east Ulster and the west of Scotland to reinforce the notion that the history of Ulster since the twelfth century is an example of a political divergence that is founded on inescapable natural differences. This was the most effective declaration of the two nations theory, and its strategic geographical remit, in which the central unit is the 'British Isles.' Irish unionists have embraced this thesis, and Irish nationalists have ignored it. Its ideological importance has always been enhanced by its claim to be a 'detached' account by an impartial foreign observer. Heslinga's book is a bible of regionalism; Northern Ireland is the political realization of objective, natural conditions for which geography and archaeology provide the scientific evidence.

Historical revisionism is the movement that derives from this view. The first issue of the revisionist journal, *Irish Historical Studies*, edited (from Belfast) by T. W. Moody and (from Dublin) by R. Dudley Edwards, appeared in 1938. The policy of *Irish Historical Studies*, to exclude subjects post-1900, operated as a fire-gap, ensuring that recent political events in Ireland (an IRA bombing campaign in Britain, de Valera's republican constitution, sectarian riots in

Belfast) were kept at a distance. Proximity would have lent disenchantment to the view that sought to make 'distance' a requirement for wisdom. This effectively garbled the differences between distance, so understood, and objectivity.

Belfast-born Moody was, from the mid-thirties until his departure for Trinity College Dublin in 1939, in charge of Irish history at QUB. He had returned from a stint at the Institute of Historical Research in London with Herbert Butterfield's rejection of the whig interpretation of history as a new weapon he would deploy to reinforce unionist rebuttals of nationalist claims on Ulster.[39] The work of Moody, whose massive history of the plantation of Derry was published in 1939, ushered in a new era in the historiography of Ulster. It also paved the way for a new generation of northern historians emanating (via the Belfast Royal Academical Institution, or 'Inst') from QUB — Beckett, D. B. Quinn, R. B. McDowell and later the more maverick figure of Stewart, all of them ready alternatively to use Butterfield's anti-whig polemic to attack nationalism or to abandon it to defend unionism.[40]

In the mid-1950s, Moody, Beckett, and the Northern Ireland Home Service of the BBC combined forces to broadcast a series of lectures on Ulster history, later published in two books of essays. These books offer a history of the province since the Act of Union. The first volume opens with a map: 'The Province of Ulster (Northern Ireland Shaded)'. The whig-loyalist teleology of that map, which inscribes the relatively recently-invented border onto a century and a half of provincial history, also manifests itself in the lectures.[41] These essays epitomize the partitionist bias of revisionist historiography.[42] In the heyday of Ulster unionism, however, these collections affirmed as history the myth of the always-and-ever separateness of Ulster. Not one of the essays questioned the legitimacy of the

border, or even addressed the ongoing debate over the issue. The discrete history of Ulster was read as a *fait accompli* to be examined and understood, not as part of an unending political crisis.

Sam Hanna Bell, in a 1951 essay on culture in Ulster, gave what at one level is a perfect description of the self-styled revisionist project:

> Our history, for historical reasons, is still warm from the hands of zealots. And here, I should like to believe, a new element enters. During the past few years a number of Ulster historians have been reassessing, and, indeed, so far as the layman is concerned, discovering the history of our country and our people. T. W. Moody, Cyril Falls, D. B. Quinn, R. B. McDowell, J. C. Beckett, J. M. Mogey, E. R. R. Green and Hugh Shearman have revealed to us the calm causality behind the frenetic story. Estyn Evans, Professor of Geography at the Queen's University, Belfast, bringing an innate sympathy from Wales to our Province, has gathered into his book *Irish Heritage* the crafts, the occupations and the ingenuities of our forefathers, a book that should be on the shelf of every Ulsterman. Here, in the work of these scholars ... is our history cooled and tempered for us.[43]

The Northern, institutionally cradled, element in this 'cooling and tempering' — the 'professionalization' of Irish history which began to reveal 'the calm causality behind the frenetic story' in the 1930s — is a neglected aspect of historiographical developments in modern Ireland. Moody's writings after 1968, for instance, show that the issue of 'the North' persisted with him as a preoccupation. In his 1977 valedictory lecture on the myths of Irish history — and the necessity of demythologizing them — there is a qualitative difference in his debunking of the myth of 'the predestinate

39 See Brendan Bradshaw, 'Nationalism and Historical Scholarship in Modern Ireland', *Irish Historical Studies*, 26, 104 (Nov. 1989), 328–51.

40 For the regionalism of Moody's *The Londonderry Plantation, 1609–41* (Belfast, 1939), see Raymond Gillespie, 'Historical Revisit', *Irish Historical Studies*, 29, 113 (May 1994), 110–11.

41 See *Ulster Since 1800: A Political and Economic Survey* (London, 1954) and *Ulster Since 1800: A Social Survey* (London, 1957), both edited by T. W. Moody and J. C. Beckett. The two collections include pieces by Beckett, Moody, Lyons, McDowell, Evans and others.

42 The later work of F. S. L. Lyons on Ulster was similarly governed by a 'two nations' approach, though far less politically complacent. See Lyons, 'Ulster: the Roots of Difference', 113–45.

43 Sam Hanna Bell, 'A Banderol: An Introduction', in Sam Hanna Bell, Nesca A. Robb and John Hewitt, eds., *The Arts in Ulster: A Symposium* (London, 1951), 17–18. This collection of essays was produced as part of the Festival of Britain celebrations.

nation' and that of 'Orangeism'. Moody describes Orangeism as 'a rich and many-sided mythology', a 'great popular force in Irish society ... down to our own day', whose 'distinctive role was that of upholding the union as the best safeguard of protestant interests in Ireland'. Echoing the language of late nineteenth-century Ulster unionism, Moody writes that the strength of Orangeism 'lay in Ulster, where protestants constituted half the population and in economic power were immeasurably superior to the other half. Industrial revolution, pioneered and sustained by protestant initiative and protestant capital, added a new dimension to the distinctiveness of the north-east from the rest of Ireland.'[44] A far more straightforward — and longer — attack on the mythology of the Provisional IRA follows. 'This myth,' wrote Moody, 'identifies the democratic Irish nation of the nineteenth century with pre-conquest Ireland, incorporates the concept of a seven (now an eight) centuries' struggle with England as the central theme of Irish history, and sees the achievement of independence in 1922 as the partial fulfillment of a destiny that requires the extinction of British authority in Northern Ireland to complete itself.'[45] Moody's politics, kept in abeyance in his early, archive-based work, came increasingly to the fore towards the end of his career, particularly when he wrote on contemporary Ulster.[46]

As already noted, Stewart's *The Narrow Ground* constituted a culminatory moment in the project to naturalize partition. Stewart sought to unearth the deep structures of Ulster's history, to trace what he called 'the shape of the past' as opposed to mere 'surface details'. This adoption of the rhetoric, if not the practice, of the French *annalistes* was a key innovation for those historians, geographers and archaeologists involved in the cultural reinforcement of partition. Stewart's 'shape

of the past' roughly corresponded to the *longue durée*, at least as far back as the Ulster plantations, and his dismissal of mere 'surface details', or *les événements*, enabled a shifting of the discursive territory away from the last fifty years, and especially away from the previous decade of violence in the North. Hence, Stewart sought to elaborate the unchanging patterns of Northern society, thereby showing that events since the late 1960s and early 1970s were not the result of the failure of the state, but were simply in keeping with a much older historical paradigm. His conclusion was that 'it' had always been thus; 'Whatever the "Ulster Question" is in Irish history, it is not the question of partition.'[47] The historical narrative of the north of Ireland, on the contrary, 'amounts to ... the delineation of patterns which cannot be changed or broken by any of the means now being employed to "solve" the Ulster question.' 'Neither pressure from London,' Stewart warned in 1977, 'nor pressure from Dublin, can alter them.'[48] Thus the strange historical narrative of 'Northern Ireland' is put firmly beyond the reach of contemporary interventions, and the maintenance of the *status quo* defended as a permanent and desirable goal.

Perhaps the most tendentious conclusion reached in *The Narrow Ground* is that the disarming of the police in the sixties was the reason for the return to what Stewart calls 'the inherited folk-memory of what had been done in the past.'[49] The disarming was 'in itself a profound shock to *society*,' he claims. As a consequence, 'the state had lost the capacity to safeguard life and property, and, stripped of that protection, the civil population turned instinctively to the only source of wisdom applicable to such circumstances'.[50] That is to say, for as long as the police remained in control, 'the monsters which inhabited the depths of the community's unconscious mind' were kept in abeyance; as soon as Westminster took away RUC guns (and disbanded the B-

44 T. W. Moody, 'Irish History and Irish Mythology', in Ciarán Brady, ed., *Interpreting Irish History: The Debate on Irish Historical Revisionism 1938–1994* (Dublin, 1994), 77–78

45 Moody, 'Irish History and Irish Mythology', 84

46 See T. W. Moody, *The Ulster Question, 1603–1973* (Dublin and Cork, 1974).

47 Stewart, *Narrow Ground*, 157

48 Stewart, *Narrow Ground*, 185

49 In 1969 the RUC was disarmed, and its notorious B-Specials disbanded, as a result of the Hunt Report.

50 Stewart, *Narrow Ground*, 184–85, italics added.

51 Stewart, *Narrow Ground*, 16

52 Quoted in Tom Paulin, *Ireland and the English Crisis* (Newcastle-upon-Tyne, 1984), 155

53 Stewart, *Narrow Ground*, 17

Specials) those monsters were let loose on the streets of Belfast and Derry.[51] The almost explicit claim here is that only when the established élite in Northern Ireland is wholly in control of 'law and order' will the re-emerging patterns of sectarian violence be contained. Thus, Stewart claims that it is the dissolution of 'Northern Ireland' that will release sectarian violence. The clear political bias of such a belief governs Stewart's treatment of Catholics in the North between 1920 and 1969 and fails or refuses to address their belief that sectarian violence was made institutional by the creation of Northern Ireland. 'Brothers and sisters in Christ,' advised the Reverend Ian Paisley after he had read it, and much to Stewart's chagrin, 'here is a great book that tells the Truth about Ulster. Go home, friend, and read it.'[52] Stewart's book has rarely been out of print since its publication in 1977.

The real problem with Stewart's historical method is that it underplays the organizational and ideological structures which have maintained the forms or conventions of 'Irish disorder'. Notwithstanding his professed concern with deep structure and its inevitabilities, Stewart is paradoxically engrossed by the contingent features of local violence, such as urban streetscapes and rioting techniques.

Although they were enacted on the same streets, he claims, there were clearly different reasons for the riots of 1886 in Belfast and those of 1921–22, 1935, 1969, or 1972. But by grouping these instances into a general 'pattern', he makes the specific problems induced by fifty years of Stormont rule disappear. Invocation of the seventeenth century to explain the present difficulties of a modern state, on one level perfectly legitimate, is on another little more than a decoy. For Stewart and other unionist historians of the North, the past is not so much a foreign country as a place which bears an uncanny resemblance to 'Northern Ireland' itself. Ultimately, Ulster's violence must be seen as another, and legitimating proof, of Ulster's difference from the rest of Ireland. The Hidden Border, long-concealed, becomes visible to the historian, who 'like the aerial archaeologist ... may glimpse the distinctive patterns of the past below the surface'.[53] The 'distinctive patterns' reveal Ulster's difference; they coalesce in one line, the border. But now that it has been so seriously challenged, it can scarcely again rely on the arguments that attempt to assert its inescapable inevitability. In the case of 'Northern Ireland', there appears to be less 'there' there than we were led to believe. ■

Photographs: Charles Hewitt. At 6.15 pm on Friday 14 December 1956, a 'person unknown' crossed the border into county Monaghan and fired six .303 rifle bullets into the Clones Customs Post. The unidentified gunman was presumed to be a unionist, protesting against a series of gun and bomb attacks by the IRA and the breakaway republican group Saor Uladh. Later that night, the IRA attacked an RUC barracks in Lisnaskea, county Fermanagh, injuring a policeman. The photographs show the damaged window in the Clones Customs Post and the RUC preparing to start a patrol in front of the battered barracks in Lisnaskea; also shown is RUC Head Constable Leslie Singer questioning an unidentified suspect after the Lisnaskea attack. See Gavin Lyall, 'Assassins on Britain's Border', *Picture Post*, 31 Dec. 1956.

Michael Scott's Busáras, Dublin's central bus station, 1955.
Photograph: Bert Hardy/Picture Post/Getty Images.

Ireland in the 1940s and 1950s
The Photographs of Bert Hardy

Sarah Smith

A working-class Londoner, Bert Hardy (1913–95) taught himself photography while working as an assistant in a photographic agency.

1   See Bert Hardy, *My Life* (London, 1985); also, see Tom Hopkinson, *Bert Hardy: Photojournalist* (London, 1975) and Robert Kee, ed., *The* Picture Post *Album: A Fiftieth Anniversary Collection* (London, 1989).

2   In 1950 the publication of Hardy's photographs of the torture of political prisoners in South Korea (with accompanying text by James Cameron) led to the firing of Tom Hopkinson, editor of *Picture Post*, who carried them against the instructions of Edward G. Hulton, the magazine's owner.

3   See A. L. Lloyd [and Bert Hardy], 'The Forgotten Gorbals', *Picture Post*, 31 Jan. 1948, and 'Life in the Elephant', *Picture Post*, 8 Jan. 1949. The Cardiff images are reproduced in Glenn Jordan, *'Down the Bay'*: Picture Post, *Humanist Photography and Images of 1950s Cardiff* (Cardiff, 2001); the journalist and historian Robert Kee wrote one of the original articles on Cardiff.

4   A. L. Lloyd [and Bert Hardy], 'Eire Takes Hobson's Choice', *Picture Post*, 21 Feb. 1948; Brian Dowling [and Bert Hardy], 'Ireland's National Drink', *Picture Post*, 22 Aug. 1953; Woodrow Wyatt [and Bert Hardy], 'One Man in Five is Out of Work', *Picture Post*, 17 Dec. 1955

Experimenting with improvised backlighting, he developed a dramatic style of portraiture and a reputation for atmospheric but unsentimental representations of the everyday lives of working-class people. In 1940 he accepted an appointment with *Picture Post*, a popular Left-leaning weekly which, along with *Life Magazine* in the US, set new standards for photo-journalism in the mid-twentieth century; he became the magazine's chief photographer, his work regularly seen by hundreds of thousands of *Picture Post* readers. His images of life in the cratered streets and dimly lit air-raid shelters of London during the Blitz have come to define memory of the 'home-front'. Called up in 1942, he worked in an army photographic unit and covered the D-Day landings, the Liberation of Paris and the Allies crossing the Rhine. He was one of the first Allied photographers to enter the Nazi concentration camp at Bergen-Belsen.[1] After he returned to civilian life, Hardy occasionally worked as a war photographer, taking assignments in Korea and Vietnam.[2] But Hardy's main interest from the late 1940s until *Picture Post* folded in 1957 was recording a period of rapid change in British working-class communities. He photographed the Cockney wide boys, working girls and horse-dealers of the Elephant and Castle district of London, West Indian immigrants in the Tiger Bay area of Cardiff's docklands and the Irish of the decaying 'closes' of Glasgow's Gorbals.[3]

Hardy completed three major assignments for *Picture Post* in Ireland in these years, providing photographs for an article on the general election in 1948, the Guinness brewery in 1953 and unemployment in the North in 1955. The articles accompanying the photographs are light. The item on Guinness's brewery, by Brian Dowling, is little more than a puff-piece for 'Ireland's National Drink', while those on the general election and on northern unemployment display little understanding of Irish society or politics. The author of the election article was A. L. Lloyd, a pioneer of the British folk music revival and frequent collaborator of Hardy's, and the piece on unemployment was by Woodrow Wyatt, then a left-wing journalist, later a fiery Labour MP and later still, as Lord Wyatt of Weeford, a confidant of Margaret Thatcher.[4] But Hardy's photos provide a compelling visual narrative of Ireland in the 1940s and 1950s that is at once familiar and surprising. Alongside despondency and poverty — visible in the pinched faces of the unemployed and, to a lesser extent, in the dreariness of midland towns and villages — there are flashes of energy and self-confidence — notably in the modernist architecture of Michael Scott's Busáras and the political fervour of the 1948 election, when the emergence of Clann na Poblachta, a new radical party, raised the possibility of a change of government for the first time in sixteen years.

Citizens of Ballaghaderreen, county Roscommon, marching out to meet Fianna Fáil leader
Eamon de Valera during the 1948 general election campaign; they are carrying a banner
depicting the nineteenth-century Land League leader Michael Davitt.

Photograph: Bert Hardy/Picture Post/Getty Images.

An elderly participant in the march.
Photograph: Bert Hardy/Picture Post/Getty Images.

Ballaghaderreen, county Roscommon: Fianna Fáil supporters listening to de Valera.
Photograph: Bert Hardy/Picture Post/Getty Images.

Preparing to meet de Valera at a Roscommon crossroads; see also inside front cover.
Photograph: Bert Hardy/Picture Post/Getty Images.

Fianna Fáil supporters in the Dublin Northeast constituency, 1948; the constituency
returned Oscar Traynor and Henry Colley for Fianna Fáil, Peadar Cowan for Clann
na Poblachta, John Belton for Fine Gael and the Independent Alfie Byrne. The
defeated candidates, whose names appear on the banner in the background, were
Eugene Timmons and John Phelan of Fianna Fáil.

Photograph: Bert Hardy/Picture Post/Getty Images.

Seán MacBride (centre), founder of Clann na Poblachta, at an election rally in
Dublin; his party won ten Dáil seats in the 1948 election.
Photograph: Bert Hardy/Picture Post/Getty Images.

Above: Innisheer, Aran Islands. Original caption: 'The scene at the polling station.
In a schoolhouse corridor the islanders of Innisheer wait their turn to vote. A poster
gives instructions for filling in the complicated Irish voting forms.'
Opposite: a woman casts her ballot.

Photographs: Bert Hardy/Picture Post/Getty Images.

A worker at the Guinness brewery at Saint James's Gate,
Dublin, taking a rest after cleaning out a kieve, 1953.
Photograph: Bert Hardy/Picture Post/Getty Images.

Architect Michael Scott, designer of Busáras, at work
in his office in Merrion Square, Dublin, 1955.
Photograph: Bert Hardy/Picture Post/Getty Images.

Derry, 1955. Hardy took several photographs of Willie Cullen, Orchard Street, Derry, one of which was the lead-image in Woodrow Wyatt's *Picture Post* article, 'One Man in Five is Out of Work'; the caption gave the following details: 'A man without work. Willie Cullen, 36. Accommodation: two miserable rooms. Dependents: four. Last job: labouring, six years ago.' See also front cover. Photograph: Bert Hardy/Magee Community Collection/University of Ulster.

Springtown. Derry Corporation housed families in the Nissan huts of
this former US navy base at the end of World War II; by the mid-1950s,
Springtown had over 2,000 inhabitants.
Photograph: Bert Hardy/Magee Community Collection/University of Ulster.

Dan Hegarty in Rose Griffin's Inishowen Bar, Rossville Street, Derry.
Photograph: Bert Hardy/Magee Community Collection/University of Ulster.

Playing on wasteland behind Nailor's Row, Derry.
Photograph: Bert Hardy/Magee Community Collection/University of Ulster.

Street-scene, Derry.
Photograph: Bert Hardy/Magee Community Collection/University of Ulster.

Barrack Street, Derry. *Picture Post*: 'Six years of standing about lie behind Francis Bradley.
It has been broken by one short period of employment — in England.'
Photograph: Bert Hardy/Magee Community Collection/University of Ulster.

Unemployed men at the corner of Barrack Street and Bishop Street, close to the Labour Exchange.
Photograph: Bert Hardy/Magee Community Collection/University of Ulster.

Lecky Road, Derry.
Photograph: Bert Hardy/Magee Community Collection/University of Ulster.

Applicants undergoing means tests for an allowance from the National Assistance Board, Derry.
Photographs: Bert Hardy/Magee Community Collection/University of Ulster.

A meeting of the Derry branch of the Unemployed Association. The original caption of the image on the bottom left reads, 'Hands willing to work are raised at a meeting of the Unemployed Association, which makes common cause of their plight — but petitioning for work creates no jobs.' An RUC man can be seen observing proceedings from the back of the hall. Photographs: Bert Hardy/Magee Community Collection/University of Ulster.

Letter from Rome
A State of Embarrassment

Conor Deane

Claretta Petacci, Benito Mussolini's last mistress, once remarked: 'It is not hard to govern Italians; it's pointless.'

It is a widely-held belief that the current Prime Minister of Italy, Silvio Berlusconi, is determined to make a fresh attempt at this pointless task, but this is not true.

Berlusconi leads a coalition made up of his own political party, Forza Italia, the anti-immigrant Northern League and the National Alliance, a party that, in its original configuration as the Movimento Sociale Italiano (MSI), had been excluded from power throughout the post-War period for its continued espousal of Fascism. Under the new and more moderate leadership of Gianfranco Fini, the National Alliance has tasted power for the first time with Berlusconi. It is certainly not a coalition of the tolerant, but this does not make it autocratic.

Since returning to power in 2001, Berlusconi has pushed through several bills that legalize the graft that he and his business associates have committed, or else that transform what had been criminal offences into technical misdemeanours. In December 2003, he attempted to enact a wide-ranging bill that is so blatantly favourable to his own extensive media interests that President Carlo Azeglio Ciampi, who usually avoids controversy, refused to ratify it. Berlusconi has also devoted a lot of energy to excluding critics from the state broadcasting company, Radiotelevisione Italiana (RAI). Foreign journalists are flabbergasted at the suppression of the free press, and the ascent of the Fascists (the National Alliance) and rabid xenophobes (the Northern League). The western press is practically unanimous in its censure of Berlusconi, who dislikes them in return. He has a particularly bad relationship with that flagship of liberal dogma, *The Economist*.

Yet the belief that Berlusconi is trying to establish repressive government is misplaced. On the contrary, he is hardly interested in governing Italy at all. In this he differs quite markedly from his late political mentor, Bettino Craxi, who made a forceful and memorable attempt to do so, and managed to stay in office for a remarkably long time (from August 1983 to April 1987, with a brief hiatus in 1986). Craxi did not suffer Mussolini's (or Claretta Petacci's) fate and end up hanging from a lamppost in Milan, but he was hounded out of office and then out of the country to die in exile. Why should this have happened? After all, his partners in crime and government stayed behind and weathered the storm. His cabinet colleague Giulio Andreotti, seven times Prime Minister, has become a respected elder statesman. Craxi's protégé, Berlusconi, was elected to office by the same Italian public whose outrage at the corruption that Craxi represented had seemed so implacable. If Craxi had simply looked after his own interests instead of also trying to govern, he might not have become such a hate figure.

In conducting a campaign to diminish the powers of the judiciary and rival media organizations, Berlusconi is not showing dictatorial tendencies. He is merely fulfilling his own personal and professional ambitions. The RAI is the only serious competitor to Berlusconi's Mediaset group, and it would therefore be very surprising were he to treat it fairly. Similarly, in seeking to undermine the judiciary, Berlusconi is acting in a perfectly coherent manner. What businessman would not take the opportunity to legalize white-collar crime and legislate to destroy prosecution cases against himself, his business associates and company? Legalizing bribery and corruption is not unheard-of either; in the US it has been institutionalized under the name of lobbying. What with all the energy that he is expending on saving himself from the courts, running his companies and generally dodging the raindrops, Berlusconi has little time left to work on becoming the next Mussolini.

Berlusconi's interest in subverting the media and the judiciary has another cause: he really wants people to like him. This claim may invite scepticism from those who are suspicious of psychological profiling to explain political action but, in Berlusconi's case, it is more akin to a job description. His first profession was that of an entertainer. He started out as a crooner on cruise ships, with the current CEO of the Mediaset empire, Fedele Confalonieri, playing piano. When delivering a political speech, Berlusconi still adopts the position of a Sinatra-era singer: left hand clasping the microphone at chest-level, right arm stretched out in a histrionic gesture of feeling. At the end of 2003, Mario Apicella, a Neapolitan singer, released a new CD with fourteen new songs written by Berlusconi. To mark the Italian presidency of the European Union, Berlusconi had an album of his favourite Italian songs compiled and delivered to all the mayors in the country. Indeed, he now looks more like a crooner

than he did on the cruise ships. After the Italian presidency came to an ignominious end in December 2003, Berlusconi vanished for a month and came back with tighter skin and darker hair. When Tony and Cherie Blair chose to spend their summer holidays in 2004 in Berlusconi's Sardinian villa, built in defiance of planning law, their host appeared with a white bandana on his head. The purpose of the bandana was to cover the scars resulting from a hair transplant.

Berlusconi does not want to be booed off stage like his friend Craxi. Apart from his businesslike approach to defending his corporate interests, he is genuinely and personally offended at the accusations lodged against him. His offensive against the judiciary, one of the powers in Italy that holds the executive in check, invites two plausible interpretations. It may be deeply sinister that Berlusconi should be making such enormous legislative efforts to ensure that top office-holders such as, well, the Prime Minister, should be doubly immune from prosecution; or it may simply be that he is reacting to a sudden burst of bad manners from the magistrates who started to throw things at him while he was entertaining. From this perspective, Berlusconi is not so much gagging the judiciary as silencing a bunch of hecklers. If his audience has anything to say, they should have the decency to wait till he has finished his gig.

This is not just a flippant use of the metaphor of spectacle, because the belief that politics is spectacle is held by many Italians, the magistrates included. Although they loftily deny political motivation, Italian magistrates belong to institutionalized political movements, and judicial appointments are made on the basis of ideological affiliation.

On 12 November 2004, Ilda Boccasini, a prosecutor whose career as an anti-Mafia magistrate earned her a reputation for fearlessness and ferocity, called for an eight-year prison sentence for Berlusconi. She made her demand in the course of the closing of the prosecution case in the 'SME Trial', which began in May 2003. Very briefly, the prosecution case is that in 1985 Berlusconi and his lawyer friend, Cesare Previti, who is also a Forza Italia MP and a former minister, bribed a judge, Renato Squillante, to block the take-over of SME, a state-sector food company, by a rival businessman. One of the lines of defence used by Berlusconi, co-defendant with Previti and seven others, was that this was a 'victimless' crime (he noted, for example, that no guns were used). Boccasini, however, argued that Berlusconi's actions since the time of the offence (amongst which she included lying to the Italian public and becoming Prime Minister) did not give her any reason to mitigate the standard sentence for the corruption of a public official.

Berlusconi's defence team and political allies were shocked and incredulous. The recurrent theme of the accusations Boccasini's proposed sentence provoked in government circles was the political bias of the judiciary. The only person who took it calmly, with the weary resignation of the perpetually persecuted, was Berlusconi himself. He endures through this difficult time with the help of his friends and of his immunity from prosecution. He cannot be jailed or even arraigned unless the parliament that elected him Prime Minister can be persuaded to vote to remove his immunity from prosecution.

The tenet that a person is innocent until proven guilty is taken very seriously indeed in Italy. Judges may not refuse leave to appeal; so a defendant charged with a serious crime, a defendant who is wealthy and, especially, a defendant who belongs to both categories, will always appeal a conviction. Sometimes years can pass before the Court of Cassation (Appeals Court) re-examines the case. If the defendant is found guilty again, s/he may appeal to the Supreme Court. Often, it takes so long for the Supreme Court to get around to hearing the case that the statute of limitations may have annulled the original offence as in the 'SME Trial' that ended in December 2004. The trick is not to be remanded in custody during the lengthy interval between conviction and appeal. The Scots have the verdict of 'not proven', but Italians have a far more nuanced version. A conviction by a court of first instance makes the defendant sort-of-guilty but not quite. It depends. If the defendant is appealing, in both senses of the word, then terms such as 'guilty' and 'convicted' are considered to be in bad taste. It becomes possible to speak of guilt only when the appeals process has been thoroughly exhausted.

Berlusconi's war with the courts certainly raises serious issues of judicial independence. When he claims the judiciary is politicized, the Italian public recognizes this is essentially true. But this does not mean that the system is corrupt. In the Anglo-American system judges have the power to interpret laws with reference to individual cases; thus, there is no need in that system for a separate body to enforce the law of equity. Under the common-law system, judges are responsible for the decisions that create equity, and if this is to be acceptable to the public, they must also be assumed to be impartial and fair. Not so in Italy. The existence of a written code that attempts to cover as many specific instances as possible limits the interpretative powers of judges. As judges are not responsible for articulating what equity is, in this system their impartiality is less important. Rather, they are expected to be seen to apply the law as it already is. If the law is manifestly bad, they must apply it regardless. A bad law must be corrected by parliament, not by a wise judge. Equity, meanwhile, is supposed to be achieved by a synthesis of argument by the prosecution and the defence. Essentially, this puts the defence on the same level as the prosecution, the defendant at the same level as the prosecutor. Given that judicial equity is not an option, both the prosecution and the defence claim that they are seeking the application of the law, and it makes sense to expose excessive interpretative efforts by the opposing side. This naturally leads to *ad personam* arguments. *La Legge è uquale per tutti* ('the law is equal for all') is inscribed and engraved in all Italian courts. In a codified system, this is not a noble aspiration but a statement of fact. The noble aspiration for which it is often mistaken is to be found in Article 3 of the Italian Constitution where it says that 'all persons are equal before the law,' which is something else entirely.

⁂

Berlusconi was back in the international, or at least the European, limelight in late 2003 when Italy held the presidency of the European Union. Misgivings about him and his government abounded; did they have the tact or democratic credentials to manage affairs with the necessary delicacy at this difficult period? But the government was

gung-ho. Italy was ready to take its place on the world stage, and the new administration was stable, efficient, dynamic. But then, in his crucial inaugural speech to the European Parliament as new President of the EU, Berlusconi suggested that the German MEP, Martin Schulz, who had raised questions about Berlusconi's judicial record, should have been a guard in a Nazi concentration camp. Deputy Prime Minister Gianfranco Fini, leader of the National Alliance, who was sitting beside Berlusconi at the time, put his head in his hands. In the silence that followed, Berlusconi continued to smile broadly, evidently pleased at his off-the-cuff quip. Only later, when he realized that he had not cut as fine a figure as he had thought, did he make sure the footage of the moment was kept off his own television stations. In a brief burst of independent broadcasting, RAI dared to transmit the excruciatingly funny moment.

Relations with Germany were further strained the following month when Italy's junior Minister for Tourism and a member of the Northern League, Stefano Stefani, told the Northern League newspaper *La Padania* that Germans were 'blonde arrogant hyper-nationalists' who, among their many other

Giacomo Balla
La Mano del Violinista
1912
oil on canvas
56 x 78.3 cm
Estorick Collection of
Modern Italian Art,
London

Jean-Baptiste-Camille Corot
Rome from the Pincio
1826–27
oil on canvas
18 x 29 cm
Hugh Lane Municipal
Gallery of Modern Art,
Dublin

faults, 'swill back vast quantities of beer and stuff themselves full of chips before engaging in noisy belching contests'. Chancellor Schröder announced he would not be holidaying in Italy. Berlusconi mollified him by pretending to have read and admired Nietzsche and Goethe and, perhaps more importantly, by forcing Stefani to resign. This was not so hard to do because the tourist industry, which is one of the mainstays of the Italian economy and whose interests Stefani was supposed to represent, was not happy to see thousands of cancelled bookings by offended Germans.

A Queer Victory

On 11 October 2004, the European Parliament's Civil Liberties Committee rejected the Italian nominee, Rocco Buttiglione, as the next commissioner for Justice and Security, and thus placed the incoming European Commission President, José Manuel Barroso, in a quandary. This was the first time MEPs had ever rejected a designated commissioner, and it raised interesting procedural problems. MEPs could not reject a single commissioner, but did have the power to reject the entire

Commission. As the dispute dragged on, it became clear that Buttiglione, who had described homosexuality as a sin and suggested that working mothers were bad mothers, was so disliked by MEPs, that they were willing to torpedo the entire European executive.

Buttiglione is joint leader of the centre-right Catholic party, the UDC (Unione dei Cristiani e Democratici di Centro — until recently, before Buttiglione joined it, Unione dei Democratici di Centro). Although he has been Minister for European Affairs in the Berlusconi government, Buttiglione, a bachelor-Catholic philosopher and personal friend of the Pope, was not the most obvious choice for Commissioner for Justice and Security, precisely because he is so closely associated with the Vatican (which is not a member of the EU). The comments he made were impolitic and remarkably forthright. It was almost as if he relished the idea of the controversy more than the job itself. After a show-down lasting most of October, the Berlusconi government finally backed down and proposed Franco Frattini, the Foreign Minister, in Buttiglione's place. Gianfranco Fini, was appointed Foreign Minister in Frattini's place.

A big fight over large issues of ethics and religion, and the first-ever hint of executive power by the European Parliament, caused a flurry of excitement precisely as Romano Prodi's depressingly dull stewardship of the Commission came to an end. Had it not been for the antics of Berlusconi and his government in Rome, Prodi's departure might have gone unnoticed. Italy has resolutely punched below its weight in Europe and yet has remained steadfastly committed to the European ideal. Prodi epitomized this workmanlike non-presence, and Berlusconi the precise opposite. When listing the achievements of his government, Berlusconi never fails to mention that his government has restored respect for Italy in Europe and abroad. Indeed, he considers foreign relations to be central to government policy, and a commitment to restore Italy to centre-stage in Europe was even one of the 'pledges' that Berlusconi 'signed' live on (his) television channel in the presence of the Italian people. He seems to be acting in the spirit of Margaret Thatcher, who also claimed to have earned 'respect' in Europe, while sacrificing Britain's status there for the sake of a closer alliance with the US. In furtherance of the newly formed foreign policy that no longer heeds the EU, Berlusconi, who is on back-slapping, arm-linking terms with President-Czar Vladimir Putin, assured the Russians in 2003 that they need not to worry about European misgivings over what are politely called 'frozen conflicts' (mass murder in Chechnya), nor about the Russian refusal to ratify the Kyoto Protocol, nor about the problem of Moldova and Transdniester, nor, naturally, about the problems relating to the judicial proceedings involving Yukos (the second-largest Russian oil company). Russia, Berlusconi magnanimously declared, could be sure of Italian support for its attempt to form a 'Permanent Partnership Council' with the EU, without the need to address these embarrassing issues. The EU took two months to unsay diplomatically what Berlusconi had managed to squeeze into a single afternoon's chat.

To mark the start of the new Italian diplomacy, Berlusconi's new government formed a 'Ministry for Italians in the World' in 2002, and then appointed an irredentist fascist-militant, Mirko Tremaglia, to head it. Tremaglia has since been trying to bully the Slovenes, partly because he does not like them for a massacre of Italian civilians at the end of the Second World War, and partly because Italy is developing a notion of its own 'near abroad', and is increasingly open about its desire for more influence in the ex-Yugoslavia, Albania and North Africa. Commenting on Buttiglione's rejection in Europe, this Minister for Italians in the World declared: 'The queers have won.' Tremaglia, born 1926 and an active member of the neo-fascist MSI from 1946 to its dissolution in 1991, lives heterosexually with his wife, whose name is Signora Italia, no less.

By appointing a neo-fascist militant as the spokesman for Italians abroad, aligning itself with the US, trying to develop an independent (non-EU) foreign relationship with Russia, putting the blame for inflation on the euro, accusing Europe of blocking public works (notably the bridge over the Messina Straits, a project on hold since the Third Punic War), picking fights with Germans in the European Parliament, proposing Buttiglione as Commissioner and then giving pre-eminence to Italy's place in Europe and the importance of foreign policy, this Italian government is the most 'Euro-sceptic' ever — although this is not a term much used in a country whose citizens are still very pro-Europe. But something has changed. Perhaps Buttiglione's comments might not have caused such a controversy had he been appointed by a different government.

Buttiglione's rejection also ran along the Protestant–Catholic fault line in Europe, and has uncovered one of the several deep political and historical fissures into which the Americans are busily packing explosives, for the day when they will find it necessary to blow the EU apart. Buttiglione's participation in an already right-wing European Commission would have been welcome in Washington as another small step towards driving a wedge into Europe and re-introducing religion as a counterweight to the secular and liberal underpinnings of the economic pact that led to the creation of the European Union. While it is unlikely that the Pentagon took time off from planning a war with Iran and destabilizing Asia to lament Buttiglione's exclusion, the liberals and the leftists in the European Parliament had good reasons for refusing his appointment, and it was not only — or even — because of his views on gays. If it seems far-fetched to see the hand of the American Neo-Cons in the affair, it should be noted that the mini-biography of Buttiglione on the Italian government website stresses his association with the American Enterprise Institute for Public Policy Research, the seed-bed of the Neo-Con revolution. In the debate that followed Buttiglione's rejection in Europe, the leftists and liberals who opposed him argued that Buttiglione was perfectly entitled to his own private views but did not have a right to bring them into the political sphere. Private and public views were seen as separate — and mutually hostile — spheres. The public man Buttiglione had no right to inflict his politics on the private life of gays, but the private man Buttiglione had every right to his own beliefs. In short, the private trumps the public.

This, however, is the very point that the Catholic Church wishes to make. Private virtue is greater than public virtue. Once it is accepted that private trumps public, then politics, which is discourse carried out in the public sphere, is automatically regarded as inferior to private practice, and an argument sustained in public will always lose to a belief held in private. Buttiglione demonstrated his contempt for public politics by expressing sincerely held private views. Contempt for public discourse has

always been a hallmark of the right, but now it has also learned to leverage the liberal reverence for the rights of private conscience. Corporations, too, have learned this trick, and demand the privileges of privacy even though they operate in the public sphere. The European Parliament, which engages in pure discourse without executive effect, was therefore the perfect body to reject Buttiglione, but its victory is pyrrhic. As long as politicians are allowed to stymie liberal objections by appealing to their private conscience, liberals can never win, because no debate takes place. Tony Blair justifies his actions by appealing to his own convictions. If he sincerely believes that bombing Iraq was the right thing, then who are we to criticise his convictions? George W. Bush is incapable of maintaining a public discourse, but is not expected to. Again, private belief trumps everything, and when he was forced to debate with John Kerry, he was shaking with rage at the affront to his internal conscience. Berlusconi simply refuses to participate in political debates with opponents, and regards demands by his opponents to explain his policies or justify his actions as invasions of his privacy. Unless carefully modulated, many of the arguments used against Buttiglione are arguments in favour of the superiority of private belief over public policy. Perhaps he should have been left in office after all.

A State of Embarrassment

'Let's be normal' is not a particularly inspiring battle-cry. If anything, it is abject. In a bid to secure the vote of the large constituency of Italians embarrassed by the image that the country is projecting, Massimo D'Alema, former leader of the leftist Democratici della Sinistra (DS), formerly the Partito Democratico della Sinistra (PDS) and, before that, of the Partito Comunista Italiano (PCI), the Italian Communist Party, made 'normalization' his battle-cry. Indeed, he even wrote a book (published by Mondadori, which is owned by Berlusconi) called *Un Paese Normale* [*A Normal Country*] in which he longingly looks forward to the day when Italy would be an ordinary decent democratic state.

D'Alema and the Centre-Left are in a constant state of disabling embarrassment that their nation should have elected Berlusconi to clown about on the world stage. But let us consider D'Alema's ideas of normality. When Berlusconi fell from office at the end of 1994 because Umberto Bossi's Northern League withdrew its support, the President of the Republic, Oscar Luigi Scalfaro, a smugly hieratic Christian Democrat, sided with the Centre-Left against Berlusconi and refused to exercise his power to dissolve Parliament. Berlusconi became incandescent and demanded fresh elections, on the very persuasive grounds that those who had voted for the Northern League believed they were voting for a right-of-centre coalition, not one that was willing to support a left-of-centre government in which D'Alema's PDS was the main party. Partly in response and partly in an effort to woo Bossi and the band of truculent xenophobes he had brought into Parliament with him, D'Alema advanced the hallucinatory suggestion that the League was in reality a party of the Left.

In spite of Berlusconi's media leverage, his repeated calls for a general election were ignored, and a new Prime Minister installed. To add insult to injury, the new Prime Minister was Lamberto Dini, a former Treasury Minister in Berlsuconi's government, who had opportunistically allied himself with D'Alema. In the meantime, the Centre-Left, which had been stunned by Berlusconi's victory in 1994, regrouped around Romano Prodi, a former minister in a Christian Democrat government. With his square glasses, square face, square shoulders, professorship in economics, Christian Democrat past and monotonous voice, Prodi, whose favourite word is the very Catholic term 'serenity', emanated a sense of stability and calm, the opposite of the mercurial and still-fuming Berlusconi (whose favoured terms were 'coup' and 'communist').

The postponed general election was finally held in April 1996. The Centre-Left led by Prodi — under the banner of the 'Olive Tree Coalition' — was narrowly elected to office. D'Alema was triumphant. The result of the election retroactively legitimized the parliamentary *coup de main* of the previous year, and the replacement of Berlusconi by Prodi was hailed as the inauguration of an alternating system of government. Prodi's vision of normality consisted in getting Italy as quickly as possible into the Economic and Monetary Union (EMU). In other words, the best way to run the Italian economy, he felt, was to hand monetary decisions over to an unelected board of central bank governors. The almost complete acquiescence of the people serves as a reminder that Italians are historically used to foreign powers running their country, and can even see advantages in it.

To qualify for permanent loss of control over its fiscal policy and relinquish its competitively undervalued currency, Italy had to make sacrifices. Government spending was drastically curbed, workers' salaries were frozen, inflation was pressed down, unemployment rose. To reduce a national debt then around 118 per cent of GDP, the state began to sell assets. Prodi, who never belonged to the Left, had no qualms about doing this. Neither did D'Alema and his party of ex-communists, but the Rifondazione Comunista, the unrepentant communists, did. Once Prodi had secured Italian membership of the EMU, it was time for him to go. In 1998, the Rifondazione Comunista, possibly encouraged by D'Alema, refused to accept Prodi's Thatcherite budget and withdrew its support. Prodi was shunted off to Brussels, then in the throes of a corruption scandal

Alfredo Ambrosi
Loreto Madonna
c.1932
oil on canvas
99.8 x 80 cm
Museo Aeronautico Gianni
Caproni, Trento; exhibited
at the Estorick Collection
of Modern Italian Art,
London, spring 2005

as the reign of Jacques Santer came to an inglorious end. (The appointment of an Italian to stamp out corruption provoked much hilarity in the northern European press.) Back in Italy, D'Alema had himself elected Prime Minister. Having taken over government by treachery and stealth, D'Alema seemed surprised that the historical moment the Left had always dreamed of — its own prime minister in power — was such an anti-climax. (D'Alema, like so many leftists who enter government, set out to prove his non-radical credentials. He oversaw major privatization operations and sought to cosy up to the Americans.) His big chance came in 1999 when the US asked Italy to participate in the bombing of Yugoslavia. D'Alema jumped at the chance to please. Far from feigning regret at the alleged need to bomb civilians, he was triumphant at the opportunity this afforded Italy to become 'normal'. With a candour that suggests Italy is unversed in the base deceit of international diplomacy, he declared: 'The crisis of Kosovo created new networks of relations ... the daily teleconferences [involve] five countries: the United States, Germany, Great Britain,

France and Italy. With Kosovo, we entered such a group ... [I]t is difficult to define the roles of membership in the noble circle of the great — there exists no statute.' The phrase 'no statute' is telling because, in permitting bombing raids against Yugoslavia in 1999, D'Alema breached Articles 11, 78 and 87 of the Italian Constitution which specify that war may not be used to resolve international conflicts (unless Italy or one of its allies is attacked) and that military action or intervention must be debated by parliament.

An Embarrassment of Choice

Although the halcyon days of Italy's trade unions were in the mid-sixties and they now represent mainly the interests of a greying population, they are still very strong. Italy also still has a Communist Party that attracts around one vote in ten; a powerful Catholic movement; a lively tradition of anarchist communes; a vociferous no-global movement; an extensive network of agricultural co-ops; a myriad of mini-parties that constantly deprive the larger parties of safe majorities; a politicized but still independent judiciary; independent universities; a council of state with regional tribunals; regional governments with real powers (and about to get more, thanks to Berlusconi); provincial and municipal governments with revenue-raising capacities; locally run health authorities; five regions (Sicily, Sardinia, Trento, Altro Adige, Friuli-Venezia Giulia) and one province (Aosta) with as much autonomy as, say, Northern Ireland; two national police forces and innumerable municipal police forces. The Italians are, of course, embarrassed by all this choice, and, in a half-hearted effort to limit it, have voted by referendum to remove the system of Proportional Representation that allows small parties to flourish. Their politicians, too, are full of praise for the British 'first-past-the-post' electoral system. It just seems that they

cannot ever get round to introducing it; thus, electoral choice remains stubbornly rich. Owing to their willingness to buy into the Anglo-American view of themselves, many Italians still see the electoral dictatorship that exists in the UK or the non-choice in the US as preferable to their own system.

Having been persuaded by Anglo-American propaganda that stronger and more efficient government is better, Italians are now being told that Berlusconi is a threat to democracy. This must surely lead to the conclusion that it is a good thing that he does not have a Tony Blair-like majority or proper executive power after all. The failure of electoral and constitutional reform might be better interpreted as a proleptic success by a healthy democracy. The reason that Italy cannot reform its electoral system to reduce the number of political parties is that there are too many political parties to agree on reform. In any case, the smaller ones tend not to believe that their own annihilation through electoral reform is worth supporting. D'Alema tried to get the larger parties to gang up on the smaller ones by conducting talks with Berlusconi (Forza Italia) and Fini (National Alliance), but he found himself in negotiation with two political opponents and without the support of the many minnows that make up the Centre-Left coalition. D'Alema, who fancies himself as something of a strategist, was surprised when he discovered that support for institutional reform had melted away.

It seems that the Italian state is good at defending itself, and is therefore stronger than is generally believed. In other European democracies, the distinction between government and state can become blurred, nowhere more than in the UK. The government can easily change the structure of the state, which eventually shapes itself into a reflection of the government. Tony Blair had to steal Thatcher's clothes to get elected (a cross-dressing that assured him

Robert Ballagh
Man and a Lucio Fontana
1972
acrylic on canvas
213.8 x 71.4 cm
Irish Museum of Modern
Art, Dublin; courtesy of
the artist

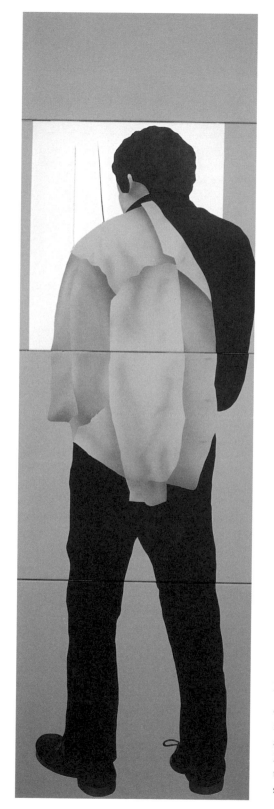

amorous advances from the Americans). In Italy, not only is this less possible, as the repeated failure of reform has shown; it is also not in the nature of Italian politicians to identify themselves with the state.

There are various reasons for the Italian government's attacks on the euro. Among them is that Romano Prodi, the person most responsible for bringing the currency to Italy, will lead the opposition coalition in the general election of 2006. Another is that the economy is in poor health, and the euro and Prodi make good scapegoats. The euro, however, is still the national currency, and so we have the curious spectacle of a government criticizing its own currency. Similarly, Berlusconi declared on 17 February 2004 that evading taxes was morally legitimate. After all, he argued, taxes in Italy are too high. Thus, in addition, we have the head of government encouraging citizens to break the laws of the state. The separation between government and state could not be clearer. This is the precise opposite of the Fascist experiment, which sought to meld the two.

When Mussolini is praised in Italy, as occasionally happens, it is for his fusion of government and state. Before the war, Mussolini seemed to have achieved that coup, but in the event, it became clear that he had not. The difficulty for any Italian government, Fascist or not, in enforcing its will is that the country has many bases of local power, whether embodied in the person of a mayor, prefect, provincial governor, trade union chief, magistrate or Mafia boss. After all, when they wanted to lever out the Fascist state from Sicily, the Americans applied for help to the Mafia. The alternative power structures, based on centuries of local tradition, proved a formidable obstacle to dictatorial rule; but another, more insidious obstacle stood in Mussolini's way. Many of those in office under him believed firmly in the Fascist state, but did not equate it automatically with government. Not all who were willing to countenance the suppression of local power structures (notably the Mafia, which the Fascists almost destroyed) in the national interest were, on that account, always willing to accept orders from the government. They had their own idea of the state, which, thanks in part to the ideology of Fascism itself, made considerations of public governance secondary and relegated political principle to an even lower rank in the hierarchy of duty. This belief in the purity of the idea of the state is often what inspires magistrates, journalists, academics and prefects to challenge the Mafia, political parties and the government. The dirtier the politicking, the purer, by contrast, the betrayed ideal of the state.

Thus, in virtue of their shallow commitment to central government and its decrees, Italians, whether for selfish local reasons or because of their internalized belief in what the ideal state should be, did not fully participate in the industrialized murder of European Jewry. The prestige of the idea (and ideal) of the state supervened over the practice of government. This meant that Italy did not become a nation of centralized collaborators like Vichy France. At the end of the war, its people found themselves in the serendipitous position of not having to participate in the mass-slaughter of German civilians either. This reluctance to follow pernicious conviction-politics earned Italy the reputation for moral ambivalence, which it still has today. D'Alema's desire to bomb the Serbs was an attempt to shake off this embarrassing reputation by committing an unequivocally immoral act. Even if one chooses to see the bombing of Serbs as thoroughly moral, that does not relieve D'Alema's motivations of their squalor.

Italy is also reputed to be extremely inefficient, an observation that is often made with a touch of gleeful censure, as if inefficiency were condign punishment for its moral ambivalence. But the fact that the British and American legislatures can rapidly turn out repressive legislation suggests that executive efficiency may even be inimical to the principle of liberty. What is regarded as poor efficiency in the Italian political system might better be regarded as an effective defence against usurpation. 'Usurpers,' as Rousseau observed, 'always bring about or select troublous times to get passed, under cover of the public terror, destructive laws, which the people would never adopt in cold blood. The moment chosen is one of the surest means of distinguishing the work of the legislator from that of the tyrant.' Even if Berlusconi wanted to become a political tyrant, the Italian state is proving an effective barrier. Rousseau's words have a more telling application for the US or the UK.

From Mussolini until Berlusconi, Italy has not paid homage to the gods of administrative and industrial efficiency. Since Mussolini is now equated with failure and humiliation, his lexicon of efficiency, technology, futurism, expansion and experimentation has long been unavailable to self-conscious Italians. Italians have also abandoned the idea that they might have a political truth to teach the world. Indeed, with the disappearance of the Soviet system, the US has practically copyrighted universalism.

The Rhetorical Gap

In the language of Italian politics, the 'lay' or 'secular' parties are the Liberals and the Republicans, neither of which counted for much in the post-war period. The other 'non-lay' parties were the major ones: the Christian Democrats, Socialists and Communists. These three were considered non-lay because they embodied different theological visions of the ideal republic. Although Italian Communists subscribed to the Marxian religion, they were not Soviets. Thanks to Antonio Gramsci, who introduced the notion of hegemony, compromise and adaptability have long been available options to even the most committed Italian Communists. Gramsci liberated the Party from much of the theological absolutism that Bertrand Russell, for example, believed to be integral to Marxism and to Marxian politics. Even a diluted Marxism, however, still used language of universalistic and epochal scope. Both the Italian Communist Party and, especially, the Socialists, blended a practical and opportunistic approach to politics with the rarefied language of visionaries, and thus exposed a highly visible, and occasionally comic, gap between word and deed. The Christian Democrats were also eminently practical people, but their very name implies final allegiance to a kingdom that is not of this world. The sublunar world of politics stood in stark contrast to the crystalline zone of their theological mission. This was no great shock for a people that had produced a long succession of venal popes with highly materialist and secular ambitions.

The Socialists eventually entered government, and they, the Communists and the Catholics, managed to co-exist in local administrations. The practical and adaptive nature of these arrangements was in conflict with the visionary and theological rhetoric that the parties continued to produce. The ex-Fascists, however, were constantly excluded from power, and were therefore not compromised by it. This helped them gain the reputation as the only party that did not indulge in double-talk. The MSI also drew on the 1930s tradition of the inspirationally vague rhetoric of the Great Leader, and used it to retain the 'spiritual' high ground by pointing up the disparity between the words and deeds of their political opponents. Fini abandoned this rhetoric and, with it, this position. He is a very good political speaker, but as soon as he entered government with Berlusconi, he adulterated the purity of the MSI tradition. After that, there was no longer any point in resisting the temptations of power, and so his distancing of the party from its Fascist roots has not been that hard.

In at least one respect, Berlusconi, with his claims of good governance, efficiency and his outdated claim to be defending the country from Communism, shares a trait that Martin Amis identified in Stalin, namely 'an infinite immunity to embarrassment'. He and his party, Forza Italia (although the name of the party is derived from a rallying cry at sports events, it also has futuristic and slightly fascist undertones) have made a valiant effort to reinstate the cult of efficiency and modernity, but, as they must operate in the context of a state which they barely govern, they are constantly open to ridicule, both from the leftist opposition at home and from foreign observers, who continue to regard the country as autochthonously devoid of political competence.

The Fascists were defeated, the Communists failed, the Socialists stopped believing, but the Christian Democrats in Italy held power continuously from 1948 to 1992. Elections were *less* frequent than in other European countries. True, governments did not last very long, but changes of government amounted to no more than what other European countries would consider mid-term reshuffles. Italy did well economically, and fought off right-wing plots, the Mafia and left-wing terrorism. The public administration of Italy may have remained ossified, but ossification provided good structural stability.

The historical basis for the Italian state is nineteenth-century liberal and secular ideology; there is already an in-built conflict between respect for the institutions of state and the beliefs of the Catholics expected to uphold it. If anything, the Communists, whose ideology is an offshoot of the same Enlightenment stock as the nationalists' liberalism, had a more natural sympathy for the Italian liberal state than the Christian Democrats who eventually presided over it. Civic virtue, in the sense of belief in the dignity of the institutions of the state and the value of the community, has therefore been more prominent among Communists and leftists than among the Christian Democrats. After almost half a century of Christian Democrat hegemony, it is hardly surprising that the practice of civic virtue was so weak. If one aspect of Italian society infuriates northern Europeans and Americans more than anything else, it is the sheer lack of civic virtue and the absence of altruism ('Look how they drive!'). Western foreigners of all political shades find themselves agreeing wholeheartedly with the Italian Left.

This version of civic virtue is a modern creation. It originated with Auguste Comte (1798–1857), father of modern Positivism and founder of the 'Religion of Humanity', a system of political belief that has had enormous influence in liberal democracies. According to Comte, the human mind develops from a theological to a metaphysical to a final positivist stage, in which humans will apply logic based on scientific observation to arrive at the truth. Naturally, the Church is hostile to Comte's belief in the superiority of human reason over faith. The idea of progress, with its various embellishments, is fundamental to both Marxism and democratic liberalism and is strongly entrenched in Italian leftist and secular opinion. Liberals and leftist Italians will often be outraged that catastrophic things (floods, child pornography, intermittent train services, administrative failure, Berlusconi) can happen 'in the twenty-first century'. Surely, they seem to be pleading, given the advances made by science, human nature should have improved by now.

Comte used the word *altrui* [others] to coin the term altruism to refer to a theory of conduct (utilitarianism) that ascribed moral value to actions the aim of which is the maximization of human happiness. These ideas, whether mediated through Herbert Spencer, Karl Marx or John Stuart Mill have become part of the generally accepted notions of civic duty in a society founded on liberal values. They are emphatically not Catholic values. According to the *Catholic Encyclopædia*, the general rules for determining the prevailing duty given by Catholic moralists are these:

- Absolutely speaking, there is no obligation to love others more than one's self.

- There is an obligation which admits of no exceptions: to love one's self more than others, whenever beneficence to others entails moral guilt.

- In certain circumstances it may be obligatory, or at least a counsel of perfection, to love others more than self. Apart from cases in which one's profession or state of life, or justice imposes duties, these circumstances are determined by comparing the relative needs of self and others.

- These needs may be spiritual or temporal; the need of the community or of the individual; the need of one in extreme, serious or ordinary want; the need of those who are near to us by natural or social ties, and of those whose claims are only union in a common humanity. The first class in each group has precedence over the second.

These rules are loose enough to stretch over the framework of a liberal state, especially where they give precedence to the community over the individual. Nevertheless, they contrast with the civic virtues imagined by the founders of the liberal state and, later, by the framers of the liberal constitution. The obligation to love self more than others, where beneficence might produce moral unease, justifies many of the practices that are associated with Italian society and especially with its Christian Democrat section: according primacy to the family to the detriment of civil society; favouring friendship over meritocratic virtue; ignoring laws that are considered contrary to the moral teaching of the Church or, indeed, to one's own moral conscience; assessing the ethical value of laws before agreeing to be bound by them; distributing wealth with reference to local rather than national interests; countenancing a devalued currency, inflation and overstaffing of the public sector in exchange for guaranteeing jobs and, generally, comparing the 'relative needs of self and others' rather than pursuing a vain 'counsel of perfection'.

Eventually, when the distortions had become too great to bear and as soon as the Christian Democrats were no longer serving the purpose of keeping the Communists at bay, the judiciary helped to force the Catholics out of power. These were first replaced by the inheritors of Communism (D'Alema and the PDS), and later by a new coalition that explicitly recalls the values of liberalism in its name (the Forza Italia–National Alliance–Northern League coalition is called *Casa delle Libertà*, which, if transliterated, yields the comic and accurate English *House of Liberties*). The end of the Christian Democrat hegemony was supposed to lead to a reaffirmation of the civic/altruistic principles they had been suppressing. The concept of 'civil society' gained ground, and moral crusaders, bearing secular badges and claiming to represent the real state, roamed the country for several years, and only now is their talk of renewal, honesty, change and reform fading.

The Embarrassing Neighbour

Surely God was joking when He decided Italy and Switzerland should be neighbours? Each seems to define itself in terms of what the other is not. The total precision of the Swiss, their staid politics, their direct democracy, clean streets, reliable banks, their hostility to European integration, their successful multinational companies, wealthy citizens and cast-iron constitutional arrangements all seem designed to underscore the absence of these in Italy. The joke works best if we compare Zurich to Palermo, or Naples, but a good deal less so if we compare Ticino to Brescia, or Geneva to Bolzano. Switzerland serves as a reminder that Italy, for centuries a land of city-states, could quite easily have chosen a completely different model, closer to the canton system; and it almost did, thanks to the efforts of Carlo Cattaneo.

The political structures in place in Italy just before the 1848 Revolution give an idea of how many possibilities were open. Rome, Bologna, Ferrara and Ancona were the chief cities of the Papal States, which encompassed many of the central regions of the country. They did not, however, include the region of Tuscany (a Grand Duchy allied with Austria), Modena and Parma, Lucca or San Marino, all of which had long traditions as independent and powerful Renaissance city-states, and one of which (San Marino) is still a separate republic. Piedmont and Sardinia were ruled by the House of Savoy, later to provide the kings of the unitary state. Milan, which had been frequently under French rule, was now, with the rest of Lombardy and Veneto, under the rule of the Habsburgs (Emperor Ferdinand of Austria); and everything south of Latium was in the Kingdom of the Two Sicilies, ruled by the Spanish Bourbons. Even after all of these were hurled together by the failure of the 1848 Revolution, followed by the improbable success of the drive to reunification, the emergence of the liberal Italian state, then a monarchy, was also fortuitous. Italy may not have been able to return to the *status quo ante*, but it might at least have been expected to acknowledge the pre-existing kingdoms and cities by introducing a Swiss-style system of cantons or instituting Cattaneo's vision of 'a united states of Italy in a united states of Europe' — an idea that still refuses to die.

Some respectable modern historians reject the whiggish idea that the national state is an inevitable outcome or some sort of culmination of events that were always pointing in one direction. Certainly, Italy made some unlikely choices but they were made in a very conscious and deliberate way, after considerable political and philosophical debate. The Italian state is, on that account, consciously constructed to a degree that other European states are not. If a state is a concept that exists more in the minds of the people than in the practice of government and enforcement of the rule of law, its collapse can occur with the suddenness of Argentines abandoning their currency, or of the nineteenth-century Irish abandoning their language. The state is a faith that needs to be reaffirmed. One of the first major public works of the new Italian state was a massive altar to the fatherland [*Altare della Patria*] in the centre of Rome. This was not just a challenge to the Catholic Church. It was part of a highly successful campaign to present the Italian state as, not merely the product of human reason, but also as a form of revealed truth. The state demands acts of worship and faith. Revolutionaries such as Garibaldi were endowed with the traits and some of the mythological power of church martyrs, and the new state set up its own secular national holidays. This ritualistic reaffirmation of the republic is visible in other Enlightenment countries. The French and the Americans, for instance, worship their flag with precisely the idolatrous awe that Protestants regard as one of the more distasteful aspects of Catholicism.

Dispassionate Italians

If we are going to accept one stereotype about Italians, it must surely be that they are not a people given to long silences. Italians greatly enjoy public debate, but often they are more concerned to find an audience than a solution. An argument between two Italians will always contain appeals to third parties, whether present or not, invocations of sympathy from real or imaginary spectators, theatrical asides, hand movements that seek to communicate inner feelings to distant onlookers. Bitter comments are oriented to the parterre rather than directly to the other person, and this abstinence from direct eye-contact mitigates the impact of the insults.

The theatricality is real. Yet rather than remark on what is most obvious — namely that such theatrics require restraint, control of language and movement, and avoidance of physical contact and violence — foreign observers mistakenly conclude that Italians are helpless prey to their own passions. Projecting their own lack of subtlety onto a sophisticated nation, northern Europeans and Americans walk gingerly through Italian cities, convinced that serious fights are on the point of breaking out on every street corner. As the visit extends in length, the foreign visitor will begin to pick up the language and notice that many apparent disagreements were not disagreements at all, and that those that are disagreements tend to remain verbal. Rather than questioning their original assumption about passionate Italians, they start speculating on the strangeness of the Italian mind in which words do not automatically lead to deeds.

Northern European and American writers and journalists also like to communicate the utter inaccessibility of the Italian psyche by filling their pages with Italian words, as if no possible English translation could exist for them. Here is a random handful from Tim Parks (*Italian Neighbours: An Englishman in Verona* [1992]): *furgoncino* (van), *afa* (clamminess), *pasticceria* (pastry shop), *motorino* (motor scooter), *tabacchieria* (tobacconist's), *contadino* (peasant, farmhand), *imprenditore* (businessman), *residenza* (residence), and *pan di spagna* (sponge cake). Refusal to translate a simple word is taken as a sign of authentic understanding of the culture. Far from being so impenetrably arcane, one of the defining features of the Italian language is the marked *absence* of untranslatable colloquialisms. This is especially true in the Italian that is used in public life and the media, where so much dissembling is supposed to take place. In some respects, Italian is the Esperanto of the Italic peninsula. Jokes, curses and slang, the truly untranslatable parts of the language, are expressed in dialect. Accordingly, a large part of the 'national' patrimony of humour is necessarily visual rather than linguistic, which may be why Italian novelists seem to be so humourless and that one of the country's chief comic exports, Roberto Begnini, is so extravagantly physical. And far from improvising their language, Italians exercise an admirable control over it. Verbal disagreement in Italian often takes some time to descend into vulgarity and familiarity, because the essentially academic and learned nature of Italian acts as a barrier. The mimetic imperative that is so much a part of public debate forces the speakers to maintain a certain distance and control over their language, rather like actors interpreting a part. The absence of a polite form (*Lei, Voi, Sie, usted, vous*)

distinguishes English from other European languages, and suggests that English-speakers, willing to use the familiar form from the outset, are less dispassionate in their mode of communication than is usual.

The control over language is very much apparent in the fields of law and politics. Circumlocution is always to be preferred, even when framing legislation. This is not, however, a failure to engage in clear thought but, rather, a recognition that wriggle room is likely to be needed before any law or political pronouncement can be made to fit its fundamental purpose. Again, it is prejudicial to claim that this is somehow a particularly Italian trait. Rather, it is a reasoned response to a codified system of law based on the Napoleonic system. The inflexibility of the codified system, in which everything has to be entered into the statute books, needs to be tempered. It makes sense to blur the terminology a little and replace prescription with description. A lengthy preamble describing what the law is supposed to do and a slight imprecision in the normative section is a sensible way of maintaining flexibility. Italian political and legal language is therefore often concerned with the veiling of intent. The effect is

Gino Severini
Le Boulevard
1910–11
oil on canvas
63.5 x 91.5 cm
Estorick Collection of
Modern Italian Art,
London

further compounded by another borrowing from the ecclesiastical tradition — the notion of *magisterium*. Language that gives its meaning up too easily is not only aesthetically impoverished, but unpersuasive, because too transparent. When an Italian political entity issues a pronouncement made up of long ciceronian periods, obfuscations, mixed metaphors and apparent contradictions, it is, like the Catholic Church, more concerned with reasserting the dignity of office than communicating a message with any great urgency.

Back to Berlusconi

Rather than regarding Berlusconi as an Italian failure, we should perhaps regard him as our future. With the arrival of a joke-telling singer turned property-developer-media-tycoon-politician to power in Italy, what Noreen Hertz called 'The Silent Takeover' became a noisy party (*The Silent Takeover* (2001)). It is appropriate that Berlusconi should be so friendly with Vladimir Putin. The two men represent a new, or at least a revamped, form of capitalism whose configurations are only now becoming clear. Russia has been the unfortunate recipient of two experiments in western utopianism in the past century. The first was Bolshevism and the second was the post-Soviet shock therapy imposed by the International Monetary Fund and World Bank, which unintentionally created an anarcho-capitalism, which is proving successful. If all goes well, Russia may develop an owner-capitalist model of business as in Italy, of which Berlusconi, Pirelli, Benetton, Agnelli and the Mafia are the best-known examples.

This economic model does not depend on the absence of government interference. Far from it. It is not the ideal 'free market' of American 'theorists' such as Francis Fukuyama. To believe that the end of Communism marked the triumph of free-market capitalism shows a lack of logic: we can say A (free market) is not B (command economy), but not conclude that Not-B equals A. Worse still, Fukuyama and others seem to have overlooked a thousand-billion-pound gorilla standing in the middle of their theory, otherwise known as the American military. Thanks to the militarization of American society and the state of permanent war in which the US now lives, government in the US is very large indeed. Bush has already amply demonstrated that America is not ideologically committed to free trade, and, in Iraq, has shown that the US is willing to use force to gain control over basic commodities.

Italy may be the first European country to have made a coherent response to global capitalism's erosion of the power of governments and transformation of citizens into consumers. Berlusconi has made the nexus between business and government explicit, but he did not emerge completely out of the blue. In the immediate aftermath of the political crisis that drove the Christian Democrat–Socialist government from power, the person appointed Prime Minister in 1992 was Giuliano Amato, Craxi's chief adviser. Amato's main qualification was his technical competence. A professor of constitutional law with a good grounding in economics, he was regarded as an ideal candidate to steer Italy through the change. Although appointed by Craxi, he managed to put himself across as a non-political crisis management expert, which he was. He was followed in 1993 by a complete technocrat, Carlo Azeglio Ciampi, who at the moment of his appointment was Governor of the Bank of Italy. He, in turn, was followed briefly by Berlusconi, but then another technocrat, Lamberto Dini, also from the Bank of Italy, took over the reins of government (1994–96). It is worth noting that neither Ciampi (later to become President) nor Dini had been elected to Parliament, yet they were both appointed Prime Minister. Romano Prodi (1996-99) too, was

essentially a technocratic figure. And Prodi went on to serve as President of the technocratic and fundamentally undemocratic European Commission from 1999 to 2004.

After this string of technocrats — interrupted briefly by D'Alema, whom the voters never chose — Berlusconi can be said to have restored some proper democratic accountability, as well as some colour, to the office of Prime Minister. The important point to note, however, is that Italy chose legal and economic technocrats in place of politicians, and then chose Berlusconi, a businessman. If Prodi or Berlusconi wins in 2006 and hangs on in office until 2011, Italy will not have had a politician's politician in power for an entire generation, apart from a few months of D'Alema.

It has been some time since the social democratic parties in Europe displayed any real policy differences from their Centre-Right opponents, or since the Democrats in the US differed greatly from the Republicans. This has also been true in Italy, and perhaps the Italian Socialists were among the first to toe the capitalist line completely. Now, however, Berlusconi has shifted the Italian Centre-Right to a new position that is hard to pinpoint. At a moment when many European citizens feel helplessly lost in a political world in which Left and Right no longer provide meaningful direction, the Italians are drawing up a new map. ∎

Genoa, 2004 © John-Barry Lowe, Dublin

Globalization and Its Discontents

Benedict Anderson

The buzzword 'globalization' is used in many different ways to mean many different things. Inevitably, what are thought to be its discontents vary accordingly.

World-systems theory has generally held that an early form of globalization came into being as early as the sixteenth century, with the vast European conquests in the hitherto unknown New World, the turning of the Pacific into what the Spanish rulers called *mare clausum*, the lockhold on trans-Asian maritime commerce by, successively, the Portuguese, the Dutch, and eventually the British, and the subjection of the western shores of Africa to a vast, cruel trans-Atlantic trade in human flesh. Some decades back, world-systems theory also posited as a central phenomenon the division of the world into cores/metropoles with overweening military and economic power, and in receding planetary circles around them, subordinated semi-peripheries and Pluto-like outer-peripheries. I have a good deal of sympathy with this large, historical, and Marxist-derived perspective.

Those, however, who think globalization is really something modern have different ideas. One view is that globalization (politically speaking) was born with the normative standardization of the nation-state around the world. Here the decisive period is 1911–19, when the Ottoman, Hohenzollern, Ching, Romanov, and Habsburg 'multinational' empires were undone. In that decade, the age-old normalcy of monarchy came to an abrupt end (politically active monarchs lingered only in scattered locations, like Japan and Ethiopia, but for not very long). With it went any means of long-term continuation of the colonial order (created

overwhelmingly by monarchical states). Perhaps the clearest sign of this was that the UK, one of the victors of World War I, lost one quarter of its 'home' territory, what came to be Éire, within five years of the war's end. Sinn Féin was already a household term in colonial Burma, whose young patriots translated the name *(Thakin)* and applied it to themselves. As for France, the other major European victor, the same 'five years war' saw the beginnings of a modern form of resistance both in Vietnam and Algeria — a sign that the discontents of this form of globalization were producing effective political oppositions. More powerfully and deeply, the normative hegemony of the nation — there were no more multinational empires inside Europe itself — was gradually understood to be fundamentally incompatible with colonialism, which could therefore no longer be regarded as a permanent condition, but rather as a period of tutelage for eventual emancipation of new 'normal' nation-states. Within forty years the French and British empires were largely gone, and with astonishingly little violence — although with big exceptions like Vietnam, Algeria, Kenya, and Cyprus, to say nothing of Ireland.

The ground had been laid for this new nation-state order for more than a century, starting with the explosion of new independent ex-colonial states in the Americas (from 1776 to about 1830), followed by struggles all over Europe from about 1820 onward. Its culmination — the

Margaret Corcoran
An Enquiry I
2002
oil on linen
46 x 61 cm
courtesy of the artist

formation of the League of Nations — also required the elimination of serious dynasticism. The striking thing about the League was that it was, as intended, a global political institution — and, historically, the first of its kind. South America was there, along with China, Japan, Thailand, and even, quite soon, Lenin's ostensibly supranational Soviet Union. The only significant power outside it from the start was the petulant United States; in the 1930s the main fascist powers — Germany, Japan, and Italy — withdrew from it, but they could not destroy it. One notes certain dates of birth: Mussolini 1883; Tojo 1884; Hitler 1889 (and one could add perhaps Stalin, 1879). These figures grew to adulthood in the last decades of the old system. They all shared twisted versions of nineteenth-century empire. But they were aberrant transitional figures. After their crushing defeat, the United Nations quickly came into being. Stalin put Byelorussia and the Ukraine into it, and made no attempt to incorporate (aside from the small Baltic states) the League's eastern European nations into the Soviet Union. Mao's China wanted in as well. The US was now the major player in the institution. Indonesia was the only country to leave and it was back within two years, when Sukarno was overthrown in a torrent of blood by the incoming Suharto dictatorship. No longer did anyone reject the normative order for which the UN stood. Decolonization swelled the UN's numbers to more than four times the League membership, and 'micro' nation-states, such as Nauru or St. Lucia, for the first time could be accepted. By the 1960s it was becoming plain that the age-old system of territorial conquest had become obsolete. Nation-states could break up into smaller pieces, but they could not expand except in the most marginal ways.

A third view of globalization focuses, with many variations in emphasis, on the century between 1848 and 1945, opening with *The Communist Manifesto* and the attempts to create a Workers' International. Marx was the first person to see and to demonstrate that industrial capitalism was a ravenous global force far more powerful than any given empire or nation; and also the first person to come to the conclusion that it could only be effectively combated on the same global stage. Combated is really the wrong word to use; Marx believed that it could and would be overcome, dialectically, through revolution, by a new world order based on the socialization of the means of production. His successors in the Comintern and also Trotsky's Fourth International understood they were engaged in a global political struggle. This was not just official piety or rhetoric; it was a struggle they took seriously. The Soviet Union was conceived originally, not merely as a supranational polity and economy, but as one with no permanent borders, and with a vast transnational constituency. This state of affairs did not end till the Comintern was abolished by Stalin, to be replaced later by the 'European' Cominform. Independent national-communist states emerged in Asia and Europe in the late 1940s. Although today we tend to emphasize the *volkisch* and nationalist aspect of Fascism, in its heyday it followed the Soviet Union in seeing itself as a global political force, with adherents in many countries — not excluding Ireland. The so-called 'Free World' after 1947 can, in many respects, be seen as a late variant on these original models. All this implied what Habermas has called 'world domestic politics'.

The most recent conceptions of globalization largely stress the 'unprecedentedness' of the transformations especially of the past two decades. The points discussed here are familiar: the collapse of any serious form of Communist or even Socialist state, as well as the collapse of any formal, institutionalized radical global politics; the 'revolution' in communications made possible by the rapidly spreading use of computer

William Orpen
Reflections: China and Japan
1902
oil on canvas
40.5 x 51 cm
Collection Hugh Lane Municipal Gallery of Modern Art, Dublin

technology; massive transnational migrations from the Third World; the hegemony of Free Market liberalism around the globe; transnational corporations of huge size and world-wide operations; movements of finance capital on a colossal scale and at lightning speed; the linguistic domination of American English; the apparent consolidation of the European Community with the Maastricht agreements; and last, but by no means least, the position of the United States as world-hegemon, dwarfing all other nation-states in its military, political, economic, technological, and pop cult power. Also, one is tempted to add to this list, in the scale of its hypocrisy.

That list looks spectacular, but distinctions have to be made. For example, the really huge migrations into Western Europe from the Third World took place between 1945 and 1973 — on the scale of twenty million

people. In the US, however, it began only in the 1970s, when the annual intake was larger than even the highpoint immigration years around the turn of the nineteenth and twentieth centuries. France actually had higher immigration rates than the US in the fifty years before World War I. There are two significant differences between then and now. First, the movement has been ever more increasingly from Asia, Africa, Spanish America and the Middle East, rather than from Eastern Europe (understood in the widest sense). Second, the migrants are no longer fleeing empires, but 'their own' nation-states. It is still worth noting their means of transportation are simply upgraded versions of what was already around in the aftermath of World War I — the airplane, gasoline-fuelled motor vehicles, steamships, and railways.

It is easy to forget that in the late nineteenth century the telegraph already made near-

Gino Severini
Quaker Oats –
Cubist Still Life
1917
oil on canvas
62 x 51 cm
Estorick Collection of
Modern Italian Art, London

1   The Republic of Ireland helped crucified East Timor to join the UN. No country in Europe did more, and no country did it so unselfishly and so 'globally'; but what if the East Timorese had been Buddhist or Muslim, rather than Catholic?

instantaneous communication around the world not only feasible but quite cheap. By the twenties, state, commercial, and personal 'ham' radio already had the same reach. Hollywood has been around for almost a hundred years. A century and a half ago, Sir James Bowring, with a panache that Madison Avenue still cannot better, had proclaimed that 'Free Trade is Jesus Christ, and Jesus Christ is Free Trade.' And until about 1900 imperial Britain was more genuinely free market than the USA has ever been. It is also easy for people without much historical memory to overlook the scale, speed, and speculative character of finance capital as it had already developed a century ago — witness the celebrated works of Hobson, Hilferding, Rosa Luxemburg and others. What is really unprecedented is primarily the current hegemony of the United States, the largest debtor in world history; 'globalization' is simply an academic-bureaucratic euphemism for that hegemony.

If this diagnosis of globalization is accurate, what are its peculiar social, political, and cultural outcomes — including its discontents? Many of these can be listed under the terms 'dispersion', 'fragmentation', 'localization'. It is striking, for example, that as 'globalization' speeds up, the number of new states in the UN increases, inevitably by the break-up or fragmentation of other states. The most spectacular example is the former Soviet Union.[1] Tibet, Taiwan, Kurdistan, Assam, Western Sahara, West Papua all wait in line. It is not at all clear that transnational capital will find such entities that much easier to deal with than Turkey, Indonesia, Morocco or even China. For all its weaknesses, the nation-state remains an indispensable institution through which those who so wish can work to restrain today's 'evil empire', helping to create compliance with the elementary rules needed to preserve the planet from environmental disaster, and from the worst

instruments of violence. One can see this need from looking at the history of labour's struggles; a myriad of strikes, slowdowns, demonstrations, fistfights and sabotage were the indispensable first steps. But the gains could only be made durable when they were incorporated into generally applicable legal statutes, and when bureaucracies with enforcement powers had been created. When a statute was in place forbidding the use of child labour in mines, and mine-owners had to fear prison if they disobeyed, this kind of abuse really did largely come to an end.

When I first went to study about Asia in the United States, over forty years ago, there was still a unified Hit Parade of popular music, New York City still had several reasonable newspapers, and television was ruled by the hegemonic triumvirate of CBS–NBC–ABC. All of this has long disappeared. The popular music world has been completely fragmented, with a dozen or more mini-Top Tens — Rhythm and Blues, Bluegrass, Rap, Soul, Blues, Dixieland, Folk, Rock-folk, Reggae, and so on. Intensification of advertising, technical development, and the rise of vast conglomerates, have enormously extended 'consumer choice'. The most striking outcome is that the listener can stay tuned twenty-four hours a day to specialized niche-stations which play only the kind of music she likes. She is no longer 'forced' to listen to the wide spectrum which in music means the 'public sphere'. Niche-marketing has had a further strange consequence. In the 1960s, when Gil Scott-Heron's foundational 'The Revolution Will Not Be Televised' came at you out of the blue, sandwiched between something by Sinatra and something by Earl Scruggs and his Kentucky Bluegrass band, it still could be felt as a riveting personal cry in the wilderness. But niche-ing has made it quite feasible to have 'The Revolution' and its grandchildren on all the time, so that it has lost its aura and faded into the tundra of

UNDERGROUND The Great Bear

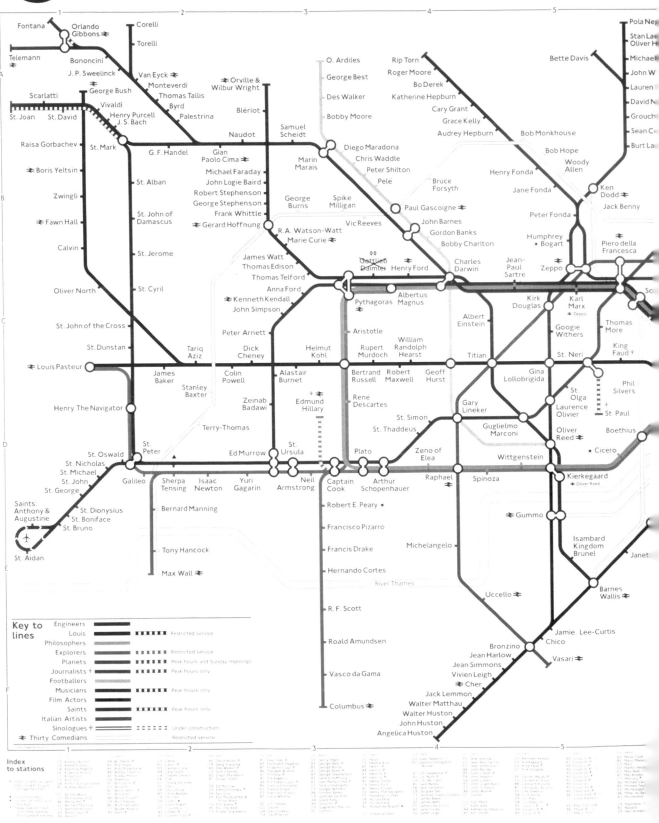

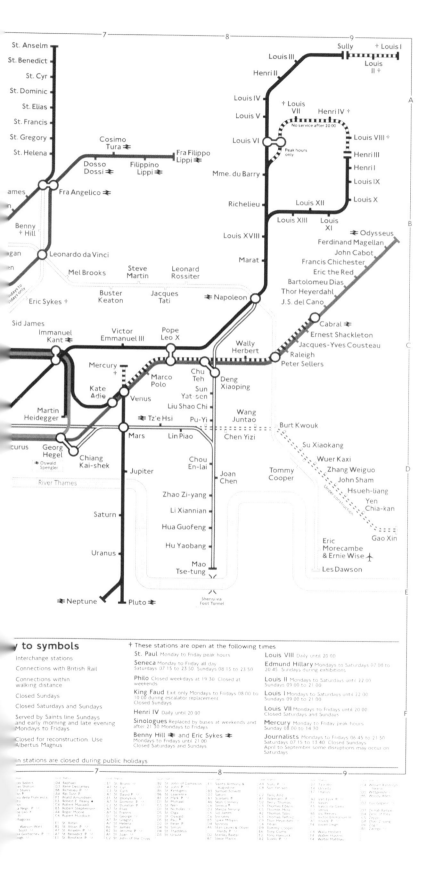

Simon Patterson
The Great Bear
1992
four-colour lithographic print
109 x 134.8
Lisson Gallery, London:
courtesy of the artist

background music. The local competitors of
The New York Times have been driven out
of business, but the paper of record is still a
provincial newspaper, though it has been
proliferating 'niche' sections alarmingly. The
triumvirate of old TV conglomerates has
now less than a third of viewers' loyalty,
because their 'broad general public' is
decayed and my own TV offers me, if I wish
to pay, more than 150 channels, virtually all
of which are 'niche' in one form or another.
The great public institution of the cinema
has long been in decline. The experience of
watching, as an eleven-year-old in
Waterford, the latest *Lone Ranger* at the
local Savoy, along with shawlies, shame-
faced young priests, mothers and snivelling
children seeking some warmth in winter,
hordes of pubescent boys and girls; or of
watching *The Battle of Algiers* in the 1970s,
in a cinema located in my small town's
small black section, is difficult to find any
more. Roars of the audience, advice to the
hero or heroine, curses at the villains, and
repartee between the viewers, have been
replaced by the solitude of home-watching
via videotapes, DVD and so on. In the
shops, these too are arranged strictly on the
niche basis, except for the most recent.
Home, hotel room, privacy: the places
farthest from politics, from the crowd, and
from public solidarities.

There are obviously parallel transformations
in the political sphere. When I was a
modestly radical student in the 1960s,
I went quite often to the Free Speech
Movement's Berkeley campus, and devoured
the local radical rag, famously entitled *The
Berkeley Barb*. The rag's editors were,
I think, real socialists of a sort; but what
struck me then was the contrast between
their editorials calling for solidarity in what
would later be termed a 'rainbow coalition',
and the contrary implications of the layout
of the rest of the paper, which had sections
for gays and lesbians, later separated from
each other, for women, for blacks, for
Chicanos, for workers, for Native
Americans, for Asian-Americans, for

environmentalists, for health food devotees,
and so on; and each of these sections
seemed to the reader a world of its own.
This niche-ing process, which also has had
its good sides, to be sure, has since
developed ever more broadly. The American
political system has adapted to the process,
making fragmentary local concessions to
this group or that. Yet at the same time, for
three decades now, electoral participation
has been in steady average decline; political
scientists continue to debate what this
means — mass alienation, or not? The
political parties are a shadow of what they
were a generation ago, single-issue
campaigns proliferate, while the informal
'permanent government' silently
consolidates itself.

These processes also have their analogue in
the global arena. I have described the trend
variously as the rise of internet, email, and
long-distance nationalism. The vast
population flows across national borders
and generally in the direction of the richest
and safest countries in the North are
creating sizeable numbers of people for
whom citizenship and nationality are largely
distinct. A spectacular, and less serious
aspect of this, is that a millionaire Canadian
computer-mogul not so long ago ran against
Lech Walesa for the presidency of Poland.
Less spectacular, and a little more serious,
are rich Mexicans in New York, running for
the mayoralties of their hometowns in
Oaxaca and Michoacan out of Manhattan
apartments. But most significant — and this
develops with the steady rise of dual or even
triple nationality — is making use of global
information and financial networks and
facilities to play politics in the countries
they have, for various reasons, abandoned.
The famous examples are the global reach
of the Tamil Tigers through the Tamil
diaspora especially in Europe and North
America; the destruction of the Babri
mosque in India, which led to the worst
sectarian violence since partition, steered by
the World Hindu Council with headquarters
in Britain; and most recently Al-Qaeda. One

could say that networks of this type existed in earlier decades, with the Irish republican operations in England and the United States as fitting examples. But the differences are striking. In earlier times the dog was usually wagging the tail, the activists in the homeland directing appeals for support in the diaspora; but this condition threatens to change to one where the overseas tails wag the home dogs. Croatia in the 1990s is an especially clear example.

Thus, diaspora identity politics typically means a divorce between nationality and citizenship. The new 'citizen' pays taxes, obeys the law and maybe votes once in a while in his country of chosen exile; but his real politics — which can mean propaganda, arms-running, financial interventions — are done in a place where he is not accountable, not arrestable, not taxable, and probably does not even bother to vote. This political type has been enormously stimulated by computer technology and the internet, where it is possible, twenty-four hours a day, to keep up almost instantaneously, with persons thousands of miles away, or to intervene in events at any moment he wishes. Furthermore, the crucial nets are typically self-enclosed niches. So one does Tibet twenty-four hours a day on *Tibetnet*; Sri Lanka on *Tamilnet*. The crucial thing is the contrast with even the most one-sided newspaper: the absence of a 'general public'. On the Armenian net one need never read a single thing from an Azerbaijani, but in the newspaper there is always the chance of a letter to the editor from an angry resident of Baku. These niches do not inevitably promote a delusional and even paranoid politics, but they certainly form a friendlier space for them than the older forms of public mediation. A Slovenian student of mine, an immigrant to Australia, has been studying the diasporic Croatians, Serbians, and Slovenians in that country; and his findings suggest that these people often have deluded visions of their faraway motherland, and are often more sectarian

and bigoted than the folks back home. It would be easy to find examples of the same thing among Irish in the United States, Ukrainians in Canada, Filipinos in the Netherlands, Iranians in Sweden, and the like. It is also quite likely that into these long-distance nationalisms are channelled the frustrations of immigrant marginality in the country of residence. Is it possible that the US — where about fifteen million immigrants arrive every decade — has so low a rate of electoral participation because many newcomers, and probably even their children, live their political passions out on the screens in their homes? Al-Qaeda is by no means a 'nationalist' movement, and its fanaticism is nothing novel in the world. But it is self-enclosed in the new hi-tech manner.

Finally, there is globalization, understood simply as America's domination of the planet to an extent never achieved by any previous power. There is no question about US military muscle; its economic power is formidable, but rests on the inflow (until 2001) of about one billion dollars a day in foreign deposits and investments, and the biggest external debt in world history. Much is made of the might of Hollywood, but it is likely that its impact is mainly among the young, and that it fades as the young grow older. In any case, as Gramsci argued long ago, real hegemony rests on a mix of force and consent. This consent in turn rests, Joseph Conrad showed us, on its self-representation of universalist ideas. The US has for long had two big ones — Liberty/Freedom and Equality. Freedom was a trump in the American hand in the Cold War; Equality remains a powerful symbol against bondage, against discrimination, against aristocratic privilege and the rest. These are by no means Ideas-Just-For-Export. In the 1950s, after South Africa, the United States was the second most unequal major society in the world. Within the Western world it was almost certainly the most sexist and homophobic. But by the early 1970s most of its formidable system of segregation had collapsed; women's emancipation (within limits) followed, then that of gays and lesbians. In both cases, the US example of self-emancipation has had vast, and mostly good, consequences in other countries.

But Freedom and Equality are in fact not natural dancing partners, and have a complex dialectical relationship to each other. Today the United States has the second largest prison population in the world (after China) in which black males make up a monstrously disproportionate part — one generation after desegregation. Freedom (of choice) has been used to cripple trade union solidarity; the same freedom has created an economic inequality far beyond that of any other advanced industrial country. In some industries, CEOs have been making almost 420-times the wages of their basic workers. In the huge battle over abortion, it is characteristic that the pro-legal abortion forces describe their position quite successfully in terms of 'Freedom of Choice' (the unborn foetus of course has none). Their adversaries, successfully deploy 'pro-life' (which is also the equality of the foetus) while typically being stalwart supporters of a death penalty which is nearly obsolete in all other advanced countries. It is no matter for surprise that these aporias and paradoxes are even more apparent in the US's global activities. This suggests that this conception of globalization isn't in fact fully globalized. During the Cold War — fought in part in the name of Freedom — the US created or gave heavy backing to many frightful régimes, including for a time those of Saddam Hussein's Iraq, Guatemala, Nicaragua, Chile, Brazil, Argentina, Uruguay, South Africa, South Korea, Chiang Kai-shek's Taiwan, Indonesia, South Vietnam, Pakistan, Saudi Arabia, Mobutu's Congo, Marco's Philippines, even quasi-apartheid Israel. Directly, or through its proxies, Washington killed far more foreigners than any other country in the world. In the 1960s and 1970s it dropped a higher tonnage of bombs on Laos

(population five million) than were dropped on Germany and Japan combined in World War II. Things have become more difficult since the collapse of the Soviet Union. North Korea is not an American creation and has a sizeable nuclear arsenal; Saddam Hussein would have disappeared twenty years ago in the Iraq–Iran War if the US had not rescued him and his poison-gas-armed forces. Support for Israel's aggressiveness could be defended in the Cold War as essential to containing 'totalitarian' Soviet advances; today it looks more like spinelessness before the powerful domestic Jewish-Israeli lobby. The language of 'We'll do it ourselves, no matter what anyone says / We'll do whatever we need to keep what we have' is the language of apartheid South Africa, not a true hegemon.

Part of Freedom was always Free Markets, in spite of the fact that historically the US has mostly been protectionist. The Bush administration's flagrant tariff-defence of the outmoded and inefficient American steel industry, the huge anti-free market subsidies for American agribusiness, gravely undermine the ideological power of Free Markets everywhere. It is too easy to interpret all this as 'You open your markets to us; but we won't open ours to you.' During the Asian and Mexican financial crises, Washington endlessly and piously denounced cronyism, lack of transparency, corruption, and so on in the name of truly Free Markets. But recent financial scandals in the United States dwarf anything that transpired in Seoul, Bangkok, Mexico City or Jakarta. Furthermore, Korean and Indonesian presidents have come to trial, the former Mexican president fled overseas, and the Thai prime minister was actually formally indicted. No one expects Vice-President Cheney, let alone President Bush, to experience a similar legal fate.

Speaking of equality and freedom is more chancy when the United States, with 5 per cent of the world's population, produces a quarter of its gas emissions, and brusquely

Margaret Corcoran
An Enquiry VIII
2002
oil on linen
46 x 61 cm
courtesy of the artist

rejects the Kyoto Protocol. The US is also a major part of that 20 per cent of the world's population which controls 8 per cent of the world's assets. This level of inequality in the global frame far exceeds any domestic ratio anywhere, and in any nation-state would be completely intolerable. A further difficulty is that most historical studies have shown that the successful industrial powers were, for most of their history, highly protectionist; and that more and more contemporary research is showing that the forcible introduction of neo-liberal free market policies has been ruinous for many Third World countries. None of this is lost on the rest of the world, even if it is not understood by many in the United States.

Blowback in different forms is bound to arise. Among these are foreign resistance to the anti-free market doctrines of 'intellectual property rights'. Pirating on a huge scale is the commonest practice. But India and Brazil, against huge American pressure are producing generic anti-AIDS drugs that their populations desperately need. This trend will certainly continue. Then there is the enormous proliferation of NGOs in the last two decades, including many based in the United States. With their international networking and their low institutionalization, these organizations are harder to bully and

bribe than are many heads of states and governments. We also now have the return of nationalism and protection of local industries from American penetration, visible in parts of America, as well as in Europe. One symbol of cultural revitalization is Al Jazeera, which is far more open to conflicting views than any American television network, and has huge appeal in the Arab world. After an initial battering by CNN, Thailand has responded by producing its own world news programme which is far better than CBS or NBC. The creative places in world cinema are not in Hollywood but in Taiwan, Iran, even Thailand. And there are the global political movements symbolized by the words Seattle, Genoa, Rio. It is astonishing just how vulnerable this new world-system is at its technological — therefore, its financial — centre. A teenager in Manila can create a computer virus that costs the speculators of Wall Street many millions of dollars. Anarchism is not dead; it is only beginning to realize its new-found opportunities. The distance between Hegemon and Rogue State is shorter than many people are accustomed to think. ■

This is a version of a lecture given at the Notre Dame Irish Studies Summer Seminar in 2002.

Edward Said (1935–2003)

A Late Style of Humanism

Seamus Deane

Why did Edward Said — uniquely among literary academics — command so wide an audience? First, he was *the* minority voice in the West for Palestine in the conflict with Israel.

1   Edward Said, 'Always on Top', *London Review of Books*, 25, 6 (20 Mar. 2003), 3–6 (3); see also Robert J. C. Young, *Colonial Desire; Hybridity in Theory, Culture and Race* (London and New York, 1995), 159–66; 'The Intellectual in the Post-Colonial World; Response and Discussion' [Panelists: Conor Cruise O'Brien, Edward Said, John Lukács] *Salmagundi*, 70–71 (Spring–Summer 1986), 65–81.

Second, his book *Orientalism* (1978) unforgettably revealed how important it was to know and further discover how the 'East' (Near East, Middle East, Far East, the Orient) had been created and observed under the supervision of Western eyes that always saw in it a counter-image and confirmation of what they saw themselves to be. In a wider perspective, Said also demonstrated in this book that the very act of the apprehension of the Other as an object for study is itself a model of the kinked relationship between rationality and domination so fatal to whatever or whoever the West considers to be beyond the pale cast of its thought. Third, because of his own involvement in these Easts and Wests, Said made the writing of literary criticism and political commentary an ethically urgent, inescapably political and complex activity. He was indeed a *chef d'école*, but postcolonialism — along with the swarms of those who deride it as a phantom and of those who welcome it as a revelation — is not at the centre of his work, although it obviously lies close to it. He thought that what he called postcolonial criticism, which began under the spiritual aegis of Fanon and Césaire, had the great virtue of showing the intertwined histories of colonizer and colonized, although without ever ignoring the realities that separated them. But since the end of the Vietnam War, and the subsequent proliferation of apologias for imperialism, postcolonialism has discovered that its very name is premature; at its weakest, it is the intellectually delayed Western response to the decolonization process of the 1960s in what is now called the 'Third World'; at its strongest, it has continued to take the lead from Said, then Homi Bhabha and Gayatri Spivak, in its examination of the discursive operations of colonialism. Said, since the late 1970s, remained alert to the workings of present-day imperialism and to the complicity of writers of all kinds — Gérard Chaliand, Conor Cruise O'Brien, V. S. Naipaul — in cleansing its record and defending its practices by their ready adaptation of the inherited discourses which he so memorably illuminated.[1]

Paradoxically, what made Said a leading exponent of postcolonialism, was his vexed, yet loyal adherence to the humanist tradition in which he had been educated and by the limitations of which he so often was dismayed. While he saw, along with many others, that the historical conditions for humanism had almost disappeared in the twentieth century — particularly with the rise of Fascism — he still sought to create conditions for the survival of some of its deepest values. Even a hostile commentator on Said, such as Aijaz Ahmad, who considers the material conditions of Said's position as a Western intellectual to expose the 'idealism' of his intellectual stance, says (erroneously) that 'the

Photograph:
© Brigitte Lacombe.
Courtesy Columbia
University Press

systematic awareness of the role of literature in imperialist ideology' had not been in the communist tradition before the anti-war movements of the late sixties and Said's *Orientalism*.[2] Yet Said's battles were not merely a reprise of those Adorno had fought earlier — against Fascism, Stalinism, late Capitalism, the Luciferian fall of the aesthetic into the abyss of popular culture and consumerism. *Orientalism* is the most influential late modern account of the various histories of collusion between military coercion, commercial greed, scholarship and the astonishing intellectual work involved in the creation of a global system that has been in the making for well over two hundred years. It liberates and entraps Said as a writer. It illuminates a predicament in which an accelerating logic of domination and control is realized by humans who are themselves commanded by it. This is not to say that Said leaves us in any doubt that it is those who are dominated who are by far the more damaged by subjection, whatever corruption may attend upon it for its practitioners, at least some of whom are as anxious to persuade themselves as they are to convince others of the beneficial and unavoidable nature of their massacres, annexations, misrepresentations and thefts. But Said wants to find the space for and confidence in an emancipatory project of the kind offered by the great eighteenth-century Italian philosopher, Vico, who imagined a secular and humane world as the ultimate historical creation of humankind. This faith was constantly challenged for Said by the often reluctantly admitted force of Foucault's thought, in which that emancipatory possibility seemed to him to have been dimmed or extinguished. The battle is visible in his own work. *Orientalism* is Foucauldian; many of the later essays in which he — more effectively than most of his critics — laid siege to his own garrisoned achievement, are Viconian in inspiration. Said fought a battle, related to but distinct from Adorno's, not against

the destruction of humanism as such, but against the damaged and ghastly afterlife it continued to lead in American foreign policy and in its most murderous variant, the destruction of the Palestinians by the Israelis in the name of 'Western' values. The Zionist project was born-again Fascism, a more enduring enemy than its first form, of which it was an inversion.

György Lukács, the Hungarian Marxist (and later Stalinist) critic made it a commonplace of European cultural belief that the central art-form of humanism was the novel, 'the epic of a world that has been abandoned by God', the most famous sentence of a description of the form which Said described as 'certainly the most brilliant ever offered'.[3] Lukács also went beyond Mazzini's work on the historical novel to make it the genre or sub-genre that most crucially and visibly bore the legible imprint of 'history'. In addition, he provided a dual theory of the evolution of the novel as a form, claiming it derived from the epic, and then, after a brilliant phase of development in the nineteenth century, culminated in the failure of the bourgeoisie in the European revolutions of 1848, falling thereafter into the 'novel of disillusionment', in which 'the incongruence of interiority and the conventional world leads to a complete denial of the latter'.[4] Tolstoy revealed how much the novel 'is the necessary epic form of our time', because in him the unbridgeable gap between nature and culture was disclosed, how the best efforts of Tolstoy (or later Dostoyevsky) could not restore that pristine and harmonious condition.[5] This is a prelude to the famous conclusion to Lukács's classic Cold War essay 'The Ideology of Modernism', with its attacks on Joyce, Musil, Benn, Kafka and others for their 'rejection of narrative objectivity, the surrender to subjectivity'; in effect, 'modernism leads not only to the destruction of traditional literary forms; it leads to the destruction of literature as

2 'Nationalism, Post-Colonialism, Communism', Aijaz Ahmad interviewed by Gregory Elliott, Francis Mulhern and Peter Osborne, *Radical Philosophy*, 76 (Mar.–Apr. 1996), 29–38 (29–30)

3 Edward Said, *Reflections on Exile and Other Essays* (Cambridge, Mass., 2000), 560

4 Georg Lukács, *The Theory of the Novel*, trans. Anna Bostock (London, 1971), 144; first published in German in 1920.

5 *Theory of the Novel*, 146

6 *The Meaning of
Contemporary Realism*,
trans. John Mander and
Necke Mander (London,
1963), 24, 45; probably
composed in 1955.

7 *Contemporary Realism*,
15–16; see also a more
detailed, if not more
convincing, temporal
sequence for the
development of the novel
in the 1935 essay, 'Il
romanzo come epopea
borghese', translated into
Italian in 1976 in
*Problemi di Teoria del
Romanzo*, ed. Vittorio
Strada (Torino, 1976),
133–78. Adorno's view
of Lukács's aesthetics,
and especially of his faith
in the bourgeois novel's
'realism' is fierce,
although Fredric
Jameson sees the
problem of 'realism' in
Lukács's work more
clearly. See Theodor
Adorno, Walter
Benjamin, Ernst Bloch,
Bertolt Brecht, Georg
Lukács, *Aesthetics and
Politics*, with Afterword
by Fredric Jameson
(London, 1977), 151–76,
199–204.

8 See Said's essays
'Between Chance and
Determinism: Lukács's
Aesthetik'; 'History,
Literature, and
Geography'; 'Traveling
Theory Reconsidered', in
Reflections on Exile,
61–69, 436–52, 458–63.
See also Abdirahman A.
Hussein, *Edward Said:
Criticism and Society*
(London and New York,
2002), 216–23, for a
splendid account of Said
and Lukács.

9 *Contemporary Realism*
in the essay 'Franz Kafka
or Thomas Mann', 47

such'.[6] Throughout, Lukács is defending a particular notion of 'realism', with Thomas Mann as his exemplary practitioner, in which the fine but necessary balance between nature and culture is struck, although it is always at risk. For Lukács, realism is the antithesis of modernism because it is founded on 'a common social attitude', always historically specifiable in the particular shape that it takes, which for him then was the expression of a human solidarity through the 'humanist revolt against imperialism' and against Cold War ideology.[7] This Lukácsian faith in the durability of the great literary novel as an expression of human solidarity and the accompanying suspicion of the dazzling melancholia of modernism and its alienated interiorities remains part of the heritage of American literary criticism in general, even as one of its allergies, and, more specifically, of Theodor Adorno (who is part of that heritage), of Fredric Jameson and of Edward Said.

Many American intellectuals of the twentieth century were deeply indebted to Marxism, which in the 1930s especially had offered the most effective analysis of the contemporary triumphs of Fascism and failures of Capitalism. Said recognized the debt he owed to Lukács's work, especially *Soul and Form* (1910), *The Theory of the Novel* (1920), *History and Class Consciousness* (1923), and *The Historical Novel* (1947); *Studies in European Realism* (1948) and *The Meaning of Contemporary Realism* (1957) had less impact. He first incurred it indirectly through the influence Lukács had exerted on Kenneth Burke and R. P. Blackmur in particular.[8] It was from Lukács that he learned how to see the affiliative connections between exile, alienation and linguistic displacement in the early modernists; in short, Lukács helped him to read Conrad. But as the prestige of Lukács — and of his disciple, Lucien Goldmann — waned and as the New Criticism became the aesthetic weapon of

choice during the Cold War, a specific American version of militant humanism began to intensify into the chronically inflamed condition that still endures. It then became doctrinal to see the Russian Revolution as a replay of the French Revolution and to say that revolutionary, utopian and atheistic visions of global transformation lacked the precious sense of human complexity and unpredictability that the liberal, Western (Anglo-American), anti-revolutionary and Christian cultures displayed in their economic, political and artistic achievements, all of which were monuments to the spirit of the individual rather than that of the collective. It was in that setting — scarcely altered in the last fifty years — that Said's *Orientalism* appeared to be so scandalous to the captains of Western propaganda. For it showed how doctrinally bound the West was; how given to creating cartoon enemies for the purpose of imaging its true self; and how clearly its aim had been and still was world domination. One of the most unnoticed features of the book is how closely its themes are repeated in the pulp fiction (print and visual) of the era from the Cold War to the present — the cults of the abnormal, the perverse, the existence of the world-threatening Evil Enemy, the Other, and the tiresome but tireless variations on the older forms of detective and thriller fiction, of which Lukács observed in the mid-fifties:

> Or take the detective story. With Conan Doyle the genre was firmly grounded in a philosophy of security; it glorified the omniscience of those who watched over the stability of bourgeois life. Now the basic ingredients are fear and insecurity: at any moment terror may break through; only luck can avert it.[9]

Said realized that the exposure of imperialism as a system in which culture was politics by other means — although he was not the first by any means to so expose it — had serious, perhaps inescapable, consequences for humanistic study. He recognized that the production of such a system and of an analysis of it, such as his own, had the same source in rationality. Thus he raised a central question about enlightenment itself. If rationality is so given to domination is domination integral to it? Or is domination the sad road taken since the eighteenth-century Enlightenment originally gave to reason the crown formerly (and latterly) worn by all kinds of irrational or non-rational agencies? These were questions that Adorno, Horkheimer and others, standing in the afterlight of Fascism and Stalinism, had raised and attempted to answer. They had wanted to renew reason's alliance with emancipation. But it was Foucault who seemed to make that renewal impossible, because of his equation of knowledge with disciplinary power and because of his peculiarly seductive way of regarding the exercise of reason as a species of covert police operation that had only one purpose — to capture and intern all that it considered to share in a nature not its own. This position clearly informs Said's in *Orientalism*; and he adheres to it in the late seventies, sufficiently so to make his intervention in the Foucault–Derrida debate seem decisive for his subsequent career. What I want to suggest is that for Said to side with Foucault in 1978 was perfectly coherent with the vision of his great book *Orientalism*.[10] For Said the postcolonial critic, Foucault was right, and he saw that; for Said the humanist, Derrida was right, but he did not see that. Derrida's 1963 lecture-review 'Cogito and the History of Madness' of Foucault's *Folie et Déraison* strikes at the central weakness of Foucault's work, 'writing a history of untamed madness … before being caught and paralyzed in the nets of classical reason, from within the very language of classical reason itself'.[11] Said could not abide by Foucault's position and remain a defender of humanism; he could have found support

for his humanism, however elusive it might have proved to be, in Derrida. To clarify his position for himself and for some others, he dismissed both as authors whose effect was to depoliticize writing and even to trivialize it to a game in which 'undecidability' was always the trump card. This was unfair, but effective. Postmodernism and deconstruction were both flushed out of the system and Said, besieged by Zionists, imperialists, and their fellow travellers in the media and the academy, turned to defend his book on the same humanistic grounds that they in turn claimed to be protecting. Anyway, no theoretical misgivings could rob *Orientalism* of its force in relation to US policies in the Middle East — Palestine, Lebanon, Iran, Iraq — and their dependence on the 'three sets of illusions [that] economically buttress and reproduce each other in the interests of shoring up the Western self-image: the view of Islam, the ideology of modernization, and the affirmations of Zionism.'[12] Moreover, its analysis of the essentially anthropological position of detachment adopted towards strange and threatening ethnic groups gains in power with every intensification of the tsunami of the propaganda 'war on terror' that rampages through the Islamic countries targeted by it.[13]

Said's defence of Western humanism, rather than of the 'anti-humanism' of Foucault and others, does not now seem as surprising as it might have done in the early 1980s. Said was always an American intellectual, although more than usually alert to the differences and interconnections between modern American, European and Arab traditions of commentary and analysis. At Princeton and Harvard 'he had the privilege to be trained in the German philological tradition of comparative literature'.[14] He was also a university teacher and an admirer of the university as an ideal and as a place. His friend and colleague Michael Wood remembered, in a tribute to him after his death, that

10 'The Problem of Textuality: Two Exemplary Positions', *Critical Inquiry*, 4, 4 (1978), 673–714

11 Jacques Derrida, *Writing and Difference*, trans. Alan Bass (London, 1978), 31–63 (34); see also Christopher Norris, *Derrida* (London, 1987), 213–23.

12 'The Formation of American Public Opinion on the Question of Palestine', in *The Politics of Dispossession: The Struggle for Palestinian Self-Determination 1969–1994* (London, 1994), 61–62

13 'Identity, Negation and Violence', in *The Politics of Dispossession*, 345–49

14 Cited in Tariq Ali, 'Remembering Edward Said 1935–2003', *New Left Review*, 24 (Nov.–Dec. 2003), 59–65 (60)

15 Michael Wood, 'On Edward Said', *London Review of Books*, 25, 20 (23 Oct. 2003), 3
16 Edward Said, *Musical Elaborations* (London, 1991), 95, 93
17 'Sense and Sensibility', in *Reflections on Exile*, 15–23

... he was as anxious to save cultural spaces from politics as he was to remind us that most people who say culture should be free of politics mean only that culture should be free of the politics they dislike. I was always moved by Edward's repeated (and I think romanticized) claim that the American university is 'the last remaining utopia', and his books are full of tributes and references and acknowledgments to a vast assortment of scholars, a sort of textual community of inquiry.[15]

I too remember that Edward was pleased to be shown Cardinal Newman's highly orientalist (although ecumenically inspired) University Church in Stephen's Green in Dublin, largely because of his admiration for Newman's 'Idea of a University' and also because of the conjunction, commemorated in a plaque on the adjoining Newman House, of the most famous names associated with it — Newman, Gerard Manley Hopkins and Joyce. That trio represented the kind of internal dissonance only a university, among all institutions, would seek to generate and celebrate. Although he did not to my knowledge write of Newman, they shared a faith in the communal yet lonely life of the intellectual in the university. In Newman's style, so famously saluted by Joyce, there is a timbre, redolent both of solitude and communion, that Said himself time and again achieved, so much so that it might be taken to be his 'authorial signature', the *air de la chanson* as Proust put it, or, in Said's own comment on the Proustian passage, 'the ultimately solitary intimacy by which the special music of an author impresses itself upon a receptive critical intelligence.'[16]

So it was ultimately on a particular version of the Ivy League university tradition that Said drew most deeply, particularly as that had developed at Columbia, with F. W. Dupee, R. P. Blackmur and, to a lesser extent, Lionel Trilling and, later, Richard

Poirier. There were various extensions of this, most notably in the so-called Geneva School of critical phenomenology, dominated by the work of Georges Poulet and Jean Starobinski. But their Geneva was a suburb of Columbia, Harvard and Princeton, which had themselves become cosmopolitan under the influence of German philological scholarship. Erich Auerbach's *Mimesis*, a work that became more emblematic for Said as time went by, was regarded as its masterwork. His *Orientalism* was a companionate achievement. In both, a whole tradition of writing and scholarship was summarized with a force that suddenly gave to an amorphous 'field' a cartographic reality that endowed it with a degree of definition by which its occupants would be forever stimulated, even if only at times — and vainly — to escape. In both cases, the authors were, like their readers, beneficiaries and casualties of the fame and completeness of these works, besieged by adulation and animosity.

What Said found in the writings of Blackmur, Poulet and others was the capacity of such critics to immerse themselves in the texts under scrutiny and yet to be able, perhaps even via such immersion, to gain a perspective on and detachment from them.[17] This was for him the essence of the idea of critical distance which he believed the intellectual needed to achieve; it was also the source of his own search for those critical terms that would accelerate his capacity to mould the perceptual into the conceptual in relation to an ensemble of works, textual or musical. The terms 'filiation' and 'affiliation' are instances of this. 'Filiation' is, so to say, a natural condition, the one into which a person is born. 'Affiliation' is a cultural condition, one into which that person might develop. This is not a simple progress from a singular to a plural condition. The words operate energetically in relation to one another. Yet there is also within these terms an observance of limitation. What is given, the filiate, is given by a specific set of circumstances and possibilities; so too is the affiliate controlled by the opportunities, internal and external, in which it can develop. A well-known example is Stephen Dedalus in Joyce's fiction. Someone dominated by those 'nets' he wants so urgently and famously to fly beyond, he grows beyond his origins to an extraordinary degree and yet his growth is marked by those origins, as is the heretic by the beliefs he repudiates. Indeed the more refined and supple the heresy, the more embedded the filiate conditions that promoted it. Yet the filiate is not altogether a destiny. For the affiliate condition is not capricious or a form of boosterism — 'you can be what you want to be' — or of any of the similar popular slogans that rotate endlessly on their commercial axes. It always has an element of retroactive recognition; this — and it need not be anything 'fulfilling' — is what lay dormant in a person, a generation, an historical epoch. Stephen Dedalus is one incarnation of this; but so too is Julien Sorel awaiting execution, both of them little Napoleons. Said is uneasy with the trouble he finds in these terms, although Blackmur surely taught him about the rewards of the punitive aspects of appreciation and thinking. Only great art has this capacity for making great trouble and enchantment arrive together, like dormant possibilities that can only awake, if they do, simultaneously. So it is only in speaking of art that, as is proper, his critical terms are stretched to the limit.

Said constantly returned to the novel to understand its particular mode of creating values by the most severe and exquisite testing of the possibility of people ever having or of ever developing the resource to live by the relatively few and basic principles they could conceive or imagine. Joseph Conrad was the most important of all novelists for him in this regard. His first

book (originally his doctoral dissertation) was on Conrad; some of the finest pages in his next book *Beginnings* dwell on Conrad's example and on his great novel *Nostromo*; and Conrad never moved out of his range of regular reference thereafter. The initial attraction is easy to understand, although it ultimately develops into a very difficult relationship. They were both from countries — Poland and Palestine — subject to massacre, the bloodstain from which had been regularly rinsed away in the detergent waters of global politics; each belonged to the presiding imperial power and culture of his time — respectively Britain and the US; each had produced an outstanding critique of imperialism; each had made the condition of exile prototypical of modernity and its various forms of domination and alienation; each was culturally attached to the politically scandalous systems he analysed and to which he was not entirely native.

It is to Conrad's novels that we must go to find the besetting image that corresponds to his presence within Said's writings — that of the informing ghost, the secret sharer, the sinister intimate who is a companion to the hero on his crusade to discover the grounds for a rational faith in human action or, alternatively, to face up to the usual polysyllabic Conradian fate of looking into the incomprehensible, or yielding to the suction of the fathomless whirlpool of unbelief that, for Conrad, had its political correlative in Russian anarchism — his version of what is now called Terror. In Conrad's *The Secret Agent* (1907) as in *Under Western Eyes* (1911) — both titles have a strong Saidian flavour — the terrorist is no military threat to the empires (British and Russian) he lives in. He threatens instead to expose the illusions by which they (or any organizations, including the conspiratorial kind) bonded themselves together — the illusion that their forms of solidarity had a foundation in the real. This attracts Said's attention, but not because he agreed with the notion that imperial and/or

18 Joseph Conrad and Ford Madox Hueffer, *Romance, A Novel* (London, 1903), 462

human solidarity have no such foundation. Instead, he wanted to argue that such a solidarity does indeed exist, but that it can survive only in the specifically human, not the imperial, form. What makes an empire frail is that the reality of human solidarity is anti-imperial. Empire, as a system or as an idea, betrays human solidarity; human solidarity, as an idea or as a system, threatens empire.

Said recognized but did not endorse the abyssal possibility that Conrad regularly insinuates. Nor was he receptive to the contrastingly grandiose sentimentality that Conrad occasionally intones, as in an early collaborative effort like *Romance* (1903), where he tells us that 'suffering is the lot of man' but bears within it 'a hope of felicity, like a jewel set in iron'.[18] Still, this strain in Conrad, with which he hoped to win a popular audience, is an important, if unsuccessful, counter to the bleaker vision that he more convincingly establishes in his best work. Said empathized with this struggle, noting that the anguish and physical ailments Conrad complained of were perhaps bound up with the impasse that he confronted almost daily when he wrote. Was the act of writing itself an exposure of an abiding nullity in all experience or, as an act, did it sanction a hope that pure reflection on existence never could? Moreover, Conrad's anxieties about money and artistic integrity did not simply rehearse the modernist anxiety to pretend that art was somehow excluded from the zone of commercial exploitation. They were anxieties, that Said also shared, about the possibility of reaching an audience in a language that would avoid the contrasting fates of ultra-refinement or of journalistic debasement. It was only with the publication of Said's memoir *Out of Place* (1999) that the resemblance with his own condition became clear; for Said too found himself plagued by a similar tension, parental in origin, between the appeal of the harsh disciplines of work and the

ravishments of aesthetic pleasure. Through one, he was an Arab who could become an American; through the other, he was an American who could again become an Arab. Yet it was in a fusion of both appeals that he founded his humanist faith in a form of solidarity that escaped the notional and national binaries that moulded his upbringing in those Eastern-Western worlds of Palestine, Libya, Egypt and the US.

His humanism refused both sentimentality and negation; Conrad's disquieting attempts to transmute the sense of human endeavour's emptiness into the affirmations required by the mass audience led to his endorsement of the British imperial adventure, which, in its propaganda, assigned to such sentiment a salient role. Said, by contrast, wanted to establish the existence of a human solidarity that rejected all forms of world domination, especially the British or American kinds, that claim universality for their provincial and cynically sentimental versions of 'freedom', 'democracy', 'way-of life'. These claims were dangerous because they were so close to the truths they perverted. They came from cultures that, to justify their attempts at domination abroad, had distorted the central tenets of the humanist tradition that had been developed at home. They displayed greater expertise in this regard than those fated to be humanism's enemies (as, for instance, Conrad thought Russia was). Perversion of principle, achieved on such a scale and with such success, came from intimacy with principle, not from ignorance of it. It is no wonder that *Nostromo* was the Conrad novel Said explored in the most searching and illuminating detail.

Perhaps this feature of Said's work also helped him to win a wide readership. His humanism had and has an appeal beyond the walls of the academy. Many would say that it had greater appeal outside than within those walls, because it has long been a belief, promoted by the popular media, that humanism had been destroyed by the academy's bulimic passion for the junk food of 'Theory', especially sinister because the plain beef-and-beer diet of the Anglo-American menu had been dismissed by a French cuisine. Although such an attitude completely deforms any understanding of Said, whose contempt for the Allan Bloom–Saul Bellow–Harold Bloom version of the intellectual life was always clear, it has merit for those who admire his brilliant, essayistic style in which the needs of the educated, rather than the specialized, audience were rarely forgotten. His work is free of the numb vocabularies and anti-humanist declarations that allegedly characterized the largely-unread but widely-caricatured work of authors such as Barthes, Derrida, Foucault, Lyotard, Baudrillard, Deleuze and Guattari — to name only a short list of the demonic practitioners. Said's position on the question of good and bad writing 'is simply to avoid jargon that only alienates a potentially wide constituency'.[19] Yet, for all that, Said never quite came to grips with the philosophical/stylistic problem of the esoteric in writing, represented by influential modern thinkers as diverse as Adorno or Leo Strauss. It is not at all enough to argue the case by identifying the esoteric elements in a discourse as 'jargon', or to say that writers such as these are exceptions, who may be allowed to be cryptic or obscure, because they are so extraordinarily gifted. This is the kind of stalwart defence of humanism that reveals the internal intellectual strain it must undergo to escape what he calls 'the impoverishing dichotomy' between jargon and 'a nostalgic celebration of some past state of glory associated with what is sentimentally evoked as humanism'.[20]

Said seems to be in agreement with Adorno on the crucial question of the status of the aesthetic in relation to the historical, political or any other form of production. Both say it is different; the only realm resistant to commodification, according to Adorno *because* it has found in the esoteric a resistance and resource against absorption. Said too asserts 'that there is always the supervening reality of the aesthetic work without which the kind of humanism I am talking about here really has no essential meaning, only an instrumental one'. But when Said then goes on to invoke the authority of the great classical humanist critics of modernity — Leo Spitzer, Erich Auerbach, Ernst Robert Curtius — for a particular kind of close reading and reception that is based 'only in the inner faith of the humanist "in the power bestowed on the human mind of investigating the human mind" [the quotation is from Spitzer], as well as an abiding sense that what one finds in the work is generally worth investigating', the chasm separating his view from Adorno's is revealed.[21] Most immediately, we can see that Said's defence of the plain style and Adorno's defence of the cryptic or esoteric are founded in completely different views of the aesthetic. While both regard it as uniquely important and different from other categories, for Adorno the shrunken audience for the aesthetic is a tragic indication of the unavoidable power of Capitalism's colonization of almost all intellectual as well as geographical space. The fate of the aesthetic, revealed in its esoteric modern or modernist forms, is part of the logic of Capitalism. For Said, the aesthetic can be acknowledged through extreme care and conscientiousness, but it is in effect, as a category, emancipated from the logic of Capitalism because, he argued, the aesthetic can never be reduced to or be identical with the historical conditions that produce it. For Said the great modernist novel was *Nostromo*, in which 'material interests', as represented by the silver of the mines, swallow everything individual into an impersonal system of power; for Adorno, the great modern novel was Mann's *Doctor Faustus* (1947), in which the musical genius Leverkühn articulates through his art an

19 *Humanism and Democratic Criticism* (New York, 2004), 72
20 *Humanism*, 70
21 *Humanism*, 64–65

22 See George Lichtheim, *Lukács* (London, 1970), 84–92; James Schmidt, 'Mephistopheles in Hollywood: Adorno, Mann and Schoenberg', in Tom Huhn, ed., *The Cambridge Companion to Adorno* (Cambridge, 2004), 148–80; Michael Maar, 'Teddy and Tommy: The Masks of *Doctor Faustus*', *New Left Review*, 20 (Mar.–Apr. 2003), 113–30.

23 Theodor Adorno, *Minima Moralia: Reflections from Damaged Life*, trans. E. F. N. Jephcott (London, 1974), 89; first published in German in 1951.

24 *Minima Moralia*, 222. See also James Schmidt, 'Mephistopheles in Hollywood', in *The Cambridge Companion to Adorno*, 168.

25 Ara Guzelimian, ed., *Parallels and Paradoxes: Explorations in Music and Society* (New York, 2002), 79–110, 169–84

26 *Representations of the Intellectual* (New York, 1994), 82

27 Edward Said, 'My Encounter with Sartre', *London Review of Books*, 22, 11 (1 Jun. 2000), 42–43

28 'Edward Said in Conversation with Neeladri Bhattacharya, Suvir Kaul and Ania Loomba, New Delhi, 16 December, 1997', *Interventions: International Journal of Postcolonial Studies*, 1, 1 (Oct. 1998), 81–96 (94)

authoritarian politics that was latent within the humanist tradition that it destroyed. (It should be noted, however, that both Lukács and Adorno were victims of self-delusion about Mann's attitude towards them and towards the history of humanism in Germany, especially as it is represented in *Doctor Faustus*.) [22] The barbarity of the modern era is created in politics; but its rupture with the past is, on closer inspection, an outgrowth of what was already there. Because of the connivance between culture and politics — a central theme in *Orientalism* — the depths of such unwelcome continuities can be plumbed more effectively in art than in or by any other activity. Said in part agrees with this; his recognition of the presence, within Jane Austen's novels, of the slave trade's sustaining a whole economy of leisure would be one instance. Yet he did not go as far as Adorno in 1945, stricken by how Fascism had gained support for its programmes of extermination against the Jews, in saying that, 'In the innermost recesses of humanism, as its very soul, there rages a frantic prisoner who, as a Fascist, turns the world into a prison.'[23] Adorno believed that art was possible without humanism and further, that the moment of humanism's extinction had been illuminated in the blaze of an art which lit up the landscape of barbarism of the war period and of the post-war period, and not just in Germany. But there was always the appeal of art to beauty and pleasure, even when it was representing mass slaughter (say in Schoenberg's composition *A Survivor from Warsaw*, which shares a birth date with *Doctor Faustus* and the great Adorno/Horkheimer polemic *Dialectic of Enlightenment*). 'Art is magic delivered from the lie of being truth.'[24] Said could not have gone so far; his belief in the conditioning existence of humanism left him instead with the older and vexing questions of the relation of art to the artist's opinions, one that he and Daniel Barenboim debated in relation to Wagner's anti-Semitism and his music, with all its accompanying history from Wagner's day to the present.[25] In the end, on the old premises, one has to say that the opinions do and do not matter; that they must and must not be taken into account in the consideration of the work as art. This may be a dialectic; but it looks more like a game of shuttlecock.

Nevertheless, despite the severe strains involved in remaining loyal to the fundamental values of the academy, Said could still aver in the 1993 Reith lectures for the BBC that 'To my mind, the Western university, certainly in America, still can offer the intellectual a quasi-utopian space in which reflection and research can go on, albeit under new constraints and pressures.'[26] His challenges to propaganda, commodification and inhumanity were the more effective because they were of such a classically 'intellectual' kind, commonly linked with a figure like Sartre in France, or Raymond Williams in England. They had both been at times dismissively indulged because they were Marxists — although Sartre's opposition to the Algerian War provoked real and vicious responses, while it also made him the icon throughout the world of the engaged intellectual — like Zola before or Said after him. (Yet Sartre and his *cénacle* were Zionists and Said's one meeting with him was an unpleasant experience.[27]) Said often spoke of the need of the intellectual to keep a 'critical distance' from power while remaining engaged; when his Reith lectures were published under the title *Representations of the Intellectual*, there was a great stir when in the Arabic version 'a word which means "not committed" in Arabic was substituted for the phrase "independent intellectual", and I don't mean it that way.'[28] Neither too far out, nor too in deep; not detached to an inhuman degree, not immersed to the point of blur — or complicity; this is a somewhat emaciated summary of his credo. But, although committed politically, he was so sturdy in his avowal of widely shared humanist beliefs, that it took a concerted and polemical strategy of misreading and then of insult to misrepresent him as a sinister influence.

Said was no Marxist; nor was he a structuralist, post-structuralist, or deconstructionist; nor did he merit any of the other terms widely canvassed in the media as equivalents for 'terrorist'. If he had a model for the engaged and frequently enraged intellectual, whose radical challenge to the corruption of traditional beliefs was sustained by the breathtaking stylistic balance he consistently struck, it was Jonathan Swift. Like Swift on Ireland or on early Capitalism, Said on Palestine showed that a humanist faith was scandalously betrayed by those who used the lexicon and the tones of civility to justify murder and exploitation. Israel was not and is not, he claimed, a country of the Western enlightenments; it has become the dark state that destroys those enlightenments by the nature of its claim to embody them. In that one battle between Palestine and Israel, Said revealed the depth and danger of the Western world's investment in coercion and hypocrisy and the pressing need to dissolve that investment.

For his appeal to survive at all, his rhetoric had to have more savour than is usual in the decaffeinated world of the American academy in particular. He won friends because he wrote so well; equally, on that account, he attracted hostility from those who were sorry to see the case against them put so cogently. He seemed to be able to negotiate successfully between the alternatives of self-referential aestheticism, with its separation of art and criticism from social praxis, and what was once the almost mandatory modernist despair about the incapacity of language to represent the real. As we have seen, he was aware of and greatly influenced by the great power of the conceptual reconfigurations achieved by Derrida and, more so, Foucault. Yet for the

sake of vigour if not rigour he had to be decisive in his repudiation of their baneful contribution to what he called 'the regulated, not to say calculated, irrelevance of criticism'. [29] Although his view of all the various moments of 'theory' was extremely conventional and far too readily dismissive, its forthrightness was part of his engaged and engaging style. All the strategic keywords in Said's vocabulary — such as molestation, filiation, affiliation, worldliness, counterpoint — accentuate the secularity of his ambitions for criticism; both to be conscious of the particular world in which it was created and to know the specific historical nature and heritage of the materials, including the works of art, which it addressed. No epistemological relativism was allowed as an excuse for escaping from ethical judgement; no ethical judgement supervened over aesthetic appreciation. He created a conceptual tempo rather than a conceptual structure in his writing; his essays are Goldberg variations on a set of basic themes, ultimately astonishing in their virtuosity but also astonishing in their revelation of the intrinsic richness of the themes themselves. In later years, as the tonic climate of his earlier writings, clear and bracing, became more autumnal, Adorno's influence returned to enrich and modify Said's thinking. One sign of this was Said's characteristically direct rejection of what he thought of as the Hegelian School's habit or routine of reconciling oppositions in a larger synthesis; instead, he thought of his position as that of bearing witness, like Adorno, to irreconcilability, allowing opposed positions to be held in a dialectical tension that was not slackened by any wish to see them coalesce under the impetus of any supposed inner logic of their own or of any borrowed ritual gesture of completion. Adorno reinforced Said's hatred of the claptrap of reconciliation, especially when, among its promoters were criminals, 'world leaders' among them, who hoped to use it as a way to efface their own actions and responsibility.

29 *The World, the Text, and the Critic* (Cambridge, Mass., 1983), 25

30 For a startlingly fine specimen of this, see Christopher Hitchens, *Orwell's Victory* (London, 2002).

31 *Minima Moralia*, 41

Postcolonialism requires a theory of power that abandons 'them' and 'us' as its governing terms. Those who are not like 'us' can only be understood in the terms the presiding 'we' dictate; this is true even if it can be shown that one term depends for its reality on the other. It is a tight, closed situation, made none the less so by the revelation that it is produced discursively. We produce alterity; it does not precede our production of it, even though believing that is the condition of the operation's success. Said, along with Bhabha and Spivak, long understood the jeopardy of a position, that had been argued too well — as he seemed to believe Foucault's had been. Rather than repay his debt to Foucault, he cancelled it. Bhabha and Spivak, on the other hand, and in their very different ways, repaid their debts to 'theory' by developing their own particular styles in the direction of the esoteric and the specialized, seeking the arcane where Said sought the familiar. For they wanted and found an exit, not from discursive power, but from the range of reference Said had ascribed to it. Bhabha, for instance, wanted to develop a subtle, taxing discourse for hybridity that would, as far as possible, escape or seem to escape from what appeared to be an almost fundamentalist binarism; Spivak, found in subalternity other populations below the horizon for whom everything, even their liberation, had been already so spoken-for that the effort was to enable these people — mostly women — to begin to speak and thereby create an alternative form of power to that which had silenced them. Said left himself no such options, largely because he did not believe either of these had the immediacy that the battle with and for knowledge and power demanded in the various places in the world (Palestine above all, of course) where it had become focused as a global issue. Further, it seemed to him that his own political connection with Palestine and the Palestinian National Authority charged his writing with an energy and demanded of it a clarity that it

would otherwise have lacked. Thus, he often regarded jargon or obscurity as a form of intellectual narcissism that is itself a consequence of having no urgent or actual involvement in a loaded political actuality; it is a fate to which academic criticism often consigns writers especially if they are — like Swift or Lukács — degraded and nullified thereby. This is obviously not a view that postcolonial criticism has taken especially to heart. But it needs to be distinguished from the notion that tough guys don't dance, that the to-tell-it-as-it-is school of writing, greatly favoured by essayists who are converts from an earlier 'fashionability', part Humphrey Bogart, part George Orwell, need not punish the language to express its thought.[30] Said had even less time for them than for the writers of jargon. Adorno remembered the politics of such straight talkers and writers:

> Behind the pseudo-democratic dismantling of ceremony, of old-fashioned courtesy, of the useless conversation suspected, not even unjustly, of being idle gossip, behind the seeming clarifications and transparency of human relations that no longer admit anything undefined, naked brutality is ushered in. The direct statement without divagations, hesitations or reflections, that gives the other the facts full in the face, already has the form and timbre of the command issued under Fascism by the dumb to the silent. Matter-of-factness between people, doing away with all ideological ornamentation between them, has already itself become an ideology for treating people as things.[31]

Thus, for all his avoidance of jargon, Said sought always to find a way of agreeing with Adorno's belief that the intrinsic difficulty of thought requires a style of writing wholly answerable to it. This view was amplified in Adorno's account of modern art — literature and music in particular — in which the esoteric nature of

the art was both an avowal of the
conditions of exile and obscurity to which
art had been reduced in modernity and also
a safeguard against art's co-optation by the
'culture industry'. It was the monopoly
exercised by that industry which, in Miriam
Hansen's phrase, 'makes technological
progress all the more a catalyst of
regression'.[32] It was, however, with Said's
adaptation of Adorno's ideas of 'late style'
that he found at last a means of
incorporating into his thinking and writing
a combination of the mandarin-esoteric
attitude and stylistic intricacy that has made
Adorno so disliked in the popular culture
world, and the civic democracy of his own
essayistic style. Lukács and Adorno had
both claimed for the essay as an art-form a
special privilege in the broken world of the
modern in which totality as a concept had
been refused asylum.[33] Adorno's 1937
essay, 'Late Style in Beethoven' and the
1959 essay 'Alienated Masterpiece: The
Missa Solemnis' seem to be the most likely
sources for Said's meditations on last or late
works by people such as Beethoven, Freud,
Auerbach, Lampedusa, Adorno himself and,
in a manner that is both subtle and obvious,
Edward Said too. His own fatal illness,
fought with over almost eleven years, clearly
gave a melancholy lustre to his work, one
that has been burnished the more by the
deaths of Sebastiano Timpanaro in Italy in
2000, of Yasser Arafat in Paris and of Susan
Sontag in New York last year. A whole
constellation of intellectual practice,
political adventurism, and stoical courage
that had a peculiarly late (!) twentieth-
century configuration faded with them in
the light of the first years of the new
century. What Edward Said set out to do
was to capture something of the
consciousness of lateness that is, of course, a
feature of the end of any century (and in
this instance of a millennium) but that can
also help concentrate attention on the effect
in works of art of the creator's
consciousness of his or her own

approaching death and of the link between
it and the death of an historical era or
system which can only at this late moment
be glimpsed or seen in retrospect, yet retains
or re-creates all the intensity of the past life,
now understood to be also a passing era.

The first two paragraphs of Proust's *À la
recherche du temps perdu* provide a well-
known instance of the enormously intricate
relations that can be caught in the sequences
of tenses — present, past perfect and
imperfect — and in the chemistry between a
word like *temps* with its continuities and
pastnesses embalmed within it and a word
like *fois* with its punctual singularity and
traces of the peremptory summons of and
by memory that is both voluntary and
involuntary. Said had of course published
Beginnings: Intention and Method in 1975
and it seems on the face of it appropriate
that lateness should be the dominant theme
of his work at the end. But beginnings and
lateness signify more than a superficial
contrast or tidy arrangement. They are
Said's final pairing of critical terms, like
filiation and affiliation, and they share the
same kind of relationship. They are not
merely opposites; they are effective,
hermeneutic terms because within the
process of generating their oppositeness,
they reveal their similarity.

There is nothing amiable in this
contradiction; it produces a disturbance that
is not to be quelled by any of the systems of
control — aesthetic conventions, for
instance — that are introduced to do that.
Rather the controlling system heightens the
sense of disturbance, like police entering a
district that has not internalized the idea of
law-and-order; it is an idea that will be
accepted if at all only through force, the
patrolling of an area that previously had no
consciousness of the boundaries that have
now made it an area and a condition. This
is what fascinated Said about both
beginnings and endings. This is *Orientalism*

32 Miriam Hansen, 'Mass
Culture as Hieroglyphic
Writing', in Nigel Gibson
and Andrew Rubin, eds.,
*Adorno: A Critical
Reader* (Oxford, 2002),
57–85 (66)

33 See Lukács's 'On the
Nature and Form of the
Essay', in *Soul and
Form*, trans. Anna
Bostock (London, 1974),
1–18; Adorno, 'The
Essay as Form', in Brian
O'Connor, ed., *The
Adorno Reader* (Oxford,
2000), 91–111.

34 Theodor W. Adorno, *Essays on Music*, notes and commentary by Richard Leppert, trans. Susan H. Gillespie (Berkeley and Los Angeles, 2002), 517
35 *Essays on Music*, 572
36 *Essays on Music*, 579

replayed as a drama of interiority, but with all the régimes of discourse and control now seriously threatened by an internal rebellion which is native, not foreign, to them. The East, as mortality, faces the West as the system that has to regard that mortality as its Other and must, to that end, create all sorts of countering myths about it that deal with everything but finality.

The similarity of beginnings and endings lies in the element of the arbitrary they both possess. Begin and end where? And why there? Each has a logic that operates prospectively and retrospectively. Each faces an insoluble question. What is it that constitutes an origin? When did a society or a story, that bears within it the whole concept of a society, begin? Was there an agreement, a contract, a pre-existing condition out of which society emerged, a system out of nothingness? These are of course the Rousseau questions that Derrida asked again. It is strange to see the force of his thought manifest itself on Said's meditations so belatedly. It is in these reflections that Said begins to repay the debt he had cancelled earlier. Yet the largest, ultimately unpayable debt is to Adorno. For he had already asked the other question, over and over again — what is an ending? Given the generations that had seen so many endings in the twentieth century, why had apocalypse ended in the mortified consciousness of the intellectually and emotionally illiterate masses of the present? Part of his answer is that this is what constitutes the apocalypse. After Auschwitz, Hollywood. It is fortunate that he did not live to see the reproduction of Auschwitz by Hollywood.

In brief, according to Adorno, Beethoven in his late works became unlike 'Beethoven' by becoming very obedient to musical convention and amnesiac about harmony. These are not symptoms of age, decrepitude or some psychological malfunction. He repudiates these attempts to read 'lateness'

as a psychic condition of the composer. Instead, he claims that the somewhat ravaged state of these works is their deepest art; it indicates how Beethoven has abandoned the harmonies and consolations of art, as he previously had produced it. Yet in doing so, he has still produced art and in producing art he has still produced some hope for a future. But not a lot. 'Harmony suffers the same fate in late Beethoven as religion in bourgeois society: it continues to exist, but is forgotten.'[34] This is very far indeed from the trumpet solo in *Fidelio*, generally heard as the announcement of the triumph of freedom for and by the bourgeoisie; or even more so from the triumphalism and rhythmic pulsations of the choral finale in the Ninth Symphony, the 'Ode to Joy' that is now the anthem of the European Union and again was once heard as a celebration of liberal individuality. In the essay on the *Missa Solemnis*, the position is reversed. The work is not musically incoherent according to Beethoven's standard practice; rather it can be said 'to contain little that exceeds the circumference of traditional musical language'.[35] The question in part is why Beethoven composed a mass at all. The effort involved was, for Adorno, significant because by forcing himself to become obedient to the demands of an anachronistic and highly complex form, Beethoven was enacting the failure of bourgeois subjectivity. 'It is already to be counted among those efforts of the later bourgeois spirit which no longer hope to conceive and form in any concrete manner the universally human ... '.[36] This sounds curiously like Lukács writing about the failure of the novel after the bourgeois defeat of 1848. The immediate point is that the lateness involved here — an historical condition — manifests itself aesthetically in very curious ways, in works in which the affirming and consolatory features of musical composition (and of novel writing) have disappeared and been replaced by effects that are disruptive precisely because they show themselves to be clinging to outmoded conventional forms that have lost the power to generate coherence between their parts. The music they produce is the sound of the historical failure of European humanism in its usual alliance with the bourgeois class or classes.

In *Freud and the Non-European* (2003), Said claims that Freud's late works — particularly *Moses and Monotheism* — were obsessed with returning 'to the very elements of identity itself, as if that issue so crucial to psychoanalysis, the very heart of the science, could be returned to in the way that Beethoven's late work returns to such basics as tonality and rhythm'.[37] This book itself is an attempt to include the whole issue of Palestine within a foundational Western discourse, like Freud's, an attempt that was met with much sectarian fury.[38] Further, in both Freud and Beethoven, 'the intellectual trajectory conveyed by the late work is intransigence and a sort of irascible transgressiveness, as if the author was expected to settle down into a harmonious composure, as befits a person at the end of his life, but preferred instead to be difficult, and to bristle instead with all sorts of new ideas and provocations'.[39] The risk Said takes here is twofold. On the one hand, there is the risk of a banality about heroic aging, the sort of platitude that is produced nowadays on an industrial scale by the endless confection of images of elderly serenity as a guarantor of wisdom — or, more usually, of the commercial reliability of a product. This hovers dangerously near the altogether remarkable notion that in late style, in these instances as with Auerbach, Lampedusa and others, what becomes visible is the possibility that where the heart of a discourse should be, there is nothing. Discourse that can produce so much in so successful and not necessarily coercive a spirit has perhaps no way of validating itself. Only perhaps. But decisively undecidable. This is where the grumpiness occasionally evident in various late conversations and interviews, as in a

querulousness about Beethoven and what he thought he was doing — as in Said's exchanges with Daniel Barenboim — gives way to a real anxiety that has no historical parallel of the kind that Adorno can always provide. The anxiety is that the relation between reflection and activism, so central to his whole career, is denied by the very nature of the work of art as such. It is a relationship fundamental to humanism, as he understood it. But if identity, tonality, and such fundamentals are questioned in these late works by the refusal to make relationship their characteristic and consoling action, something is wrong either with art or with humanism. Or perhaps it is in the nature of each to question the other's grounds for existence, and in so doing to reveal them. This brings Said back to his beginnings with Conrad and the fiction of autobiography, as his title has it. He ended as he began, at a beginning that could not be trusted as valid but had to be taken on trust as though it would finally prove itself to be so. Yet the narrative is there. The story was told, not of Edward Said's life, but of the life of an era that his life, like that of a character in a great novel, came to represent in an unforgettable manner. ∎

37 *Freud and the Non-European* (London, 2003), 29
38 A characteristic example, Leon Wieseltier, 'The Ego and the Yid', *The New Republic*, 7 Apr. 2003, 38
39 *Freud and the Non-European*, 29–30

Review Essays

The image contains the text: "IMPERIAL FAMINE AND PESTILENCE" on the banner, "WAR" on the helmet, and the signature "AILBHE Ó MONACHÁIN"

Early Modern Ireland

Clare Carroll

It is now almost forty years since the Folger Shakespeare Library published D. B. Quinn's *The Elizabethans and the Irish* (1966), a work whose coverage of Renaissance English texts on Ireland inspired a generation of both historians and literary scholars.

Aisling Ghéar:
Na Stíobhartaigh agus an
tAos Léinn, 1603–1788
Breandán Ó Buachalla
Baile Átha Cliath: An
Clóchomhar, 1996
xii + 808 pages
ISBN 0-90375-899-7

Poets and Politics:
Continuity and Reaction in
Irish Poetry, 1558–1625
Marc Caball
Cork: Field Day and Cork
University Press, 1998
vii + 220 pages
ISBN 1-85918-162-7

Ailbhe Ó Monacháin,
untitled illustration,
reproduced from Brian Ó
hUiginn, ed., *The Wolfe
Tone Annual*, 15 (1947), 35

At that time, as Toby Barnard has noted, there was a 'mere trickle' of work on early modern Ireland, whereas now there is 'a spate'. Along with greater production have come higher standards. The best recent work not only reaches deeper into the archives, it also covers a wider range — not just the usual political but also intellectual, economic and cultural history. And it is more comparative, partly because of the example of the New British History, which has emphasized the need to relate the history of the three kingdoms to one another. Perhaps most importantly, as scholars have engaged with materials in Irish — the language of the majority of people on the island in the early modern period — they have revealed histories hidden from those locked within the limits of English. Accompanying the research into Irish language material is research into Latin, Spanish, Italian, and French sources, which has both advanced our understanding of developments within Ireland and Ireland's relation to Catholic Europe, the site of the first Irish diaspora.

For thorough archival research, broad comparative scope, and imaginative historiographical innovation, Breandán Ó Buachalla's *Aisling Ghéar: Na Stíobhartaigh agus an tAos Léinn, 1603–1788* and Marc Caball's *Poets and Politics: Reaction and Continuity in Irish Poetry, 1558–1625* stand out as, without

question, the two most important books of the last decade on early modern Ireland. Their scholarly rigour is exemplary; but it is their refreshing originality in developing a new history of the period that places them apart. This was, in part, a consequence of immersion in hitherto neglected sources, particularly in the Irish language. Ó Buachalla's book took some twenty years of research in twenty-eight archives in six countries. Yet it is not just its scope that is so formidable. It reconfigures the whole field by its examination of the impact of the *aisling*, or vision poem, upon the literary and political history of seventeenth- and eighteenth-century Ireland. Ó Buachalla interprets this visionary poetry — widely disseminated in song — both as an expression of political thought and as a motivator of political action. Ó Buachalla charts the formation of the idea of the Irish nation in the matrix of religion, kingdom and fatherland, beginning with the bardic celebration of the Stuarts as the true inheritors of the Irish kingship after the Nine Years War. He demonstrates how the *aisling* mobilized support for James II and, later, for the Stuarts in exile on the continent.[1] Although less grand in scope and ambition, Caball's *Poets and Politics* is a brilliantly executed study of the various cultural and political changes registered in late sixteenth- and early seventeenth-century bardic verse. The traditional codes of Irish bardic poetry were transformed to the reaction to conquest and colonization, which included a concerted attempt to maintain the continuity of the older culture in the face of violent change. In a way, Caball's book can be seen as taking up the challenge made by Ó Buachalla in his scathing critique of Tom Dunne's and Michelle O'Riordan's earlier work on bardic poetry. The former claimed that post-1603 bardic poetry was simply defeatist and the latter claimed that such poetry was so sclerotic that it did not register any change but simply repeated the *topoi* of the medieval tradition.[2] Free of any polemic against these earlier interpretations, Caball's readings demonstrate again and again the great variety of the responses to contemporary events that is manifested in this poetry — the horror at the change in the landscape wrought by English colonization, the hope for a sovereign with a Gaelic lineage with the accession of James I, and the development of a modern political vocabulary grounded in an emerging Irish national identity.

The new understanding of the role and function of poetry, especially in its political dimensions, in the sixteenth and seventeenth centuries, is further enhanced by the revaluations that three new biographies demand. All three embody the characteristic interdisciplinarity, multilingualism, and historiographical awareness of the innovative work of recent times. Two of them are devoted to key figures of the time, Gerard the 11th Earl of Kildare and Geoffrey Keating. The third, Colm Lennon's *Archbishop Richard Creagh of Armagh, 1523–86*, reintegrates a figure, once reserved to the hagiographical and ecclesiastical tradition, into social and cultural history. As Lennon puts it in his preface, 'the new historiographical context for Irish Reformation studies' now makes it possible for an ecclesiastical figure such as Creagh to be interpreted in relation to 'his socio-economic background, formative cultural and educational experiences, and receptivity

to ideas thrown off by the welter of his time'. Lennon gives a compelling narrative of a man who started out in life as a merchant, pursuing his well-to-do Limerick family's business, and became one of the leading intellectuals and advocates for education and, at the end, a prisoner for the faith in the Tower of London. Lennon takes us through Creagh's intellectual formation in Louvain and Rome, where his talents attracted the attention of Ignatius Loyala and Pope Pius IV, back to Ireland and his mission as bishop of Armagh, where Lord Deputy Fitzwilliam had him incarcerated because he was posing too much of a threat to the Protestant competition. A brilliant man who wrote not only theological but also historical and linguistic works, Creagh was strictly devoted to his local traditions and religion, yet always protested his allegiance to the Queen. Lennon scarcely needs to point out that it would be anachronistic to see Creagh as a nationalist, but he usefully explains how his uncompromising defence of Catholicism, as well as his erudite defence of the Irish language, expressed a specifically early modern sense of *patria*. Lennon's expert narrative, drawing on a wide array of archival sources — everything from the few scraps of Creagh's bilingual treatise on the Irish language in Trinity College Dublin to Latin manuscripts in the Jesuit and Vatican archives — deepens our understanding, not just of Creagh, but of the state of Catholicism in Ireland, and of Irish relations with Rome throughout this period.

Likewise, Vincent Carey's study of 'the "Wizard" Earl of Kildare' fully embeds its subject in his social and cultural history. He shows how Kildare earned the nickname bestowed on him by local folklore: the earl had the nimbleness simultaneously to operate in the Gaelic world of late feudal vassalage, and in the English world of court factions. Carey's closely-worked account of political and social institutions in the late medieval borderland of the Pale sets the

1 It has long been rumoured that Ó Buachalla will produce an English translation of his indispensable study, if only in a shortened version. I would reckon the hardest part of this task to be the translation of primary texts. (Indeed, the citing of over 700 poems calls for a major work of editing and translation that would make this body of literature available to a wider audience.) It is one of the terrible ironies of Ireland's postcolonial condition that one of its greatest works of scholarship remains unread by the professional historians who should be required to read it, while at the same time its translation could be seen as promoting the dissolution of the very culture that it seeks to record.

2 See Breandán Ó Buachalla, 'Poetry and Politics in Early Modern Ireland', *Eighteenth-Century Ireland/Iris an Dá Chultúr*, 7 (1992), 22–26.

Archbishop Richard Creagh of Armagh, 1523–1586: An Irish Prisoner of Conscience of the Tudor Era
Colm Lennon
Dublin: Four Courts Press, 2000
166 pages
ISBN 1-85182-473-1

scene for the wider and more enduring conflict between Gaelic and English concepts of land tenure and jurisdiction that continued beyond the rebellion of Silken Thomas (1534–35) into the reigns of Mary and Elizabeth. His account of how Kildare attempted to regain the jurisdictional and military rights that would have been part of his medieval Gaelic inheritance is based on hitherto unexplored archives in the Public Record Office of Northern Ireland. In addition to explaining Kildare's involvement in Gaelic institutions, Carey also describes his apprenticeship in and mastery of European court politics. Rescued from danger after the rebellion of Silken Thomas, Kildare was raised on the continent where he was master of the horse in the house of Cosimo de Medici and a frequent guest at the French court. Kildare was well connected with the English court. He married a lady-in-waiting of Queen Mary, Mabel Browne, whose sixty-year-old father had wed his sister, the 'Fair Geraldine'. But he had to struggle to survive the lethal ideological warfare of the 1570s and 1580s. With Elizabeth excommunicated and the Earl of Desmond bringing in papal troops to Smerwick (Kildare's own wife was said to have been involved in plotting this expedition), he struggled to maintain contradictory roles as loyal subject of the queen and leader in the Gaelic Catholic community. On the one hand, he hired hunted Catholic priests to teach his children and, on the other, he detained and surrendered the Catholic Archbishop Creagh to the Crown. The final chapter describes how Kildare's strategy was undermined by his New English rivals. Their intelligence briefs concerning his relations with the rebel Baltinglass, passed on by Walsingham's spies, ultimately convinced Lord Deputy Grey that Kildare had to be imprisoned. Although his abject apology persuaded the queen to spare him, Kildare ended his days confined to the area around Dublin, exiled from both Ireland and the court. What is so compelling about

Carey's account is that it allows the reader to comprehend the contingencies of power politics in this period from various perspectives — those of the New English élite, the Crown and Leicester factions, Kildare's Gaelicized English-Irish feudal clients, the Irish rebels, and of Kildare himself. Carey's focus is not simply on the individual story of a man, struggling to maintain a power base rooted in a customary law that was being swept away by colonization and conquest. It is sufficiently sustained and sharp to exhibit the story's representative status. This makes the account more resonant than others.

Bernadette Cunningham's *The World of Geoffrey Keating* is the third of these three important contributions to Irish biography. This book is scrupulously researched and thorough in its coverage of the intellectual and social formation of Keating and his contemporaries, and of the response to his work by both Catholic and Protestant historians. Nevertheless, it does not fully capture what is required in a biography of such a significant intellectual and cultural figure. Keating's *Foras Feasa ar Éirinn* was the first major prose work in Modern Irish; he created the modern literary language, in much the same way that Dante created Italian in his *Commedia*. Similarly, he was the first historian working in Irish to engage the humanist debates about how history should be written, according to what criteria, from what perspective and with what responsibilities to its audience. As its title implies — literally the 'Foundation of Knowledge about Ireland' — the work tackles historiographical questions. Since many manuscripts of the *Foras Feasa* are lacking the historiographical prologue, Cunningham surmises that it was the least interesting part of the work to a contemporary audience although she perceptively notes that '[in] a country that hovered between kingdom and colony, readers understood the significance of alternative readings of the past'. Whatever

Surviving the Tudors: The 'Wizard' Earl of Kildare and English Rule in Ireland, 1537–1586
Vincent P. Carey
Dublin: Four Courts Press, 2002
240 pages
ISBN 1-85182-549-5

The World of Geoffrey Keating: History, Myth and Religion in Seventeenth-Century Ireland
Bernadette Cunningham
Dublin: Four Courts Press, 2001
xv + 263 pages
ISBN 1-85182-533-9

the status of the prologue in the seventeenth century, this is the most interesting part of the work today; the questions that it asks of the historian are still valid. Does the historian have the necessary linguistic competence to write a history of a people? How does his or her relationship to the audience influence the writing of history? And how does the historian's own experience of life influence what he or she writes? To avoid these questions is to write uncritically, and to assume that these questions can be overcome through some quasi-scientific objectivity is either a form of naïveté or of the will-to-power. Cunningham's biography provides a goldmine of information for future research projects, but I wish it had made a more compelling case for Keating's cultural achievement. Keating's *seanachas* was far from being purely antiquarian in the sense that it focused merely on the preservation of the past. For example, through an implied comparison of the Norman conquest with the early modern English conquest, Keating gave a potent critique of the contemporary situation. Like Machiavelli in his *Discorsi*, he used historical knowledge as a political weapon. Keating's poetry, not the book's intended focus, nevertheless merits more attention and would certainly have enriched our sense of his overall achievement. Still, this is an excellent introduction to Keating's intellectual background, prose writings, and critical reception. My reservations are voiced here only because the responsibilities assumed in writing an account of Keating's life — and the first one at that — are so vast. Few scholars of early modern Ireland have the palaeographical and linguistic skills, which Cunningham has deployed here.

One historian who has a real knack for making early modern Irish history relevant is John McCavitt, who conceived of his book *The Flight of the Earls* as 'a narrative of compelling human interest to the general reader'. The book is eminently readable —

truly the only page-turner of the lot reviewed here — and scholarly. Both his earlier book on Sir Arthur Chichester and this one derive from his doctoral thesis. *The Flight of the Earls* contains many dramatic episodes, including 'kidnapping and hostage taking ... extramarital affairs, rape, and suggestions of homosexual liaisons'. McCavitt has chosen an intriguing topic — an event that has remained a mystery, long debated by historians. In seeking to solve it, he creates a clear narrative out of the complex events that led up to O'Neill's decision to follow O'Donnell into exile, the tumult following his departure and the defeat of O'Doherty's rebellion. In addition to explaining the flight and its consequences for those left behind, the book also serves as the second half of the biography of Hugh O'Neill. It picks up the story where Hiram Morgan left it in *Tyrone's Rebellion* and follows the great chief to his initially splendid, but ultimately frustrating, and sadly diminished end in Rome.

In contrast to McCavitt's detailed narrative of a specific event and its ramifications, Nicholas Canny's *Making Ireland British, 1580–1650* and David Edwards's *The Ormond Lordship in County Kilkenny, 1515–1642* seek to interpret a critical period in Ireland's early modern history. Each, in its own way, attempts to account for the changing configuration of land-ownership and use, the administration of law, and Crown policy, within the relationship between England and Ireland. Canny's focus is mainly on Ulster; the number of Protestant Scots who initially settled there stood in the same proportion to the total native population as that of Spaniards to the peoples of the New World. Within this context, the term 'British' came to be significantly and frequently used to describe English legal and economic institutions created by English and Scottish settlers to enforce and justify their rule over Irish under-tenants and labourers.[3] For Edwards, the focus is on Kilkenny, which since 1610

3   See, for example, *Conditions to Be Observed by the British Undertakers of the Escheated Lands of Ulster* (1610), a key document of the Ulster Plantation.

The Flight of the Earls
John McCavitt
Dublin: Gill and Macmillan, 2002
x + 277 pages
ISBN 0-71713-047-9

Making Ireland British, 1580–1650
Nicholas Canny
Oxford: Oxford University Press, 200
xiv + 633 pages
ISBN 0-19-925905-4

The Ormond Lordship in County Kilkenny, 1515–1642:
The Rise and Fall of Butler Feudal Power
David Edwards
Dublin: Four Courts Press, 2003
xiv + 378 pages
ISBN 1-85182-578-9

An Irish lackey, c.1603–06. Huntington Library, MS 25863: Album of Hieronymus Tielch.

had been, as he points out, the 'spiritual centre' of Irish Catholicism (through the work of Bishop David Rothe) and then, with the founding of the Confederation in 1642, its 'secular capital' also. For Canny, the key institution for analysis is plantation; for Edwards, lordship. Therefore, in Canny's work, the defeat of the Desmond rebellion, the Munster plantation, the Cromwellian conquest and the subsequent devastating land confiscations that ensued are the central linking events in making Ireland British. In Edwards's account of the Ormond lordship, he begins with the rule of the 8th earl, the Gaelicized English-Irish warlord Piers Ruadh, and ends with the Confederation of Kilkenny, which coincided with the demise of the Ormond lordship under the 12th earl, James Butler. These points define what is at stake. In Canny's

book we read how the drastic social change wrought by plantation brought about Ireland's increasing, if troubled, incorporation into Britain. In Edwards's we read how the persistence of English-Irish feudalism helped resist, at least for a time, such nightmares of colonial rule as the mass-executions under martial law, the confiscations of the plantation policy, and the political disenfranchisement of the Irish under English rule.

This is not to say that there is no common ground here. While focusing on what he calls 'one of the great under-explored themes of early seventeenth-century Irish history — the continuing vitality of feudalism', Edwards does not ignore the corrosive force of modernization introduced by the English administration of Ireland.

And Canny's book also reveals the resistance of older cultural forms to this process. His chapter on the intellectual resistance of the native Gaelic élites is notable, but would have profited from a greater engagement with more thorough studies of political thought in the Irish language, such as Caball's *Poets and Politics* and Ó Buachalla's *Aisling Ghéar*. In a sense, both Canny's and Edwards's books can be read as explanations of the conditions that created the rebellion of 1641. Lord Deputy Wentworth plays a key role in both narratives. In Canny's study, we see him reading, imitating, and enforcing Spenserian plans for garrisons, confiscations, and plantations. In Edwards's study, the all-too-eager cooperation of James Butler with Wentworth's plans for centralized power brings about the alienation of his Catholic gentry constituents, their rebellion, and his consequent inability to control and represent the interests of the local community. Canny convincingly shows how the appropriation and widespread adoption of the colonial model in Spenser's *A View of the Present State of Ireland* (1596) brought about the disenfranchisement and subjugation of the indigenous population, which in turn led to their rebellion in 1641. Edwards's reading of James Butler's poisoned relationship with the local community and with his grand-uncle, Richard Viscount Mountgaret, goes a long way towards explaining the strains behind the 1643 truce and 1643–46 peace talks, both of which have seemed murky in earlier accounts. I hope that Edwards will further investigate local alienation from Ormond and its long-term consequences for the Confederacy and beyond. He tantalizingly ends this magnificently researched and argued book with speculation about just this topic.

The 1640s are the subject of two ground-breaking new monographs — Pádraig Lenihan's *Confederate Catholics at War, 1641–49* and Tadhg Ó hAnnracháin's *Catholic Reformation in Ireland: The Mission of Rinuccini, 1645–1649* — and an important collection of essays, *Kingdoms in Crisis*, edited by Micheál Ó Siochrú. All three volumes owe a great deal to Ó Siochrú's *Confederate Ireland, 1642–1649: A Constitutional and Political Analysis* (Dublin, 1999), which has superseded Donal Cregan's unpublished 1947 dissertation as the standard history of the 1640s. Ó Siochrú's introduction to *Kingdoms in Crisis* — the collection is dedicated to Cregan — is one of the most succinct and comprehensible accounts both of the period and of what is needed in future histories of it; the introduction is particularly valuable for its critique of historians' neglect of Irish language materials, many of them literary, in favour of researching official state papers. In the first essay in the collection, Toby Barnard argues for an approach to 'confederate rebellion as baronial uprising' that would bring accounts of Ireland in the 1640s more into line with English and European histories of this period. It would be interesting to explore the limits of such an approach, given the very different conditions of the élites in Ireland to those in the rest of Europe. Jane H. Ohlmeyer's essay on Irish recusant lawyers draws on Donal Cregan's unpublished notes to produce a richly documented and deftly contextualized account of why Irishmen attended the English Inns of Court and what role they came to play in Confederate Ireland. In a related article, Bríd McGrath argues that the evisceration of Catholic power by successive parliaments drove recusant lawyers like Plunkett and Darcy, who had been members of parliament, into alliance with the Northern rebels and into active participation in the Confederacy. Other important articles in this volume include Pádraig Lenihan's analysis of Confederate military strategy, and Tadhg Ó hAnnracháin's reading of the relationship between the Irish clergy and the papal nuncio, Giovanni Batista Rinuccini. Lenihan argues that the Confederate army's failure to see the need for a strategy that would consolidate and

Kingdoms in Crisis: Ireland in the 1640s: Essays in Honour of Donal Cregan
Edited by Micheál Ó Siochrú
Dublin: Four Courts Press, 2001
288 pages
ISBN 1-85182-535-5

Confederate Catholics at War, 1641–49
Pádraig Lenihan
Cork: Cork University Press, 2001
xi + 260 pages
ISBN 1-85918-244-5

defend an area 'lying south of a line from Drogheda to Galway' left Ireland weaker and more vulnerable to Cromwell. Ó hAnnracháin's treatment of Rinuccini is surprisingly sympathetic, emphasizing the cardinal's good faith and sustained efforts to increase the strength of the Irish clergy. Lenihan's fascinating *Confederate Catholics at War, 1641–49* is enlivened by its sharp grasp of historiographical issues, and by its clear explanation of the conditions leading up to the war. These included the excessive taxation exacted from Catholics in exchange for limited toleration, and the ever-increasing share of land holdings by British settlers on the Ulster plantation and elsewhere. In his account of the mobilization and financing of the army, Lenihan documents the numbers of men in the various counties, their wastage, sickness, and desertion, and provides figures on taxes and pay rates. One of the main problems was lack of pay. He is even able to ascertain the economic level of the recruits, the single largest group of which was made up of domestic servants. There are also numerous maps showing campaigns, fortifications, and battle lines. Not only does Lenihan provide plenty of hard data, but he also explains such distinctive features of the Confederate army as its status as *gairm slua,* or hosting, rather than a standing force. Throughout, his analysis is made more profound by his knowledge of the Irish language — he cites Irish sources on everything from the use of the pike to O'Neill's exhortations to his troops at Benburb. Destroying the bogey of antiquated 'Celtic' warfare, Lenihan maintains that the pike was an effective weapon, and that the Confederate army, especially the Leinster section of it, was quite advanced in its ability to organize and rout cavalry formations. He ends the book with an account of Dungan's Hill, which, tellingly, in the Irish, but not in the English sources, emerges as a sheer massacre. His conclusion lays the blame for the final defeat of the Confederacy on the lack of experienced generals, although he praises

O'Neill, who seems to have had the charisma and strength both to control his troops in battle and also to exhort them to remain calm and steady. According to Lenihan, seventeenth-century warfare was psychological, even more than it was physical, in its demands.

The decisiveness of Lenihan's study is in stark contrast with the inescapable ambiguities of Tadhg Ó hAnnracháin's involved account of Rinuccini. The various perspectives of Rinuccini, the Vatican, the Old English, the Confederate army, and the plain people of Ireland, provide a series of contrasts and even contradictions. Although at first Rinuccini was welcomed with open arms in the streets of Kinsale, ultimately he was embittered and rather isolated. Whereas he antagonized the Old English by insisting upon open jurisdiction for the Church and no compromise with Protestants, he believed that he was doing so in the best interests of the Catholics of Ireland, many of them Old English. But even the Vatican's reaction to the excommunication that Rinuccini imposed on those who would agree to a truce with Protestants was less than enthusiastic. Ó hAnnracháin attempts to make sense of all this by locating Rinuccini's actions in the light of his intellectual and spiritual formation as a Counter-Reformation bishop in Italy. The largely unsympathetic cleric emerges from Ó hAnnracháin's accounts as a sincere reformer, not bent on his own advancement — he chose a posting in Ireland over one in Florence — but devoted instead to his mission to strengthen the Church in Ireland, which for a time he succeeded in doing. At the same time, Ó hAnnracháin explains the Vatican's position towards Ireland in relation to its concerns about Westphalia. Negotiating with Protestants in Ireland might compromise the Church's stand in the Protestant German-speaking territories. The larger European historiographical perspective here, which is absent from insular and British accounts of Irish history, helps set what would otherwise seem bizarre in a comprehensible context. This is a brilliantly researched book based on a wealth of Italian, Latin, Irish, and English sources that presents a deftly nuanced and often ironic narrative. The author wryly observes that 'Rinuccini's most notable accomplishment was to impede the formation of a unified party capable of resisting the 1649 invasion'.

In addition to his book on Rinuccini, Ó hAnnracháin has published a number of articles on Counter-Reformation intellectual history, one of the best of which — in *Kingdom or Colony*, a superb collection of essays edited by Jane H. Ohlmeyer — deals with varieties of Irish Catholic political thought in the mid-seventeenth century and places them within the context of wider European developments. Here, Ó hAnnracháin investigates the responses of the seventeenth-century Irish intelligentsia to rule by a Protestant king — these ranged from revolution and regicide to accommodation with Protestant monarchy and defence of the Confederate critics of Rinuccini. The Confederates who opposed the 1648 censure were in turn criticized by O'Ferrall and O'Connell in their *Commentarius Rinuccinianus* (1661–62), only published in the middle of the twentieth century and only now in the process of being fully translated into English.

Ohlmeyer's *Kingdom or Colony* is a product of seminars on early modern Irish history sponsored by the Folger Institute, as is Hiram Morgan's earlier collection, *Political Ideology in Ireland, 1541–1641*. These collections include some of the finest examples of the kind of interdisciplinary and critically self-interrogating history that is yielding innovative results, not least by interrogating the limits of inherited historiography, including the older colonial and the newer 'British' models. What emerges is a much more palpable sense of

both the ideology and the practice of colonization — how England ruled the Irish as a colonized people, with lesser rights than English subjects. The essays also give a sense of how the Irish envisaged their own sovereignty in terms that were drawn from both Irish and continental political traditions. Providing strong evidence based on the conduct of the English administration on the ground in Ireland, David Edwards's brilliant article on martial law demonstrates how summary executions without trial were the rule in Elizabethan Ireland. Investigating the roots of an Irish political tradition rooted in continental natural law, Colm Lennon's essay on 'The *Analecta* of Bishop David Rothe' shows an Irish political thinker envisaging a religious toleration in Ireland, such as that allotted to the Protestant minority in France by the Edict of Nantes. Articles by Vincent Carey on Old English bilingualism and by Marc Caball on identity formation and the critique of the English conquest in bardic poetry, show the strength of Irish language political thought. As Caball observes of the Gaelic literati, that they 'managed to formulate a transcendent ideology of culture, religion, and sovereignty in less than auspicious political and economic circumstances is indeed remarkable'. The growing concern with what Ohlmeyer, in her characteristically lucid and comprehensive introduction, terms the 'considerable cross-fertilization [that] occurred between different religious and ethnic groups at all levels' is evident in excellent articles on the representation of the king, parliament and people in Keating's *Foras Feasa* and John Lynch's *Cambrensis Eversus* (Bernadette Cunningham), popular culture (Raymond Gillespie) and Vincent Gookin's arguments against the transplantation of the Irish in the 1650s (Patricia Coughlan).

Historians are profiting from a new recognition of the pertinence to their work of literary works and of methods of

Catholic Reformation in Ireland:
The Mission of Rinuccini,
1645–1649
Tadhg Ó hAnnracháin
Oxford: Oxford University Press, 2002
x + 324 pages
ISBN 0-19-820891-X

Political Thought in Seventeenth-Century Ireland:
Kingdom or Colony
Edited by Jane H. Ohlmeyer
Cambridge: Cambridge University Press, 2000
xvii + 290 pages
ISBN 0-521-65083-6

Political Ideology in Ireland,
1541–1641
Edited by Hiram Morgan
Dublin: Four Courts Press, 2000
264 pages
ISBN 1-85182-440-5

interpretation developed in literary criticism. (For example, Nicholas Canny devotes a whole chapter of *Making Ireland British* to Spenser's *Faerie Queene*.) At the same time, the analysis of historiography itself has benefited greatly from the interpretive acuity of literary scholars. In *Language and Conquest in Early Modern Ireland*, for instance, Patricia Palmer analyses English accounts of the Irish language, and describes the activities of Irish translators in bringing about the Anglicization of Ireland. She also connects the Linguistic experience of the English in Ireland and in the Americas, unfavourably contrasting their lack of capacity or interest in Amerindian languages with the extensive production of dictionaries and transcription by the Spanish. In her final chapter, following Homi Bhabha, she argues for the need to open up a 'space of translation,' in which English and Irish languages are in dialogue with each other. I disagree with her conclusions about the English incomprehension of Irish — I would argue that the English had to have at least an instrumental knowledge of Irish to operate on the ground outside the Pale — and lament the preponderance of English language sources, largely from the State Papers, in her bibliography. Richard McCabe's contribution to David J. Baker and Willy Maley's *British Identities and English Renaissance Literature* is, like Palmer's, another significant literary intervention in early modern Irish history. McCabe sees the colonial 'rhetoric of superiority' in Holinshed's Irish *Chronicles* as 'an index of self-doubt'. Teasing out the various layers of authorship from Giraldus Cambrensis to Campion, to Stanyhurst, and Hooker, McCabe masterfully reads the conflicting impulses in each appropriation of the text, explaining the Welsh, English, and Irish dimensions of these various contexts, which might collectively be called 'British.'

Baker and Maley's introduction to *British Identities* sets up a compelling debate that runs throughout the entire volume about the possibilities and limits of the New British

history. Richard Murphy weighs in on behalf of the 'archipelagic' and 'Atlanticist' models that place Ireland somewhere between England and the Americas. In her response to this wide-ranging collection of essays on historiography, Shakespeare, the New World, Britain, and Ireland, Ohlmeyer sensibly and authoritatively insists on the use of 'British and Irish histories' — which has the distinct advantage from an historical perspective of corresponding to the term used by people writing in the early modern period.

If the archipelagic model sees Ireland between England and America, yet another historiographical approach is placing Ireland in the cultural geography of Europe. Two outstanding volumes on the Irish in Europe, one edited by Thomas O'Connor, *The Irish in Europe, 1580–1815*, and the other co-edited by O'Connor and Mary Ann Lyons, *Irish Migrants in Europe after Kinsale, 1602–1820*, go a long way toward redressing the dearth of material on the Irish on the continent. The essays in both volumes are based on hitherto-neglected continental archives, such as those explored by Ciaran O'Scea in his account of the Spanish version of what went wrong at Kinsale, and by Karin Schuller in her work on Irish migrant networks in Spain. These essays offer fresh insights into the Irish in such far-flung locations as Madrid, Poitiers, and Yorktown Heights. And they cover a range of economic levels: from the destitute families of discharged soldiers on the streets of *ancien régime* Paris, movingly portrayed by David Bracken, to the aristocratic Wild Geese at the Jacobite court of Saint-Germain-en-Laye, richly described by Edward Corp. (He has now produced an entire book on this topic as well as one on the Stuart court in Rome.) From Hector MacDonnell's narrative of his own ancestors' response to the changes of the seventeenth century, one gets a sense of the wide-ranging European connections of one of the few Catholic families that held on to

Language and Conquest in Early Modern Ireland:
English Renaissance Literature and Elizabethan Imperial Expansion
Patricia Palmer
Cambridge: Cambridge University Press, 2001
xii + 254 pages
ISBN 0-521-79318-1

British Identities and English Renaissance Literature
Edited by David J. Baker and Willy Maley
Cambridge: Cambridge University Press, 2002
xvi + 297 pages
ISBN 0-521-78200-7

The Irish in Europe, 1580–1815:
The Other Hidden Ireland
Edited by Thomas O'Connor
Dublin: Four Courts Press, 2001
219 pages
ISBN 1-85182-579-7

Irish Migrants in Europe after Kinsale, 1602–1820
Edited by Mary Ann Lyons and Thomas O'Connor
Dublin: Four Courts Press, 2003
288 pages
ISBN 1-85182-701-3

its power. Both volumes are also strong on political and intellectual developments, many of which found expression in Irish and Latin. Notably, Mícheál Mac Craith and David Worthington give a fascinating account of the 'literary activity' of the Irish Franciscans in Prague and O'Connor analyses Peter Lombard's argument for 'foreign intervention in early modern Ireland' in his *Commentarius* (1600). These books also contain a wealth of information on the Irish military-men in Europe and beyond, such as those Irish Jacobites who participated in the American War of Independence, as chronicled by the French historian Patrick Clarke de Dromantin. These are truly international and comparative studies that bring together work being done by Czech, French, German, Spanish, and American, as well as Irish and English scholars.

Another major contribution to the study of the Irish on the continent is *The Irish College, Rome, 1628–1678*, an edition of a manuscript history of the college written in 1678 by James Reilly SJ to mark its fiftieth anniversary. Printed in Rome by the Pontifical Irish College, this sumptuously produced volume features colour photographs of the architecture and art of the early years of the college, an informative historical overview of seventeenth-century Irish ecclesiastics in Rome by Thomas O'Connor as well as a very detailed introduction to the text itself by John J. Hanly. Among the alumni of the college whom O'Connor describes were the saintly scholar Oliver Plunkett and the combative rogue Terence O'Kelly, who complained a great deal during his student days and later, as vicar apostolic of Derry, 'took to himself a mistress and lived publicly with their children'. The history itself recounts such topics as the endowment of the college by Cardinal Ludovisi, the Jesuit take-over of the college administration, financial difficulties, and how various rectors dealt with them. This volume suggests the riches

in European archives yet to be mined for future histories.

Irish history has long been dominated by political and military approaches but both younger and more established historians are beginning to show the influence of European trends in cultural history, in which visual and literary, as well as popular and religious history play a role. In early modern literary studies of the 1970s and 1980s, it was almost as if religion had become the taboo that sex had once been; whereas sex and power were everywhere. If this has begun to change in literary studies, with, for instance, Stephen Greenblatt's marvellous meditation on the meaning of Purgatory for understanding *Hamlet*, the same is true for cultural history. Two striking examples of Irish historians approaching religion from an open-ended anthropological perspective are Clodagh Tait's *Death, Burial and Commemoration in Ireland, 1550–1650* and Toby Barnard's *Irish Protestant Ascents and Descents, 1641–1770*. Tait's volume includes representations of public executions, martyrdom, disinterment, and the place of monuments in the construction of honour. While I applaud her attention to material culture, I was disappointed not to find any treatment of Gaelic laments (*caointe*), through which grief was expressed in both learned manuscript and folk traditions. As she maintains, Irish poetry is 'conventional', but so, too, are funerary monuments and narrative histories, both of which provide her source material. All human linguistic expression is constructed, and it would be naïve or disingenuous to discount poetry as 'problematic as a measure of sorrow' for this reason. The point is to take the time to understand the conventions and how they work.

Toby Barnard is off the hook when it comes to Irish sources since the *Irish Protestant Ascents and Descents* that he describes largely took place in English. Nevertheless, realizing that Irish was the majority

The Irish College, Rome, 1628–78: An Early Manuscript Account of the Foundation and Development of the Ludovisian College of the Irish in Rome
Contributions by John J. Hanly, Declan Lawell, Albert MacDonnell and Thomas O'Connor
Rome: Pontifical Irish College, 2003

Death, Burial and Commemoration in Ireland, 1550–1650.
Clodagh Tait
Basingstoke and New York: Palgrave Macmillan, 2002
ix + 229 pages
ISBN 0-333-99741-7

Irish Protestant Ascents and Descents, 1641–1770
Toby Barnard
Dublin: Four Courts Press, 2004
xvi + 359 pages
ISBN 1-85182-693-9

Ireland and the Jacobite Cause, 1685–1766:
A Fatal Attachment
Éamonn Ó Ciardha
Dublin: Four Courts Press, 2002
468 pages
ISBN 1-85182-534-7

language and was particularly important for zealous Protestants bent on reforming the Irish, he has written about 'Protestants and the Irish Language'. Amongst those Protestants who studied and promoted the language were scholars such as Archbishop William King, who warned against the baleful effects of a ban on the Irish language, and William Bedell, who translated the Bible into Irish. Barnard points out how Bedell was inspired to save souls by the vernacular by the example of the Genevan scholar Diodati, who had translated it into French and Italian. Irish Protestants also travelled in European circles; such cultural connections deserve further investigation and research.

Barnard is a remarkably versatile historian. In a book which gathers together some twenty years of his essays, he explores local socio-economic and cultural experiences as expertly as he addresses issues in intellectual history; for instance, his analyses of the 'political, material, and mental culture of the Cork settlers' in the late 1600s, the power that Katherine Conolly of Castletown wielded as a hostess, and 'the uses of the 23rd of October 1641' are all exemplary. His writing displays a recurrent desire to strike an ironic note or to undo received ideas, a tendency that is at once a strength and a weakness. He revels in making observations that might overturn the strongly held opinions of other historians — that no one cared about Edmund Spenser in eighteenth-century Ireland, for example — when this is not precisely the case. It was only that there was no interest in Spenser's poetry, not that there was no interest in *A View*, reprinted twice in that century. And he also engages in distinctions that are sometimes beyond me, as in 'It could be that a scheme of 1749 to outlaw the employment of Catholics as agents arose not to safeguard the Protestant interest but the employment prospects of Protestants.' I fail to see the difference.

A book to be read in conjunction with

Barnard's is Éamonn Ó Ciardha's *Ireland and the Jacobite Cause, 1685–1766* (an opinion with which Barnard, given his own review of the book, would agree). I cannot think of a recent book in Irish history that better combines original primary research, including profound research into Irish language poetry, a continental European perspective, and a concern for both élite politics and popular culture. Ó Ciardha interprets the meaning that the Stuart cause had for expatriate Irish Jacobites who served in European armies as well as for dispossessed rapparees on the ground in Ireland, who like their shining prince, would become the stuff of song and legend. Ó Ciardha discusses some four hundred poems (all usefully catalogued by an index of first lines) which he skilfully reads in relation to the events and concerns from which they arose and the politics which they envisioned. As he repeatedly points out, such poems were intensely topical, performing the function of news from Britain and the continent. They also expressed the political aspirations of the Irish not just for a rightful king but also for the restoration of their confiscated lands. From the cultural point of view, Jacobitism was deeply bound up with Catholicism; the Stuarts in exile exercised the power to appoint bishops to Irish dioceses, and later, when the Pope rescinded that power, the laity doubted the Stuarts' claim to the Crown and scorned the clergy who had misled them. Jacobitism was also bound up with the Irish language (although, as Ó Ciardha points out, James himself disavowed any concern for it in his own writing). This is a truly original book in that it has overcome a huge imbalance of historiographical focus on 1691 and on the last decades of the eighteenth century leading up to the 1798 rebellion. The years in between have largely been written about as the history of the Protestant Ascendancy. Anyone who wants to contend with eighteenth-century Irish history from now on will have to engage with Ó Ciardha's *Ireland and the Jacobite Cause.* ■

Mission Accomplished?

Looking Back at the IRA

Brendan O'Leary

The full implementation, on a progressive and irreversible basis by the two governments, especially the British government, of what they have agreed will provide a political context, in an enduring political process, with the potential to remove the causes of conflict and in which Irish republicans and unionists can, as equals, pursue our respective political objectives peacefully. In that new context the IRA leadership will initiate a process that will completely and verifiably put IRA arms beyond use. We will do it in such a way as to avoid risk to the public and misappropriation by others and ensure maximum public confidence. From IRA Statement, 6 May 2000

For one detailed analysis of the Agreement see Brendan O'Leary, 'The Nature of the British-Irish Agreement', *New Left Review*, 233 (1999), 66–96.

Photograph: H-Block 5, B-Wing 9/25, 2003. © Donovan Wylie/ Magnum

People voluntarily kill, or die, for collective causes expressed in words that register their group's esteem, dignity and honour. Actions that provoke and rekindle resentment are catalysts of violence. Group-honour often provokes more violence than considerations of material self-interest, or material group-interest. These propositions govern what follows. Flatly stated, the IRA of 2005 has fulfilled its original volunteers' pledges, and since its mission is accomplished, consistent with its constitution, it may, should, and likely will disband. This internally valid constitutional dissolution should occur because the governments of Ireland between 1922 and 1949, and subsequently the governments of the United Kingdom and Ireland have jointly removed the constitutional resentment which created, and maintained, the IRA's reason for being.

The IRA's existence after 1922 expressed two forms of constitutional resentment:

- at the Treaty of 1921 between Great Britain and Ireland, which provocatively required the Irish Free State to imbibe the relics of British constitutionality, particularly the oath of allegiance to the Crown by members of Dáil Éireann, and

- at the denial of the people of Ireland as a whole of their right of self-determination, usurped by the unilateral decision of the Government of Great Britain to partition Ireland in 1920.

These related resentments have now been substantively redressed. The final implementation of the comprehensive Belfast/Good Friday Agreement of 1998 can be seen as the culmination of the IRA's mission, though it is not just that.[1]

Óglaigh na hÉireann

Analysis of the IRA must begin with its first name, Óglaigh na hÉireann, its title in Ireland's official national language, and its self-description in its official communiqués signed by 'P. O'Neill' on behalf of the Irish Republican Publicity Bureau.[2] IRA activists sometimes refer to the organization as 'ONH', the acronym of its Gaelic name. The etymology of Óglaigh na hÉireann is significant: *laoch* means 'hero, champion, warrior, soldier'; and *óg* means 'young', and so *óglaigh* came to mean 'vassals', 'youths of military age', or 'soldiers', and finally 'volunteers'.[3] Óglaigh na hÉireann therefore comprises the 'Volunteers of Ireland', or 'The Irish Volunteers'. The Volunteers had been founded as Óglaigh na hÉireann in 1913, in response to the formation of the Ulster Volunteer Force, a militia loyal to the Ulster Unionist Party and determined to oppose the granting of home rule to Ireland by the Westminster parliament. Óglaigh na hÉireann was the idea of the secret Irish Republican Brotherhood (IRB), otherwise known as the Fenians, who tried to run it as a front organization, although it was formally created by a broad coalition of the Ancient Order of Hibernians, the Gaelic Athletic Association (GAA) and Gaelic League revivalists, i.e. by the major cultural bodies of the Irish nationalist revival. The Volunteers divided shortly after the start of the Great War. The National Volunteers, following John Redmond, the leader of the Irish Parliamentary Party, took the majority into the British army — on the understanding that Great Britain would honour its commitment to implement home rule when the war was over. The minority retained the founding organization's title deeds, and rejected service in another English war, not least because home rule had been postponed because of the resistance of the Ulster Unionists. Óglaigh na hÉireann organized military training. Its members were subsequently partly mobilized, through an IRB conspiracy, in the launching of the insurrection of Easter

1916 — in which a Republic was proclaimed in arms, but put down by forces of the British Crown. At the start of the insurrection Óglaigh na hÉireann was renamed (in English), together with the Irish Citizen Army, as the Irish Republican Army, and it was as Commandant General of that army that Pádraig Pearse surrendered.[4] It was 'Irish' because of its national identification; 'Republican' because militant Irish nationalists since the late eighteenth century have opposed British Crown authority; and an 'Army' because only such an organization is the legitimate defender of a state or nation.

The Volunteers remained known by their original English title for a while; and ever since rank-and-file IRA members have been known as 'volunteers'. In October 1917 Sinn Féin, the political party which had originally stood for a separate Irish parliament under the British Crown, was revitalized by an influx of Volunteers, who elected Eamon de Valera, the surviving leader of the 1916 insurrection, as the party's president. Then '[u]nder the cover of the meeting, 250 delegates met in an Army Convention in the GAA grounds, Croke Park. De Valera was elected President, and Cathal Brugha Chief of Staff, but the IRB was prominently represented in the Staff: [Michael] Collins was Director of Organization'.[5] The IRA was now, in principle, subordinated to political control by a party — which claimed the right to speak for the nation, although it was in practice significantly controlled by Collins, now the President of the Supreme Council of the IRB. While subordinated to civilian authority the IRA had established its internal democracy — a general convention, and the election of the senior officers. The IRA subsequently spearheaded Ireland's War of Independence between 1919 and 1921, in conjunction with Sinn Féin, which was victorious in Ireland in the Westminster general elections held in 1918 — the first held under full male suffrage and the franchise for women over thirty. Sinn Féin won on an explicit platform of

2 Selections of recent IRA statements may be found on Sinn Féin's web-site: http://sinnfein.ie/peace/ira_statements. The BBC has a collection of the IRA's statements 1998–2003: http://news.bbc.co.uk/1/hi/northern_ireland/1144568.stm. The University of Ulster's CAIN web-site has a collection of statements from 1994: http://cain.ulst.ac.uk/othelem/organ/ira/statements.htm

3 Patrick Dineen, ed., *An Irish-English Dictionary: Being a Thesaurus of the Words, Phrases and Idioms of the Modern Irish Language* (Dublin, 1927), 631, 807, 808

4 The name had an antecedent: J. Bowyer Bell, *The Secret Army: The IRA* (New Brunswick, NJ, rev. 3rd edn. 1997), 15n.3, notes that 'As early as the abortive Fenian invasion of Canada in 1866, a green flag was used with the letters IRA.'

5 Bowyer Bell, *Secret Army*, 17

6   For fuller analyses of this
     election see John
     McGarry and Brendan
     O'Leary, *Explaining
     Northern Ireland:
     Broken Images* (Oxford,
     1995), ch. 1, and
     Brendan O'Leary and
     John McGarry, *The
     Politics of Antagonism:
     Understanding Northern
     Ireland* (London, 2nd
     edn. 1996), ch. 2.
7   Tim Pat Coogan, *The
     IRA* (New York, 4th
     edn. 2002), 30–31
8   Constitution of *Óglaigh
     na hÉireann* as Amended
     by General Army
     Convention, 14–15 Nov.
     1925, Blythe Papers
     ADUCD P24/165 (10),
     cited in Richard English,
     *Armed Struggle: The
     History of the IRA*
     (Oxford and New York,
     2003), 42–43, 394n.3.
     The word 'race' was
     used the way people
     today use 'ethnic', so it is
     anachronistic — and
     false — to interpret the
     IRA's mission as racist;
     nationalism and racism
     are not equivalents.

'abstentionism'.[6] Its MPs would not take their seats at Westminster but instead would constitute the deputies of the Irish parliament.

Two significant entities today call themselves Óglaigh na hÉireann because both claim to be the army of Ireland. Ireland's Taoiseach, Bertie Ahern, in October 2004 pointedly said, 'our Constitution states there can be [only] one Óglaigh na hÉireann. At the moment there are two'. One is the official name of the army of the sovereign, independent and democratic republic of Ireland that comprises twenty-six counties of the island, and is a member-state of the European Union and the United Nations. This Óglaigh na hÉireann has never fought a foreign or defensive war; it serves a state that is not (yet) a member of NATO; and is typical of the resource-starved military of a small European 'Venus', best known for participation in UN peacekeeping missions. Under the Irish Free State (1922–37) it was known only as Óglaigh na hÉireann, and had no official English name. The other Óglaigh na hÉireann is the secret army, *the* IRA. The two 'Óglaigh na hÉireann', official and unofficial, sprang from the winners and losers, respectively, of the Irish Civil War (1922–23). That war was precipitated by the implementation of the Treaty between Great Britain and Ireland, which led to a division within the ranks of the IRA, then over 100,000 strong. After April 1922, there were two armies, one loyal to the Free State's provisional government, the other to the IRA Executive. Pro-Treaty volunteers joined the army of the Irish Free State; anti-Treaty volunteers insisted they constituted the true IRA.

Initial Constitutional Objectives

The reformed anti-Treaty IRA's initial constitution, drafted in the spring of 1922, before the onslaught of the Civil War, stated that

The Army shall be known as the Irish Republican Army. It shall be ... a purely volunteer Army ... Its objects shall be:

1. To safeguard the honour and maintain the independence of the Irish Republic.
2. To protect the rights and liberties common to the people of Ireland.
3. To place its services at the disposal of an established Republican Government which faithfully upholds the above objects.[7]

Having 'dumped arms' — acknowledging defeat in the Civil War in May 1923 — the IRA amended its constitution in November 1925 to specify four objectives: guarding the Republic's honour and upholding its sovereignty and unity; establishing and upholding a legitimate Irish government with total control over the Republic; securing and defending citizens' civil and religious liberties and their equal rights and opportunities; and, lastly (a new item), reviving the Irish language and 'promoting the best characteristics of the Irish race'. Aside from this addition of an ethno-national agenda, the content was the same as that of spring 1922.[8]

It is vital to understand the original three quoted 'objects'. The IRA was reformed by those republicans, a majority of the Volunteers, who regarded the Treaty signed by Sinn Féin's delegates in 1921 as a fundamental betrayal of 'the honour and independence of the Irish Republic'. This was, among other things, because the Treaty acknowledged a continuing role for the British king and his successors as the (constitutional) monarch of Ireland, gave Great Britain a right of ratification over the permanent constitution of the Irish Free State by requiring that the latter comply with the Treaty, restricted Ireland's international sovereignty, and required the Free State to make its key naval ports available to the forces of the Crown. The failure of the Treaty immediately to reverse the partition of Ireland into two entities, 'Northern' and 'Southern', which the Westminster parliament had authorized in the Government of Ireland Act of 1920 without the consent of a single Irish MP, was regarded by some, but not all, opponents of the Treaty as an equally fundamental betrayal of Ireland's national honour, rights, liberties and independence.

'To protect the rights and liberties common to the people of Ireland', meant that the IRA's mission was to defend the right of the people of Ireland to what today we would call their human rights. It was also a statement of inclusive civic republican nationalism for Irish citizens, whatever their origins, and of their collective right to national self-determination.

The third object of the IRA, 'to place its services at the disposal of an established Republican Government which faithfully upholds the above objects', warrants detailed parsing. The IRA endorsed republican — and democratic — government, and, in principle, the subordination of the army to an 'established Republican Government', *provided* that government faithfully upheld the honour and independence and the rights and liberties of the people of Ireland. 'Established Republican Government' was code for the government created by 'Dáil Éireann' — the Assembly of Ireland — formed by the Sinn Féin members elected to the Westminster parliament of 1918 who had then proclaimed Ireland's own parliament. Its successor, the Second Dáil, elected in 1921, had 'established' and sworn its members' loyalty to the Irish Republic proclaimed in the rebellion of 1916.

In 1919, Cathal Brugha, Minister of Defence in the Government created by Dáil Éireann, had insisted that the IRA take an oath of loyalty to Dáil Éireann — thereby formally establishing civilian control of the military in the new and emergent state, and

attempting to reduce the influence of the IRB (and Collins) within the IRA. The Treaty precisely required members of Dáil Éireann to swear an oath of allegiance to the British Crown, thereby repudiating the establishment of the Republic. The provocative British insistence on this new oath, requiring deputies to foreswear their solemn commitments, stuck in the throat of republicans, many of whom were otherwise prepared for political compromise, e.g. Eamon de Valera, the then President of Dáil Éireann, who had sought for Ireland to have 'external association' with, but not membership of, the British Commonwealth, and was willing to recognize the British king as the head of the Commonwealth. In the perspective of the new IRA's constitution, the deputies of Dáil Éireann who obliged the Treaty by taking the oath, had done what they had no right to do, namely disestablish the Republic at British insistence, and thereby dishonoured the independence, rights, and liberties of the people of Ireland.

The Treaty, made under the duress of David Lloyd George's threat of 'immediate and terrible war', had been accepted by a bare majority (3 to 2) of Ireland's negotiators (who had then signed *en bloc*), and by a bare majority of the cabinet of Dáil Éireann (4 to 3). The deputies who accepted the Treaty included the majority of the second Dáil Éireann, led by Michael Collins (then President of the IRB), and Arthur Griffith, the founder of Sinn Féin, who had endorsed the Treaty as members of the negotiating team and the cabinet. The deputies of Dáil Éireann later dissolved themselves into the new parliament (also called Dáil Éireann) of the Irish Free State, which had 'dominion status' within the British Empire, with the British king as head of state. The defeated minority of deputies became, in the vision of the new anti-Treaty IRA, the upholders of Ireland's honourable independence, the 'established' Republic — and they, as the rump 'Second Dáil', provided the legitimate

9   The most comprehensive and elegant treatment of the early Sinn Féin is provided by Michael Laffan, *The Resurrection of Ireland: The Sinn Féin Party, 1916–1923* (Cambridge, 1999). Brian Feeney, *Sinn Féin: A Hundred Turbulent Years* (Dublin, 2002), 161–210, provides an accurate, intelligent and witty dissection of its development between 1923 and 1969 (and after).

10 The Irish title of the new party, 'Soldiers of Destiny', had been the slogan of the Irish Volunteers, and had been embroidered in their cap bands: see Feeney, *Sinn Féin*, 159.

11 English, *Armed Struggle*, 43

12 See Coogan, *IRA*, Part I; Patrick Bishop and Eamonn Mallie, *The Provisional IRA* (London, 1987), 1–88; Peter Taylor, *Provos: The IRA and Sinn Féin* (London, revised and updated edn. 1998), 1–20; Bowyer Bell, *Secret Army*; English, *Armed Struggle*, Part I; Brian Hanley, *The IRA, 1926–1936* (Dublin, 2002); Peter Hart, *The I.R.A. and its Enemies: Violence and Community in Cork, 1916–1923* (Oxford, 1998) and *The I.R.A. at War, 1916–1923* (Oxford, 2003); Uinseann Mac Eoin, *The IRA in the Twilight Years: 1923–1948, History and Politics* (Dublin, 1997). Argenta, the name of Mac Eoin's publisher, signals the author's sympathies: it recalls the ship on which IRA members were interned without trial in Northern Ireland in 1922, on which see Denise Kleinrichert, *Republican Internment and the Prison Ship* Argenta, *1922* (Dublin, 2001).

13 From 1933, volunteers were prohibited from belonging to the Communist Party by General Army Order No. 4: see Bowyer Bell, *Secret Army*, 246.

democratic authority for the IRA to oppose the Treaty. After losing the Civil War, the IRA did not disband, but endured as a significant organization of trained soldiers opposed to the Treaty and its consequences, including the partition of Ireland. The split within the IRA was mirrored at party level. Sinn Féin divided: the majority forming Cumann na nGaedheal (and the first government of the Irish Free State), while the minority maintained the title deeds to Sinn Féin.[9] Most of the members of Cumann na nGaedheal would later become, in the 1930s, members of Fine Gael, the party that was most committed to the Treaty.

The majority of the deputies of Sinn Féin left its ranks in 1926 to join the new Fianna Fáil party, which was prepared to work the dominion system while being committed to removing every obnoxious vestige of the Treaty from the constitution of independent Ireland.[10] In the meantime the IRA was pledged, by its revised 1925 constitution, provided the Republic was fully established, to acknowledge the authority of such an emergent entity: 'The Army Council shall have the power to delegate its powers to a government which is actively endeavouring to function as the *de facto* government of the republic …When a government is [thus] functioning … a General Army Convention shall be convened to give the allegiance of Óglaigh na hÉireann to such a government'.[11]

The IRA Between Two Wars in Ireland

The volatile, labyrinthine, public and secret history of the IRA (or, as some would have it, of the many IRAs) between 1923 and 1969 cannot be thoroughly traced here. It is chronicled in a range of journalists' narratives (Tim Pat Coogan, Peter Taylor, Patrick Bishop and Eamonn Mallie), in the memoirs of former IRA volunteers, and sympathizers (notably Uinseann Mac Eoin),

and in more systematic appraisals by contemporary historians (J. Bowyer Bell, Richard English, Brian Hanley and Peter Hart).[12] The story in the standard accounts, of course, is not one of complete coherence. Contradictory dispositions in and actions by the IRA abounded in the fifty years between the onset of Ireland's War of Independence and the extensive 'return' of British troops to Northern Ireland in 1969. The IRA apparently did not believe that a majority, even an Irish majority in *the* Dáil, had the right to be wrong on the constitutional status of Ireland — evidence of 'vanguardism' and 'elitism'. Yet its successive leaders genuinely sought to lead (or assist) a popular revolution against three régimes (in Belfast, Dublin and London). In the 1920s and 1930s, the IRA commended parliamentary abstentionism, which for many became an article of faith as opposed to a tactic, but one of its Army Council members was elected to the Northern Ireland parliament in 1933, and the organization actively canvassed for Fianna Fáil (which described itself as 'The Republican Party' in English) in two critical general elections in 1932 and 1933 — both of which saw the anti-Treaty party returned to power. The IRA's membership was mostly Catholic in its origins, but the Catholic clergy and bishops of Ireland regularly condemned it. The IRA proclaimed a civic Irish republicanism, true to the heritage of the eighteenth-century revolutionaries, the United Irishmen, in which Protestants and other minorities would have full citizenship rights. Yet its leaders and members were often regarded as 'sectarian' in practice. The IRA was described as comprised of highly localized sectarian militias, defenders of Northern Irish Catholics, but also as centralized internationalist left-wing revolutionaries. In one decade, the 1930s, the leadership of the IRA went from being the Comintern's closest ally in Ireland to conspiring with Nazi Germany, under Sean Russell, several years later, before returning in the 1960s to an accommodation with

Marxists.[13] In the early and mid-1930s, the IRA 'denounced partition, yet remained very much an organization focused on the overthrow of the southern rather than the northern state. It trained for warfare, yet often tried to prevent its members involving themselves in confrontation with their enemies'.[14]

Yet despite multiple zigzags, not least in orientation toward socialist politics in this fifty-year interval, one can observe a unifying theme across the IRA's history before 1969, namely, the comprehensive constitutional rejection of British determination of Ireland's constitutional arrangements. Here is a sketch of five partially overlapping phases, which correspond to the received history learned by IRA volunteers.

First, after the glorious defeat and surrender of 1916, came sudden and surprising success in guerrilla warfare against the British. The IRA refers to this moment as the 'Tan War' — after its engagements with the Black and Tans (uniformed in black and khaki), emergency reserve police recruited from Great Britain. Success affirmed for many the merits of armed struggle, particularly guerrilla warfare, which had done more to create a self-governing Ireland than fifty years of parliamentary pursuit of home rule.[15]

The second phase, 1923–48, opened after the equally sudden defeat of the bulk of the IRA in the Civil War over the Treaty. The IRA was decisively defeated militarily: significant numbers of volunteers were killed, injured, or incarcerated. Of those subsequently released many left the organization. The IRA's explicit or tacit electoral supporters became a minority in the South.[16] It became an anti-system oppositionist underground army organization in the Irish Free State — and was weaker still in Northern Ireland.[17] There was a progressive diminution both in

the strength of and the support for the IRA, even though its membership in the 1930s has been estimated as high as 30,000.[18] Volunteers were intermittently repressed, subjected to extensive surveillance, interned without trial, and gradually marginalized, even though the veterans of the Tan War retained public admiration in the South. This loss of support was largely because the IRA progressively lost its rationale in the South. Successive political leaders of political parties in independent Ireland, under Cumann na nGaedheal, Fianna Fáil, and later Clann na Poblachta, were to prove Michael Collins's perception of the Treaty to be true: it could be used as a 'stepping stone' to establish Ireland's formal — and republican — independence from Great Britain.[19] A Cumann na nGaedheal-led government confirmed the equality and independence of all the British dominions in the Statute of Westminster of 1931. From 1932 Fianna Fáil governments, under the leadership of de Valera, who had led most active republicans away from the abstentionist policies of Sinn Féin and the IRA, progressively dismantled most of the objectionable features of the Treaty. They removed the oath, abolished the post of governor general, recovered the Treaty ports, and established Ireland's external sovereignty — to the extent that it was able to remain neutral in World War II (formally in protest at the maintenance of partition). The removal of the requirement that deputies take an oath of allegiance to the British Crown, according to de Valera, removed the case for abstentionism in the South: deputies were now free to argue for the republican platform without British-imposed impediments. Ireland freely established its popularly endorsed constitution (Bunreacht na hÉireann) in 1937 without British interference and created an elected president as head of state, and external association with the British Commonwealth, i.e. a republic in all but name. Later, a Fine Gael- and Clann na Poblachta-led coalition government

14 Hanley, *IRA*, 26–27
15 Peter Hart's *The I.R.A. and Its Enemies* and *The I.R.A. at War* provide the most social scientific treatment of the IRA in these years. I cannot discuss my reservations about this excellent work here.
16 Drawing extensively on the papers of Maurice (Moss) Twomey, Hanley's *The IRA, 1926–1936* provides an analysis of the organization in this period; the idea that Ireland experienced a counter-revolution after 1921 is spiritedly advanced by John Regan, *The Irish Counter-Revolution, 1921–36: Treatyite Politics and Settlement in Independent Ireland* (Dublin, 1999).
17 Comprehensive historical treatments of the IRA in Northern Ireland between 1916 and 1969 are yet to be written: Jim McDermott, *Northern Divisions: The Old IRA and the Belfast Pogroms 1920–22* (Belfast, 2001) provides a pioneering account of divisions between the pro- and anti-Treaty IRA in Belfast.
18 This figure is 'safely assumed' by Coogan, *IRA*, 79, but Hanley, *IRA*, ch. 1, provides good reasons for thinking that the IRA numbered between 10,000 and 12,000 volunteers in 1932, before declining after a significant breakaway by the politically minded founders of the Republican Congress, and being reduced to fewer than 4,000 members by 1936.

19 Seán MacBride, the leader of Clann na Poblachta, was a former Chief of Staff of the IRA, who achieved a unique historical status as a winner of both the Lenin and Nobel peace prizes.

20 The defeat of the IRA in Northern Ireland in the 1940s was exemplified in the execution of Tom Williams, whom the Northern Ireland court identified as the key figure in a unit that killed an RUC officer. One of his reprieved comrades, Joe Cahill, later became the first Chief of Staff of the Provisional IRA: see Jim McVeigh, *Executed: Tom Williams and the IRA* (Belfast, 1999) and Brendan Anderson, *Joe Cahill: A Life in the IRA* (Dublin, 2002).

21 Bowyer Bell, *Secret Army*, 252n.1, observes that 'The situation was so bad that the IRA Intelligence had got access to a copy of a secret [Irish] government publication, *Notes on the IRA*, and used the names to make their early contacts [for reconstruction] under the assumption that if Special Branch thought a man was a troublemaker he would be a good man.'

22 Bowyer Bell, *Secret Army*, ch. 14–16; Seán Cronin, *Irish Nationalism: A History of its Roots and Ideology* (London, 1980), ch. 5

proclaimed Ireland a Republic in 1949. The 1937 constitution vested sovereignty in the people of Ireland, made it plain that the institutions established were a product of Irish will, and (implicitly) repudiated the Government of Ireland Act (1920), which had partitioned Ireland. In Articles 2 and 3 of its constitution, it affirmed that the whole island of Ireland was 'national territory', and reserved to the Irish parliament the right to govern all of Ireland, including the lost six counties. The 1949 declaration that independent Ireland was a Republic — it then left the British Commonwealth because that organization did not then accept republics — meant that the IRA was left with no meaningful grievance against Ireland's constitutional status. In short, the constitutional resentment at the Treaty in sovereign Ireland had been substantively resolved by 1937, in the view of one former IRA anti-Treaty man, who had become Prime Minister, de Valera, and by 1949, by another former anti-Treaty IRA man, Seán MacBride, who had become Minister for External Affairs.

The third phase, 1939–56, saw a strong re-orientation of the rump IRA, abandoned by many of its southern leftists, toward achieving Irish unification. Reversing partition was the last extant objectionable feature of the Treaty of 1921, arguably after 1937, and certainly after 1949. This re-orientation began with a bombing campaign in England, after a formal declaration of notice and war, in 1939–40. The campaign was a failure and the upshot was the imprisonment and the near-extinction of the IRA's volunteers in both parts of Ireland as well as of its activists in England.[20] The IRA had to be rebuilt almost from scratch after World War II.[21] The logical corollary of the orientation toward ending partition was seen in an Army Convention resolution of 1948 that there would be no military action by the IRA in the twenty-six counties — which should in retrospect be read as the IRA's first step toward formal recognition of

what it called the 'Leinster House Parliament'. It was followed, shortly, by General Army Order No. 8, which forbad volunteers from defending their arms in the South, or from any defensive actions in the South. In short, the IRA was no longer at war with independent Ireland. That armed struggle had been abandoned.

The fourth phase, the IRA campaign of 1956 to 1962, within Northern Ireland, launched from both the North and the South, was intended to liberate the six counties, and to reunify Ireland using guerrilla warfare and armed propaganda. It was preceded by significant evidence of Northern Irish nationalist discontent with the Belfast régime, expressed in successive elections of Sinn Féin candidates. But it was a small-scale conflict, quickly repressed on both sides of the border, and ended in a thorough defeat, publicly acknowledged by the IRA's Army Council.[22]

The comprehensive failure of the IRA's armed struggle to liberate the North led to a fifth phase, between 1962 and 1969, when an emergent left-wing oriented leadership tried to take the IRA, South and North, strongly in the direction of communist politics, to make 'reds' out of 'greens'. They were ready to abandon militarism, and to shift toward recognition of Ireland's parliament and the abandonment of principled abstentionism.

This capsule history is, at first glance, one of comprehensive military, political, and strategic failure for the IRA. It went to war against the government of the Irish Free State (1922–23), against the government of Great Britain in 1939, and against the Northern Ireland government in 1956. It was defeated in all three instances, and had acknowledged each defeat, and by the early 1960s appeared to have a rendezvous with a coroner. Politically most of its members had been moral conservatives, Jeffersonian republicans rather than hard-line socialists

— although socialists had been consistently the most ideologically-driven of them, believing their position had been legitimated by the incorporation of Marxist James Connolly's Irish Citizen Army into the IRA in 1916. By the late 1960s in both parts of Ireland, and within the Irish diaspora, the IRA appeared to be a relic, a group of obsessives disconnected from contemporary politics. It had never repeated its successful symbiosis with Sinn Féin of 1919–21, when a military and democratic political movement had combined and forced the UK government to negotiate with Irish republicans.

But failure was not the whole story. The IRA's founding agenda had been substantively realized in the South.[23] All southern governments from 1922 had former senior IRA men in their ministerial ranks. With the notable exception of Kevin O'Higgins, most were republicans with kindred beliefs to those of the IRA.[24] They progressively addressed its constitutional agenda, which was neither insane nor unprincipled, even if it was dogmatic, and even if it refused the right of a majority to be wrong on the constitutional status of the state. However, resentment did lead the IRA into increasingly bizarre ideological deductions. The deputies of the rump Second Dáil who had taken the anti-Treaty side, and who had withdrawn from participation in the 'partitionist' Dáil Éireann, continued to meet until the late 1930s as if they were the valid parliament of Ireland. This, in turn, meant that the IRA's mandate stemmed from the last all-Ireland parliament — one that was increasingly, as time passed, demographically as well as chronologically removed from the current preferences of the people of Ireland, North and South. The *demos* from which the IRA derived its authority was frozen in time, increasingly virtual. Eventually, the ageing deputies, the rump Second Dáil, authorized the IRA Army Council to be the government of

Ireland until the Republic could be re-established — although in the IRA's theory it had never been validly *de jure* 'dis-established'. It was, for example, in its capacity as the alleged government of the Irish Republic that the IRA declared war on Great Britain in January 1939.[25] Ideological derivations of arcane and progressively dated mandates did not stop with the view that the IRA was the Government of Ireland pending (the re-establishment of) the Republic and a validly constituted Dáil. The last surviving member of the rump Dáil, General Tom Maguire, was to live long enough to be twice asked to decide which section of the republican movement was the true inheritor of the mandate of the last valid Dáil (and thereby the valid government of the Republic of Ireland). In 1969, he decided that the mandate belonged with the Provisional IRA, and in 1986 that it belonged with those who rejected the decision of Sinn Féin to recognize the legitimacy of the Dublin parliament. On his death Maguire handed the baton on to Michael Flannery.[26]

This excursus into the repercussions of republican constitutional ideology might occasion laughter if the stakes were not so serious. In considering policy responses to political violence, it is too customary for analysts and policy-makers to treat ideology and normative constitutional doctrine as masks for other interests or grievances, or as easily moulded plasticine that can be rapidly reshaped as and when a movement requires. Policy-makers tend to focus on either the incentives or opportunities that encourage or discourage the use of political violence, or on the material grievances held to underpin insurrectionary movements. These are not pointless dispositions. But ideologically barricaded organizations may be best induced to withdraw from violence if an internally principled path can be found for their members to abandon their use of violence. Governments that directly engage the ideological propositions, and the

23 The most incisive analysis of de Valera's long-term legitimizing of independent Ireland through constitutional republicanism is Bill Kissane's *Explaining Irish Democracy* (Dublin, 2002), 165ff.

24 O'Higgins, the strongman of the Cumann na nGaedheal government, seriously sought to have George V separately crowned as King of Ireland, following thereby the original 'dual monarchy' proposal made by Arthur Griffith earlier in the century, and claimed that 'republicanism' was a foreign ideal. Griffith died in 1922 so we do not know whether he would have supported this reasoning.

25 Its ultimatum addressed to Lord Halifax is reproduced in Cronin, *Irish Nationalism*, Appendix XIV.

26 For a ninety-page statement of calcified orthodoxy, see Ruairí Ó Brádaigh, *Dílseacht: The Story of Comdt. General Tom Maguire and the Second (All-Ireland) Dáil* (Dublin, 1997).

27 In the 1950s and 1960s, judging by their publications and statements, Irish nationalists did not consider that Ireland's progressive unwinding of the Treaty had entrenched Ulster unionists' wish to remain part of the United Kingdom. Denis Kennedy, in an analysis of unionist newspapers 1919–49, argues that it in fact widened the gulf between both parts of Ireland (by which he means the gulf between Ulster unionists and Irish nationalists): see *The Widening Gulf: Northern Attitudes to the Independent Irish State, 1919–1949* (Belfast, 1988).

28 Bishop and Mallie, *Provisional IRA*, 104; Paul Arthur, 'Republican Violence in Northern Ireland: The Rationale', in John Darby, Nicholas Dodge and A. C. Hepburn, eds., *Political Violence: Ireland in a Comparative Perspective* (Belfast, 1990), 48–63 (49)

constitutional norms of such movements, may have greater success in promoting their internal transformations. That is one lesson one can extract from the progressive termination of the IRA as a serious subversive threat to the government of the Irish Free State, and its successor, the government of the Republic of Ireland. By progressively eliminating the obnoxious features of the Treaty, by transforming Ireland's constitutional status and laws, successive Irish governments rendered outmoded the IRA's constitutional objections to the 'actually existing' Republic of Ireland. This assisted in the demobilization and constitutionalization of the IRA's members in the South, and their withdrawal from the politics of armed struggle. There is a forgotten logical counterfactual to this proposition. Had Irish governments not followed this path, and had not British governments reconciled themselves to it, whether by accident or design, independent Ireland's Civil War over the Treaty would have been renewed, and the IRA would have had greater support for attempting a *coup d'état* in the South.

Normative constitutional engagement with insurgents is not sufficient for making political settlements and peace, nor is what might be termed 'constitutional appeasement' always appropriate or sufficient. The long-run success of Irish governments in marginalizing the IRA in the South owed a great deal to the regularly renewed democratic and majority mandates of such governments, their successful use of civil policing, extensive surveillance, intermittently severe repression under the rule of law, and the imposition of multiple hardships which induced many IRA veterans to leave the organization or to emigrate. One must not forget that the institutionalization of the Irish state, supported externally by Winston Churchill, was preceded by the thoroughly brutal — and frequently lawless — suppression of the majority of the IRA in the Civil War,

including executive-authorized executions. Nevertheless, where military nationalist movements have constitutions that guide their conduct, and are organized around coherent constitutional resentment, constitutional engagement may be a necessary condition for conflict-resolution. Having shown how the argument applies to the IRA in the South, I will later attempt to show that a similar argument can be used to interpret the IRA's willingness to sustain ceasefires in the 1990s and presently to consider its own disbandment.

Provisional IRA: Objectives and Nature

The IRA could, and did, object to the failure of Irish governments to achieve Irish unification, but its volunteers knew that the major obstacle to Irish unification lay not with what they persisted in calling the Free State. After all, governments of Ireland had diplomatically campaigned for Irish unification after 1937. Rather the obstacles lay with the UK government, and with the wishes of Ulster unionists, the strongest beneficiaries and supporters of the Treaty settlement.[27] The Provisional IRA was created in December 1969 in full knowledge of these facts, its twin-sister, Provisional Sinn Féin, shortly afterwards. The new IRA's first declaration affirmed its allegiance to 'the Thirty-two County Irish Republic proclaimed at Easter 1916, established by Dáil Éireann in 1919, overthrown by force of arms in 1922 and suppressed to this day by the British-imposed Six County and Twenty-six County partitionist states', a re-statement of the IRA's traditional stance.[28] The 'Provisional' title served three functions. It echoed the 'Provisional Government of the Irish Republic' proclaimed in 1916; and, secondly, it repudiated the 'Official' IRA's leaders, who had just sought to manoeuvre the IRA to end political abstentionism, and had, it was thought, used unconstitutional means to do so. Thirdly, 'Provisional' suggested a temporary designation, pending the reorganization of the IRA. This mission was proclaimed accomplished in September 1970, but the name 'Provisional IRA', and its derivatives 'Provos', 'Provies', stuck.

The split between the Provisionals and the Officials is generally attributed to three cleavages. The Officials were Marxist, or on the verge of becoming so; the Provisionals were more nationalist; and the Officials preferred to build a political liberation front to military struggle.[29] There is truth in this characterization. The historian Roy Foster further maintains that the Officials were 'woolly radicals dreaming of a national liberation front', whereas the Provisionals are typecast as 'Defenderists' and as 'fundamentalists'.[30] The Defenderist motif is commonplace in accounts of the Provisional IRA.[31] It suggests a lineage from the clandestine eighteenth-century agrarian Catholic nativist militia of Ulster who defended their co-religionists from Protestant settler vigilantes, the 'Peep o' Day Boys', organized killers and expellers of Catholics. It insinuates that the Provisionals are more sectarian than ideological, and less committed to the civic citizenship agenda of Ireland's first eighteenth-century republicans, the United Irishmen (who fused the Defenders into their organization before the 1798 insurrection). It treats the Provisionals as atavistic.

The Defenderist motif appears to make sense because the impetus for the formation of the Provisional IRA was the unpreparedness of the IRA, North or South, for the assaults on Catholics, especially Belfast Catholics, by Protestant mobs, in collusion with the Royal Ulster Constabulary and its auxiliaries, the B Specials, in August 1969. These assaults, which led to deaths, injuries, and expulsions, and the burning out of Bombay Street, are standardly described as 'pogroms' in the memories of post-1969 Provisional IRA volunteers.[32] These assaults were responses to the then peaceful civil rights movement, which republicans had helped

organize from 1966 to mobilize against deep injustices within Northern Ireland, modelling the protests on the US civil rights movement.[33] The Provisionals were organized in immediate response to urban defencelessness, and to remonstrative graffiti on Belfast walls that declared 'IRA = I Ran Away'. But the post-1969 Provisionals were not atavistic throwbacks. Their new members were, mostly, urban working-class activists who saw themselves, initially, as defenders of their communities against contemporary loyalists, partisan police and partisan British troops. Their founding leaders soon persuaded them that active offence against the British state was the only or at least the best way to address the unreformable polity of Northern Ireland. To typecast the Provisionals as religious 'fundamentalists' is as misleading as reading them as throwbacks. Their early and their later members included many self-styled socialists; and although the Provisionals have been overwhelmingly Catholic in social origin they have not, generally, been pious believers, have not followed the political advice of their Church's bishops — or the Pope — and are less overtly and traditionally Catholic than the volunteers of 1916 or of the 1920s. There has never been a serving priest, let alone a bishop, in the IRA's Army Council, or, to my knowledge, among its volunteers.[34] The IRA's symbolism may be suffused with a Catholic heritage, as some maintain, but it is the Irish nation rather than the Roman Catholic Church which they affirm, and to which they pledge allegiance. That said, the Provisionals were founded by 'republican' fundamentalists, men who had fought in the failed 1956–62 campaign, such as Ruairí Ó Brádaigh, Dáithí Ó Conaill, Seán Mac Stiofáin, and Joe Cahill, and who believed in the republican traditions, i.e. in rejecting the Treaty's institutions, and undoing partition by force.[35]

The Provisionals soon declared themselves at war with the British army, which had been deployed in Northern Ireland in 1969

29 Bishop and Mallie, *Provisional IRA*, 89–105; Bowyer Bell, *Secret Army*, 355–72; Coogan, *IRA*, 365–84; English, *Armed Struggle*, 81–147; Henry Patterson, *The Politics of Illusion: Republicanism and Socialism in Modern Ireland* (London, 1989), ch. 4–6 and James M. Glover, 'Northern Ireland: Future Terrorist Trends', Ministry of Defence [United Kingdom], D/DINI/2003 MOD Form 102: s25/II/82, 2 Nov. 1978, reprinted in Cronin, *Irish Nationalism*, 339-57

30 R. F. Foster, *Modern Ireland: 1600–1972* (London, 1988), 589

31 Kevin Toolis, *Rebel Hearts: Journeys Within the IRA's Soul* (London, 1995), 28ff. Toolis writes of the IRA through investigative and personalized studies of 'defenders', 'brothers' [the Finucanes], 'informers', 'volunteers', 'chieftains' [McGuinness], and 'martyrs'. In its story-telling and prose *Rebel Hearts* is the best journalistic foray into the IRA. It is, however, a social science-free zone, and its policy proposals are shallow. But it has the quality of enduring literature, and many of its stories read like realist film or drama scripts.

32 See the interviews in Robert White, *Provisional Irish Republicans* (Westport, Ct., 1993), ch. 4.

33 Bob Purdie, 'Was the Civil Rights Movement a Republican/Communist Conspiracy?', *Irish Political Studies*, 3 (1988), 33–41; *Politics in the Streets: The Origins of the Civil Rights Movement in Northern Ireland* (Belfast, 1990)

34 Fr. Michael Flanagan was Vice-President of Sinn Féin (1917–21), and its President in 1934. He was disciplined by the Roman Catholic Church and was the sole priest in Ireland to support the Spanish Republic against General Franco (Cronin, *Irish Nationalism*, 279n.140). Fr. Patrick Ryan, whose extradition to the UK was refused by the Irish Courts in 1988, was accused of being a member of the IRA.

35 Hereafter, unless otherwise stated, the Provisional IRA will be treated as *the* IRA, and Provisional Sinn Féin as Sinn Féin because that is how the volunteers and members describe their organizations, and because, officially, the Official IRA no longer exists, having been disbanded by its party, the Workers Party, the heir of the defunct Official Sinn Féin.

36 James Kelly, *Orders for the Captain?* (Dublin, 1971); *The Thimble Riggers: The Dublin Arms Trials of 1970* (Dublin, 1999)

37 O'Leary and McGarry, *Politics of Antagonism*, ch. 3–4

38 She almost certainly authorized indirect negotiations during the first batch of hunger strikes in 1980: see David Beresford, *Ten Men Dead: The Story of the 1981 Irish Hunger Strike* (London, 1987), 40, 292–93. After the Anglo-Irish Agreement of 1985 Thatcher and Secretaries of State Tom King and Peter Brooke were aware, and approved of, a 'pipeline' to and from Gerry Adams via priest Alex Reid: see Ed Moloney, *A Secret History of the IRA* (New York, 2002), 246–60, *passim*.

39 For example, see the information in Moloney, *Secret History, passim*.

40 See Coogan, *IRA*; Brendan O'Brien, *The Long War: The IRA and Sinn Féin from Armed Struggle to Peace Talks* (Dublin, updated paperback edn. 1995); Taylor, *Provos*; White, *Provisional Irish Republicans*.

41 O'Brien, *Long War*, Appendix 1; Martin Dillon, *Twenty Five Years of Terror* (London, 1996), 353–84; and see the commentary in Coogan, *IRA*, 544–71.

in 'support of the civil power', apparently in a peacekeeping role, and to head off a potential intervention by the Irish government — which had arranged at least one clandestine supply of arms to protect Northern Catholics.[36] The new IRA, which some, wrongly, maintain was brought into being through the active planning of the Irish government, argued that only a British disengagement would resolve the conflicts on the island, but focused its initial attention on removing the Stormont parliament — through which the Ulster Unionist Party had organized a systematic system of discrimination for nearly fifty years.[37] In 1970–71, the Provisionals rapidly surpassed the Officials in militancy and recruitment amongst Catholic youths; and from 1969 until 1997, with breaks in 1972, 1974–75, and between 1994 and 1996, this new IRA organized a sustained insurrection. It has not succeeded in unifying Ireland, but regards itself as having removed the majoritarian and tyrannous Stormont parliament in 1972. It was not militarily defeated by what is widely acknowledged as the most capable European army, nor, after 1976, by an extremely large, armed, reorganized, and well-funded police force, the Royal Ulster Constabulary.

Operating mostly within a territory with just over one million and a half people, and for most of that time within a support base of a minority of the minority cultural Catholic population of approximately 650,000, the IRA's organizational endurance was impressive. It survived the efforts of five UK prime ministers to crush it — Harold Wilson, Edward Heath, James Callaghan, Margaret Thatcher, and John Major. The IRA's leaders negotiated, directly or indirectly, with all these prime ministers. The leader of the UK's opposition, Harold Wilson, who was to be prime minister again between 1974 and 1976, met the IRA in Dublin in 1971. In 1972, an IRA negotiating team, including the young Gerry Adams and Martin McGuinness, met with Heath's Deputy Prime Minister, William Whitelaw, in London. The IRA would later indirectly negotiate with Wilson's government in 1974–75, and with Major's between 1990 and 1996. Thatcher must have authorized Peter Brooke, then Secretary of State for Northern Ireland, to open negotiations about negotiations by proxy with the IRA in 1989.[38] And since 1997 the IRA has been indirectly — directly on some interpretations — negotiating with another British prime minister, Tony Blair. In the same period it has negotiated, indirectly or directly, with four Irish prime ministers — Charles Haughey, Albert Reynolds, John Bruton and Bertie Ahern. In short, 'talking to terrorists' has been considered a necessary risk by six British premiers, and at least four recent Irish premiers.

What is known about the contemporary IRA? Transparency cannot be the dominant trait of an underground army. The names of the IRA's Army Council and Executive leaders, although widely guessed, reported, and denied, are organizational secrets, which Ed Moloney claims to know. Presently many of its serving volunteers freely supply journalists with extensive information about intra-IRA debates, apparently in violation of IRA General Army Order No. 3, 'No member ... shall make any statement either verbally or in writing to the press or mass media without General Headquarters permission'.[39]

Most studies of the IRA are dependent upon authorized interviews.[40] There are, of course, some documentary materials. The IRA, since its first effective organizer Michael Collins, has been textual. Its 1979 'Green Book' is a manual of lectures on constitutional commitments and rules for recruits, and guidance for volunteers facing interrogation.[41] The IRA tries to keep fastidious records in notebooks and electronic media. This trait has, of course, often compromised secrecy. Peter Taylor's remarkable account of an interview with

Ruairí Ó Brádaigh shows that the IRA's leaders keep extensive minutes, and that these minutes are authoritative.[42] It is equally clear that no journalist, let alone historian, has had access to full copies of such records, and whether they will eventually become available, or revelatory, cannot be known. They are, however, more likely to be reliable than some of today's literature and pulp fiction that goes into successive editions for the denizens of airport lounges and the generally male consumers of books on war and conflict. For source materials on the IRA serious analysts are dependent upon the organization's formal communiqués; transcripts of its authorized interviews with journalists and academics; public police and court records of volunteers and prisoners; stolen, lost or leaked British or Irish army, police, MI5, MI6, and Ministry of Defence intelligence reports; accounts of conflictual incidents and victims of incidents; and what can be gleaned from the memoirs, autobiographies, and authorized and unauthorized biographies of the IRA's leaders and volunteers, or from the National Graves Association, which provides a roll call of the republican war dead.[43] There are also the suspect but potentially informative accounts of volunteers turned spies or who have abandoned the cause.[44] What follows is a provisional summary of what is known about the IRA from a critical but impartial appraisal of these sources.

Structure: Division of Labour, Recruits, and Numbers

Until 1977 the IRA was organized, as it had been since the Irish Civil War of 1922–23, as a shadow or underground version of the British army, complete with officers, staff and line, and territorial brigades, battalions, and companies. From 1976–77 it was reorganized in smaller cellular structures, active service units (ASUs), each intended to be specialized (e.g. in sniping, executions, bombings, robberies), and to comprise a small number of volunteers. The idea was to intensify the division of labour, and to create a more compact organization, less vulnerable both to volunteers' surrendering information and to intelligence losses through informants.[45] In this reformation, several hundred volunteers, especially many ex-prisoners, were excluded from the ASUs as security risks, either because they were easily monitored security-risks, or because they were otherwise regarded as unreliable. Nevertheless, after the change some of the old nomenclature of battalions and brigades was preserved — and in Crossmaglen and Tyrone lip-service was paid to the change.[46]

Presented in a formal organizational chart the top tier of the IRA consists of the Executive (12 members), elected by the General Army Convention, which did not meet between 1970 and 1986, because of the danger of mass arrests. As the agency responsible for the IRA's constitution, the Convention is its sovereign. The Executive elects and, nominally, holds to account the Army Council (7 members), the operational executive chaired by the Chief of Staff. The General Headquarters of the IRA staff is organized functionally into 'offices': Quarter Master General, Operations, Engineering, Intelligence, Finance, Training, Security, Publicity and Political Education. Operations are organized by area: England, Europe, and, since reorganization, two Irish Commands, 'Southern' and 'Northern'.[47] The role of Southern Command is to act as the supplier and stockist for Northern Command — and for many operations in England. Judging by arms, guns, ammunition, explosive devices, and bomb-making equipment found by the Garda Síochána (the Irish police) in the decade preceding the ceasefires of the 1990s, most matériel was kept in the border counties, or in the Greater Dublin region, which makes logistical sense, although extrapolating from the location of 'finds' may be misleading because matériel may be more successfully hidden elsewhere in rural Ireland. Before and after reorganization the IRA

42 Taylor, *Provos*, 181
43 For police and court records, see Kieran McEvoy, *Paramilitary Imprisonment in Northern Ireland: Resistance, Management and Release* (Oxford, 2001); for a key intelligence report, see Glover, 'Northern Ireland: Future Terrorist Trends'. For accounts of victims, see David McKittrick, Seamus Kelters, Brian Feeney, Chris Thornton, *Lost Lives: The Stories of the Men, Women and Children Who Died as a Result of the Northern Ireland Troubles* (Edinburgh, 2001); Malcolm Sutton, *Bear in Mind the Dead: An Index of Deaths from the Conflict in Ireland, 1969–1993* (Belfast, 1994). For autobiographical and biographical accounts of republican figures, see Gerry Adams, *Falls Memories* (Dingle, 1983); *Cage Eleven* (Dingle, 1990); *Before the Dawn* (London, 1996); *An Irish Voice* (Dingle, 1997); *An Irish Journal* (Dingle, 2001); *A Farther Shore: Ireland's Long Road to Peace* (New York, 2003); Anderson, *Joe Cahill*; Liam Clarke and Kathryn Johnston, *Martin McGuinness: From Guns to Government* (Edinburgh, 2003); Seán Mac Stiofáin, *Memoirs of a Revolutionary* (London, 1975); Laurence McKeown, *Out of Time: Irish Republican Prisoners, Long Kesh 1972-2000* (Belfast, 2001); Shane Paul O'Doherty, *The Volunteer: A Former IRA Man's True Story* (London, 1993); Bobby Sands, *The Diary of Bobby Sands* (Dublin, 1981); *Prison Poems* (Dublin, 1981); *One Day in My Life* (Cork, 1982); David Sharrock and Mark Devenport, *Man of War, Man of Peace? The Unauthorised Biography of Gerry Adams* (London, 1997). There is also Danny Morrison's prison journal, *Then the Walls Came Down: A Prison Journal* (Cork, 1999), which I have not read.

44 Martin McGartland, *Fifty Dead Men Walking* (London, 1997) and *Dead Man Running: The True Story of a Secret Agent's Escape from the IRA and MI5* (Edinburgh, 1998); Eamon Collins (with McGovern), *Killing Rage* (London, 1997); Sean O'Callaghan, *The Informer* (London, 1998). Collins's book seems to me the most interesting, honest, revealing and least self-serving of the apostate accounts.

45 John Horgan and Max Taylor, 'The Provisional Irish Republican Army: Command and Functional Structure', *Terrorism and Political Violence*, 9 (1997), 1–32. Details of the reorganization, spelled out in a 'Staff Report', allegedly thought through by Gerry Adams and others when interned in Long Kesh, became known when IRA Chief of Staff Seamus Twomey was arrested in December 1977. The changes may have been implemented when Martin McGuinness was Chief of Staff (1978–82): see O'Brien, *Long War*, 107ff; see also Coogan, *IRA*, 464–74.

46 Collins, *Killing Rage*, 83

47 According to Moloney, *Secret History*, 573, the operational units in Northern Command are formally organized around Belfast and six other areas (Derry, Donegal/ Fermanagh, Tyrone and Monaghan, Armagh (North and South), and Down), and each has ASUs operating under Brigades; in slight contrast, O'Brien, *Long War*, 105, 110, maintains the Northern Command is organized over all of the six counties of Northern Ireland and the five adjacent border counties of the Republic (Louth, Monaghan, Cavan, Leitrim and Donegal), and has Belfast, Derry, Donegal, Tyrone/Monaghan and Armagh as the Brigade areas.

48 Bowyer Bell, *Secret Army*, 468–69

sought to establish a pyramidical command and control organization, like a functioning army. But, of necessity, the IRA has been extensively decentralized, reliant on the initiatives and flair of its semi-autonomous units:

> The Army Council and the GHQ were engaged in oversight, not command. Operational matters were often controlled by those close to the target. Intelligence was apt to arrive rather than be sought. GHQ spent a great deal of time balancing demands and seeking resources rather than in directing a war. All the strategic decisions had been made. Most tactical decisions were shaped by opportunity and vulnerabilities. Initiative was seldom punished … in reality the IRA ran on a consensus achieved largely unconsciously … Operational freedom often meant blunders, innocent people killed, incompetents sent in harm's way, bombs detonated when quiet was needed; but there was every indication that tight control from the centre would hardly have changed matters.[48]

Two more elements of IRA organization require comment: its security and its finances. The IRA has its own internal security, colloquially known as the 'nutting squad', whose mission is to interrogate, court martial, and, where deemed necessary, to execute suspected spies or informants.[49] It also organizes vigilante justice through punishment squads of auxiliaries, a lower tier of generally lower calibre volunteers, who are not members of the ASUs, although they can graduate to them.[50] The administration of 'punishment beatings', what I call policing without prisons, may take the form of brutal beatings of limbs with baseball bats or iron bars, or of 'knee-cappings' with gunshots. This is one of the most politically and morally sensitive subjects for the IRA's supporters and apologists. It is clear from interviews that republican leaders would be delighted to be

divested of any association with the system — even though one standard analysis is that the IRA's leaders support punishment beatings to entrench their local power. The punishment-beating system, which has its counterpart among loyalists, has been both a demand and a supply problem for the IRA. Rough justice is demanded for alleged offenders and petty criminals within nationalist working-class communities, especially where the IRA is dominant, and where calling on the services of the police, especially the unreformed RUC, has been unimaginable — not least because police officers have often been unwilling to provide standard security where they fear that they might be set-up and shot. IRA leaders in Belfast felt it necessary to meet some of this demand — and at least some of its auxiliaries have performed punishment beatings with sadistic enthusiasm. The supply problem has been occasioned when the IRA has a surplus of potential volunteers who might otherwise either join other republican organizations, or dilute the calibre of the core organization. Organizing the surplus in auxiliaries and punishment squads solves some of this problem. The system is one of the grisliest by-products of the absence of legitimate state institutions.[51]

The last item in considering organization is the IRA's finances. These are, of course, not 'known', but are subject to extensive speculation. Journalists regularly report Irish police and RUC estimates as authoritative, but they cannot be, at least not without confirmation from the IRA's internal 'accountants' and 'auditors'.[52] Albeit dated, the most interesting evaluation, precisely because it was not intended for publication, remains that of the stolen report of Brigadier James Glover of 1978.[53] It estimated IRA annual income at UK£950,000, and expenditure at £780,000, i.e. with an annual surplus of £170,000, 17.9 per cent, available for arms, ammunition and explosives.[54] Glover estimated expenditure as devoted, in descending order of importance, to four items: volunteers' pay, travel and transport costs, propaganda, and prisoner support. He considered the IRA had four principal sources of income, in descending order of importance: theft and robbery in Ireland, racketeering in Ireland, overseas donations, and the Green Cross (a prisoners' aid organization). 'Overseas donations' were estimated at £120,000, i.e. 12.7 per cent of revenues, and were not expected to rise.[55] Glover assumed that the IRA's commercial undertakings were marred by 'dishonesty and incompetence', and poor sources of revenue, other than its black taxi service. He listed no domestic Irish donations at all, which seems incredible. His estimated outlay per volunteer assumed that a £20 per week supplement was paid to 250 volunteers drawing UK unemployment benefit, and that a further 60 were paid £40 per week (implying a part- or fully- paid cadre of just over 300 volunteers). More recent estimates of the IRA's annual income range from US$10 million to the figure of £10 million usually cited by contemporary police sources to journalists.[56] These figures imply a significant growth of revenues since the mid-1970s, even allowing for inflation. Sources of income, contra Glover's expectations, have included commercial undertakings — social clubs, service and hospitality centres also serving as money-laundering operations — as well as extortion, armed robberies, and, no doubt, domestic donations. Kidnapping, as Glover makes clear, has been regarded as counter-productive, and unauthorized, although it took place in the 1970s. If one compares Glover's report with subsequent estimates of the IRA's income and expenditures, in my view three judgements cannot be avoided. First, running the IRA is a relatively cheap operation, primarily dependent upon the donated time and sacrifices of its volunteers.[57] Secondly, the IRA demonstrates the power of the weak. It does not need large expenditures to have dramatic and powerful impacts. Small numbers of determined militants can build and use relatively cheap 'home-made' or

improvised explosives (fertilizers and mortar bombs), install bespoke sleeper-devices with devastating effects, and own, maintain and use relatively cheap guns. Thirdly, the low estimates of the IRA's financial surplus, and of resources available per volunteer, strongly suggest that 'rent-seeking' or 'greed-based' accounts of its maintenance lack empirical foundation — Glover acknowledged that 'we cannot accurately judge the extent to which they line their own pockets'.[58] In short, the focus of policy-makers on closing down or squeezing the IRA's finances, while a necessary and predictable response, was never likely to be pivotal in affecting its performance.

Who volunteered to join the IRA? Here there is fair degree of consensus. First of all, most volunteers have been young males, although there are female members, and there is a long-standing women's republican organization, Cumann na mBan. Secondly, the founding membership of the Provisionals was from families with long ties to the IRA, dating back to the 1920s, and in some cases back to the Fenians of the 1860s.[59] This core provided the nucleus around which the IRA had survived after the 1940s. (Familial socialization, of course, is not pervasive: many males with such relatives did not become volunteers.) Thirdly, IRA recruits are nearly all young males, of Catholic origin, who are mostly from working class, small farmer or lower middle-class occupations. The list of the occupations of ninety-five IRA prisoners, imprisoned for more than three years in Belfast Prison between 1956 and 1960, is revealing.[60] It included just one businessman. Construction workers, farmers, clerks, and industrial apprentices predominated. They were neither prosperous professionals, nor 'lumpen-proletarians'. Twenty years later the Glover Report (1978) stated: 'Our evidence of the calibre of rank and file [IRA] terrorists does not support the view that they are mindless hooligans drawn from the unemployed and the unemployable.'[61] Two surveys of

49 The IRA's internal rules of court martial procedure are documented in Coogan, *IRA*, Appendix II. Collins's *Killing Rage* describes his participation in these internal courts.

50 Collins, *Killing Rage*, 84

51 A clear-headed appraisal of vigilantism and punishment-beatings is found in Andrew Silke, 'Rebel's Dilemma: The Changing Relationship between the IRA, Sinn Féin and Paramilitary Vigilantism in Northern Ireland', *Terrorism and Political Violence*, 11, 1 (Spring 1999), 55–93. Unlike standard critics he shows how much it is a response to local demands. Silke correctly argued that only with major police reform will the IRA and Sinn Féin be able to terminate their involvement in the system, but in my view was too pessimistic in assuming that both organizations are 'irretrievably' committed to vigilantism.

52 Many of these are summarized in Horgan and Taylor, 'The Provisional Irish Republican Army,' Table 1.

53 Glover, 'Northern Ireland: Future Terrorist Trends', published in *Republican News* and reprinted in Cronin, *Irish Nationalism*, 339–57

54 Cronin, *Irish Nationalism*, 344. Hereafter, unless otherwise indicated, all references to pounds are to pounds sterling.

55 Foster, *Modern Ireland*, 590, writes of the Provisionals that 'American money, local support and the army's record in house-to-house searches established them firmly in the urban ghettos'. This implicit order of ranking is not consistent with the evidence. It would have been more accurate to write that local support for defence against loyalist and police attacks, the British army's record of repression, and donations from Ireland and America, firmly established the Provisional IRA in many nationalist dominated areas.

56 Scott Anderson, 'Making a Killing: The High Cost of Peace in Northern Ireland', *Harpers Magazine*, 288, 1725 (Feb. 1994), 45–54

57 See also Robert White, 'Commitment, Efficacy and Personal Sacrifice among Irish Republicans', *Journal of Political and Military Sociology*, 16 (1988), 77–90.

58 Cronin, *Irish Nationalism*, 343

59 White, *Provisional Irish Republicans*, passim

60 Cronin, *Irish Nationalism*, Appendix XVI; the list was compiled by Eamon Timoney, one of the prisoners.

61 Cronin, *Irish Nationalism*, 342; Coogan, *IRA*, 468

62 Kevin Boyle, Tom Hadden, and Paddy Hillyard, *Ten Years on in Northern Ireland* (London, 1980), 19; see also Kevin Boyle, R. Chesney, and Tom Hadden, 'Who Are the Terrorists?', in *Fortnight*, 7 May 1976 and *New Society*, 6 May 1976. Ex-IRA Volunteers Gerry Adams, *The Politics of Irish Freedom* (Dingle, 1986), 67–68, and Patrick Magee, *Gangsters or Guerrillas? Representations of Irish Republicans in 'Troubles Fiction'* (Belfast, 2001), 16, both approvingly cite the Glover Report, and the Boyle, Hadden and Hillyard (1980) appraisal, as independent assessments of the non-criminal nature of IRA recruits.

63 Magee, *Gangsters or Guerrillas?*, passim. The 1984 bombing of the Grand Hotel Brighton, the site of a Conservative Party conference, killed five people, injured senior Conservative Norman Tebbit, seriously disabled his wife, and came close to killing Margaret Thatcher. Magee received five life sentences for the bombing. He served fourteen years before being released under the terms of the Good Friday Agreement.

64 Anderson, 'Making a Killing'

65 Michael Ignatieff, 'The Temptations of Nihilism', in *The Lesser Evil: Political Ethics in an Age of Terror* (Princeton, 2003), 122

republican offenders coming before the courts found that the data 'beyond reasonable doubt' established that the bulk of them were young men and women 'without criminal records in the ordinary sense, though some have been involved in public disorders [but] in this respect and in their records of employment and unemployment they are reasonably representative of the working class community of which they form a substantial part [and] do not fit the stereotype of criminality which the authorities have from time to time attempted to attach to them'.[62]

IRA recruits are therefore not criminals, gangsters or mafiosi, despite the aforementioned auxiliaries involved in punishment squads. The gangster motif, as the former IRA volunteer Patrick Magee, known as 'the Brighton bomber', shows in an intelligent published doctoral thesis is the most stale cliché in the popular or pulp fiction generated by the conflict.[63] It is also a theme highlighted in British press and broadcasting reportage, and cartoons. Journalist Scott Anderson wrote under the heading 'Making a Killing' to popularize the gangster idea in the US.[64] It is more startling to find the contention reproduced by a thoughtful liberal intellectual, my friend, Michael Ignatieff, who has lived in the UK and reported on Northern Ireland. His *The Lesser Evil* maintains 'there will always be a gap between those who take the political goals of a terrorist campaign seriously and those who are drawn to the cause because it offers glamour, violence, money and power. It is anyone's guess how many actual believers in the dream of a united Ireland there are in the ranks of the IRA. But it is a fair bet to suppose that many recruits join up because they want to benefit from the IRA's profitable protection rackets'. He footnotes Taylor's *Provos* and Coogan's *The IRA*, without pagination, before continuing, 'The IRA bears as much relation to the Mafia as it does to an insurrectionary cell or a radical political party and the motivations that draw young

people into the movement are often as criminal as they are political ... The criminal allure of terrorist groups and the cynicism of those who join them are additional reasons why it is a mistake to conciliate or appease a group like the IRA with political concessions'.[65]

There is no serious empirical warrant for these views, certainly not in the books of Coogan and Taylor. 'Believing in the dream of a united Ireland' is not an impartial characterization, and while this belief may not be the primary motivation for all members to join, affirmation of the goal is a condition of membership. Ignatieff's assumed knowledge of volunteers' private inner desires is just speculation, and he appears unaware that experience of state repression or of attacks by loyalists is the most widespread shared feature of post-1969 IRA recruits.[66] These considerations undermine the 'criminal' characterization of the IRA's volunteers. Robert White's interviews, and statements by republican leaders, show convincingly that surges in applications to join the IRA are directly linked to political events, rather than to 'rent-seeking' opportunities. Attacks on the civil rights movement, loyalist mobs burning-out Catholics from their homes in Belfast, the Falls Road curfew by the British army, internment without trial, Bloody Sunday, and the British government's response to the hunger strikes of 1980–81, were more potent sources of recruitment than the meagre material 'rewards' facing volunteers. The evidence is in fact strongly against the criminal motivation thesis.[67] IRA 'surpluses' do not enrich its leaders, and if they did, this would be a major UK media theme. Gerry Adams has doubtless become prosperous, after the peace process, but from his published writings. There is no evidence that he was enriched through his IRA or Sinn Féin roles. IRA members do not personally profit from takings; if they do, they are excluded from the organization, punished or suffer moral disapproval. This can be seen in the critical accounts of

McGartland (1997) and Collins (1997). Volunteers in ASUs rely on minimal support, as do those 'on the run'; and the auxiliaries' role is to punish petty criminals, not to lead them — though, of course, some may behave contrary to the organization's norms. Earning respect from local peers rather than profits is a better explanation of membership of vigilante and punishment squads.[68] The IRA's resources, however dubiously or criminally obtained, are overwhelmingly channelled back into mission-related activities. The IRA recruited those willing to risk their lives or long jail sentences for what they warned would likely be a dangerous and short career. In short, group-oriented, non-pecuniary and non-egoistic motivations have been key, both to recruitment and retention. The costs of membership have been high: the risks of death or of long-run imprisonment plain, and the costs have also been borne by family and loved ones, even if support is provided to the families of imprisoned volunteers. Famously, IRA volunteers have been resistant to prison management techniques that 'ordinary criminals' generally accept without organized protest or rancour.[69] This is not to say that all IRA recruits epitomize austere republican virtue, merely to affirm that personal criminal opportunism amongst volunteers is punished. The IRA, famously, does not 'do drugs', and has attempted to 'close down' a rival republican organization, the INLA, when it started this mode of 'self-financing'. Northern Ireland, by contrast with the rest of the UK and Ireland, as many have observed, has been politically rather than criminally violent.[70]

Ignatieff and others have the direction of causality wrong. Defeated violent nationalist organizations may become mafias, but they do not originate as such, nor will they have extensive legitimacy if they become such. One priority of the Irish peace process is to ensure the rehabilitation of former republican paramilitaries — and, to date, rates of recidivism, political or criminal,

among ex-IRA prisoners have been strikingly low, and further evidence against the criminal motivation thesis. The IRA, the INLA and the Continuity and the Real IRAs may come to resemble mafias in the course of their respective dissolutions, but this will constitute the corruption of their missions, not their starting motivations. Indeed one may argue that the policy implications of the criminality thesis have been tested to destruction in Northern Ireland.[71] The hunger strikes of 1980–81, which led to the revitalization of support for both the IRA and Sinn Féin, were a demand for recognition as political prisoners and not as criminals. The authorities faced the obvious problem that most of those incarcerated were incarcerated under 'scheduled offences', i.e. under special procedures for politically motivated special offences. Precisely because the IRA was a political agency, it needed to be treated politically as well as legally (though plainly any politically violent agency in a liberal democratic state violates the criminal law). Had Ignatieff's counsel been followed — i.e. not to conciliate or appease the IRA with political concessions — then there would never have been a Good Friday Agreement in 1998, and perhaps another 1,000 people would have died since 1994 because of a false theory of motivation.

Fourthly, there is no sustained evidence that the IRA's recruits are psychologically abnormal. Studies have been made comparing the murderers committing political as opposed to non-political killings in Northern Ireland. They confirm this appraisal (e.g. Lyons and Harbinson 1986), and thereby support the general finding in research on political violence and terrorism that ethno-national terrorists are 'normal', i.e. representative of their social bases.[72] Yeatsian-tinged psychological portraits of Irish republicans nevertheless abound in the literature. Patrick Bishop and Eamonn Mallie title the Prologue to their *The Provisional IRA*, 'Fanatic Hearts', after Yeats's lines, 'Out of Ireland have we come /

66 Robert White, 'From Peaceful Protest to Guerrilla War — Micromobilization of the Provisional Irish Republican Army', *American Journal of Sociology*, 94 (1989), 1277–302; White, *Provisional Irish Republicans, passim.* Collins's *Killing Rage* provides the fullest narrative of his movement into the IRA — it includes the mistreatment of his mother and the beating up and false arrest of his father, his brother and himself by British paratroopers, knowledge of left-wing ideology and exposure to a left-wing (English) academic, disillusionment with the prospects of reform and power-sharing, and the impact of the campaign for political status by republican prisoners. 'I was full of a heady mixture of anti-imperialism, anger, sympathy and self-importance' (23); greed played no role, and he despised volunteers and auxiliaries who engaged in petty theft.

67 Reviewed further in McGarry and O'Leary, *Explaining Northern Ireland*, ch. 6–7.

68 Frank Burton, *The Politics of Legitimacy: Struggles in a Belfast Community* (London, 1979); Silke, 'Rebel's Dilemma'.

69 See McEvoy, *Paramilitary Imprisonment.*

70 Ken Heskin, 'Societal Disintegration in Northern Ireland — A Five Year Update', *Economic and Social Review*, 16, 3 (1985), 187–99

71 See also Brendan O'Leary, 'The Labour Government and Northern Ireland, 1974–79' in John McGarry and Brendan O'Leary, *The Northern Ireland Conflict: Consociational Engagements* (Oxford, 2004), 194–216.

72 H. Lyons and H. Harbinson, 'A Comparison of Political and Non-Political Murderers in Northern Ireland, 1974–84', *Medicine, Science and the Law*, 26 (1986) 193–98; Clark R. McCauley, 'Terrorism Research and Public Policy: An Overview', *Terrorism and Political Violence*, 3, 1 (1991), 126–44; Andrew P. Silke, 'Cheshire-Cat Logic: The Recurring Theme of Terrorist Abnormality in Psychological Research', *Psychology, Crime and Law*, 4 (1998), 51–69; Andrew P. Silke, ed., *Terrorists, Victims and Society: Psychological Perspectives on Terrorism and Its Consequences* (London, 2003), ch. 1–2

73 Bishop and Mallie, *Provisional IRA*, 5

74 For example, see Moloney, *Secret History*.

75 Bishop and Mallie, *Provisional IRA*, 1; Mallie is identified as the interviewer and Bishop as the author.

Great hatred, little room / Maimed us at the start / I carry from my mother's womb / A fanatic heart.' It is good poetry; it is not social psychology. Kevin Toolis claims to have journeyed 'within the IRA's soul' — fine words, but not convincing science. Bishop and Mallie see IRA violence as an inevitable psychological product of partition: 'Even if the leadership were to abandon violence, another violent organization would spring up in its place. As long as Ireland is divided, violent republicanism will be an ineradicable tradition.'[73] This is an extreme psycho-political claim that will be tested when the IRA disbands.

Fifthly, there is agreement that the spatial origin of IRA recruits has changed. In the 1956–62 campaign significant numbers of southerners were involved. Today it is agreed that, except, of course, in Southern Command, northerners predominate, at all ranks — although there are still significant numbers of volunteers from or living in the southern border counties. The IRA's evolution is, in part, the story of it being taken over by northerners, i.e. those with most to complain about the long-term repercussions of the Treaty of 1921.

Sixthly, IRA volunteers are Irish nationalist, in identity, and as a result of experience. They did not all grow up in Irish nationalist households, and, indeed, there have been a small number of Irish Protestant and English-born volunteers, but most are Irish nationalists, by birth, or culture and learning. They believe that Great Britain denied the Irish people its right to self-determination when it partitioned Ireland, and that Northern Ireland is an artificial entity which cannot function as a democracy, and, until recently, have believed it is unreformable, i.e. Catholics or nationalists cannot be treated as the equals of Protestants and unionists within the UK. The IRA's nationalist character bears emphasis because it is so often portrayed in international media as religiously motivated.

It is vital to preserve the distinction between nationalist agents who use political violence (whether in democratic or undemocratic settings) and the salvationist violence of apocalyptic religious fundamentalists (like Al-Qaeda). The distinction is not just important for analytical accuracy. Nationalists prepared to use force may be repressed (but rarely fully), or negotiated with (successfully or otherwise), or both. By contrast, cosmopolitan religious fundamentalists can be thoroughly repressed in some circumstances, because they are likely to be territorially infrequent and isolated, but they cannot be negotiated with as long as they retain their beliefs. It is an error, into which Ignatieff slips, to conflate liberal opposition to nationalist violence with liberal opposition to apocalyptic religious fundamentalism.

A last word about the IRA's recruits since 1969 is required on numbers. We do not have the IRA's personnel records. Widespread uncertainty is suggested by the fact that in the major books on the IRA *none* has 'numbers' in its index — some do not have indexes.[74] It is standard to estimate between 300 and 500 volunteers in ASUs, a measure of the 'stock' of militant activists that probably derives from leaks of the IRA's own organizational planning changes of 1976–77, which informed the Glover Report. It seems reasonable to assume approximately an equivalent number of 'cadets' in training, and in the auxiliaries, at any one time, suggesting an annual stock of ASUs and reserves and auxiliaries of about 900. As for total flow, Martin McGuinness, a former Chief of Staff, is widely cited as having suggested that over 10,000 people have been in and through the IRA's ranks since 1969. One journalist, Eamonn Mallie, reports that the IRA told him that between 'eight and ten thousand' of its personnel had been imprisoned before 1987.[75] The gap between estimates of current stock and total flow make sense when one recognizes the high attrition rate of volunteers, through death, injury, incarceration, flight — or resignation. The IRA is not like 'Hotel California' — one can leave. Most volunteers are expected to retire after having served a sentence. A formal check on the 10,000 estimate of the total flow is the stock and flow of the prison population. The average daily number of prisoners in Northern Ireland's jails in 1969 was approximately 600; by 1979 it had reached nearly 3,000 — a figure that excluded IRA volunteers in jails in Great Britain and Ireland, but included loyalist prisoners. From 1985 until 1997 the Northern Ireland prison population stabilized at around 2,000 as a daily average.[76] The cited estimate of a total flow of IRA volunteers of 10,000 is therefore credible (especially given that a significant number may never have been incarcerated). It suggests that an extraordinarily high proportion of Northern Irish working-class Catholic males who matured after 1969 have been through IRA ranks.

Tactics, Strategy, Costs of Conflict

Between 1919 and 1921 the IRA improvised to create a standard template in modern violent politics, inventing contemporary guerrilla warfare, flying columns that avoided facing the imperial power in the field of formal war, and modes of resistance and rejection which attacked the state's sovereignty and its core functionaries, especially its police and intelligence agencies, but in conjunction with a wider democratic movement, of which the most important component was a political party, Sinn Féin. This party's name, standardly translated as 'Our Selves', can also be translated as 'Ourselves Alone', or even as 'Self-Determination', according to Bill Kissane. Sinn Féin, backed by the IRA's cutting edge, established a parallel state, creating what is nowadays known, after Trotsky, as a situation of 'dual power'. The forte of the IRA, orchestrated by Collins, was killing policemen and intelligence officers — which broke the imperial state's

surveillance and control capabilities. It ensured that the IRA was far more effective than all previous Irish insurrectionary movements; it showed how a war of the flea could confound an imperial elephant, provided that the elephant felt restrained from destroying the habitat of the flea.

The contemporary IRA also innovated. It invented new modes of urban guerrilla warfare, donating the 'car-bomb' to the known repertoires of political violence. Political murders, assassinations, tit-for-tat shootings, and 'human bombs' made the IRA infamous, as did 'tarring-and-feathering' and kneecappings. It was arguably less effective in killing senior military, police and intelligence officers than the old IRA. It failed to assist its party in creating dual power or a parallel state — unless one counts the vigilante system. It also showed greater political and moral weakness than its predecessor by its expanded conception of legitimate targets — including non-uniformed off-duty police and soldiers, retired police and soldiers, and workers in organizations supplying non-military services to the army and the police. (But, as Glover noted, it generally has not attacked the families of police and soldiers.)

The IRA is not proud of its techniques of disciplining its own membership and its community, but it has undoubtedly been resourceful. The IRA's campaign has been conducted in Northern Ireland, Great Britain, and in places as far apart as Gibraltar and British military bases in Germany, leading to the deaths of approximately 200 people outside the main 'war theatre'. Fund-raising and weapons running were organized in places as distinct as Carter's and Reagan's USA and Colonel Gaddaffi's Libya.[77] It tied down tens of thousands of UK soldiers for three decades, imposed immense economic damage on the region, and on the UK exchequer, assassinated key members of the British political élite, including Lord Louis Mountbatten, a member of the royal family,

76 McEvoy, *Paramilitary Imprisonment*, 16
77 Jack Holland, *The American Connection: US Guns, Money and Influence in Northern Ireland* (Dublin, 1989), 27–113; Moloney, *Secret History*, 1–33

78 See Figure 1, and O'Leary and McGarry, *Politics of Antagonism*, ch. 1, and Brendan O'Leary and John McGarry, *The Politics of Antagonism: Understanding Northern Ireland* (London, 3rd edn. forthcoming).

79 English, *Armed Struggle*, 380

80 F. Zimmermann, 'Political Unrest in Western Europe', *Western European Politics*, 12 (1989), 179–96, cited in O'Leary and McGarry, *Politics of Antagonism*, ch. 1

and twice came within a whisker of blowing up the UK Prime Minister and Cabinet. The bulk of the IRA's violence, of course, was organized within Northern Ireland, where it was spatially concentrated, notably in Belfast. Allowing for the ceasefires, the IRA's thirty-year campaign is one of the longest nationalist insurgencies in the post-war world, certainly the most enduring in the established liberal democracies.

The Provisional IRA developed a fearsome capability and reputation. Between 1969 and 1994 it was responsible for more deaths, over 1,750, than any other agency in the conflict.[78] It out-killed all other republican organizations; all 'loyalist' (i.e. pro-régime) paramilitaries combined; and all loyalist *and* all other republican paramilitaries combined. It significantly out-killed the individual and combined official forces of the UK: the British army, the Royal Ulster Constabulary, the B Specials — and their successors, the Ulster Defence Regiment and the Royal Irish Regiment. According to *Lost Lives*, by David McKittrick, Seamus Kelters, Brian Feeney and Chris Thornton, the (Provisional) IRA was responsible for 48.5 per cent of the over 3,600 deaths arising from the conflict between 1966 and 2001. By contrast, the IRA lost nearly 300 of its volunteers, 8 per cent of the total victims. Richard English, using the same data-source, maintains that

civilians formed the largest single category of IRA victims (642), followed by the British forces (456), the RUC (273), the Ulster Defence Regiment or Royal Irish Regiment (182), republicans (162), loyalists (28), prison officers (23) and others (12).[79] His conclusion depends upon disaggregating the security forces and aggregating civilians. A different way to frame the same data, as I have done in Figure 1, is to observe that 967 of the IRA's victims were military, police, prison officers, or loyalist paramilitaries — i.e. the IRA killed more of its self-defined targets than civilians. But that still means only just over 54 per cent of its victims fell within its official legitimate targets, roughly one in two. In any military appraisal of its war, this must constitute the strongest indictment.

The IRA's violence made Northern Ireland the most politically violent region in the European Community (later the Union). The numbers killed between 1969 and 1990 exceeded those killed as a result of political violence in *all* other EC countries put together. In 1973–82 violence in Northern Ireland alone placed the UK at the top of a league table of nineteen western European states in deaths from political violence and political assassinations.[80] The absolute death toll naturally pales in contrast with the major civil, colonial, and ethnic wars of the post-war authoritarian world. The

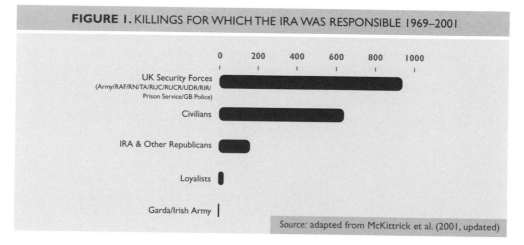

FIGURE 1. KILLINGS FOR WHICH THE IRA WAS RESPONSIBLE 1969–2001

Source: adapted from McKittrick et al. (2001, updated)

British authorities have not suppressed the population which explicitly or tacitly supports the IRA in the manner experienced by Algerian Muslims, the Kurds of Iraq, Kashmiri Muslims, Palestinian Muslims and Christians, South African blacks, or Sri Lankan Tamils. The British authorities treated incarcerated IRA prisoners relatively mildly by contrast with what was meted out in Latin American, African, or South Asian jails. Yet these observations can mislead. Nearly all wars and civil wars between 1945 and 1990 were exacerbated by superpower rivalries, or by regional powers and neighbouring states. These factors did not operate in Northern Ireland — which proves how deep ethno-national conflict can become in geopolitically isolated regions. The US government deplored violence in Northern Ireland and sought to prevent unofficial support from Irish-Americans, in the form of guns and money, from reaching the IRA. The 'special relationship' with the UK consistently proved more important for American geopolitical interests during the Cold War than the ethnic sentiments of some Irish-Americans. The Soviet Union, by contrast, used the Northern Ireland experience to embarrass the UK, e.g. in reference to the jailing of innocent Irish people in Great Britain, like the Guildford Four, the Birmingham Six, and the Maguire Seven, but played no role in fomenting the conflict. The two states with most at stake, the UK and Ireland, despite multiple disagreements, generally sought to co-operate to contain the conflict. The IRA did not champion and were not championed by Ireland — although the British regarded Ireland as the IRA's 'safe haven'. Loyalist paramilitaries embarrassed British politicians — and such support as they received from the security forces (so far) appears to have been unauthorized by ministers. The sole third-party state that sought to inflame the conflict, Libya, was neither a regional power nor a neighbour. Its supplying of arms in 1974–75, and again in 1988, was retaliation for American and British actions against the régime of Colonel

Gaddaffi. The conflict of the last thirty years has therefore been extremely intense given that it took place in a small region, in the presence of moderately amicable relations between the relevant neighbouring states, and regional powers, and in the absence of operational superpower rivalries. In duration, the present conflict easily outranks all others in twentieth-century Ireland, and only the Irish Civil War exceeds it in intensity.

How did people die? In assassinations (a plurality of all deaths); in gun-battles, crossfire, through snipers' bullets, and in ambushes; in explosions or from anti-personnel devices; and a small proportion died in riots or affrays. Over half of republican killings, mostly by the IRA, took place during gun-battles/crossfire, sniping incidents, ambushes, or through explosives and anti-personnel devices; by contrast most loyalist killings were assassinations.[81] But a third of deaths caused by republicans were assassinations. There were, in effect, two wars. First, a war of national, ethnic, and communal assassination, executed by IRA volunteers, loyalist paramilitaries and by some UK security personnel. There was also a guerrilla and counterinsurgency war, with riots and affrays, especially in the early years, enhancing the numbers killed. In aggregate, paramilitary killings of civilians outnumbered those killed in the guerrilla war between republican paramilitaries and the security forces. The number of civilians killed through targeting, or through 'collateral damage', by republicans, loyalists, and the UK security forces amounted to approximately half of the total number killed. The paramilitary 'defenders' of the two major communities had dramatically fewer casualties than the civilians they claimed to be defending. The IRA failed to make and present the war as a clean fight between Irish republicans and the British state; the British state failed to make and present the conflict as just a dispute between two unreasonable communities, but had some success in doing

81 See O'Leary and McGarry, *Politics of Antagonism* (3rd edn.).

so; loyalists helped veto a British disengagement.

The annual death tolls and responsibilities for them are in Figures 2 and 3. The high death toll in the early years is explained by three factors. The first was the 'loyalist backlash', both proactive and retaliatory, against civil rights demonstrations in the late 1960s, *and* then against the IRA's war. The British government's decision to abolish the Northern Ireland parliament in 1972, and its efforts between 1973 and 1976 to establish a power-sharing government with all-Ireland institutions increased loyalist fears. Very high numbers of Catholic civilians were victims of sectarian assassinations by loyalists between 1971 and 1975. The intention was to deter Catholics from supporting the IRA, but because loyalists did not have reliable information on IRA volunteers, 'representative' killing of randomly selected Catholic civilians, identified by their first names, surnames, or residences, predominated. The second factor was the decision by the IRA to launch its war, employing classical guerrilla techniques against UK army and police personnel. But it also extensively engaged in large-scale bombings of commercial targets, such as factories and shopping centres. Guerrilla warfare produced large numbers of casualties among inexperienced police and soldiers, while commercial bombings led to significant numbers of civilian deaths, especially in Belfast; Martin McGuinness, by repute, organized the urban bombing of Derry with far less collateral damage. The third factor was the repressive — and counter-productive — policy of internment without trial of suspected terrorists, which lasted between 1971 and 1975. Initially targeted (inaccurately) exclusively at republicans the policy produced widespread resentment throughout the Catholic population, acted as a recruiting agency for the IRA, and added fuel to the fire. Explanations for the fall-off in deaths after 1976 complement this analysis. Loyalists reduced their killings of Catholics, both absolutely and as a share of the total death toll, because their fears of a British withdrawal had diminished — and were not revived until the Anglo-Irish Agreement of 1985. Loyalists were arrested and jailed, and their organizations became more factionalized, corrupt, and directionless. The IRA changed its organization, and strategy, in ways that reduced the annual death toll.

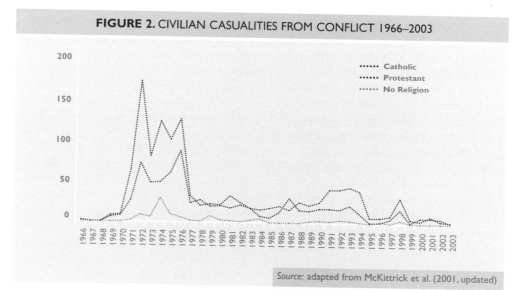

FIGURE 2. CIVILIAN CASUALITIES FROM CONFLICT 1966–2003

Catholic
Protestant
No Religion

Source: adapted from McKittrick et al. (2001, updated)

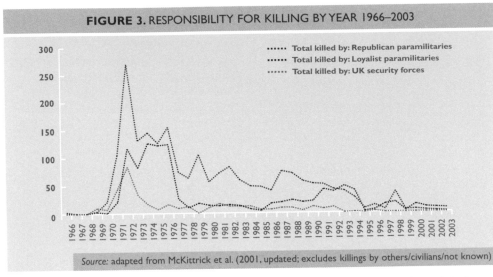

FIGURE 3. RESPONSIBILITY FOR KILLING BY YEAR 1966–2003

..... Total killed by: Republican paramilitaries
..... Total killed by: Loyalist paramilitaries
..... Total killed by: UK security forces

Source: adapted from McKittrick et al. (2001, updated; excludes killings by others/civilians/not known)

82 W. D. Flackes and Sidney Elliott, *Northern Ireland: A Political Directory, 1968–88* (Belfast, 1989), 394

Many of its volunteers had been jailed; and in response the ASUs were developed. After 1976 the IRA primarily aimed to attack 'military' and 'police' targets, and until the early 1990s reduced its urban commercial bombing which had threatened to undermine its support. The IRA became responsible for a lower annual death toll, but a higher share of the total death toll. Furthermore, more effective surveillance and intelligence among the security forces reduced the levels of violence. The authorities abandoned internment in 1975–76. A battery of new containment techniques was employed. Up to 30,000 personnel patrolled the countryside and city-streets, establishing armed 'check-points'. Forts and observation posts with the latest surveillance technologies were established in the heart of nationalist districts, including in school premises. House searching and civilian screening took place on a massive scale, backed up by computerized databases on over one quarter of the population. Armoured vehicles, bomb-disposal robots, and 'jelly-sniffers' were used to protect security force personnel. Entire 'town-centres' were cordoned off, and everybody entering such areas subjected to rigorous searching. Emergency legislation weakened civil liberties and facilitated the apprehension and sentencing of suspected paramilitaries. Finally, all experienced

'learning curves'. In 1970, the IRA had to make an average of 191 attacks to kill a single member of the security forces; by 1984, 18 were sufficient.[82] The security forces became more vigilant to defend themselves. They also, formally, became more restrained: in the early 1970s they were permitted to shoot at identified petrol-bombers but now are supposed to use 'minimum force' weaponry, like plastic bullets. The return to 'police primacy' in 1977 was associated with a reduced level of killings. Armed police are more restrained than soldiers trained to kill in combat. Personal and collective surveillance and security management by ordinary citizens also increased. They travelled warily in 'shatter-zones' or 'frontiers', or avoided them altogether; and migration from 'mixed areas' to ethnically segregated residences in the 1970s reduced the opportunities for 'soft' or 'easy' killings. The time-series show a dramatic falling-off in the number of deaths sustained by the British army — excluding the locally recruited regiments. The local security forces (UDR, RIR, RUC and RUC Reserve) suffered an increasing proportion of the deaths sustained by the security forces. This was the predictable product of 'Ulsterization', the UK's post 1975 policy-preference for local security forces — which reduced the UK's vulnerability to the loss of British-recruited

83 Compare the evaluations of Brendan O'Duffy, 'Violence in Northern Ireland: Sectarian or Ethno-National?', *Ethnic and Racial Studies*, 18, 4 (1995), 740–72, and Robert White, 'The Irish Republican Army: An Assessment of Sectarianism', *Terrorism and Political Violence*, 9, 1 (1997), 20–55, with those of Steve Bruce, 'Victim Selection in Ethnic Conflict: Motives and Attitudes in Irish Republicanism', *Terrorism and Political Violence*, 9, 1 (1997), 56–71.
84 For example, see Bruce, 'Victim Selection'.

troops, but increased its dependency upon local Protestants who were less likely to be impartial. It also occasioned a switch in the targets chosen by the IRA: it was easier to kill local security force members, at their homes, or off-duty, than to kill soldiers in fortified barracks or in armoured vehicles.

Who suffered most in the conflict? Who was most sectarian among the paramilitaries? These questions are not amenable to easy empirical treatment. Estimates of numbers of victims are available, under various labels. Since each choice of label affects numbers, all appraisals are contested.[83] It is extremely difficult to code motivations, or even the primary motivations of the killers. Taking civilians alone, the largest single category of victims has been Catholic, and since Protestant civilians outnumber Catholic civilians by approximately 3 to 2, Catholic civilians suffered more deaths, absolutely and relatively, than Protestant civilians. Appraisal cannot rest there. Catholic civilians were the primary targets of loyalist paramilitaries, and the security forces were the primary targets of the IRA, but these facts obscure an important consideration. The local security forces were recruited primarily from Protestants. A simple comparison of Catholic and Protestant civilian death-rates therefore obscures the victims suffered by the Protestant community. That said, the nearly 300 dead mostly Catholic IRA volunteers almost directly match the over 300 mostly Protestant dead police in the RUC and its reserves. The dead in the B Specials, UDR and RIR also nearly match the other republican dead. The data and interpretation of Sutton (1994), presented in Figure 4, with slight adjustments, suggest that IRA violence has been primarily strategic, aimed at its official legitimate targets, rather than sectarian, i.e. the deliberate killing of Protestant civilians: he classifies 12.4 per cent of IRA killings as sectarian, and a very high proportion of these occurred in 1975–76. This viewpoint is supported in the sophisticated analyses of

O'Duffy (1995) and White (1997). The IRA killed far more members of the security forces than Protestant civilians, partially fulfilling its mission of fighting 'a war of national liberation'. But, that does not definitively settle the question of IRA 'sectarianism' — even if one codes the IRA as less sectarian than loyalists, as the death-evidence warrants. Protestants interpret and will interpret the targeting and killings of Protestant members of the local security forces as sectarian. White points out that the small proportions of Catholic members of the security forces killed matched their numbers in these forces (which suggests no special effort on the part of the IRA to target Protestant members of the security forces), but such killings are simply coded as sectarian by unionists, loyalists and their sympathizers.[84] The IRA unquestionably carried out some overt and intended killings of uninvolved Protestant civilians — as opposed to killing such persons through 'collateral damage'. These actions were defended by IRA volunteers as necessary acts of deterrence against loyalist killings of Catholic civilians, especially in south Armagh, or shamefacedly acknowledged — or simply denied.

Violence extended far beyond killings. Data on injuries sustained as well as the annual number of explosions, the number of bombs neutralized, the scale of findings of explosives and firearms, the number of shooting incidents, the use of rubber and plastic bullets, the number of armed robberies, and the money taken in armed robberies are available. They show the same patterns as the death toll data: very high levels of violent activity in the years 1971–76 with subsequent 'normalization'. Close to one in fifty of the population suffered serious injuries. Available data do not include the mental injuries suffered by those kidnapped; held hostage in their homes during 'stake-outs'; arrested when guilty of no crime; or otherwise maltreated. Nor do they measure the distress caused by intimidation, being the friend or relative of

85 Irish Information Partnership data, cited in O'Leary and McGarry, *Politics of Antagonism*, ch. 1
86 Bob Rowthorn and Naomi Wayne, *Northern Ireland: The Political Economy of Conflict* (Oxford, 1988), *passim*

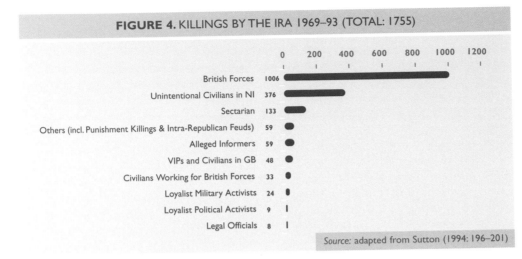

FIGURE 4. KILLINGS BY THE IRA 1969–93 (TOTAL: 1755)

British Forces	1006
Unintentional Civilians in NI	376
Sectarian	133
Others (incl. Punishment Killings & Intra-Republican Feuds)	59
Alleged Informers	59
VIPs and Civilians in GB	48
Civilians Working for British Forces	33
Loyalist Military Activists	24
Loyalist Political Activists	9
Legal Officials	8

Source: adapted from Sutton (1994: 196–201)

a victim or being a witness to violent deaths, injuries, and other episodes.

The IRA's campaign, as intended, resulted in heavy financial burdens on the UK exchequer. It also placed costs on Ireland's exchequer: the extra security costs ensuing from the crisis between the years 1969 and 1982 were estimated at over IR£1,050 million. For the same period additional expenditure on security incurred by the UK government was estimated at UK£4,150 million. One 1985 audit estimated that the annual direct costs of violence of the conflict incurred ran at £1,194 million — a figure that excluded the indirect economic costs of lost output and employment arising from the political crisis.[85] Providing security in Northern Ireland in the fiscal year 1990–91 cost just under £1 billion — more than three times the per capita UK average, and certain costs were not apparently calculated, e.g. those entailed in tightening security at military bases in Great Britain and Germany, intelligence-gathering and surveillance in Great Britain, and protecting the political and civil establishments. Other economic costs included the stress on and infrastructural damage to the public services: health and welfare and housing administration, public utilities, and the penal services. Telephone exchanges, post offices, railway networks, bus garages, gas depots, power stations and reservoirs were bombed or robbed and their staffs intimidated. Frauds against public-sector organizations ran into millions of pounds. Compensation payments to victims of violence or owners of destroyed properties ran much higher. Claims for compensation exceeded 13,000 cases per annum. Protection rackets affected the profitability of many private-sector organizations; as did the requirements imposed by insurance companies upon shops and offices. The insurance costs of private transport rose to reflect the high numbers of vehicle thefts, hijackings, and car-bombings. The incredibly high proportion of the population involved in security led economist Bob Rowthorn to describe the Northern Ireland economy as a 'workhouse', in which most were employed in controlling or servicing one another.[86] The most obvious economic costs are the least measurable: the 'opportunity-costs' of three decades of conflict, in lost investment, output, and productive employment.

The human-rights costs and the impact on liberal democratic institutions must also be counted. The legal authorities of Northern Ireland, Great Britain, and Ireland were granted formidable emergency powers. The ratios of arrests to charges, and of charges to convictions, were relatively high, suggesting large-scale screening, and systematic deprivation of many innocent

87 Peter Wright, *Spycatcher: The Candid Autobiography of a Senior Intelligence Officer* (New York, 1987) and Paul Foot, *Who Framed Colin Wallace?* (London, 1989)

88 Michael L. R. Smith, *Fighting for Ireland? The Military Strategy of the Irish Republican Movement* (London, 1995) is an unusual Clausewitzian treatment, which I examined as a PhD dissertation.

89 On the blanket protest and hunger strikes, see Tim Pat Coogan, *On the Blanket: The H Block Story* (Dublin, 1980), Beresford, *Ten Men Dead* and Liam Clarke, *Broadening the Battlefield: The H-Blocks and the Rise of Sinn Féin* (Dublin, 1987).

citizens of their liberty. Departures from traditional legal procedures become normal: no-jury courts were used because jury-trials were not safe from perverse verdicts or the intimidation of jurors and witnesses. Confessions became admissible as the sole basis for conviction on charges of having committed scheduled offences — including confessions subsequently retracted. In 1988 the UK government abandoned the traditional common law 'right of silence' — courts and prosecutors were entitled to draw inferences from the silence of suspects. Delays of several years became routine in holding inquests on persons killed by the security forces. Belief in the impartiality of British justice was severely damaged. The most notorious cases of wrongful imprisonment demonstrated police-fabrication of evidence against innocent Irish people; incompetent or malevolent forensic practices; judicial wishful thinking and partisanship; and ethnic bias in media reporting. The conflict impaired other key institutions. Certain sections of the British intelligence services ran amok in the 1970s. Believing that the authorities were 'giving in to terrorism', they plotted directly against the elected Labour government, and spread false rumours.[87] Collusion with loyalist paramilitaries also occurred on a significant scale from the late 1980s. The media were censored in both jurisdictions.

What was the IRA's strategy, and how could it justify such costs? Appraisals of its strategy are rare.[88] The simplest answer is that had no single strategy, but multiple strategies. In the first phase of conflict, 1970–75, the IRA expected a short war, a replication of what had happened in 1919–21, in which the British government would be forced to negotiate its withdrawal from the remainder of Ireland. It overestimated its capacity to hurt the UK state, underestimated the costs that loyalists and the security forces could impose on its volunteers, neglected the rooted determination of the majority unionist population within Northern Ireland to oppose a compulsory united Ireland, and overvalued southern support for an offensive — as opposed to a defensive — IRA. The IRA played a role in the overthrow of Stormont, but over-reached in thinking it could produce a quick British disengagement, and lacked any overt evidence of a popular mandate. It was also completely unsuccessful in negotiations — and out-manoeuvred in 1975. In the second phase of conflict the IRA's leadership foresaw and organized for a long war of attrition. It was capable of maintaining itself, but underestimated the extent to which it could be contained within Northern Ireland. Taking the war to Great Britain and Europe involved spectacular activities, but these could not be as logistically sustained as those in Northern Ireland. The IRA initially lacked a convincing political strategy to match its military activities. A new and apparently more effective strategy emerged almost by accident, in 1980–81, when the impact of the republican hunger strikes on public opinion created opportunities for Sinn Féin to emerge as an electorally significant political party in the North.[89] To continue the novel electoral momentum and search for broader allies the republican movement was obliged to reconsider abstentionism, first within local government in the North, and then toward Leinster House in the South. It endorsed change, and modified its constitution. That led to the first significant split in the movement — though not within the IRA. Older pre-1969 southerners in protest formed Republican Sinn Féin. The strategy of combining the ballot box and the Armalite, as Danny Morrison described it, superficially resembled the Sinn Féin and IRA alliance of 1918–21, but with a major difference: the lack of a majority mandate within the North, not even among the Northern nationalist population, or among the nationalist population in Ireland as a whole. The IRA was persuaded to accept the end of abstentionism by Sinn Féin in the belief that the army would not be run down — and hard-liners were temporarily sweetened by the prospect of major arms supplies from Libya. Sinn Féin, the IRA's party, because originally it was little more than that, then placed limits on the IRA. It gained greater autonomy, and sometimes its needs had to be placed first. Bobby Sands and his colleagues had died on hunger strike 'to broaden the battlefield', and had succeeded beyond their expectations. Sands's hunger strike, his victory in a parliamentary by-election, and his death, followed by the deaths of nine other prisoners, cemented the political status of the IRA, but would end up limiting its military actions, and subjecting it to electoral discipline.[90] The party gathered one in three northern nationalist votes on a platform of supporting its army, the IRA, but to grow later on, it had to distance itself, or place constraints on its army. In the interests of electoral gains, reinforced by their materialization, Sinn Féin has, therefore, slowly displaced the IRA as republicans' preferred organizational means of struggle, and not without dissent within the ranks of the volunteers — and the creation of two small break-away organizations, the Continuity and Real IRAs.[91] The party now has many members, probably an overwhelming majority, with no record of service as volunteers; and many of these are now prominent parliamentarians. Combining the ballot box and the Armalite, contrary to what Morrison thought at the time, proved unsustainable. Success with one undermined use of the other. From being the inspirer of the party, the army became a constraint. The IRA's decision to organize a ceasefire in 1994, and later to renew it, had one primary beneficiary: Sinn Féin. The party doubled its vote share in the North within a decade, recently winning four seats in the Westminster parliament, five in Dáil Éireann, and becoming, just, the largest nationalist party in the (suspended) Northern Ireland Assembly — and it has had one of its former Chiefs of Staff serve as a Minister of the Northern Ireland Executive.

How did this transformation happen? One: the IRA was not winning its long war to compel the UK state to disengage, even if it was not losing, and even if it could plant devastating bombs in the City of London. No victory on the 'battlefield' meant that there could be no victory at the negotiating table. Two: demographic transformations pointed to the possibility of a Northern nationalist majority that could create a constitutional path to end partition — and to a currently large enough nationalist bloc to leverage a power-sharing settlement given existing UK policy commitments to the Irish government. Three: republicans began properly to assess the full recalcitrance of unionists and loyalists toward the idea of a unitary Ireland, and the possible development of indifference toward reunification in the newly prosperous Ireland. Four: political agents inside and outside the republican movement persuaded sufficient IRA leaders, volunteers and prisoners that a peace process, building up a wider alliance of nationalists, was the best way to advance the IRA's objectives, even if that meant the IRA's disbandment before the attainment of a unitary Ireland. Key sections of the IRA leadership eventually determined on a peace process without express assurances that their declared war-objectives would be met through negotiations, and called a 'complete cessation' of military operations in August 1994, after a careful and protracted process of negotiation among Irish nationalists, and then between the UK and Irish governments, had produced the Joint Declaration for Peace of December 1993. The divided IRA resumed military operations by a majority vote of its Army Council in February 1996 in protest at the Conservative government's unwillingness to engage with Sinn Féin, but formally declared a ceasefire again in 1997. The full complexity of this transformation, its necessary ambiguities, and consequences, is beginning to emerge in a range of studies and publications, and we will likely not know the full details of intra-IRA manoeuvres and disputes for some time.[92] Given space constraints I will use just two texts to complement my earlier argument on

90 See the discussion of the hunger strikes in Padraig O'Malley, *Biting at the Grave: The Irish Hunger Strikes and the Politics of Despair* (Belfast, 1990), critically reviewed in Brendan O'Leary, 'Review [of O'Malley 1990]' *Irish Political Studies*, 6 (1991), 118–22.

91 See Feeney, *Sinn Féin*.

92 Important here are Feeney, *Sinn Féin*; English, *Armed Struggle*; Eamonn Mallie and David McKittrick, *The Fight for Peace: The Secret Story Behind the Irish Peace Process* (London, 1996); McGarry and O'Leary, *Explaining Northern Ireland*, ch. 10; McGarry and O'Leary, *Northern Ireland Conflict*; Anthony McIntyre, 'Modern Irish Republicanism: The Product of British State Strategies', *Irish Political Studies*, 10 (1995), 97–122; Moloney, *Secret History*; Brian Rowan, *Behind the Lines: The Story of the IRA and Loyalist Ceasefires* (Belfast, 1995).

the old IRA, those of Richard English and Ed Moloney. English, a unionist with roots in Northern Ireland, and a professor at Queen's University, Belfast, has written a dispassionate evaluation in *Armed Struggle*. In his concluding chapter, he identifies seven arguments that motivated the IRA. First, its resurgence 'began primarily in response to defensive need', providing 'muscular defence' in 1969–70 for oppressed nationalists in Belfast and Derry against a partisan RUC and loyalist sectarian mobs. Second, there was deep-rooted unfairness toward the nationalist minority in Northern Ireland, where the Ulster Unionist Party ruled without interruption from the formation of the régime until 1972, and which created, thereby, the social base of the IRA. Third, and relatedly, there was the cause of Irish national self-determination — to which he arguably pays insufficient attention. Fourth, the IRA regarded Northern Ireland as 'unreformable'. The treatment of the civil rights demonstrations of the 1960s confirmed this belief, as had the introduction of internment without trial between 1971 and 1975, and events such as the Falls Road curfew of 1970 and Bloody Sunday in 1972. Fifth, IRA volunteers defined the conflict as a national liberation struggle, and for over two decades stressed socialist as well as republican commitments. Sixth, they saw unionists as 'a residue of British colonialism in Ireland'. Lastly, they regarded themselves as, and often succeeded in behaving as, non-sectarian republicans committed to creating a common democratic state for all of Ireland. One of the many merits of English's book is that he evaluates these arguments seriously, and shows that these convictions were sincerely held, and were sane.

Naturally, he addresses the deficiencies and disputable elements in the IRA's arguments, dealing *seriatim* with the IRA's frequently offensive role, and its contribution to serious injustice in Northern Ireland and elsewhere, both through actions and provocations. He adds minor (unionist) qualifications to the picture of a discriminatory unionist régime before 1972; observes that Ulster Unionists have a case for self-determination and regarding Northern Ireland as legitimate; argues for the empirical (and normative) importance of the autonomous dispositions of unionists and loyalists, who often resisted the policies of Westminster and Whitehall; and stresses the counterproductive nature of the IRA's violence in stiffening unionist resistance to Irish reunification, and in inhibiting a political settlement; and, not least, emphasizes the IRA's intermittent descent into sectarian killings. But, English scrupulously acquits the IRA of sole responsibility for the conflict of the past thirty years, distributing blame across a range of political groups, and on British and unionist policies and dispositions without which the IRA's actions or persistence would have made little sense. None of his writing avoids the elemental emotions and tragedies involved in IRA actions and their repercussions for both the organization's target-victims and its members. He forgets neither the 'Fanonist rage' of some volunteers, nor the local status and petty power sometimes achieved through being in 'the 'RA', but refuses to overemphasize the tabloid components of the IRA, which he treats as neither corrupt nor as ruthlessly efficient as it would have liked to have been. From this measured study we may conclude that the IRA has failed militarily to drive the British state out of Ireland, and to achieve a united Ireland in the immediate future. If Ireland is to be reunified in future, it will be through ballot boxes and institutionalized negotiations.

But what English misses is the constitutional path through which the IRA must disband itself, if it is to dissolve itself in good order. That requires its volunteers not only to believe that military means cannot win their objectives, and are therefore best replaced through democratic — and consociational — politics, but to do so consistent with their own constitution, to which they are pledged, or else face the danger of further splits and the departure of their matériel into the hands of irreconcilables. Thanks to Ed Moloney's *A Secret History of the IRA,* the current IRA constitution, as amended in 1986, and again in 1996, is a matter of public record. It has five objects, recognizable successors to the founding aims, namely, 'to guard the honour and uphold the sovereignty and unity of the Irish Republic as declared by the First Dáil'; 'to support the establishment of an Irish Socialist Republic based on the 1916 Proclamation'; 'to support the establishment of, and uphold, a lawful government in sole and absolute control of the Thirty-two County Irish Republic as constituted by the First Dáil'; 'to secure and defend civil and religious liberties and equal rights and equal opportunities for all citizens'; and 'to promote the revival of the Irish language as the everyday language of the people' (Art. 3. 1–5). Until these objects are achieved the organizational integrity and cohesion of the IRA, and its military capabilities must be maintained (Art. 8. 5.1–2); and 'until a settlement has been agreed, leading to a united Ireland' the IRA must retain its arms (Art. 8. 5.5).[93] So, the question presently before all is this: how may the IRA constitutionally disband itself if the sovereignty and unity of the Irish Republic, 'as declared by the First Dáil', has not been achieved?

Before answering this question let me sweep aside some side-issues. Let us assume that socialism on the basis of the 1916 proclamation, civil and religious liberties, equal rights and opportunities for all, and promoting the Irish language, do not require the existence or use of the IRA's arms — a proposition with which the current Irish prime minister, who has declared himself a socialist, would certainly affirm. Note, secondly, that it is now the First — not the Second — Dáil's mandate (for an autonomous Ireland that would exercise its self-determination) that is defended by the

IRA. It is this constitutional change that has enabled the IRA not to oppose Sinn Féin's participation in elections to and membership of Leinster House.

One way the IRA's constitutional self-transformation may go in future would be to argue that since the Belfast/Good Friday Agreement of 1998, endorsed by the people of Ireland, North and South, and now on the verge of full implementation, the partition of Ireland presently rests on a decision of the people of Ireland, as do the power-sharing institutions, agencies and policies embedded in that Agreement. In short, the Agreement is the necessary act of Irish national self-determination that repairs the constitutional wound of 1920. That was certainly how constitutional nationalists, North and South, defended the Agreement, and in instructing its voters to endorse it in the two referendums, Sinn Féin became complicit with that argument. The Agreement recognizes (present) partition as an Irish, not a British decision, and recognizes Ireland's right to achieve (re-)unification through consent in both jurisdictions. It also, of course, establishes consociational institutions within Northern Ireland and cross-border all-Ireland arrangements that may legitimately be construed as harbingers of a federal Ireland.[94] Once the Agreement is on the verge of being fully implemented, notably with the withdrawal of British troops to barracks, comprehensive police reform, major changes in the administration of justice, and with the Northern Ireland (Suspension) Act of 2000 removed from the UK's statute book, then it becomes possible to argue two things. One is to say that 'a settlement leading to a united Ireland', without any British external interference over Irish self-determination, has already been accomplished. A united Ireland has been achieved through the Agreement, but not a unitary Ireland, rather an Ireland united by the institutions of the Agreement. The people of Ireland, North and South,

93 Moloney, *Secret History,* Appendix 3
94 See O'Leary, 'The Nature of the British-Irish Agreement'.

have the right of national self-determination, but also the right to choose how to exercise national self-determination, and if that involves having one territorial unit with revisable linkages to the United Kingdom, that need not be a denial of the underlying principle. This would probably be too much for most republicans to stomach — it may seem lawyerly, or specious, although it has its attractions. Secondly, and probably more persuasive to most republicans, it is possible to argue that 'a settlement has been agreed [and implemented] leading to a united Ireland', even though the latter has not (yet) occurred — 'leading to a united Ireland' is not the same as the 'attainment of a united Ireland'. Either of these arguments permit republican volunteers in good conscience to amend the IRA's constitution to say that the object of the First Dáil has been met — which would then authorize the ratification of decommissioning by an Army Convention (required by Art. 8. 5.5), and the subsequent disbanding of an organization which had met its constitutional mission.

A united Ireland need not necessarily be a unitary Ireland; and a sovereign Ireland may take many forms, including a divided form, through a federation or confederation, or through two units within a European confederation. Moreover, a Northern Ireland Assembly — and legal system, and even UK parliament — which does not require oaths of allegiance to the Crown on the part of ministers is surely in some respects like a Dáil Éireann which has no such requirement. The new Northern Assembly and North-South Ministerial Council create forums in which all the objects of the IRA may be pursued without recourse to arms, and with some prospects of success (although the chances of the Irish language must be less than those of a unitary state). Arguments of this nature may have occurred — or be anticipated — if the IRA is, as is clear, willing comprehensively to decommission its weapons. We shall find out.

If such an internal constitutional transformation occurs the IRA will not have failed politically to the degree that it failed militarily. The IRA, in action or on ceasefire, made it necessary for a political settlement to address the denial of Ireland's right to self-determination in 1920 — and, for that matter, to undertake the radical police reform that has been negotiated since 1998, as well as range of other anti-discrimination measures that might not otherwise have materialized. The IRA did not fight for power-sharing in a Stormont parliament, nor did it design those institutions, nor did it initially endorse the Good Friday Agreement. But its existence, and the skilled trading of its capacities for constitutional and political concessions, obliged others to create comprehensive power-sharing institutions in and across Northern Ireland, Ireland and Great Britain all of which are consistent with the core idea of Irish national self-determination. In that idea the 'Irish' include both Irish nationalists and Irish unionists who identify with Great Britain. In that idea self-determination may take a concurrent as well as a unitary form. The IRA may in good faith amend its constitution to accomplish its own dissolution in a manner that the majority of the ghosts of the First Dáil would approve, although the vote might be too close to call among the ghosts of the rump Second Dáil. ∎

Postscript

This essay was completed toward the end of 2004. Three events since have led readers of my draft to ask whether I wish to modify or update my views. They are, first, the failure of the two governments to oversee a renewal of the Agreement of 1998 with the active consent of the DUP and Sinn Féin. The second is a major bank robbery in Belfast which the Police Service of Northern Ireland rapidly blamed on the IRA. It persisted in this claim, despite vehement denials by both Sinn Féin and the IRA, and was joined in its accusation by the two governments and the Independent Monitoring Commission, which additionally alleged Sinn Féin's involvement. The accusations prompted the IRA to withdraw all past offers it has put on the negotiating table, but not its cease-fire. The story of the robbery has, to date, climaxed with the arrest in the South of Sinn Féin members, 'suspected' IRA members, and one suspected 'dissident republican' according to the head of Ireland's police. The third event is the murder of Robert McCartney in the North, which eventually led the IRA to deny its involvement, to describe such murders as contrary to its principles, and to encourage those with knowledge to do as the victim's family wants, which means informing the police.

These events do not require any revision of the analysis given above. They are reminders that history records few tidy end-games to conflicts. It is worth emphasizing that Sinn Féin and the DUP had reached an astonishing level of agreement. The gap separating them was narrow — the precise form of publicity to accompany the verification of decommissioning. It was also huge because it involved group-honour, emphasized above. The IRA and Sinn Féin sought to avoid humiliation; they believed that was precisely the DUP's price-tag on the prospective bargain. As matters have unfolded different humiliations awaited republicans. The interpretation of the bank robbery still requires some caution. It is not yet known whether it was the action of unauthorized IRA operatives, or of conspirators within the IRA opposed to the peace process. It seems incredible that it would have been authorized by the IRA's Army Council. At the very least the unfolding evidence suggests a loss of control within the IRA that has damaged and embarrassed Sinn Féin's leaders. Neither the IRA nor Sinn Féin is a monolith, and it would be no surprise to find some Sinn Féin figures handling the IRA's finances. The argument presented above was that the IRA has been an instrumentally rational nationalist paramilitary organization, politically rather than criminally motivated, and, with the right political management, on the verge of dissolution. That argument withstands scrutiny despite these events. Group-honour is essential both to understanding the IRA's longevity, and how it must be managed, and the bank robbery and the murder have magnified its importance. One can and should condemn crimes without rushing to brand an organization's leaders as guilty without a trial. To step on a group's honour may arouse anger rather than reason. The IRA's dissolution should be sought, but with sufficient care to prevent the type of fragmentation associated with ETA in the Basque country. Sinn Féin will need to cleanse itself, both because that is right and to avoid electoral damage, but it is always more difficult to reform when shamed. These events have rendered resolution far more awkward, coming as they do in the run-up to elections in both parts of Ireland and in Britain. They have postponed the resolution which this essay foresaw; they have not terminated that prospect.

Thanks are owed to the late Marianne Heiberg, to Sharon Burke, Bill Kissane, John McGarry, Brendan O'Duffy, Stephan Stoeler, and to people whom I cannot name.

Reviews

The Book of the Cailleach:
Stories of the Wise-Woman Healer
Gearóid Ó Crualaoich
Cork: Cork University Press, 2003
xvii + 302 pages. ISBN 1-85918-372-7

The *Cailleach* of this book's title is probably best known as *Cailleach Bhéarra,* the Old Woman, or 'hag', associated since eighth-century literature to modern folklore with the Beara peninsula, county Cork. Many other landscapes in Ireland and Scotland have *Cailleach* stories of their own, several of which Gearóid Ó Crualaoich presents and analyzes, but his book is not in any sense a catalogue. Instead, as the subtitle suggests, it goes beyond literary analysis and geography to examine questions of wisdom and therapy. Healing is as old as human society, but university-trained scholars and practitioners have been slow to accept that ethnomedical practices do produce therapeutic effects, while anthropological studies that take vernacular healing systems seriously tend to be concentrated on non-European cultures.[1] Ó Crualaoich's scholarly exploration, through literature and oral tradition, of what he identifies as an indigenous Irish form of psychotherapy, is therefore both highly original and important. Among its virtues is the map it offers of a territory long colonized by Christianity in Ireland — the human spirit, brought alive in a landscape of rock and water and land, both tilled and untilled, its imagination richly grounded in the feminine.

The Book of the Cailleach is not only ambitious, but courageous: at once a theoretical intervention, providing richly complex readings of texts transcribed from oral storytellers, and a sort of speech-act between covers, designed to make whole a communal imagination that had been broken. The illustrations therefore include reproductions of work by visual artists, as well as photographs of Irish landscape, and of one performer. George Pickow's evocative image of Mrs. Elizabeth Cronin at her county Cork fireside in 1952 is not contextualized; instead it appears on page 78 as though to introduce the tales through the person of a woman storyteller. Taking as his own canvas the whole history of human consciousness, Ó Crualaoich tracks two groups of Irish mythological legends across it: stories about larger-than-life manifestations of the feminine, and extraordinary episodes of affliction and healing. The oral legends he studies and offers for contemplation are mapped onto familiar landscapes, physical and social, but in his exegesis at least, they comprehend the cosmos. Their elements are offered as 'transactional symbols' (76), onto which, Ó Crualaoich suggests, listeners, and now readers, may attach emotions in such a way as to allow them to be manipulated therapeutically. Irish legends of healing, he argues (286–87), are 'non-prescriptive articulations of a hermeneutic of the human experience of affliction among whose functions was the provision of a communal therapeutic resource of archetypal dimensions and provenance'. Divided into three parts, the last of which is a corpus of thirty-four oral legend texts in their original Irish (or mixed Irish-and-English), this book is both a study of the figures of the *Cailleach* ('supernatural old female') and *Bean Feasa* ('wise woman'), in Irish tradition, and an engaged attempt to recover the emotional and imaginative resources of a vernacular psychotherapy.

Following a review of the literature, the second half of Part One is devoted to a thirty-page survey of medieval to modern literary texts in Irish. The examples discussed show early medieval authors devaluing, degrading and dethroning the autonomous female otherworld figures of earlier tradition, reducing them to the role of accessories in patriarchal political structures. Meanwhile, other kinds of dynamic cultural production have kept the essential characteristics of those same figures alive and available to the popular imagination. Ó Crualaoich argues persuasively that reflexes of the despised feminine — the *Cailleach* — are to be found in the figures of the death-messenger *Bean Sí* (Banshee), the seductive *Spéirbhean* of *aisling* poetry, the fairy queen Aoibheall in Brian Merriman's 'Midnight Court', and the *Bean Feasa* of apparently recent memory.

Part Two, which takes up half the book, is an imaginative exegesis of the thirty-four oral narratives which Part Three presents in the original. Rather than submitting the stories to a common paradigm, Ó Crualaoich takes them one by one, and provides translations, followed by readings that are compelling, if at times repetitive. The first sixteen deal with the figure of the *Cailleach.* This is a representative, rather than a comprehensive, selection, so Seosamh Laoide's 1913 edition of *Lúb na Caillighe,* as told by

1 See, for instance, Michael Winkelman and Philip M. Peek, eds., *Divination and Healing: Potent Vision* (Tucson, 2004).

Micheál Mag Ruaidhrí, gardener at Patrick Pearse's St. Enda's, does not receive mention, for instance, nor does Máire Mac Néill's essay, 'Poll na Seantuinne and Poll Tigh Liabáin' (*Béaloideas*, 39, 41 (1971–73), 206–11), which made an authoritative case for associating certain spectacular landscape features — notably coastal blowholes in the west of Ireland — with the figure of an elderly otherworld woman. The range of stories presented here makes vivid both the engagement of traditional narrative with the power and mystery of wild nature, and the prevalence in shared imagination of a feminine presence 'of a larger order than can be accommodated in any human dwelling' (124). It is in the examination of narratives of legendary wise-woman healers (174–229), however, that we find the clearest articulation of Ó Crualaoich's thesis. Here he establishes that notwithstanding widespread belief in the historicity of various 'wise women', both healer and client in the 'wise woman' legends are symbolic fictions, designed, he suggests, to project experience beyond the immediately personal. Noting that such legends reassure their listeners that experience always has meaning, he maintains (223–24), that 'premodern vernacular culture in Ireland shows a grasp of the psychodynamic of therapy, making it available [to individuals] ... in the public domain of oral narrative performance rather than in the private domain of the professional individual consultation'.

The stories considered in *The Book of the Cailleach* make available a wealth of imagery and evocation not found in English translation from Irish since Máire Mac Néill's *The Festival of Lughnasa*, but aspects of their presentation leave something to be desired. Early on in his text (14), Ó Crualaoich acknowledges that he has left unresolved 'a multitude of properly textual considerations regarding [the] status and ... transmission' of the texts he presents. While this is understandable in a work that aims primarily at poetic insight, many readers might prefer to find at least the names of storytellers and collectors noted in some consistent form, with dates and places of recording or transcription. It is a pity, too, that reading this fascinating book should be made difficult by so many misprints and eccentricities of punctuation. (At times it seems as though the panda of Lynne Truss's *Eats, Shoots and Leaves* had strolled through the text,

inserting and deleting commas just for fun.) And after careful reading I remain mystified by the attribution to me of the notion that it is somehow 'not permissible' to analyze literary and folklore texts within a common hermeneutic frame (15). Quibbles aside, however, this book will be indispensable to students of Irish vernacular culture and richly rewarding for readers from many other backgrounds. For the scholar of Irish traditions it offers a strong and flexible framework within which to consider and interpret a multitude of texts, both literary productions and those derived from oral performance; for the growing number of readers who approach traditional narrative as a resource for psychotherapy meanwhile, it will be a rigorous and authoritative guide.

Angela Bourke
University College Dublin

Ar Chreag i Lár na Farraige:
Amhráin agus Amhránaíocht i dToraigh
Lillis Ó Laoire
Indreabhán: Cló Iar-Chonnachta, 2002
389 pages + CD. ISBN 1-902420-36-5

A Hidden Ulster:
People, Songs and Traditions of Oriel
Pádraigín Ní Uallacháin
Dublin: Four Courts Press, 2003
540 pages. ISBN 1-85182-738-2

Ar Chreag i Lár na Farraige is a ground-breaking study of Gaelic song as social and aesthetic practice on Tory Island off the northern coast of Donegal. By focusing on singing as cultural process rather than on song texts as cultural products, the author — himself an accomplished traditional singer — has undertaken an ambitious ethnographic field study which takes the reader under the skin of a contemporary Irish-speaking island community. The theoretical basis for the enquiry is provided by narrative theory and the hermeneutics of culture expounded by Hans-Georg Gadamer and Paul Ricoeur. Central to the approach adopted throughout is the concept of action as text, and this is expounded in a manner which includes the social and psychological aspects of an art-form practised in a context where individual actions and interpretations are shaped by communal social and aesthetic values. While Ó Laoire is building on the work of Irish-language and folklore scholars such as Breandán Ó Madagáin (on the functions of folk song), Angela Bourke (on the texts and contexts of devotional song) and Gearóid Ó Crualaoich (on the practice and reception of oral culture), his dialogical methodology owes more to the insights of anthropologists such as Clifford Geertz, James Clifford and Lauri Honko, especially in its attention to the finer details of cultural practice and to the practitioners' own perceptions of the form and function of their art. Combining observation and participation, the personal testimony of his *oidí* or mentors (especially the singers Éamonn Mac Ruairí, Teresa Mhic Claifeartaigh and Séamas Ó Dúgáin), and a self-reflexive or 'framing' meta-narrative, the author manages to produce an analytical account which is simultaneously objective and intimate.

Each chapter focuses on particular aspects of song as cultural practice (processes of acquisition and transmission, chapter 3; folk aesthetics and criticism, chapter 4; the importance of context in the performance, reception and interpretation of song, chapters 5–9). The main concern throughout is with the social significance of song, a significance which is inextricably linked to an aesthetics of form and of performance. The over-riding insight of this study is that in a community like Tory Island, traditional song serves clearly defined social, emotional and psychological functions and that both practitioners and audiences are very conscious of these functions. The analysis of the place of song performance at island gatherings such as the school-house dance, illustrates the role played by such performance in differentiating between groups in the community and between the different functions of the social gathering itself. A native lexicon is employed to expound an aesthetic understanding which includes an expectation that individual performances will adhere to communally agreed standards. Central ideas here are the concept of correct form — that the song should be rendered accurately in correct sequence (*cuma cheart*); and the concept of effective execution — that the performance should exude energy and conviction (*brí agus misneach*). The singers themselves, highly aware of the transformative and restorative power of their art, emerge as the most discerning of critics. The detailed analysis of the relationship between particular song texts and the personal circumstances of both singers and audiences shows how traditional singing serves individual and communal needs by facilitating the successful expression of emotions in a range of social contexts. Interesting also is the recognition that the traditional process of acquisition has the capacity to accommodate non-native song material, while at the same time non-native material may on occasion be consciously chosen by a singer unsure of his or her ability to satisfy traditional aesthetic standards. This apparent inconsistency is indicative of the kind of insights to be gained when the focus of the study is on the dynamics of a functioning system rather than simply on the performance or reception of a particular body of texts.

Pádraigín Ní Uallacháin's *A Hidden Ulster: People, Songs and Traditions of Oriel,* is a very different kind of book. Focusing on the historical region of Oriel ('Oirialla'), which comprises parts of counties Armagh, Monaghan and Louth, this publication is a marvellous work of cultural salvage whose central purpose is the preservation, dissemination and historical contextualization of the extant song texts associated with the region. Oriel is a region where aspects of Gaelic tradition persisted, although in residual forms, into the early twentieth century. Ní Uallacháin — a native of the region and herself also an accomplished traditional singer — was able to draw on the work of previous generations of collectors and editors to compile a comprehensive collection of songs in Irish which are published here with English-language translations, historical notes and, wherever possible, musical notation and discography. One of her central purposes in compiling the book was to remarry published song texts to their original airs, thus making them available to contemporary singers. While the difficulty of this task is acknowledged at the outset, nevertheless she has succeeded, by assembling all the available evidence in a body of fascinating linguistic, literary and musical material.

While this book will be an invaluable resource for singers, its main interest for the social and literary historian must lie in the wealth of lore and historically documented accounts of the composition and performance of particular songs assembled in it. Of particular interest are the songs associated with calendar customs and with women's work. The discussion of song texts such as 'Amhrán na Craoibhe' and 'Thugamar Féin an Samhradh Linn', which were traditionally associated with Bealtaine (May time) celebrations, and the connected 'Cuacha Lán de Bhuí', which may have been associated with Samhain (Halloween), reveals the role of song as one performance element in seasonal dramatizations which also included dance, costume and ritualized role-play. It is apparent from the discussion that women played a central part in the transmission of all aspects of the Oriel song tradition. Thirty-six of the sixty-seven singers from whom songs were collected in the region were women, and the book's discussion of their song repertoires and biographies serves as a valuable contribution to nineteenth-century and early twentieth-century women's cultural history. The evidence adduced for specifically female forms of composition and performance is particularly notable. Ní Uallacháin's discussion of a spinning song such as 'Túirne Mháire', for example, foregrounds the collective nature of such songs and points to the need for further research, in the Irish context, into the relationship between female labour and female creativity.

Our knowledge about the song traditions of Oriel would be much poorer were it not for the efforts of language revivalists such as Énrí Ó Muiríosa (Ó Muirgheasa) and Lorcán Ó Muirí (Ó Muireadhaigh), whose pioneering work in the field of song collection during the first half of the twentieth century is acknowledged throughout the book. Certain details related to these collectors illustrate how the cultural losses associated with language shift can sometimes be offset by new kinds of cultural exchange. The fact that an Oriel song such as 'An Chailleach Riabhach' could become popular in the repertoire of the singers of Rannafast in the Donegal Gaeltacht because it was a favourite of Carlingford-born Ó Muirí (founder of the Irish College, Coláiste Bhríde, in Rannafast in 1926), who sang it there, is merely one small example of the dialogic nature of all genuine cultural encounters. On the other hand, details relating to the censorship of traditional song material by Ó Muiríosa, Ó Muirí and others illustrate the difficulties of reconstructing a corpus of song from the published work of those who found certain aspects of that tradition objectionable. Here Ní Uallacháin's account benefits from the testimony

of contemporary traditional singers, including that of her father Pádraig.

Though the methodology employed in these two volumes is very different, as studies of the role of song in the lives of particular communities they complement each other wonderfully. The material in both books is presented in a clear and lucid manner, and excellent use is made of visual material, including, in the case of A Hidden Ulster, many previously unpublished early twentieth-century photographs of singers, storytellers and musicians. The authors in both cases are concerned with the dynamics of living cultures and their discussion of songs and singing successfully combines the rigour and detachment of the professional researcher with the experience and passion of the engaged practitioner.

Máirín Nic Eoin
Coláiste Phádraig, Droim Conrach

Ag Dul ó Chion:
Cás na Gaeilge, 1952–2002
Máirtín Ó Murchú
An Aimsir Óg: Paimfléad 1
Baile Átha Cliath: Coiscéim, 2002
iv + 40 pages. ISSN 1649-3079

Dúshlán agus Treo d'Eagraíochtaí na Gaeilge:
Limistéar na Síbhialtachta
Helen Ó Murchú
An Aimsir Óg: Paimfléad 2
Baile Átha Cliath: Coiscéim, 2003
iv + 64 pages. ISSN 1649-3079

Beir Leat do Shár-Ghaeilge!
Súil Siar agus ar Aghaidh
Alan Titley
An Aimsir Óg: Paimfléad 3
Baile Átha Cliath: Coiscéim, 2004
vi + 44 pages. ISSN 1649–3079

Pobal, Féinmheas, Teanga:
Todhchaí d'Éirinn
Peadar Kirby
An Aimsir Óg: Paimfléad 4
Baile Átha Cliath: Coiscéim, 2004
viii + 45 pages. ISSN 1649–3079

Cosaint na Daonnachta:
An Cultúr Gaelach
Breandán Ó Doibhlin
An Aimsir Óg: Paimfléad 5
Baile Átha Cliath: Coiscéim, 2004
iv + 41 pages. ISSN 1649–3079

These five *An Aimsir Óg* pamphlets, edited by Mícheál Ó Cearúil, despite their diverse foci, spring from a single belief — the Gaelic League's language revival philosophy no longer suffices. Moulded by nineteenth-century cultural nationalism and empowered by *fin de siècle* tensions, it inspired and authorized the Gaelic League to speak in the early decades of the twentieth century and attracted wide support. But a new philosophy is required if the language project is to prosper in the twenty first century. The present time demands a new approach because, as Alan Titley argues (translated) 'the rhetoric has become barren' (33). While previously the Gaelic League undisputedly spoke for the language movement, these publications illustrate the gradual demise of that once powerful body and the erosion of its pre-eminent position. The editor conceives the series as a means 'to encourage a forum in Irish for balanced thought on all aspects' of the language. The authors, of which there are five to date, set themselves the task of formulating a new vision for the Irish language and repositioning Irish in the political and cultural mainstream. Written for non-specialists in clear Irish, they avoid over-indulgence in jargon and terminology.

In the first volume in the series, *Ag Dul ó Chion? Cás na Gaeilge, 1952–2002* [Devaluation: The Case of Irish, 1952–2002], Máirtín Ó Murchú lays out in stark terms various governments' and political parties' retreat from supporting Irish since 1952. His chronologically structured report makes for sobering reading. Not alone does he chart the withdrawal of official support for Irish, but he concludes that just as tangible results began to emerge from the Free State's linguistic policy, confidence in the project faltered. Currently, the political importance attached to Irish is greatly reduced and parliamentary parties need not concern themselves with language policy. Yet, Ó Murchú finds optimism in the sustained widespread support for Irish among the general public. Helen Ó Murchú, in the subsequent volume, *Dúshlán agus Treo d'Eagraíochtaí na Gaeilge: Limistéar na Síbhialtachta* [A Challenge and Guide for Irish Language Organizations: The Sphere of Civility], advocates in lucid prose, a new approach for Irish language organizations. Drawing on her considerable experience, she argues that language promotion groups based in the voluntary sector should align themselves with cultural and sporting bodies to broker a new deal with the government as part of the national strategy on social development. While each pamphlet offers practical suggestions on appropriate and immediate action, Ó Murchú's has most merit and practical application. It remains to be seen, however, if the inevitable petty jealousies and internecine rivalries of the language movement and the voluntary sector will entertain or even enact such a bold strategy. Time is not on their side.

Alan Titley in the third pamphlet, *Beir Leat do Shár-Ghaeilge! Súil Siar agus ar Aghaidh* [Take Your Snazzy Irish and Clear Off! Looking Back and Forward], argues that Irish is the most practical language choice for Ireland if its inhabitants wish to learn about the island's culture and heritage. Detailing the image of Irish throughout recorded history, he suggests that a rediscovered interest in the magic of the spoken word would help stimulate a linguistic revival. Irish, he asserts, honed the human imagination on this island; the Irish aural and visual imagination are formed by the language. Titley and his fellow authors view Irish not as a means to an end, but as an integral part of a wider project not limited to linguistic affairs alone. In a similar vein Peadar Kirby writes authoritatively in the fourth pamphlet, *Pobal, Féinmheas, Teanga: Todhchaí d'Éirinn* [Community, Self-respect, Language: A Future for Ireland], of recent ideological shifts in Irish politics toward what Garret FitzGerald describes as 'new right-wing liberal ideology antithetical to further redistribution' and its effects on wider society. Pity any social, cultural or language group reliant on state intervention; market forces alone dictate policy. The most controversial statement contained in the five pamphlets is Kirby's declaration that Fianna Fáil are (translated) 'the greatest enemies of the language cause, as they feign affection but act contrarily' (34). Acknowledging Éamon Ó Cuív as an exception, he accuses Fianna Fáil of manipulating Irish for their own benefit and suggests the Greens as a logical party for those committed to promoting the language.

Breandán Ó Doibhlin draws on philosophical and political theory in *Cosaint na Daonnachta: An Cultúr Gaelach* [The Defence of Humanity: Irish Language Culture] to identify the major challenge facing future Irish generations: how to function in a global economy while retaining a distinct Irish identity? Ó Doibhlin's somewhat vague answer is that we discover a lifestyle that allows communities to develop organically, based on the identity which history bequeaths them. He calls, not for a simple increase in census figures for language usage, but for a fundamental change that would motivate public spirit. Should Ireland undertake such a process, he argues, Irish would be the logical, indeed, the only choice for Irish people seeking to retain their cultural identity while functioning in the global economy. Much of Ó Doibhlin's stern prose is polemical and relies on the reader's acceptance and indeed acquiescence in a higher moral authority and purpose. Without this, his argument loses impetus. At a period of intense flux when Ireland, as several commentators have recently observed, is intent on disavowing traditional Catholicism with an intensity and fervour equalling its rejection of Irish in the nineteenth century, these pamphlets seek to identify a role for the language in the new post-Celtic Tiger, post-nationalist, post-Catholic Ireland. The appearance of these pamphlets, the quality of their thought and the candour of their assessment is to be commended. If the Irish language is to play a role in the future of Ireland, then these essays may well represent a watershed. Whether the proposed venture comes to fruition, or whether the petty politics condemn it to naught, remains to be seen. The pamphlets, deserving of extended treatment, are essential reading for anyone interested in contemporary Irish language culture and politics, and offer a snapshot of the cultural, political and intellectual state of Irish, and indeed of Ireland, at the start of the twenty-first century.

Brian Ó Conchubhair
University of Notre Dame

Maeve Brennan:
Homesick at The New Yorker
Angela Bourke
London: Jonathan Cape, 2004
xvii + 333 pages. ISBN 0-224-06260-3

Elizabeth Bowen:
The Shadow Across the Page
Maud Ellmann
Edinburgh: Edinburgh University Press, 2003
xiv + 241 pages. ISBN 0-7486-1703-5

Irish feminist criticism has tended to focus more on the archival retrieval of collective endeavours than on the solitary writer. In *The Dictionary of Munster Women Writers 1800 to the Present* (Cork, 2005), edited by Tina O'Toole, and the volumes of *The Field Day Anthology of Irish Writing* (Cork, 2002), centred on Irish women's writing and traditions, edited by Angela Bourke, Siobhán Kilfeather, Maria Luddy, Margaret Mac Curtain, Gerardine Meaney, Mairín Ní Dhonnchadha, Mary O'Dowd, and Clair Wills, communalities matter more than the distinct trajectory of the lone author. *Maeve Brennan: Homesick at* The New Yorker by Angela Bourke and *Elizabeth Bowen: The Shadow Across the Page* by Maud Ellmann make good such omissions by concentrating attention on two crucial Irish women writers whose literary legacy deserves far more scrutiny than it has hitherto garnered. In reclaiming and elucidating their subjects, these critics adopt different modes. Bourke's study is a luminous, pioneering biography of a writer who has only recently been rediscovered, while Ellmann writes a searching, critical monograph about a novelist whose idiosyncratic work has enjoyed a much more continuous reception. Despite this, however, both investigations suggest that one of the primary and besetting areas of concern for feminist criticism is teasing out the hidden but defining interconnections of life and work in the *œuvre* of the individual woman writer.

Separated by a generation, Maeve Brennan (1917–93) and Elizabeth Bowen (1899–1973) stemmed from opposing worlds. Bowen was the last descendant of a Protestant, colonial family whose declining fortunes mirror the gradual eclipse of this land-owning class with its ill-defined pro-British and imperialist leanings, while Brennan belonged to the burgeoning nationalist,

Catholic culture that was to predominate in the new Ireland that emerged in the political upheavals prior to and after the 1916 Rising. Bowen remained faithfully wedded to her heritage, while Brennan was catapulted into American exile and the assumption of identities far removed from her family origins. Both writers, however, were fated to live existences that were often painfully stretched between different spheres: Bowen roved between the ramshackle milieu of Ascendancy Ireland and metropolitan London, while Brennan uneasily conjoined *petit bourgeois* Ranelagh in suburban Dublin and the deracinated cosmopolitanism of New York. As a result — but in very differing ways — the themes of exilic or diasporic identity and of displacement and loss dominated their fictions. Even though both writers were fascinated by modernity, they depicted the insidious hold that the past and family structures have on the present and on the female psyche.

Angela Bourke warns the reader that Maeve Brennan will not occupy centre stage in her own biography until chapter four of the work. To some degree, this remains the dilemma throughout as Brennan is a curiously shadowy figure who becomes increasingly enigmatic even as aspects of her life begin to be fleshed out. Bourke's method is not to attempt an unwarranted resolution of the contradictions and evasive silences of her subject but to give us a sense of the material densities of her life. She is particularly adept at unearthing the influence of family and of cultural and social contexts on the development of the writer. The initial chapters vividly and with winning exactitude portray the nuances of Irish rural life in early twentieth-century Wexford and also trace the remarkable careers of Brennan's parents, both of whom were active members of the Gaelic League and supporters of the fight for Irish independence. Brennan's father was continuously on the run, due to his republican activities and his work as a journalist, during her early childhood in Ranelagh. As Bourke persuasively argues, her later peripatetic life in Manhattan — when she moved restlessly between rented apartments, the holiday homes of her ever-generous friends, and the vacant back rooms and corridors of *The New Yorker* — seems an ineluctable re-enactment of an intergenerational fate. The virtue of the even-handed, non-judgemental perspectives of this biography is that they allow the positive force

and the oppressiveness of both this rich family background and of a nationalist, Catholic upbringing to become evident.

Brennan was significantly moulded, personally and professionally, by her engagement as a journalist, first at *Harper's Bazaar* and then for several decades at *The New Yorker*. Here, Bourke shows how this career path encouraged her to develop a brittle public persona, poised between sophistication and vulnerability, and to adopt the sometimes prescriptive house style fostered by William Maxwell, who became a lifelong friend and mentor. The spare surrealism, icy control, and quirky indirection of Brennan's stories seem at once the by-product of habits of mind encouraged by *The New Yorker* as well of her own peculiar imagination. Even though she continuously produced both fiction and journalism revolving around New York life, her stories also obsessively revisit her childhood in Ranelagh and sketch shadowy renderings of the marriage of her parents in the tales of her two troubled fictional families, the Derdons and the Bagots. One of the signal achievements of this biography is that it painstakingly pieces together the genesis and multiple redraftings — often years apart — of these Irish fictions and draws upon this history of creative production to counterpoint Brennan's turbulent professional and personal life. Bourke resists the view that Brennan's fiction is merely a form of psychodrama. Instead, she persuasively makes the case that Maeve Brennan is a writer of considerable stature who left behind a body of work that should earn her a place in the Irish literary canon alongside Joyce and Beckett.

Joyce and Beckett are points of reference, too, in Maud Ellmann's comprehensive and revelatory analysis of the novels and short stories of Elizabeth Bowen. The themes of paralysis and nullity that pervade her work signal her affinities with both these writers. As well as pinpointing Bowen's position in the history of twentieth-century literature, Ellmann is also at pains to unearth the specificities of her writing, an endeavour at which she excels. Utilizing narratology and insights gleaned from psychoanalytical theory, she catalogues the numerous recurrent motifs and devices in Bowen's fiction, including the demonic child, the alluring, siren-like older woman, and the entombing house which is at once enticing and repellent. Eliciting further patterns from her adept close readings, she also brilliantly observes that architecture becomes a substitute for psychology in Bowen and that objects in general tend to usurp the subject position in her plots.

Yet, Bowen's work is not simply reducible for Ellmann to a circumscribed list of involuntary mannerisms and self-replicating themes. Rather, she sees it as propelled by a peculiar dynamics of desire which has the deep-seated function of a grammar or mathematical code. Here, once again, Ellmann's gift for elucidatory close reading is to the fore. Building on Sean O Faolain's perception that there is a diminishment of human agency in Bowen's fictions, she reveals in her interpretations of novels such as *The Hotel* and *The Death of the Heart* how human interaction is configured in the strained worlds that they depict. In particular, she isolates the way in which desire in Bowen is always mediated by what she terms a 'shadowy third', a ghostly other or others who at once conduct and deflect emotion. The transactional nature of love further explains why the twinned themes of locomotion and of fixity predominate in her fiction. Their presence for Ellmann signals the operations of a death drive which she links at once with Bowen's membership of the decaying Anglo-Irish Ascendancy and with the death of her mother which she deduces left an irrevocable scar on the author.

Overall, Ellmann's study proffers its persuasive and original readings of successive novels as cumulative proof of its main propositions. However, it also views Bowen's fiction as a nodal point in which psychology, memory, and imagination meet. As a consequence, its fluidity and ability to respond to historical circumstance are also highlighted. In this light, a final chapter mounts a concerted defence of *Eva Trout*, a novel often deemed — like its heroine — an oddity or misfit. For Ellmann, Bowen in this final, playful work anticipates the future by producing a proleptic postmodern fiction in which identity depends on surface display and masquerade rather than unplumbed depths.

The continuing marginalization of women writers in contemporary Irish literary histories and cultural debates has frequently been noted. Such gaps are due not just to tokenism or residual misogyny but to the dearth of studies of key artists that would allow us to deepen our understanding of Irish female creativity and the pressures which shape or stifle it. Angela Bourke's *Maeve Brennan:* and Maud Ellmann's *Elizabeth Bowen:* are of moment not just because they are scholarly, informative, and pleasurably readable. They are also valuable contributions to Irish feminist criticism that at once consolidate its work to date and lastingly widen its ambit.

Anne Fogarty
University College Dublin

Peace in Ireland:
The War of Ideas
Richard Bourke
London, Pimlico, 2003
xvi + 462 pages. ISBN 1-84413-316-8

The Northern Ireland Conflict:
Consociational Engagements
John McGarry and Brendan O'Leary
Oxford: Oxford University Press, 2004
xiii + 448 pages. ISBN 0-19-926657-3

These are two big books on Northern Ireland. Despite their very different perspectives and totally divergent bibliographies the authors converge on analysis and, to some extent, on prescriptions. It is significant that they do so without any serious reference either to one another or to the data the other relies on.

It is hard to be original these days, and in this book John McGarry and Brendan O'Leary do not try. They reprint a set of articles on institutional provisions in Northern Ireland, which have already been published in political science journals or edited books, and add an introduction outlining the consociationist perspective which guides them and an extensive bibliography of their joint and individual works. Consociationism — proportionality in the electoral system and in public institutions, executive power sharing, mutual veto rights, and a degree of segmental autonomy — is argued to be a necessary tool to achieve group protection and equality in ethno-nationally divided societies like Northern Ireland. The broad thrust of their arguments is convincing. Consociational institutions are undoubtedly the best representative institutions for Northern Ireland at present. McGarry and O'Leary are undoubtedly the best technicians of consociational institutional design and they write with verve and robustness. They come to clear conclusions — they do not like ambiguity — and if these are sometimes proven wrong, they revise them. This set of articles from different periods of the conflict and peace process demonstrates a clear development of policy recommendations in the light of experience. It is simply the best book going on institutional design in Northern Ireland and the authors know it.

Sometimes, however, the authors seem to think that the intricacies of institutions or voting systems are the only intellectual problems left. Consociationism — the institutional form for which they argue in this book — is an institutional structure, not a set of moral principles. Nor is it the only institutional form compatible with the liberal egalitarian principles which they champion. Consociationism answers a relatively limited set of political demands, and in the case of the Good Friday Agreement, as they point out, it is supplemented by intergovernmental management and a level of all-Ireland integration. Nor does consociational theory even begin to answer the questions of how the conflicting groups whose demands it mediates are constituted, or how consociational institutions may themselves provoke change in these groups. McGarry and O'Leary are impatient and dismissive of such questions, and this leads to flaws in their analysis. They seem to believe (16–21) that constructivist or systemicist analyses which open conceptual possibilities of conflict transformation must lead logically to prescriptions for integrationist institutions in Northern Ireland. (Integrationism gives equal citizenship to individuals within one state without group protections.) This is simply a mistake, although it is one shared by some of the transformationalists whom they criticize. These are different levels of analysis and the prescriptions which follow from systemicist analyses are long-term and strategic rather than immediate and institutional. There is no contradiction between seeing totalizing and persistent communal conflict (in Northern Ireland or elsewhere) as a complex and contingent product of a multiplicity of social elements and relations, which is in principle changeable, and seeing

the best short- to middle-term institutional arrangement as consociational and intergovernmental. This is my view and, while it converges with McGarry's and O'Leary's analysis of the institutions of the Good Friday Agreement and with many of their immediate policy recommendations, it provides a very different analysis of the causal mechanisms which produce conflict.

Richard Bourke's book is a well-referenced, well-researched and well-written set of historico-philosophical reflections. Although he does not tackle the technical literature on consociationism, he shares the broad political perspective of McGarry and O'Leary, arguing that settlement became possible only when the parties moved from majoritarian to more egalitarian notions of democracy. Bourke refers to the political science literature on Northern Ireland on only a handful of pages, where he dismisses ethnic interpretations of the conflict without a great deal of understanding of what is at issue in the debates. He, like McGarry and O'Leary, fails to grasp the conceptual (and political) possibilities which open when one analyzes the multiplicity of interlocking factors which feed together in path-dependent ways to constitute what appears to be a simple communal conflict. What Bourke does is done well. However, his analysis of changing views among unionists and republicans would have benefited from reading the social scientific literature — at various points in the book he reinvents the wheel, by showing once again that indeed unionists and nationalists had different views of democracy (as the literature shows, they also had different views of justice, of freedom, and of equality). He shows that unionist and nationalist conceptions of democracy have changed, but this is narrative analysis rather than an explanation of why they changed or an identification of the precise extent of change. This is a case where disciplinary specialization, and in particular the divisions between the humanities and the social sciences, has prevented what is a good solid book from living up to its own ambitions and actually moving the debate further. Both books begin from a liberal egalitarian and democratic perspective, and both show that this presently requires a non-majoritarian concept of democracy in Northern Ireland. Bourke argues against the majoritarianism of the guarantee that

Northern Ireland's constitutional status as part of Britain or Ireland is to depend on the express will of a majority there. McGarry and O'Leary would defend this guarantee on egalitarian grounds. Short of full joint British-Irish authority, there is no reason why one national preference should perpetually prevail over another, and if unionists today (and for the past eighty-five years) have had their majority status respected, there is no reason to change the rules once they fear losing that status.

Both books are well presented. The Bourke volume is in colourful and (relatively) cheap paperback. The McGarry and O'Leary volume is presently only available in expensive hardback, presumably aimed at library rather than individual sales. The geometric cover-design is effective; it is in many shades of green, which will no doubt confirm the views of their unionist critics.

Jennifer Todd
University College Dublin

The Politics of Irish Drama:
Plays in Context from Boucicault to Friel
Nicholas Grene
Cambridge: Cambridge University Press, 1999
xvii + 312 pages. ISBN 0-521-66051-3

Gender and Modern Irish Drama
Susan Cannon Harris
Bloomington: Indiana University Press, 2003
xi + 307 pages. ISBN 0-25334-117-5

Theatre Stuff:
Critical Essays on Contemporary
Irish Theatre
Edited by Eamonn Jordan.
Dublin: Carysfort Press, 2000
xvii + 326 pages. ISBN 0-95342-571-1

The Theatre of Nation:
Irish Drama and Cultural Nationalism,
1890–1916
Ben Levitas
Oxford: Oxford University Press, 2002
viii + 278 pages. ISBN 0-19-925343-9

Revival:
The Abbey Theatre, Sinn Féin, the Gaelic
League and the Co-operative Movement
Critical Conditions 13
P. J. Mathews
Cork: Field Day and Cork University
Press, 2003
viii + 208 pages. ISBN 1-85918-365-4

A History of Irish Theatre, 1601-2000
Chris Morash
Cambridge: Cambridge University Press, 2002
xviii + 340 pages. ISBN 0-521-64117-9

Twentieth-Century Irish Drama:
Mirror up to Nation
Christopher Murray
Manchester: Manchester University
Press, 1997
Syracuse, New York: Syracuse University
Press, 2000
x + 278 pages. ISBN 0-8156-0643-5

Theatre and the State in Twentieth-Century
Ireland:
Cultivating the People
Lionel Pilkington
London: Routledge, 2001
x + 256 pages. ISBN 0-415-06938-6

It is often remarked that Irish theatre transformed itself completely during the 1990s, undergoing a second — or perhaps even a third — renaissance. While the extent of that transformation is sometimes exaggerated, there have been many important developments during the last fifteen years. New theatre companies, with innovative methodologies and fresh ideas, have been established throughout Ireland. The Celtic Tiger period has made more funds available for the construction of theatre spaces, and has encouraged a shift in audiences' expectations about the social and cultural function of Irish theatre. And dramatic writing has changed too: established dramatists such as Friel, Kilroy and Murphy have set out in intriguing new directions, and lively new voices are emerging all the time.

One of the most notable transformations is in the quality of theatre criticism, both journalistic and academic, during the last five years. The 1990s were, for the most part, a lean period for writing about Irish theatre. Although many valuable studies of Irish drama were published outside the country, there were few examples of serious theatre criticism being produced by Ireland-based writers for Irish audiences. *Theatre Ireland* ceased publication in 1993; thereafter, Irish theatre discourse was generally restricted to the daily newspapers, with coverage dominated by pre-publicity interviews, 'Second Opinion' columns, and overnight reviews of 350 words. Some of this work was of a high quality; but most was written by journalists who lacked specialized training in, knowledge of, or interest in the theatre. This gave rise to a sense of mutual antipathy between theatre practitioners and critics in Ireland.

The severity of this problem became apparent in a 1995 review of the theatre sector, carried out by the Arts Council. Practitioners were asked to give their opinions on the professional standards of the personnel involved in Irish theatre — the writers, directors, actors, marketers, and so on. Theatre critics fared far worse than any other grouping in the survey. A majority of respondents — 57 per cent — described critics' level of professionalism as 'poor', while 21 per cent thought it 'adequate'. Only 14 per cent thought it 'good', and none of the respondents regarded Irish theatre criticism as 'excellent'. People working in theatre have never needed an excuse to complain about critics, but the level of hostility discernible in these results is noteworthy.

Things began to change in 1998, when two significant events occurred: the publication of the first issue of *irish theatre magazine,* and the establishment of Carysfort Press, the Dublin-based publisher dedicated exclusively to the production of books on Irish theatre. One of its first publications was *Theatre Stuff,* a collection of essays on contemporary Irish drama. According to its editor Eamonn Jordan, the book was an attempt to come to terms with the perception that Irish theatre had changed 'both fundamentally and radically' (xi) since the early 1990s. It described that transformation effectively, presenting a variety of essays that charted the emergence of new companies, new writers, and new

ideas. *Theatre Stuff* was most exciting, however, for the diversity of methodologies, styles, and ideologies employed by its contributors: academic writing appeared side-by-side with articles by journalists, and both were complemented by the writings of practitioners. The collection was important because it placed at its centre the notion that essays on textual analysis are as important as essays on performance, and that there need not be any substantive distinction between journalistic and academic writing. The book showed the strength of Irish theatre criticism by including the work of Declan Kiberd, Christopher Murray, Terry Eagleton, and other established writers. But it also pointed to the emergence of a new generation of theatre scholars, publishing work from (at that time) pre-doctoral writers such as Melissa Sihra and Karen Vandevelde. The book thus made an important declaration about the growing coherence of writing about theatre in Ireland, showing that, although the field involves many different groups, it is possible for all interested parties to work within the same discursive framework.

Since the appearance of *Theatre Stuff,* there has been an explosion of books about Irish theatre, many of them of an extremely high quality. While differences in style, subject matter, and objectives are apparent, these publications share a desire to find new ways of writing about Irish theatre. They also attempt to tackle (and in many cases to reinvigorate) old questions — about the relationship of literature to society, and about whether drama that is conceived for audiences in London can really be considered 'Irish'. But one of the most interesting suggestions that arises from these books is also made clear by *Theatre Stuff:* that great Irish theatre acts as a stimulus for the development of a sophisticated, socially-grounded criticism.

This notion is expressed most clearly by Christopher Murray's *Mirror up to Nation.* Introducing his study of Irish drama during the twentieth century, Murray provides an overview of the development of criticism in Ireland during that period. He draws attention to the quality of three publications that emerged during the late Revival: Cornelius Weygandt's *Irish Plays and Playwrights* (1913), and Ernest Boyd's *The Contemporary Drama of Ireland*

(1918) and *Ireland's Literary Renaissance* (1922). Although, Murray writes, 'no study of Irish drama has looked in detail at the interrelationships of history, politics and performance … the[se] earliest books undoubtedly blaze a trail' (11). He then points out that the mid-century decline of the Abbey coincided with a series of books that avoided political analysis, instead aiming to define the Irish dramatic canon. This comparison reveals that, at times when Irish dramatic writing is of a high quality, theatre critics demonstrate a curiosity about the political context of that writing — whereas times of theatrical stagnation seem to encourage scholars to give more attention to canon-formation and textual analysis.

Murray himself blends both approaches, moving freely between social context and close-reading. His book is organized chronologically, establishing linear relationships between writers; and its first four chapters are devoted to Yeats, Synge, Gregory, and O'Casey. We then have a valuable reminder of the importance of the neglected mid-century dramatists — Robinson, Johnson, Carroll, Shiels, D'Alton, and Molloy — and interesting work on contemporary drama. So there is an obvious desire here to refine our understanding of the Irish dramatic canon.

Yet this analysis is always accompanied by considerations of writers' relationships with Irish society. For Murray, theatre does not just represent Irish life, but also imagines what Ireland might become: 'mirror and dream are two sides of the same mimetic process,' he suggests. He implies that criticism should fulfil a similar mimetic function. 'Theatre,' he writes, 'provides at communal level the record and representations which enable self-discovery. The history of Irish drama in the twentieth century is thus based on a need for a narrative of identity. The more problematic and fragmented identity becomes the greater the need for images of wholeness' (246). The success of Murray himself in imposing wholeness on fragmentation — by organizing disparate events into this history — shows that the roles of dramatist and critic may overlap: both can shape a country's sense of itself.

Since the publication of Murray's book (first published in 1997 in the UK, and reissued by Syracuse in 2000), many writers have sought to define the relationship between 'history, politics and performance' in Irish theatre. One of the most explicit treatments of the political is Lionel Pilkington's *Theatre and the State in Twentieth Century Ireland.* As with *Mirror up to Nation,* Pilkington's book devotes almost half of its pages to Irish theatre during the revival period, and it also sets about retrieving forgotten plays, devoting important attention to such writers as T. C. Murray and George Shiels. The main thesis here is that Irish theatre during the twentieth century has allowed ruling élites to 'cultivate the people' — an argument that provides interesting ways of thinking about many important events in modern Irish theatre history, from *Blanco Posnet* to *Translations* and beyond.

Pilkington begins by considering the foundation of the Abbey in the context of the Tory government's policies of constructive unionism, and suggests that, throughout its subsequent history, the theatre has tended to reflect the *status quo* in Irish society, rather than attempting to imagine alternatives. The book is particularly interesting in its discussion of Northern Ireland, however: Pilkington shows how theatre productions in the Irish Republic often reflected official policy in relation to the Troubles, and he also considers how the Stormont government used theatre during the post-1922 period. The strength of this analysis is not just that it describes the history of Irish theatre, but that it also establishes a model that might be used to consider the relationship between the state and other cultural forces in Ireland — notably cinema — during the twentieth century.

Judging from the content of *Revival,* P. J. Mathews might disagree with some of the conclusions of *Theatre and the State.* But he still places Pilkington's suggestion that there is a need to 'counteract the long-standing assumption that Irish drama exists outside of politics' (1) at the centre of his own book. Whereas Pilkington analyses theatre in the context of the operation and distribution of power, Mathews considers it as one element in a broader social framework, arguing that the energies that went into the establishment of the Abbey Theatre should be seen in the context of a 'self-help' ethos that emerged in Ireland in response to the failure of Parnellite nationalism. The growth of the Irish

Literary Theatre, argues Mathews, occurred not just simultaneously, but in tandem with the emergence of Sinn Féin, the Gaelic League, and the agricultural co-operative movement. He shows how these movements began with similar objectives, often sharing the same personnel — and he accounts interestingly for their divergences too.

Ben Levitas also sees the fall of Parnell as central to the development of Irish theatre during the Revival period, establishing a relationship between Irish theatre and the development of cultural nationalism from 1890 to 1916. This choice of chronology makes transparent Levitas's desire to study theatre against a political map, to 'plot the course of this discourse through the turns and twists of its expression, from the disgrace of Parnell to the crisis of *The Playboy* 'riots' and the dénouement of the Easter Rising'. What makes Levitas's book stand out, however, is his desire to show that the Abbey was only part of a broader theatre movement. He also considers regional theatre, for example, devoting particular attention to the Ulster Literary Theatre — an institution that is attracting increasing attention at present. Levitas seems aware that the focus on the Abbey can produce an excessive interest in the category of the nation at the expense of the region. While he treats that theatre's national(ist) credentials seriously, he also stresses the importance of 'regional difference and the impact of class, gender, and generational rebellion on public perception of artistic norms' (8). It is this breadth that makes his book so welcome.

The combined effect of the work of Pilkington, Mathews, and Levitas is to draw attention to the limitations of textual analysis within a nation-centred theatrical discourse. These authors draw attention to the variety of responses to theatre throughout Irish dramatic history, an approach that works against the view that literature produces and communicates an essentialized category of 'Irishness'. This is especially notable in these authors' treatments of the controversies that attended the production of Synge's works. Mathews's discussion of *The Shadow of the Glen* and Levitas's and Pilkington's consideration of *The Playboy* all show that the hostility excited by these plays arose from competing visions of what the nation, and national theatre, ought to be. There is an interesting contrast, however, between the largely homogenous representation of Irishness presented by Synge, and the variety of responses provoked by his work. Pilkington, Mathews and Levitas all illustrate that, although Synge may have been 'inventing Ireland', the category of nation might be more useful when used to consider the *multiplicity* of Irish responses to his work. By focusing on audiences and performance, these authors construe the category of nation not as an abstraction, but as a description of a communal or civic process, which involves a variety of perspectives — none of which should (necessarily) be privileged. What we are witnessing here is the beginning of a shift in our conception of 'Irish theatre' — which is increasingly being understood not as literature produced by Irish writers, but as drama watched by Irish audiences.

Susan Harris's *Gender and Modern Irish Drama* covers similar territory, but uses an entirely different approach. Harris points out the preponderance of images of blood, birth, and sacrifice in drama by Yeats, Synge, O'Casey and Pearse, and considers their interplay in relation to the construction of gender within nationalist discourse. Harris establishes many intriguing parallels between productions of plays and contemporaneous events; indeed, the highlight of her book is a fascinating chapter on how *The Playboy* appeared at a time when Irish journalists were preoccupied with issues of public health and vaccination. It is difficult to tell sometimes whether Harris is describing context or coincidence, however. Irish audiences at the turn of the twentieth century certainly had a well-developed sense of the symbolical importance of gender. But did they understand it as Harris does? The field of evidence provided here does not answer this question clearly. Quotations from periodicals are employed regularly to substantiate Harris's argument, but those sources rarely become part of the argument themselves — which means that the book could be accused of being over-dependent on textual evidence. Its work on constructions of gender in Ireland in the early twentieth century is valuable, but it doesn't consider the extent to which those constructions were a product of the militarization of Europe prior to World War I, rather than a direct outcome of nationalism. And although Harris's book includes many fascinating readings of Irish plays, it doesn't provide a historical account of how those plays were received by Irish audiences. So the tone of this book is speculative at a time when most other publications on Irish theatre are grounded in the archive. This makes Harris's book a fascinating contribution to the debate, since it establishes alternative ways of thinking about Irish theatre.

Nevertheless, there does seem to be a growing conviction that the exclusive use of textual sources is no longer an appropriate response to the complexity of Irish theatre history. This point is made most clearly by Chris Morash's wonderful *History of Irish Theatre*. The first major achievement of this book is that it thoroughly disproves the notion that there was no Irish theatre before 1891. Morash starts his history in 1601, and devotes half of his book to the period before 1904. His treatment of Irish theatre in the eighteenth century is fascinating, particularly its discussion of Smock Alley and Thomas Sheridan. And his work on the nineteenth century shows how the idea of an Irish 'national' theatre was in circulation long before Yeats turned his attention to the matter — an aspect of the book that's important in its own right, while also shedding new light on the foundation of the Irish Literary Theatre. Morash shows that the movement that culminated with the foundation of the Abbey 'chose to ignore the existing Irish theatre history', so that it was 'compelled … to imagine afresh its relationship to Irish history'. This meant that the theatre completely ignored 'the existence of discerning and sophisticated theatre audiences, who were familiar with an increasingly wide range of theatrical forms' in Ireland at that time. In a memorable formulation, Morash thus declares that the ILT came into being 'by imagining an empty space where in fact there was a crowded room' (117). This book will inspire others to explore the 'crowded room' that Morash has unlocked for us, but it is also important that he has presented the foundation of the Abbey to us in these terms.

His second achievement is to define a new, more inclusive, methodology for the study of Irish theatre. 'A history of the Irish theatre is a history of Irish audiences,' Morash states. 'Who they were, how much they paid for their tickets, where they sat, whether they watched reverentially or threw oranges at the orchestra'. Conceding that we can 'never fully know what it was like to sit in an Irish theatre in 1662 or 1754 or 1904', Morash proposes that we can still 'reconstruct a reasonably accurate picture of what those vanished audiences expected, and of what they saw on those now-darkened stages' (1). He attempts these imaginative (but well-informed) reconstructions in seven 'nights at the theatre' — brilliantly written accounts of key moments in Irish history, which are presented from the perspective of the audience. By insisting on the use of archival evidence — as well as textual interpretation — Morash demonstrates that Irish theatre criticism may be speculative without being fanciful, imaginative without being undisciplined.

All of the books discussed above share a preoccupation with the national features of Irish theatre. Nicholas Grene's *Politics of Irish Drama* broadens this perspective by showing that, since at least the time of Boucicault, Irish drama has been 'created as much to be viewed from outside as inside Ireland' (3). Grene establishes an important link between national self-expression and international endorsement, suggesting that, if Irish drama during the twentieth century has involved the production of a 'narrative of identity', that production also requires *validation* by non-Irish audiences.

To be viewed inside Ireland, a play's action must be meaningful to an Irish audience; to be successful abroad, the central 'Irish' narrative must be framed or mediated in a way that will provide an interpretative or moral anchor for an urbanized, cosmopolitan audience lacking in specialized knowledge of Ireland. In the nineteenth century, Grene suggests, this involved the use of 'stage interpreters', such as the English gentlemen who populate Boucicault's plays: characters whose interaction with feckless, devious Irishness was both a source of comedy and a mediator for non-Irish audiences. This 'outsidedness' also operated importantly *within* Ireland. The dramatists of the Irish Revival recalibrated Boucicault's presentation of Irishness as 'other' as a way of constructing an emergent national identity. Otherness thus became a key feature of the Revival, especially with the use of the 'Stranger in the House' motif.

While it makes sense for a colonized culture to deploy ideas of otherness as a counter-hegemonic device, it is surprising that Irish drama continues to use this strategy. As Grene notes: 'On the whole,

Irish drama has continued to look to social margins for its setting, whether the western country districts or the working-class inner city. It is thus typically other people that a largely middle class urban audience watches in an Irish play, other people who speak differently — more colloquially, more comically, more poetically' (264). The 'politics of Irish drama' are thus wrapped-up in its use of otherness — in the fact that Irish drama is always written to be comprehensible to Irish *and* non-Irish viewers. Grene points out the paradox at the heart of modern Irish theatre — Irish audiences simultaneously watch other people while experiencing a form of theatre they regard as representative of their own nation. Friel's notion that in Irish theatre we hear the nation 'talking to ourselves' while being overheard by people from abroad, thus needs to be slightly reformulated: Irish audiences perform *both* roles, imagining themselves as included in the stage representation of the nation, while simultaneously judging that representation from the perspective of an outsider.

The variety of approaches and methodologies used by these books reveals that Irish theatre criticism is currently enjoying a dynamic and creative period, characterized not only by scholarly rigour, but also by excellent, accessible writing. Particularly encouraging is that all of these books identify important issues for further scholarship. Irish drama before the 1890s remains in need of much work; so too does drama at the Abbey between 1926 and 1960. The issue of gender in modern Irish drama also needs more attention, especially in terms of the practical involvement of women in Irish theatre. There is certainly room for a detailed history of the contribution of Irish women to theatre on this island — a work that could consider groups like Inghinide na hÉireann to Charabanc, and such writers as Teresa Deevey, Una Troy, Lady Gregory, and Johanna Redmond (daughter of John Redmond) as well as the younger generation of Irish women writers who have between them produced over 150 new plays since 1990.

But perhaps the most intriguing question is, why are we getting so many books on the Revival now? Undoubtedly, some of the momentum has been generated by a desire to capitalize on the Abbey Theatre centenary of 2004. And the strength of Irish theatre during the 1990s must also be a factor. But perhaps the most significant reason for the renewed interest in the Revival is because of its relevance to our present — a point made brilliantly by P. J. Mathews: 'At a time when homogenizing pressures of globalization on local cultures have registered as a major concern within cultural criticism, the achievements, as well as the failures, of the Irish revival may have much to teach us about the cultural dynamics of Ireland in the twenty-first century' (148). This intriguing — and inspiring — statement nicely encapsulates the achievement of these new books on Irish theatre, which use the past as a way of explaining where we are right now.

Patrick Lonergan
National University of Ireland, Galway

Charles Trevelyan and the
Great Irish Famine
Robin Haines
Dublin: Four Courts Press, 2004
xvii + 606 pages. ISBN 1-85182-755-2

In 1977 the late Austin Bourke published two articles in *The Irish Times* which, under the title, 'Apologia for a Dead Civil Servant', set out to defend the record of Sir Charles Trevelyan as assistant secretary to the Treasury during the Great Famine. A quarter of a century later, Robin Haines has taken up Bourke's challenge and expanded the case for the defence. The result is a sprawling and rather disorganized, if nonetheless important, monograph.

The case set out by Bourke and elaborated by Haines has at its core two central propositions: that Trevelyan did not bear ill-will towards the Irish poor, and that as a civil servant he cannot be held responsible for political decisions over relief made by ministers. Considerable evidence can be deployed to support these propositions, and Haines presents an effective (if hardly original) case against wilder historical claims of genocidal intent, racial antagonism, total indifference to human distress, or dictatorial control over relief on the part of her subject. Instead we are given a portrait of the civil servant as hero — labouring with utmost skill and efficiency to implement well-intentioned, if complex and imperfect, relief policies in the face of extraordinary natural, administrative and political constraints, yet receiving for his trouble only unwarranted contemporary and historical brickbats as the public face of the Treasury.

Haines is, however, not content with an 'only obeying orders' defence of Trevelyan, and it is here that she parts company with Bourke. This departure recognizes the reality that Trevelyan was not merely a neutral conductor of policy, but was often an active participant in certain fields of policy-making (as well as frequently an enthusiastic promoter and apologist for such policies). Identifying the precise nature and extent of his political as opposed to administrative agency is complex, and readers may quibble with Haines's sometimes arbitrary assessments, but the acknowledgement of the fact leads her into a more general defence of government (or more accurately, Treasury) relief policies in the Famine years. Running throughout this monograph is an unresolved strain between two modes of discourse — a polemical drive to refute virtually all criticism of her subject (necessitating a reductionist and caricatured presentation of other interpretative positions); and a professed desire to present a contextualizing historical analysis of Irish famine relief and Trevelyan's part within it. The failure of this book lies within this conflict; all too frequently, polemical point-scoring overwhelms careful analysis and throws up a series of contradictions, unsubstantiated assertions and interpretive distortions. This analytical weakness is in great part attributable to the author's evident unease with the intellectual and ideological context of the period. Discussion of the ideas and applications of contemporary political economy is minimal and superficial; its central place in Trevelyan's mental world is evaded as posing a distraction from the preferred portrait of the administrator as an enlightened pragmatist. Similarly, discussion of the related question of Irish land is muddled and incoherent. Haines cannot deny Trevelyan's preoccupation with promoting a reconstructive 'social revolution' in Ireland, but there is no real engagement with the economic and sociological underpinnings of a policy she regards as simply common sense.

The treatment of Trevelyan's religious opinions is also problematic. Haines admits his self-professed 'evangelicalism' (albeit of an ecumenical and 'moderate' form), but denies that this was of any significance in the public sphere. Regarding any discussion of providentialism in Trevelyan's thought as the product of hostile criticism, the author employs a strategy of evasion and suppression with respect to his frequent public and private employment of providentialist concepts to explain both events and the correct moral response to them. Haines seems frequently bemused by her subject's general 'optimism' about Ireland's prospects; perhaps a deeper excavation of his mental foundations might have thrown more light upon this.

The book's interpretive limitations are exemplified in its treatment of the concept of 'self-government'. This idea was central to the ideological position adopted by both Trevelyan and the Whig Chancellor of the Exchequer, Charles Wood, and denoted the enforcement of collective local responsibility for relief on ratepayers and landowners, through representative local bodies such as relief committees and boards of guardians. Obsession with the moral improvement connected with enforcement of this object is evident throughout the correspondence of these men (and lay behind the premature removal of salaried vice-guardians in 1848–49 — a contributory factor in Twisleton's resignation as chief poor law commissioner). Yet Haines misinterprets the phrase as relating to Irish national self-government, and confounds this by erroneously associating it with the proposed abolition of the lord lieutenancy (a policy aimed at further integration of Ireland within the United Kingdom rather than devolution).

Haines's exclusion of the ideological is evident also in her treatment of intra-governmental conflicts over Irish famine policy — the source of much of the contemporary criticism of Trevelyan's role later taken up by historians. Two propositions are strongly argued; firstly, that the civil servant Trevelyan served as a useful (but unwarranted) proxy in altercations between ministers; and secondly, that these disputes were primarily driven by personality clashes rather than substance. Both appear plausible, but Haines's insistence on these to the exclusion of all other dimensions is unconvincing.

The repeated claim that Trevelyan simply took the political flak really intended for Chancellors Goulburn in 1845–46 and Wood in 1846–50 is greatly overstated. Ministers were acutely aware of where the power of decision making lay within the administration and cannot be accused of mistaking their target; moreover, they were more than capable of attacking each other in their correspondence without the need for an intermediary target (Lansdowne, Bessborough and Clarendon all criticized Wood directly in letters to Russell). The inclusion of Trevelyan in these attacks at least accorded him the dignity of treating him as a political agent in his own right. Haines's reduction of all conflict to the politics of the personal — following from her rejection of the existence of any substantial intra-party factions — is also ultimately unsatisfactory. Her vindication of Trevelyan and the Treasury's position in these disputes leads her into the character-assassination of critical politicians: Graham is hysterical and vacillating, Lincoln irritable and fuelled by personal misery, Bessborough an idle and bibulous womanizer, Clarendon an alarmist manipulator, and so on. So single-minded is this focus on weaknesses of character and personal infighting that Haines ignores structural explanations for strains between the Treasury and spending departments such as Dublin Castle. But it is the refusal to contemplate the existence of real, substantial, differences over relief policy lying behind these disputes that is most striking, and ultimately most trying.

This can be seen most clearly on pages 517–18 where the author seeks desperately to spin the overt criticisms made of Trevelyan by Clarendon in letters to Russell. 'I only hope,' wrote the Lord Lieutenant on 6 December 1848, 'that [the crisis] will not be unnecessarily aggravated and our position made worse by crude Trevelyanism. The theories and the influence of that gentleman alarm me exceedingly.' 'I have for months past not disguised from you my fears', he added on 12 February 1849, 'that the doctrinaire policy of Trevelyan, reflected through C. Wood and supported by Grey would prevail.' In December 1849 he was still lamenting the 'harsh Trevelyanism' which had prevailed too much. Haines tries various ploys to rationalize these charges — that it was the product of political calculation by the hypocritical Clarendon, that it is absurd that the young and ill-connected Trevelyan could act as mentor to ministers (forgetting, temporarily, that he was Macaulay's brother-in-law), and that the real target was Wood. But in the context of sustained conflict between the Treasury

and Dublin Castle over relief expenditure, and between Clarendon and Russell on one side and 'moralist' ministers on the other over major reconstructive projects to lift the burden from the poor law (including waste-land reclamation and assisted emigration) — and in which Trevelyan acted as an assured and empowered advocate of the Treasury line — this is difficult to sustain.

There are a smattering of factual errors; Earl Grey was indeed an aristocrat (45); the Devon Commission reported in 1845, not 1838 (95); Lord Monteagle was not an MP (98); Twisleton was not chairman of the Poor Law Commission in 1846 (148); polenta is not maize meal but a porridge produced from it (179); Lord Devon was a Conservative (228); Fitzwilliam was a Whig (311); the Martin estate was at Ballinahinch, not 'Ballinahuish' (515); the MP for Kerry in 1849 was Henry Arthur Herbert, not Sidney Herbert (534). There are also contradictions. We are told (xiii) that Trevelyan's 'constant refrain' was that the people not be allowed to starve, only for it to be later admitted that this phrase disappeared from his repertoire shortly after the fall of Peel's government. The plausible claim that there was an entrenched culture of resentment towards Treasury officials at Dublin Castle is later (156) reversed by the observation that Lincoln's arrival as Chief Secretary initiated animosities. Haines assures us (360) that all Trevelyan's letters to the press were delivered as personally signed letters for publication — 'with no hint of scheming' — but later provides numerous examples of his leaking official documents to *The Times* with an explicit view to shaping that paper's commentary on Irish policy (see 504, 514). There are striking gaps: the claim that Peel's policy after 1846 would have been no different from that of Russell rests on the total omission of any mention of Peel's March 1849 initiative on Irish policy. These flaws, along with the extensive amount of repetition in the text, might have been checked by effective editing. The book overall would have benefited from opting for either extended analysis based on a critically-evaluated hypothesis, or for a much shorter and controlled polemic; the attempt to combine them cannot be regarded as a success.

Charles Edward Trevelyan was a complex individual, who managed to combine a commitment to private charitable exertion for Ireland with the 'harsh Trevelyanism' towards further relief that so infuriated Clarendon and Twisleton in the later years of the Famine; who could combine minute attention and mastery of the details of administration with a capacity for economic abstraction and rationalization of mass mortality; and who could join marginal and pragmatic interventions with a dogmatic and providentialist defence of the principles of relief policy. All of these are evident in the pages of his 'Irish Crisis', which the author attempts to portray as joint-authored, but which Trevelyan evidently regarded as essentially his own production. In seeking to rescue Trevelyan from the hostility of history, Haines gives us not a picture of a complex individual but rather a counter-caricature of the (almost romantically) heroic civil servant, along with his deluded, scheming critics, past and present.

The concluding evaluation of the 'success' of famine relief policy is both provocative and facile. The ill-informed parallels with modern disaster relief border on the ludicrous. On the fundamental policy decisions made during the Famine which can be connected with unnecessary mortality — the failure (unlike the governments of France and Belgium) to secure sufficient food stocks on the international market in autumn 1846; the failure to pay adequate survival wages on the public works in 1846–47; the excessive delay in replacing the public works with effective soup kitchens in 1847 and the refusal to reintroduce this form of relief after that summer; the failure to relieve the poor law and devastated Irish economy with extensive remedial projects (whether creating relief entitlements through reproductive employment or assisting emigration); the withdrawal of significant assistance to the distressed western districts in 1848–49 — there is little persuasive discussion here. Of course it would be foolish to attribute these policies solely to Trevelyan, but he enthusiastically endorsed and implemented them, and bears a share of the responsibility for the government's failure to honour both his and its own early commitment that 'the people must not be allowed to starve'.

Peter Gray
University of Southampton

'Captain of All these Men of Death':
The History of Tuberculosis in Nineteenth- and Twentieth-Century Ireland
Greta Jones
Amsterdam and New York: Editions Rodopi, 2001
263 pages. ISBN 9-04201-031-2

When the Irish make claims to distinction, it has often been noted, the claim is more often based on misery than on accomplishment. Ireland's claims to uniqueness have in many respects fallen away under the pressure of new research in recent decades, but one remains: the appallingly high death rates from tuberculosis (TB) that afflicted the island as late as the 1960s. Well after the Irish, like other Europeans, had virtually eliminated deaths from many infections diseases, and well after other Europeans dramatically reduced the impact of TB on their populations, thousands of Irish people died of the disease each year, and many more survived with badly impaired health.

Tuberculosis held a special place of horror not just for its ubiquity, but for who it affected and how. Most infectious diseases preyed primarily on the very young or the very old. TB could strike anyone, but teenagers and young adults comprised a large share of the afflicted. In contrast to most infectious diseases, then, TB struck down those just starting out in life. Most infectious diseases also killed quickly, if at all, and those they spared did not suffer serious long-term consequences. Death from TB, on the other hand, was a lingering, long-term affair, and TB's survivors could be badly impaired: crippled, with scarred lungs, hard-pressed to find a mate or to earn an income.

Surprising, then, that TB in Ireland has never been the subject of a detailed, full-length historical study. Greta Jones's book is thus most welcome. A contribution to the Wellcome Series in the History of Medicine, the study's aim is to survey the development of the TB epidemic in the second half of the nineteenth century, and especially to explore the various attempts to contend with it. Jones emphasizes the medical and institutional responses to the problem, but along the way she provides a solid overview of the disease's incidence within Ireland, and discusses various explanations for why the problem was so bad in this one part of the British Isles.

TB affected virtually every Irish community to some extent, but it was especially bad in urban areas and in the textile mills of the industrializing north. The remarkable prevalence of the disease among Irish emigrants to the United States helped support the notion that TB (or at least proclivity to it) was genetic, but with Koch's discoveries in the 1880s, the medical community at least came to understand that TB was caused by a bacterium. That discovery explained why tuberculosis was so common in overcrowded housing in both rural and urban areas, and why the damp, poorly ventilated textile mills were especially good at spreading infection.

Jones focuses on what set Ireland apart: once the medical basis of the disease was understood, other European countries undertook strenuous, systematic efforts to reduce its incidence; Ireland did not, at least until the 1950s. The obstacles were many, ranging from the country's inability to afford the more expensive remedies that were in use on the continent, to nationalist, sectarian, and party-political squabbles within the medical community and later within the governments of both the six and the twenty-six counties. Some of the problems were the Irish themselves. The most obvious prophylactic measure, strict segregation of the infected, struck many people as cruel and the infected themselves as a sort of social death.

Jones succeeds admirably in calling attention to both the importance of TB in Ireland's recent history, and to the many ways that this history can be used as a lens in studies of other issues. Her efforts highlight the need for several further, more detailed studies. One important arena is the actual incidence of the disease: the relative impact on males and females, on the rural and urban, on rich and poor, etc. A first step here would be to query the accuracy of the death-rates reported by the Registrar General, and on which she and others (myself included) have relied. The birth-rates reported by the Registrar-General are known to be badly deficient until the 1890s, grossly understating the number of births in many rural areas. The apparent rise in births the Registrar General's figures suggest reflected not increased fertility, but better reporting of births.[1] Might something similar have happened with tuberculosis? That is, some of the apparent rise in the disease in the late nineteenth century might reflect better record-keeping rather than a worsening situation. To follow a different line of thought, many historians, myself included, think that much of what was genuinely distinctive about late nineteenth-century Ireland reflected the enormous emigration of that and earlier periods. Those who remained in Ireland were those who did not want to emigrate — or could not emigrate. Might this have a role in the apparently enormous impact of TB in Ireland? If the sick were less likely to emigrate, then some of Ireland's distinctiveness in this respect might reflect the force of emigration, not infection. At the very least a detailed demographic study is in order.

Another path for study would be to use the ineffective efforts against TB until the 1950s to further probe some well-worn themes in the history of the post-partition Irish states. One theme Jones suggests is sectarian conflict in the six counties, and the Roman Catholic Church's efforts to cement its role in the twenty-six counties. Party politics also played a role. As a leading figure in the Free State and later Republic's medical service, Dr. James Deeny was pivotal in the formulation of the government's efforts to eradicate TB. But his efforts were partly undone by his clear (and mutual) enmity towards Dr. Noel Browne, who was Minister of Health in the Republic's first government. The conflict was partly one of class, with the well-off Deeny more comfortable with the status quo than was Browne, who had been raised in tough circumstances. The conflict also reflected personal histories: Browne himself had suffered from the disease, and lost family members to it. He could hardly credit the government's hitherto half-hearted efforts when he knew the consequences of that policy all too well. And Deeny, his memoirs suggest, also found Browne insufficiently nationalistic. Deeny attributes to Browne a vociferous attack on the Fianna Fáil government's health policy, and insinuates that Browne's membership in the new Clann na Poblachta coloured his methods if not his motives.[2] Browne's efforts were largely successful, but one wonders how many more such conflicts frustrated earlier efforts against TB.

1 Cormac Ó Gráda, 'New Evidence on the Fertility Transition in Ireland 1880–1911', Demography, 28, 4 (1991), 535–48

2 James Deeny, To Cure and to Care: Memoirs of a Chief Medical Officer (Dublin, 1989), 162–64

Jones provides a clear overview of tuberculosis's history in Ireland. Her study points to the importance of this epidemic in modern Irish history, and to the need for more detailed studies to fully understand its causes, impact, and end.

Timothy W. Guinnane
Yale University

Semicolonial Joyce
Edited by David Attridge and Marjorie Howes
Cambridge: Cambridge University Press, 2000
x + 269 pages. ISBN 0-521-66628-7

Ireland's Others:
Gender and Ethnicity in Irish Literature and Popular Culture
Critical Conditions 10
Elizabeth Butler Cullingford
Cork: Field Day and Cork University Press, 2001
xi + 304 pages. ISBN 1-859-18251-8

Irish and Postcolonial Writing:
History, Theory, Practice
Edited by Glenn Hooper and Colin Graham
Basingstoke: Palgrave Macmillan, 2002
viii + 265 pages. ISBN 0-33392-966-7

Gaelic Gothic:
Race, Colonization, and Irish Culture
Luke Gibbons
Galway: Arlen House, 2004
96 pages. ISBN 1-90363-139-4

In 1982 the late Edward Said wrote about the phenomenon of 'travelling theory'. Said's argument was that all too often when 'radical' cultural and literary theory 'travels' from one political, intellectual and institutional location to another — Said's example is Lukács's great theory of reification and totality — it undergoes a kind of declension and moves from being an insurrectionary weapon to being an academic tool. In the recent Irish context, the major 'travelling theory' has been so-called the postcolonial theory with which Said's own name has been associated, and the overdue question must be: what has been the fate of this travelling theory here?

In the volumes under consideration in this review, we witness a number of kinds of engagement. In the essay collection edited by Glenn Hooper and Colin Graham, *Irish and Postcolonial Writing,* we find a book that perhaps demonstrates a healthy degree of metacritical unease in both its rather peculiar name, and in its structure, which is divided into sections entitled 'Theories', 'Comparisons' and 'Readings'. In *Semicolonial Joyce,* edited by Marjorie Howes and Derek Attridge, again, the title uses Joyce's own language to flag the degree to which the editors and authors acknowledge the partial fit between Joyce's career and writings, and postcolonial theory. Elizabeth Butler Cullingford's volume of essays, *Ireland's Others: Gender and Ethnicity in Irish Literature and Popular Culture,* in its title provocatively declares its intention of examining that Ireland or Irish culture have 'Othered', women and ethnic minorities, instead of treading the more familiar ground of Ireland's status as 'Other' itself. Luke Gibbons's essay, *Gaelic Gothic: Race, Colonization, and Irish Culture,* arguably treads that more familiar ground, but does so with an unusual degree of philosophical sophistication and breadth of reference, as well as bringing Irish culture into the realm of the colonial Gothic.

The Hooper and Graham volume opens with a useful and cogent introduction by Hooper, which traces both the history of that amorphous discourse, 'postcolonial theory', and also examines the ways that this discourse has gradually intersected with Irish literary and cultural studies. This is a much-needed exercise, ably executed. Theoretical essays by Graham, Richard Kirkland and Shakir Mustapha follow. Of these, that by Kirkland is the strongest, examining the complex and conflicted figure of Roger Casement and the ways that his career and its interpretation by subsequent writers — Yeats, Dora Sigerson, Lucy McDiarmid, David Rudkin — might complicate Irish postcolonial theorizing. Colin Graham's essay on the 'textual fetish' of nineteenth-century Irish writing is a formidable exercise in theory, drawing on Freud, Bhabha and Bakhtin; but it seems really to stand more as a prelude to further work than as a fully worked-out argument. Mustapha's essay on revisionism seems to add little to this perennial debate. Moving into the section of the book on 'Comparisons', we find some interesting essays, but 'comparisons' that are loose to the point of lacking much utility. So Tim McLoughlin's essay comparing Maria Edgeworth and Doris Lessing as 'settler writers' seems unhistorical and without much sense of context; and Joshua Esty's essay on scatology and excremental thematics in Joyce and Beckett, and in Wole Soyinka and Ayi Kwei Armah, seems intelligent and interesting but fails fully to press the actual points of comparison. David Johnson's essay on Lady Anne Barnard ambitiously focuses analysis of the evolution of British nationalism through her experiences and attitudes to rebellion in both Ireland and the Cape. Lyn Innes draws out the analogies between the roughly contemporaneous discourses of Orientalism and Celticism. The final section of the book, 'Readings', offers Hooper's intelligent and cogent re-reading of J. G. Farrell's Irish fiction in the light of both his Empire fiction and of postcolonial theory, cleverly forcing the question as to why readings of Farrell as an 'Anglo-Irish' writer appear to have precluded viewing him as a writer of the end of empire more generally.

Semicolonial Joyce offers more confident assertions of Irish postcoloniality, and some virtuoso readings. Seamus Deane, whose 1982 essay 'Joyce and Nationalism' helped to pioneer the current historicist/postcolonial emphasis in Joyce studies, here offers a splendid essay on *Dubliners*. 'Dead Ends: Joyce's Finest Moments' is an exemplary exercise in concision and intelligence. David Lloyd's essay on Irish masculinity and temperance nationalism focuses on Joyce's story 'Counterparts', for a reading which uses theory powerfully to focus close reading. Joseph Valente's essay on 'the double-bind of Irish manhood' uses the 'Cyclops' episode of *Ulysses* to provide a meticulous teasing-out of issues of gender, masculinity and the Victorian discourse of 'manliness'. Essays by Enda Duffy and Marjorie Howes focus on a still relatively-neglected theme in Irish literary studies — the politics and representation of space in cultural forms. Katherine Mullin offers an excellent and comprehensively-researched background to 'Eveline', locating that story at the nexus of fears about the white slave trade. Luke Gibbons, in a characteristically sparkling essay, moves from the use of the term 'paralysis' by Filson Young in a 1903 essay on Ireland, by way of analysis of hysteria in Europe more generally, to a discussion of the representation in Joyce of the domestic sphere, and the suppressed energies it is barely able to contain. And notably, Emer Nolan offers a thoughtful and engaged critique of Lloyd's earlier work on Joyce, particularly his essay

'Adulteration and the Nation'. Nolan's work is valuable for its metacritical turn, its willingness to examine whether a particular theoretical model really fits an Irish text, and what the intellectual and even political consequences of that model might turn out to be.

Luke Gibbons's *Gaelic Gothic* is a useful addition to readings of the Irish Gothic such as those of Terry Eagleton, Seamus Deane, Siobhán Kilfeather and W. J. McCormack. Where Gibbons is most impressive, and perhaps advances further than these scholars, is in his interest in developing the argument that in the case of Ireland, racial discourse intersected with the Gothic, in identifying the *invisible* degeneracy of the Irish. Gibbons then brilliantly traces this heritage all the way from Renaissance portrayals of the Irish to variations on this theme, including its political reversal in the late nineteenth century (where Ireland is seen as the victim of vampiric British taxation, for example).

In these books, as with Elizabeth Butler Cullingford's *Ireland's Others* (in spite of that volume's tendency towards political caution and a residual Leavisite ambivalence about even 'applying' theory), we find extensive evidence of the energies that Irish literary and cultural studies have gained from their intersection with postcolonial theory over the last ten years or so. What we nevertheless find in far lesser measure is a sense of the real politics that this most 'political' of literary-theoretical discourses works within. In spite of the bravura deployment of rhetorics of geopolitics and of the colonial state, Irish postcolonial criticism seems as yet generally unwilling to turn its batteries on its own discursive locations, institutions, and worldly affiliations. Some will say that that is a task for another day, but this reviewer is not so sure.

Conor McCarthy
Mater Dei Institute of Education
Dublin City University

Irish Orientalism:
A Literary and Intellectual History
Joseph Lennon
Syracuse, New York: Syracuse University Press, 2004
xxxi + 256 pages. ISBN 0-8156-3044-1

In a 1996 reading of Oliver Goldsmith's *Citizen of the World* (1762), Tao Zhijian strongly criticized the Irish author's Chinese letters for their typically Western caricature of the cultural and political stagnation of China. Goldsmith's imperial facetiousness was exemplified, for Zhijian, in a passage where Goldsmith's Chinese commentator writes to his Peking correspondent that, though he always expects accounts of social revolutions in China, he discovers that it is 'only the rapidity of my own motion gives an imaginary swiftness to objects which are in some measure immovable'. However, exactly the same sentiments are expressed in Goldsmith's 1757 letter to brother-in-law Daniel Hodson, still residing in the Irish midlands: 'it was the rapidity of my own motion,' he supposed, 'that gave an imaginary one to objects really at rest'. Goldsmith understood that Chinese and Irish realities were, for the exile in London, irretrievably mediated. As such they became fungible, mutually allegorical places of origin for the critic of imperialist Britain.

Goldsmith's disguise is just one instance of the general ploy according to which Irish authors could allegorize their nationality and anti-imperialist grievances through oriental and pseudo-oriental devices. In reproducing certain stereotypes they could inveigle themselves into imperialist discourse in order subtly to effect its undoing. Zhijian's oversight, however, demonstrates an abiding danger of the post-colonial critique, and much of the blame for undifferentiated or wilful 'occidentalism' has, rather unfairly, been directed towards the influence of Edward Said's landmark *Orientalism* (1978). In his introduction Joseph Lennon includes a concise survey of the theoretical issues and arguments attending the book's legacy, and enumerates the ways in which Irish orientalism corrupts and complicates Anglo-French norms. Like Lisa Lowe's *Critical Terrains* (1991) before it, this is a stimulating and constructive addition to the theoretical and scholarly body of work begun by Said.

'Long before it was treated as Celtic, Irish culture was linked to the 'Orient'; the link, writes Lennon, was based in their being perceived as similarly antithetical to 'modern, enlightened Europe' (xv). The link between Ireland and the Orient would be further developed by cultural nationalists who 'created anti-imperial and cross-colonial narratives for this ancient semiotic connection' (xvii). The dominant strains in

European orientalism, as delineated by Said, were French and British; Irish orientalism, Lennon demonstrates, has a distinct history which stems from its colonial predicament. Accordingly, Irish authors deployed a greater degree of 'allegory and linguistic play' (xxi) through which nationalist and decolonizing sentiments might be voiced.

The book is helpfully divided into two broad but coherent sections. Its first, diachronic, part is concerned with Irish orientalism before the Celtic Revival; the synchronic second part deals with the Revival itself. Lennon gives a satisfying chronological account of legends advancing the Greco-Roman and Oriental origins of the Irish, and describes the development of pseudo-historical origin myths in Irish antiquarianism and philology. As origin legends were emptied through the late eighteenth and early nineteenth centuries, the Romantic Irish orientalisms of Lady Morgan, Thomas Moore, and James Clarence Mangan turned speculative weakness into allegorical, critical, and literary capital. This literariness took on a mystical and occult augmentation in the early part of the twentieth century. Lennon's Revival is a stimulating account of 'cultural syncretism' in W. B. Yeats's Celtic Orient, in George Russell's orientalist theosophy, in James Stephens's 'eastern sensibility' and, finally, in James Cousins's political solidarity with India. If there is to be a criticism, it is that the non-Revival counterpoint of James Joyce's East might have been included more substantially.

For Stephens, Ireland could best visualize itself by looking at other nations. In drawing analogies between itself and the Orient, Ireland could discover some of the imperialist iniquities of representation to which it was victim. Irish orientalism, then, was less a representational subordination of the Eastern 'periphery' to the European 'core' than it was a knowing sphere of 'periphery to periphery' interaction. As an account of this phenomenon, Lennon's book is empirically exhaustive and theoretically sophisticated. *Irish Orientalism* is an important and admirable contribution to Irish literary and intellectual history, and to the study of orientalism generally.

Michael Griffin
University of Limerick

Revolutionary Dublin, 1795–1801:
The Letters of Francis Higgins to Dublin Castle
Edited by Thomas Bartlett
Dublin: Four Courts Press, 2004
480 pages. ISBN 1-85182-754-4

Francis Higgins was the proprietor of one of the English government's Irish newspapers, *The Freeman's Journal*, and one of its principle informants about first the Catholic Committee, and then the United Irishmen. Besides providing information, he recruited informers, he placed spies, he raised a mob, he caused one to be dispersed, he rigged a jury, he recruited thugs to make people take their hats off at the theatre during the singing of 'God Save the King,' and, decisively, he helped to locate and capture Lord Edward Fitzgerald. He began life as an errand boy, rose to a shoeblack, learned to forge documents and became a fraudster (he could never quite shake his lifelong moniker as 'the Sham Squire' after deceiving a young woman of many acres to become his bride). He was familiar with the brothel and gambling scenes of Dublin. He was an amusing dinner guest, and a liberal host himself. He rode about town and environs in his own carriage.

Thomas Bartlett, professor of modern Irish history at University College Dublin, and a brilliant historian of the military, political, and intelligence aspects of the 1798 rebellion, introduces these letters and annotates them. He explains how the government's intelligence rose from Post Office interceptions, Customs House surveillance, military intelligence, bookshops, newspaper editors, and finally from individual Castle informants like Higgins who was a municipal type comparable to Vidoq (Paris) or Colquhoun (London). Higgins was Catholic, persistent, loyal, sacrificing, and apparently possessed of judgement unclouded by bigotry, though his property interests were a source both of strengths as a spy (for information he forgave rent), and limitations which are not explored. The annotations are exact, scrupulous, and informative about the individuals Higgins mentions. Bartlett avoids the temptation of the raconteur, he reports rather than judges or amuses. The notes make this volume an essential reference for students of the rebellion.

These could be letters sent directly from hell, if we accepted Higgins's vocabulary at face value.

Sometimes he settles on a more mundane register — 'set of seditionists,' 'incendiary republicans,' 'the murderous crew,' 'the armed circuitous horde' — and once in these seven years he adopts more descriptive, ideological designations — Paineites, Democrats, Levellers, and United Irishmen. But by and large he prefers to refer to hell: 'the present infernal crew,' 'the infernal brotherhood,' 'the infernal banditti,' 'the infernal confederacy,' 'the infernal fraternity,' 'the infernal band,' 'the infernal society,' 'the infernal constitution,' 'the infernal banditti of conspirators,' 'the revolutionary infernal crew,' or 'the jacobinical infernal confederates.' It is a tic of his writing. Perhaps it began as a way of pleasing his superiors at Dublin Castle, or perhaps it arose from a fear of losing his properties. But it was widely practised at the time by those who were reactionaries.

His standard repetitions would be tiresome were his observations about the Protean organization of the United Irish not so cool and detached. He identifies the shifting 'splits' of the cellular organizations of the United Irish: a Druid's Lodge is a front; the Houses of Call of the weavers and other skilled workers were doubtful; the Telegraph Club was radical, and Freemason lodge number 21 was another one of the masks of sedition. He was sceptical of all lottery and charity clubs and he had a healthy fear of the 'five committees of silence'. Funeral societies were subversive; the 'Brotherhood' at Stephen. St. Chapel was doubtful; the Prisoner's Relief Committee was subversive as was a group formed to support a Charity School, readers at a Public Library, 'Swadlers' or Methodists in an evening prayer group, Furniture Clubs, and Watch, Clock, and Plate Societies. On examination, Higgins's 'inferno' consisted of institutions of prayer, debate, reading, schooling, banking, employment, hire purchase, burial, relief, conviviality, scepticism, and eating. Not to mention, which he does not, football or hurling! There is thus considerable overlap between the plebeian organizations of civil society and the clandestine organization of revolutionary independence.

In addition to the frequent tic, there is a single slip. On 8 March 1798, he wrote, 'There will be no insurrection or rising of the lower ordeal of the people on Patrick's Day. I am ashamed to write more, I am so sleepy.' He meant to write of the 'lower orders,' but here his mask falls off for a moment. It is not even quite clear why he is ashamed. The tic is a defence against the repressed conscience. Later he inveighs against the profiteers. 'It would be more than presumption in me to guess at the services! the utility! or the cause! why the government permit a set of men, under the pretext of making corn a speculative article of commercial dealing, to sport with the wants of the people!'

He knew the small deeply-mortgaged property holders who hoped for a revolutionary 'clearing off'. Some of his own rural tenantry expected land 'to be their own and divided equally'. He quoted the United propaganda, 'all men desirous of recovering the property of their forefathers', or the 'antient rights of Ireland'. He owned tenements and manufactories in Dublin's Liberties where the textile workers were concentrated, and he became a quiet advocate for them after the failure of the 1798 uprising, at least to the extent of supplying the Castle with information against the monopolists and forestallers responsible for the high price of bread. That there was no Dublin insurrection in 1798 among the lower orders who afterwards instead suffered greater ordeals than ever, became a source of shame to such as Thomas Russell, Robert Emmet, and Edward Despard, if not to the 'Sham Squire' who died in 1801.

Peter Linebaugh
University of Toledo, Ohio

Irish Political Prisoners, 1848–1922:
Theatres of War
Seán McConville
London: Routledge, 2003
xii + 820 pages. ISBN 0-415-21991-4

Simply read as a chronicle relating political prisoners to seventy years of politics, this book is a singular contribution to Irish Studies; it succeeds as a history, however, by leaving the implicit and explicit tensions between official records and the stories of the individual Irish political prisoners intact. The vast research that comprises what the author calls 'a history of politics, penology and administration written to the standards of scholarship and within its conventions' defers to its institutional content. The

form of the volume adapts a contrasting tone as the narrative history of a succession of rebels is organized from 'episodes, characters, sayings, heroes, villains, fools, sages, tragedies and even some comedy.' The book works as a history by preserving rather than eliding the conflict between the bureaucratic density of official records and the more personal narrative sources — the unrealized costs of a more concentrated analysis of the tactics, technologies and absurdities of the prison are outweighed by the benefits of a good story, well-told. The 'theatres of war' are translated into the composition of the work itself with sound scholarship guided by the principle 'the human element should never be forgotten as the final reference'.

Seán McConville, a legal scholar and prison historian, brings a distinguished resumé to this overwhelming but neglected field of inquiry. Writing from his own principled perspective, he doles out ethical and legal critiques of prisoners, their sympathizers, prison administrators and government officials. The study works with a permissive, inclusive, and flexible definition of the prisoner of conscience. With these ghostly demarcations resolved, the work transforms the exceptions McConville discovered while writing the previous two volumes *(History of English Prison Administration Vol. I: 1750–1877* and *English Local Prisons, 1860–1900: Next Only to Death)* into the story of Irish political prisoners, including the gentlemen prisoners of Young Ireland, the Fenians, Michael Davitt, and the Dynamitards. Much of the book is spent addressing the Easter Rising and the dizzying bureaucratic shuffling in its wake, among them the internment of 1,775 republicans at Frongoch; the imprisonment of Constance Markiewicz, Maud Gonne and Kathleen Clarke in Holloway; and the detention of Michael Collins, Eamon de Valera and other familiar figures of the Anglo-Irish War.

Some may mistakenly reserve judgement on this volume until its sequel, *Irish Political Prisoners, 1920–1998,* offers a more contemporary perspective. Whatever one's sensibilities, the depth and detail of scholarship herein ensure this will be a volume to contend with for the foreseeable future. While studies of groups of Irish prisoners and the better-known personas in this period often address prison as a component, *Irish Political Prisoners, 1848–1922: Theatres of War* positions the many iterations of institutional incarceration at the centre of the volume — making one wonder why this has not been done before. This book leaves the reader with many questions, perhaps substantially more than before it was begun. But the inquiries are refined by a clearer sense of the contradictions and conflicts that make the prison and the prisoner crucial, if discrete, fields of study.

Sean T. O'Brien
University of Notre Dame

Verse in English from Tudor and Stuart Ireland
Andrew Carpenter
Cork: Cork University Press, 2003
xx + 598 pages. ISBN 1-85918-354-9

Andrew Carpenter's superb anthology stands as a fitting a sequel to *Verse in English in Eighteenth-century Ireland* (Cork, 1998). Like the earlier volume, it reproduces an admirable range of verse composed in English that Carpenter's masterly introduction then situates in a wider historical and literary context. *Verse in English from Tudor and Stuart Ireland* draws on manuscript archives and printed materials (often unique copies) housed in the Public Records Office in Kew, the British Library, the Bodleian Library, Oxford, the Royal Irish Academy, Trinity College, Dublin, and the Beinecke Library, Yale University, New Haven. The Yale material is particularly noteworthy. Over a period of forty years James Butler, first duke of Ormond, assembled a remarkable 'literary scrap book' of fifty-nine manuscripts that include copies of verse, anagrams, satires, elegies, panegyrics, prose, speeches, pictorial and other addresses. Of these Yale verses twenty-two are in Latin, one is in French, one in Irish (a panegyric written by an Irish Franciscan in 1680) and the remainder are in English. Interestingly, two-thirds of the items that Ormond collected date from the period before 1660. Given that so little verse has survived from Ireland in the 1640s and many of these manuscripts appear to be unique (and certainly never appeared in print), these items are of particular significance.

The verse selected for inclusion in the anthology is diverse and embraces low and high culture: almanacs, anthems, ballads, carols, ditties are reproduced alongside anagrams, elegies, funerary inscriptions, panegyrics and conventional poetry. Carpenter has also uncovered the text of an early masque, performed in 1610 at Rathfarnham castle to celebrate the marriage of Lady Cassandra Ridgeway and Sir Francis Willoughby. While some of the writers whose verse is included are well known — Sir John Davies, Payne Fischer, Sir William Petty, William Shirley, Edmund Spenser, Richard Stanihurst, Jonathan Swift, Nahum Tate, and the earls of Orrery and Roscommon — others are not. They include female writers (Katherine Philips and Lady Ann Southwell), priests and preachers (Edmund Arawacker, John Bale, Cornelius O'Mahony, Jeremy Taylor, Faithfull Teate and Luke Wadding), together with verse composed by doctors, lawyers, soldiers, teachers and, excitingly, those from the 'middling sorts' (whose work, sadly, often lacks attribution).

Like the writers, the nature of the verse is varied and reflects the priorities, preoccupations and perceptions of the religious and ethnic groups living in sixteenth- and seventeenth-century Ireland who chose to express themselves through the medium of English. Some of the poems bristle with humour and satire, others with learning and sophistication, with bawdiness and sex, with love, with desperation and despair and so on. For example, Richard Nugent's sonnets, which were published in London in 1604, recapture Nugent's unrequited love for his Old English sweet heart, Cynthia. The anonymous 'The Life and Death of John Atherton' luridly recounts the crimes — adultery, buggery, incest and rape — allegedly committed by the New English bishop of Waterford (he was tried and executed in December 1640). Equally salacious is another anonymous poem collected by Petty (and probably dating form the 1670s), which vividly relates the antics of Dublin prostitutes and their titled clients (including the earls of Ardglass, Arran, and Drogheda, together with Viscounts Blessington and Galmoy and Sir William Talbot).

The equivalent of modern-day tabloids, bawdy verses such as these illuminate aspects of everyday life in early modern Ireland otherwise lost and provide invaluable insights into popular (and élite) culture. Equally fascinating is the way in which many of these writings illustrate the levels of interaction between native and newcomer and in particular the extent of cultural and linguistic cross-pollination. For instance, the influence of the Irish language can be detected in a hunting song, 'Ye merry boyes all that live in Fingale' (c.1634). The ravages of the rebellions and wars of the sixteenth and seventeenth centuries are well covered. Sir John Harington's 'Of the warres in Ireland' captures in verse his experiences during the Nine Years War as a cavalry commander under the earl of Essex. In a similar vein, 'England's Hope against Irish Hate' forcefully depicts the Irish as barbaric rebels and murderous traitors. This anti-Irish rhetoric also characterizes the verse written by Protestants during the wars of the 1640s which is reproduced in the anthology alongside verse composed by Catholic writers. For example, the confederate 'lawyer-poets' — Sir Edmund Butler, Oliver Martin, Sir Richard Blake and Richard Bellings (who continued Sidney's *Archadia* into a sixth book during his years as a student at Lincoln's Inns) — use verse to trumpet their loyalty to the Stuart cause and to the Ormond dynasty. The Catholic verse of the 1640s also documents key political and military episodes: the death of Sir Charles Coote (1642), the siege of Duncannon (1645), the battle of Benburb (1646), the First and Second Ormond Peaces (1646 and 1649), and the execution of Charles I (1649).

A short review such as this can not begin to do justice to the richness of the verse which this anthology reproduces. The poems themselves, combined with Carpenter's superb introduction, have already proved invaluable as teaching tools. Equally important, topics worthy of further research and areas that would particularly benefit from cross-disciplinary collaboration (such as representation, royalism, literary patronage or discussions of honour and of virtue) are clearly identified throughout the anthology. One can only hope that Carpenter's two anthologies will inspire companion volumes — one on 'verse in Irish' and the other on 'verse in Latin', which was after all the *lingua franca* of the early modern world.

Jane H. Ohlmeyer
Trinity College Dublin

The Irish Face: Redefining the Irish Portrait
Fintan Cullen
London: National Portrait Gallery
Publications, 2004
240 pages. ISBN 1-85514-290-2

The Irish Face is one of the handsomest books on an art-related topic to have appeared on the Irish publication lists to date. Published by the National Portrait Gallery in London, the production values have all the hallmarks of serious institutional support and, as one would expect from Fintan Cullen, the methodological approach is new in Irish art historical writing. The book offers the first and most stimulating and well-researched resumé of the issues and debates surrounding the foundation of the national portrait collections in Ireland. It provides a rich contextual background to a number of celebrity portraits alongside the first serious study of the issues surrounding a hitherto ignored body of reportage sketches of Irish peasants. It is a tantalizing book. It bristles with potential, posing a series of challenging questions such as what makes a portrait an *Irish* portrait, what gives a portrait an *Irish* face, what constitutes a *national* portrait. And we know from the outset that these questions will not be answered simplistically. Cullen, himself, tells us that it will not be about Celtic physiognomy, nor will it offer a traditional art historical outline of Irish portraiture. What he is after is Irish subject matter expressed through the portrait.

That clear statement did not prevent this reader from being confused at times about the presence of portraits of King George IV or, for that matter, the Elizabethan adventurer Thomas Lee, who was not Irish and never even visited the country, but he did dress up in the gear. They had a relationship with Ireland of one kind or another, mainly political. Kings George IV and V certainly had Irish connections but did they impact on the nature of their portraits and, if so, how? If the face is *Irish* because the person it belonged to had a connection with Ireland then might not John F. Kennedy, or the Pope, have been better choices, or, to help the gender balance, the Virgin Mary? At least their images were displayed all over Ireland for decades while Thomas Lee's face was unknown in this country until now.

The book aims to be something other than a history of Irish portraiture yet at times that is precisely what it seems to be. In a preamble to one of the most innovative sections of the book, a discussion of Irish peasants at the Parnell Commission, the author says, 'Any discussion of the genre of portraiture as an artistic genre must involve exploring the full range of output, rich, poor, known and unknown' (190). Inevitably there will be differences of opinion about the choices that represent that range but the most serious criticism of this book hangs on those choices. With only one exception, the images in the book are all academic, realistic and conventional. Apart from a self-portrait by Louis le Brocquy there is not a single expressionist portrait in the 140-odd portraits discussed. That might not matter if it did not mean the exclusion of Brian Maguire's subversive portraits of prisoners, hospital inmates, travellers, and the marginalized. Maguire successfully undermines the hierarchical and exclusive nature of the genre through his mode of presentation and his empowerment of his sitters and went on to give his practice an international context with his portraits of the disappeared in São Paolo in 1998. At another remove Sydney Nolan's shocking portraits of miners in Australia or the Irish exiles in his *Wild Geese* series provide another powerful counter-statement to the conquerors and colonized in the book. Maguire and Nolan challenge the celebrity hold on portraiture within the terms of the genre. The peasant 'portraits', fascinating though they might be, reinforce it.

Cullen acknowledges the gender imbalance in his book, claiming that it reflects the contents of the collections of the National Portrait Gallery in London and the National Gallery of Ireland. That is no excuse. To omit Sarah Purser's pastel portrait of Maud Gonne is a mistake on several counts but, to play down the importance of Mary Robinson, by including an attractive but unremarkable domestic portrait of herself and her husband, rather than representing her as first woman President of Ireland, and influential human rights spokesperson, is perverse. In 147 images in this book approximately 20 women are portrayed. Curiously one of these is Hazel Lavery (not Irish of course), represented in a photograph by Baron Adolf De Meyer but there is no discussion of the face that dominated the modern Irish state through her presence on Irish banknotes. Perhaps that would have been more useful than the information that she may have been the lover of Michael Collins.

Cullen is to be admired for his wide reading of contemporary literature but his analysis of the visual object is less rigorous. This reader found the discussion of James Barry's *Self-Portrait* in the National Gallery of Ireland, which affirms a position already rehearsed by Luke Gibbons, fascinating but was not at all convinced by Cullen's reading of the painting. To support the view that Barry makes a powerful statement about the victimization of the Roman Catholic artist in early nineteenth-century Britain in this work, Cullen calls attention to another Barry painting — his portraits of Edmund Burke and himself as *Ulysses and Companion Fleeing from the Cave of Polyphemus*. Cullen claims that Barry, the companion in this picture, is really Christ, simply because he has sweat on his brow. No artist then, not even one as self-obsessed as Barry, would have portrayed Christ as the junior companion, looking to his mentor for a rescue plan.

In another instance Cullen critiques Dorothy Walker's interpretation of Edward McGuire's portrait of Seamus Heaney, in which she described the sitter as a besieged nationalist poet. Instead Cullen sees the portrait as 'less an image of "fending off ... attackers", and more one of a rising Irish literary figure in an era of growing confidence in the country's international potential' (15). Walker had the sitter's cramped position to support her interpretation whereas Cullen contests it on the basis that the portrait was executed in 1973, when Ireland joined the EEC and that Heaney's sideburns look relaxed in contrast to the window frame behind him. The timing of the portrait is as relevant for one interpretation as the other; is wavy hair enough to swing the reading?

'Portraits declare a history,' Cullen asserts, and 'it is that history, the role of the portrait in explaining the past that concerns this book.' If the history of Ireland and Irish art was confined to men, and to hierarchical approaches to art-making, then this book would go a good way to meeting his concern. Happily the Irish face and the national portrait are more inclusive.

Catherine Marshall
Irish Museum of Modern Art

The Continuing Story of Irish Television Drama:
Tracking the Tiger
Helena Sheehan
Dublin: Four Courts Press, 2004
x + 178 pages. ISBN 1-85182-688-2

In 1987 Helena Sheehan published, *Irish Television Drama: A Society and Its Stories,* a pioneering study of Irish television drama over a twenty-five year period, from the first broadcasts of RTÉ in 1962 through 1987. *The Continuing Story of Irish Television Drama: Tracking the Tiger* picks up where the earlier study left off, now tracking that popular media form for another fifteen years, through 2002. Her new volume belongs to a Four Courts Press series that includes Richard Pine's *2Rn and the Origins of Irish Radio* (2002) and Iarfhlaith Watson's *Broadcasting in Irish: Minority Language, Radio, Television and Identity* (2003). Recently John Horgan completed an addition to the series, addressing the evolution of current affairs programming in both Irish radio and television.

At first glance Sheehan's short book reads as a collection of plot summaries of the plays produced by RTÉ and a number of independent production companies. But despite her somewhat pedestrian presentation of evidence, Sheehan contributes significantly to our understanding of television's role in Irish society by providing invaluable data and making discriminating judgements about recent media production.

As she completed her first book in 1987, Sheehan voiced high expectation for Irish television drama. She hoped that contemporary debates about pressure for change within society would enable RTÉ to offer dramatic programming dealing 'with dilemmas at the cutting edge of contemporary experience, drama that would stop ending up in conventional cul de sacs'. However in her new work, she argues that the authority's record over the past fifteen years has been uneven and disappointing. Irish television drama during this period has more often than not has been 'too derivative, too myopic, [and] too mundane'.

Despite her disappointment with the overall quality of programming, Sheehan notes some exceptions to that record — television dramas that have engaged viewers in dialogue about topical and often controversial contemporary issues. She singles out *Family,* written for television by Roddy Doyle, co-produced by RTÉ and the BBC in 1994, as provoking considerable debate about social problems Irish television had traditionally avoided. A dark exploration of urban working-class life, this four-part series depicted a dysfunctional family headed by an abusive father, portrayed as a menacing threat to his wife and children. *Black Day at Blackrock,* written and directed by Gerard Stembridge in 2001, is also singled out for addressing contemporary issues in the era of the Celtic Tiger. Based on an actual incident, the drama is set in a small Irish town thrown into turmoil when the government decided to settle thirty refugees temporarily there. It was aired during a period of vigorous debate about Ireland's response — including fear and racism — to the swift transformations taking place in a once profoundly homogeneous society. Another television drama singled out for praise is *The Truth About Clare,* also directed and produced by Stembridge. This dramatic programme followed a young twenty-six-year-old married woman from Cork, who was expecting her third child. Travelling first to Dublin to stay with an old school friend and then to London for an abortion, she returns home to Ireland and commits suicide. Sheehan argues that *The Truth About Clare* succeeded because, not simply an 'issue-based drama', it ambitiously explored a range of views about an emotionally charged subject animating much debate and discussion.

In addressing the uneven production history of recent television drama, Sheehan contributes to the growing field of media studies. *The Continuing Story of Irish Television Drama: Tracking the Tiger* will be an important resource for interdisciplinary students interested in the complexities of broadcasting in a rapidly changing society.

Rob Savage
Boston College

Gaelic Prose in the Irish Free State, 1922–1939
Philip O'Leary
Dublin: University College Dublin Press, 2004
xi + 753 pages. ISBN 1-904558-13-5

The revival of the Irish language has a mixed track record. Its primary stated objective, formulated in Douglas Hyde's lecture on 'The Necessity of De-Anglicizing Ireland', was to rescue Irish from extinction and to have it oust English as Ireland's premier language. Those ambitions were not overly far-fetched: language revivals occurred at the time in the Baltic area (Finnish, Estonian, Latvian, Lithuanian, even Ukrainian) as well in the Balkans (Albanian, Macedonian). All these languages had degraded by the mid-nineteenth century to a despised and dwindling vernacular of a rustic, underprivileged populace, and all of them have now become the unchallenged national language of sovereign states. In comparison, and even in comparison with the successful revival of regional languages such as Catalan or Galego, the revival of Irish must be considered a failure. Its demise as a living language in daily use was, it is true, arrested and postponed — but only for a while.

However, the language revival had enormous consequences beyond the field of linguistic demographics. It provided an enabling focus for separatist nationalism following the death of Parnell, and became the carrier of a notion of Irishness that motivated political activists and the state which they managed to set up in the teeth of the British empire. As a result, while Irish did not become the dominant daily language in Ireland, it gained enormous prestige as the state's official language and indeed its anthropological justification. No longer the vernacular of illiterate rustics, it was cultivated and consecrated as the main carrier of the nation's moral identity, gaining a status comparable perhaps to Hebrew in worldwide Jewish culture (outside Israel), or Latin in the pre-Vatican II Catholic church: spoken by no-one as a native or daily language, but available to all as a linguistic ambience in more formal or ritual circumstances.

The newly raised status of Irish was expressed in the instruments and protocols of the new state, and suffused the educational system in the early decades of Irish independence. It was perhaps this symbolical, even hieratic investment of the language that worked against its viability. Its new, great dignity ensured its official status in the town halls and schools, but hampered its everyday adoption in the kitchens and garages, of Mullingar and Arklow. Within a society that, although culturally fixated on its national past, was feeling the forces of twentieth-century urbanization and technological innovation, anything like a populist revival of Irish was a lost cause.

Yet again, the Irish language was capable of generating a literature which has produced a remarkable body of important work over the last century. That literature was initially rooted in the Western Gaeltacht, which harboured some extraordinary intellects and traditions, and also provided the capital, Dublin, with an Irish self-image of a prelapsarian, pristinely native-Gaelic populace in the West. Alongside this Gaeltacht base, writing in Irish in the course of the century came to involve writers who by education, profession or situation formed part of the metropolitan atmosphere of European modernism. The two streams — Gaeltacht rootedness and *an domhan mór* — have coexisted throughout the course of Irish literature in the last century until the present day. Only recently has that duality started to lose its edge, now that we're getting blasé about global mobility and postmodern hybridity. Bouzouki-cum-bodhrán, or Country 'n Western in West Kerry, has become normal.

For most of us, literature in Irish is represented by a few Great Names: authors whose works have been translated into English, or who wrote in the two languages, and who are therefore accessible as presences even to those who cannot read Irish with facility. A fragmented cluster of names is current by way of a canon-by-reputation: the Blasket authors, Flann O'Brien, Máirtín Ó Direáin, Máirtín Ó Cadhain, Seán Ó Ríordáin, the Behan of *An Giall*, Nuala Ní Dhomhnaill. Yet these names represent only isolated exponents of what is after all a literary tradition. They are the visible peak, not of an obelisk, but of a pyramid; and its base, broad and wide though it is, is shrouded from our view. Their context, the networks of fellow-authors, readers, publishers, critics, reviews and editors; the positive or negative literary influences they underwent in their formation as writers or poets; the influence they exerted; their quarrels, their careers; in short: their context and source-tradition — all that is hidden from view unless one is oneself involved in Gaelic culture either as a native speaker or at least as a literate reader.

How many of us were even aware of the depth of our ignorance? The twentieth century witnessed the rebirth of a literature which had been pauperized into illiteracy by 1860; but the twentieth-century history of its revived growth has scarcely been written. We had, to be sure, some anthologies, and some surveys — but they often concentrated on poetry, mostly post-1945, and were often written in Irish themselves: the criticism of Seán Ó Tuama or Frank O'Brien for instance. For the rest, an entire literary tradition was untraced in its developments, known only in a few exemplary names. A vague notion of l'Irlande à papa which was summarized and dismissed in the same gesture as 'all the sort of interwar stuff that was published by An Gúm and satirized by Flann O'Brien'.

It is the great achievement of Philip O'Leary to have brought to light, in a comprehensive and even-handed study, this foundational base of twentieth-century Irish-Gaelic literature. O'Leary, who teaches Irish Literature at Boston College, with the true twangy blas of Massachusetts, is the world's acknowledged expert in twentieth-century Irish prose writing — narrative fiction, but also journalism, criticism and the discourse of political and cultural debate. The book under review here is his second major work in presenting this corpus — so central to our understanding of modern Ireland, yet so inaccessible and neglected — to a wider readership. To some extent Gaelic Prose in the Irish Free State, 1922–1939 is a continuation of his earlier, invaluable study (published in 1994) on the attitudes and ideologies of language revivalists in the early twentieth century, The Prose Literature of the Gaelic Revival, 1881–1921.

This is a literary history, and more. O'Leary's main concern is to chart cultural policies and attitudes in an Ireland that owed its independence to the revivalism of Pearse and Griffith, and that felt the need to legitimize itself by the cultivation of its own language and literature. An Gúm fostered Irish authors by facilitating publication, offering them additional employment by a demand for Irish translations of foreign books. The authors themselves, often dedicated language revivalists with close ties to the more important institutions of the new Ireland, had a literary agenda and a cultural idealism which quite spontaneously matched the state's political and ideological outlook: a preoccupation with country life, with the national experience, with the tension between Ireland's heroic past and its modernizing present, with the dubious idea of translating foreign books for Irish readers, with the unsettling proximity of the English language. Above all, it is the history of their self-awareness: all of these authors (and O'Leary gives many quotations to bear out the fact) were conscious that they were creating a 'national literature', and reflected a good deal on this position between heritage and future. These concerns form the thematic subject of the various chapters of O'Leary's voluminous study, which surveys and analyzes hundreds upon hundreds of texts and authors in order to inventorize the corpus and chart the waters.

O'Leary's book has its primary value, then, as a history of the Free State — a cultural history, or intellectual history, or even mentality history, traced through its Gaelic-language writings and literature. Indeed, also a literary history — but literary history as a branch of history-writing, as much as a form of criticism. O'Leary has done for the intellectual and cultural history of early-twentieth-century Ireland what Joe Lee has done in the field of social and political history.

A literary history of the Gaelophone Free State has one problem: much of the stuff dealt with here is simply woeful. O'Leary must have mustered all his irony, benevolence and humour to make it through all those earnest, stodgy narratives and posturings which reek of floor polish, stale incense, the coal scuttle, and rain-dampened tweed jackets: the high-minded reek of a navel-gazing Ireland before the opening of Shannon airport. While wholesale dismissal would not be a good attitude from which to undertake a history, O'Leary cannot really claim to have discovered a Gaelic Virginia Woolf or even a

Gaelic Isaac Bashevis Singer. In many cases he is therefore content to briefly summarize the narratives of literary works in Irish, and saves his space and quotations for the meta-literary discourse: the criticism, the programmes, manifestos and historical assessments. Indeed that remains the focus of his book: the expression of ideals and opinions concerning Ireland, the ideology of Irish writing in the inter-war years. Much more would not have been possible, for these were lean years. The actual flourish of creativity in Irish started in the 1940s, and this book does not reach that far into the century. But O'Leary's survey is indispensable if we want to understand the connection between Irish nostalgic nationalism and Irish modernity, the bridge that spans across the 1920s and 1930s from Patrick Pearse to Máire Mhac an tSaoi.

And were they fools, for all that? By no means. A writer like Liam Ó Rinn, singled out by O'Leary as the 'most erudite, versatile, and enterprising critic writing in Irish at this time', had a clear appreciation of his generation's dilemma:

> The work writers of Irish will have to do is harder for the fact that we still have no great modern literature, and therefore they have nothing available to help them like what is available in so many ways for the apprentice writer of English. There is, for example, no one to judge their first efforts. (189–90)

O'Leary's survey thus raises poetical issues alongside the ideological ones. The generation of '22–'39 had to bootstrap itself from the level of the simple early-revival stories (Séadna, Íosagán) to altogether higher standards, from a separatist agenda to an autonomous national outlook, from the juvenile or learner's register to adult proficiency and mature interests; and all the time, Ireland's prestigious, limelight-stealing talents were working through the medium of English. Within Gaelic, the most fecund living traditions, as well as the most versatile and poetically flexible language, were anchored in those parts of the country and those parts of society which were least in touch with metropolitan modernity. The greatest themes for literary inspiration lay in the past, not in contemporary life. Those were the dilemmas with which authors like

the Ó/Mac Grianna brothers, and critics like Ó Rinn, had to cope. They overshadow the period, and its aftermath. The Kierkgaardian scowling of an uprooted Ó Direáin, or the Internment caesura in Ó Cadhain's development, stand out in greater relief now that we know the climate of their early development. Looking forward further beyond 1939, we can more clearly appreciate Ó Ríordáin's high seriousness, and the great comic genius of Flann O'Brien, who resolved the dilemmas of the previous half-century by short-circuiting them. But even Flann O'Brien, for all the wayward frolics of An Béal Bocht and the Cruiskeen Lawn squibs, never quite lost that anxiety which we see emerge as the condition of Free State modernity: the claustrophobic desire to explore new perspectives, and the agoraphobic reluctance to take one's identity for granted.

Philip O'Leary is keenly sensitive to these dilemmas, and to the fact that many of these authors were themselves sensitive of them. He traces, through literary debates and exchanges, the thwarted urge towards a Gaelic modernism within Depression Ireland, which wore its independence as a tight-collared Sunday suit. The debates and issues that are traced here are complex, sometimes embarrassing, often (amidst all the period stodginess of the rhetoric) at times painful and moving to read. O'Leary has read it all, and by no means uncritically; but at the same time with sensitivity and understanding. He recognizes nationalist tunnel-vision when he sees it, and some of the quotations are chosen with a mischievous whimsy; but O'Leary's judgements are never facile or flippant. Rather than dismissing a given author or line of thinking on principle, he places them in their mutual interaction and context. If anything, he is too indulgent with his sources; he passes very lightly, for instance, over the tendency (widespread in Europe at the time, and also in Ireland) to seek ethnic regeneration in a fascist-style glorification of collective discipline and hero-worship.

Philip O'Leary has done us all an enormous service by performing an Ordnance Survey of this transitional generation and its culture-political mentality, lost between romantic nostalgia, institutional conformism and modernist, often misdirected, energy. To present this entire breeding ground for modern Irish literature fairly, and to a wide audience less familiar than he with the Irish language, is something we should all be grateful for. This study will prove its great value over many decades to come, and in many different ways.

Let me mention by way of PS the excellent production of this great big book by UCD Press. Over 750 pages, with indexes, extensive notes (containing the Irish originals of translated quotations), and an indispensable gazetteer of names and pseudonyms with mini-biographical notices, are brought together into a book that is attractive and easy on the reader's hands and eyes.

Joep Leerssen
University of Amsterdam

Acknowledgements

Our thanks to the following without whose support this journal could not have been produced: Donald and Marilyn Keough, Carmel and Martin Naughton, Christopher Fox, Éamonn Ó Ciardha, Luke Gibbons and Kevin Whelan and the Notre Dame Irish Studies Summer Seminar in Dublin.

Contributors

Authors

Benedict Anderson has published several books on the political and literary culture of Southeast Asia and on the rise of nationalism, notably *Imagined Communities* (1983). He is Aaron L. Binenkorb Professor of International Studies at Cornell University where he is director of the Modern Indonesia Project.

Angela Bourke writes on oral culture and literature. She received an *Irish Times* Literature (Non-Fiction) Prize for *The Burning of Bridget Cleary* (1999). Jonathan Cape published her biography of the Irish-American author Maeve Brennan in summer 2004. She teaches Irish language and literature at University College Dublin.

Mary Burgess teaches at the University of Notre Dame. She is completing a book on the cultural politics of partition in twentieth-century Ireland.

Clare Carroll is director of Irish Studies in Queens College, City University of New York. She is the author of *Circe's Cup* (2002) and the editor (with Patricia King) of *Ireland and Postcolonial Theory* (2003). She has also published scholarly editions of *Orlando Furioso* (1532) and (with Vincent P. Carey) of *Solon his Follie* (1594).

Conor Deane lives in Rome.

Seamus Deane teaches at the University of Notre Dame where he holds the Donald and Marilyn Keough Chair of Irish Studies. He is the author of several books on Irish literature and was general editor of *The Field Day Anthology of Irish Writing*, 3 vols. (1991). Cork University Press will publish his *Foreign Affections: Essays on Edmund Burke* in 2005.

Anne Fogarty is general editor of the *Irish University Review*. She works on treason and sedition in early modern Britain and Ireland, women's fiction and poetry and cultural memory in Joyce. She is a senior lecturer in English at University College Dublin where she is chair of the board of Drama Studies.

Luke Gibbons holds the Keough Family Chair of Irish Studies at the University of Notre Dame. His most recent books are *Gaelic Gothic* (2004) and *Edmund Burke and Ireland* (2004). He is currently engaged in a major study of Joyce.

Peter Gray specializes in the history of Anglo-Irish relations, especially the Great Famine and the politics of poverty and land in the nineteenth century. He teaches at the University of Southampton where he also directs the electronic cataloguing and full digitization of British parliamentary papers on Ireland. His publications include *Famine, Land and Politics* (1999).

Michael Griffin is completing a book on Oliver Goldsmith and working on another on the late eighteenth-century poet Thomas Dermody. He teaches English at the University of Limerick.

Timothy W. Guinnane is professor of economics and history at Yale University. His *The Vanishing Irish* (1997) won the Donald Murphy Prize of the American Conference for Irish Studies in 1999.

Joep Leerssen is the director of the Huizinga Institute at the University of Amsterdam. He has published extensively on the cultural and literary history of Ireland and Europe; his most recent book is *Hidden Ireland, Public Space* (2002).

Peter Linebaugh is an historian at the University of Toledo, Ohio. He is the author of *The London Hanged* (1991) and (with Marcus Rediker) of *The Many-Headed Hydra* (2000).

David Lloyd has been a key figure in bringing the perspectives of critical theory and postcolonial studies to bear on modern Irish culture. He teaches at the University of Southern California. He is the author of several books, including *Anomalous States* (1995) and *Ireland after History* (1999).

Patrick Lonergan is review editor of *Irish Theatre Magazine*. He recently completed a doctoral dissertation on contemporary Irish theatre at the National University of Ireland, Galway.

Sylvère Lotringer teaches French literature and philosophy at Columbia University. He is the author of many books on French critical theory and on art, including *Nancy Spero* (1995) and (with Jean Baudrillard) *Forget Foucault* (1987). He is the founder and general editor of the independent press Semiotext(e).

Breandán Mac Suibhne has published on various aspects of Irish social and cultural history and is the editor (with David Dickson) of Hugh Dorian, *The Outer Edge of Ulster* (2000).

Catherine Marshall is a senior curator at the Irish Museum of Modern Art. She is the author of *Irish Art Masterpieces (1994)* and numerous catalogue essays on contemporary Irish art.

Amy Martin is assistant professor of English at Mount Holyoke College. She is working on a book on the relationship between British imperial nationalism and Irish anti-colonial nationalism in the nineteenth century.

Conor McCarthy teaches Irish Studies and English at the Mater Dei Institute of Education, Dublin City University. His *Modernisation, Crisis and Culture in Ireland, 1969–1992* was published in 2000.

Máirín Nic Eoin received an *Irish Times* Literature Prize for *B'Ait Leo Bean* (1998), a study of gender in the Irish language literary tradition. Cois Life will publish her *Trén bhFearann Breac*, an analysis of cultural displacement in modern Irish literature, in summer 2005. She teaches at St. Patrick's College, Drumcondra.

Seán T. O'Brien is completing a PhD on Irish prison literature at the University of Notre Dame.

Brian Ó Conchubhair recently curated the *Free State Art* exhibition in the Burns Library at Boston College and he is the editor (with Nollaig Mac Conghaíl) of *Scéalta Éireann* (forthcoming), a collection of writing in Irish from the 1930s. He teaches Irish at the University of Notre Dame.

Cormac Ó Gráda has published several books on Irish economic and demographic history, most recently *Black '47 and Beyond* (1999). He is Professor of Economic History at University College Dublin.

Jane H. Ohlmeyer is Erasmus Smith Professor of Modern History at Trinity College Dublin. She is the author of *Civil War and Restoration in the Three Stuart Kingdoms* (1993) and the editor of several collections of essays on early modern Ireland.

Brendan O'Leary is an authority on nationalism, electoral systems and power-sharing arrangements and he was recently a constitutional adviser to the Kurdistan Regional Parliament. He has published many books, including a number on Northern Ireland, the most recent of which is (with John McGarry) *The Northern Ireland Conflict* (2004). He is Lauder Professor of Political Science and Director of the Solomon Asch Center for the Study of Ethnopolitical Conflict at the University of Pennsylvania.

Philip Pettit is the William Nelson Cromwell Professor of Politics at Princeton University. His recent books include *A Theory of Freedom* (2001) and a collection of essays, *Rules, Reasons and Norms* (2002). He is also author (with Geoffrey Brennan) of *The Economy of Esteem* (2004) and (with Frank Jackson and Michael Smith) of *Mind, Morality and Explanation* (2004).

Rob Savage works on Irish political and cultural history. He has written a biography of Sean Lemass and a history of television in Ireland; he is also editor of *Ireland in the New Century* (2003). He is one of the directors of the Irish Studies programme at Boston College.

Sarah Smith lectures in historical and critical studies at the Glasgow School of Art. She won the James McTaggart Prize for Filmmaking for her 2001 short film, *Walker*, and is currently completing a PhD on avant-garde film and video art.

Jennifer Todd teaches political science and philosophy at University College Dublin. She has published extensively on the politics and political culture of Northern Ireland, including (with Joseph Ruane) *The Dynamics of Conflict in Northern Ireland* (1995), and is editor (with Joseph Ruane and Anne Mandeville) of *Europe's Old States and the New World Order* (2004).

Artists

Robert Ballagh is one of Ireland's best-known artists and designers. His work is in many important collections including the National Gallery of Ireland, the Irish Museum of Modern Art and the Albrecht Dürer House, Nuremberg.

Margaret Corcoran exhibited *An Enquiry* in Dublin in 2002; it is a critically acclaimed series of eight small paintings of a young woman making her way around the Milltown Room of the National Gallery of Ireland. It will be shown at the Snite Museum of Art in the University of Notre Dame in April–May 2005; two of the paintings are reproduced in this issue.

John-Barry Lowe is an architect and photographer. He established Eden Architects in central Dublin in 2004.

Mick O'Dea has exhibited widely in Ireland, Britain and America. His *The Split* (1997), reproduced in this issue, was first shown in 1998 in *Art into Art*, an exhibition in the National Gallery of Ireland in which a number of Irish artists responded to paintings in the gallery's collection. His *Audience*, an exhibition of forty-four portraits, was in the Dunamaise Arts Centre in Portlaoise in January 2005. His work can be seen in the Kevin Kavanagh Gallery, Dublin.

Simon Patterson was nominated for the Turner Prize in 1996. Much of his work from the early 1990s, such as *The Great Bear* (1992), which is reproduced in this issue, subverts familiar classification systems. He is a contributor to *Re Views: Artists and Public Space* which will be published by Black Dog in June 2005.

St. Patrick's College
Drumcondra, Dublin 9

Founded in 1875, St Patrick's College is one of Ireland's oldest colleges now offering programmes to doctoral level in arts, humanities and education. A college of Dublin City University, winner of the Irish University of the Year Award 2004 (*Sunday Times*), its Humanities faculty is distinguished, dynamic and innovative.

PhD/MA in Humanities

Applications are invited for places on graduate programmes

- Taught two-year, part-time MA (Irish, History, Children's Literature, Theatre Studies, French, Music)
- One-year full-time MA (History, Theatre Studies)
- MA by major thesis (English, Irish, French, Geography, History, Music or interdisciplinary)

Qualified applicants will normally hold honours bachelors degrees, minimum grade of second-class honours grade two or equivalent in the specified subject or a cognate area.

Application forms and further details from: Admissions Officer, St. Patrick's College, Drumcondra, Dublin 9.

Email: admissions.office@spd.dcu.ie
Tel. 003531 8842013/2025
Fax 003531 8376197

Closing date for receipt of applications: 30th April 2005

Centre for Irish Studies
National University of Ireland, Galway

The Centre for Irish Studies was established as a centre of excellence at NUI Galway and is dedicated to interdisciplinary research and advanced teaching on the cultural, social, and political endeavours of Irish people, on the island of Ireland and beyond. Contributing disciplines include History, Archaeology, English, Geography, Irish, Economics, Philosophy, Women's Studies, Political Science and Sociology.

Taught Programmes

- MA in Irish Studies
- On-line Diploma in Irish Studies
- Part-time Diploma in Irish Studies
- Customised Programmes for Visiting Students
- Irish Studies Summer School

Research Degree Programmes

- MLitt in Irish Studies
- PhD in Irish Studies

National University *of* Ireland, Galway
Ollscoil na hÉireann, Gaillimh

Critical Conditions

General Editor: Seamus Deane

In 1996 Field Day (in association with Cork University Press) commenced publication of *Critical Conditions*, a series of essays and monographs by geographers, historians and critics that made innovative and provocative work usually confined to specialist journals available to a wider readership; the University of Notre Dame Press published the series in the United States. To date, fourteen books have appeared in the series. The final two volumes, Seamus Deane's *Foreign Affections: Essays on Edmund Burke* and William J. Smyth's *The Forging of Ireland*, will appear in 2005. All the *Critical Conditions* books remain in print and are available in good bookstores.